Complex Emergencies

DAVID KEEN

polity

First published in 2008 by Polity Press

Reprinted 2008, 2009, 2010 (three times)

Polity Press
65 Bridge Street
Cambridge CB2 1UR, UK.

Polity Press
350 Main Street
Malden, MA 02148, USA

ISBN-13: 978-07456-4019-8
ISBN-13: 978-07456-4020-4 (pb)

A catalogue record for this book is available from the British Library.

Typeset in 11.25/13 pt Dante
by Servis Filmsetting Ltd, Manchester
Printed and bound in Great Britain by the MPG Books Group

The publisher has used its best endeavours to ensure that the URLs for external websites referred to in this book are correct and active at the time of going to press. However, the publisher has no responsibility for the websites and can make no guarantee that a site will remain live or that the content is or will remain appropriate.

Every effort has been made to trace all copyright holders, but if any have been inadvertently overlooked the publishers will be pleased to include any necessary credits in any subsequent reprint or edition.

For further information on Polity, visit our website: www.politybooks.com

Contents

Acknowledgements

This project has evolved over quite a long time period, and many people have helped and influenced me along the way. Among the scholars and aid workers who have been particularly helpful, I would like to thank: Adekeye Adebajo, Astier Almedom, Philippa Atkinson, Edward Balke, Mats Berdal, Matthew Bolton, Mark Bradbury, Roddy Brett, Teddy Brett, Dennis Bright, Peter Cutler, Chris Dolan, Comfort Ero, Valpy FitzGerald, Elliot Green, Francisco Gutierrez Sanin, Barbara Harrell-Bond, Barbara Harriss-White, Wael Ibrahim, Dominique Jacquin-Berdal, Wendy James, Douglas Johnson, Marcus Lenzen, Philippe Le Billon, Yang Li, Jeremy Loveless, Jon Lunn, David Malone, Roland Marchal, Zoë Marriage, Maria Teresa Mauro, Andrew Mawson, Omar McDoom, Karen Moore, Thi Minh Ngo, Melissa Parker, Ricken Patel, Nirad Pragasam, Alessandro Preti, Paul Richards, Hugh Roberts, John Ryle, Klaus Schlichte, John Seaman, David Shearer, W.P.S. Sidhu, Hugo Slim, Frances Stewart, Nick Stockton, David Turton, Megan Vaughan, Tony Vaux, James Vincent, Eftihia Voutira, Gavin Williams and Ken Wilson. Let me extend particular thanks to Mark Duffield and Alex de Waal for their inspirational work in this field and for personal support at various points. I also owe a major debt to two distinguished Indian intellectuals: Amartya Sen, for awakening my interest in this topic, and Amrita Rangasami, for guiding me towards a radically different point of view. I would like to extend a special thank you to my inspirational schoolteacher, David Jones.

Perhaps most importantly, let me thank the many people who have given time for interviews – often in the face of extreme suffering – and who, at various points, encouraged me to see things a little differently from the mainstream. I particularly thank those in Guatemala, Sudan, Sierra Leone, South Africa, the former Yugoslavia and Iraq. I have tried to convey some of the insights of ordinary citizens – and not just their sad stories and experiences.

In terms of my experience at the London School of Economics, I would like to say a special thank you to John Harriss for his faith in me as a teacher in the field of complex emergencies at the Development Studies Institute; also to my co-conspirator Tim Allen and to my friend and minder Sue Redgrave, as well as Jo Beall, Drucilla Daley, Stephanie Davies, Dennis Rodgers and many others in what has usually been a bizarrely happy department. Of course, I would like to extend a special thank you to my Masters students over the years for their lively intelligence and awkward questions.

At Polity, I would like to thank Ellen McKinlay for coordinating this project with great kindness and enthusiasm, desk editor Justin Dyer for his great diligence and extreme patience, Chantal Hamill for the index, the rest of the production team at Polity, and lastly David Held for encouraging me to pursue this book and for warning me that it would not all be fun!

Closer to home, let me thank my dear sister Helen and her husband Roy as well as my favourite aunty, Ann. Most of all, I would like to thank my mum for being a great mum and extending such sustained love and encouragement. Among many friends who have helped me along the way, let me give special thanks to Cindy, Simon, Hartmut, Chandima, James, Angela, Anne, Clive, Andreas, Klaus, Gabi, Haro, Eric, Georgia, Huw, Clare and Martin. I would like to thank my mother-in-law, Joanne, for her support and kindness, particularly in the last stages of this project.

To stay sane in the course of this project, I have needed the presence of a grace and love as sweet and strong as the topic is bleak. I would like to thank my wife Vivian for all that love and support, for her faith and intelligence – and most of all for lighting up my life!

Introduction

The aim of this book is to analyse the abusive systems that surround and produce complex emergencies. The book argues that these disasters cannot be properly understood or addressed without comprehending their *functions*. The study has its origins in a series of lectures given at the London School of Economics in a Development Studies course called 'Complex Emergencies', though I have restructured significantly and added a good deal of material.

But what is a 'complex emergency'? The term is employed here in accordance with common usage in the aid world, which is to say that complex emergencies are humanitarian crises that are linked with large-scale violent conflict – civil war, ethnic cleansing and genocide. To echo a phrase used by Joanna Macrae and Anthony Zwi in their 1994 edited volume *War and Hunger*, complex emergencies are 'conflict-generated emergencies'.[1] Complex emergencies should be distinguished from natural disasters – that is, from disasters caused primarily by drought, floods, earthquakes, hurricanes, tidal waves or some other force of nature.[2] The United Nations Office for the Coordination of Humanitarian Affairs (OCHA) has emphasized that complex emergencies are linked to 'internal or external conflict'.

Another title for the book might have been 'complex humanitarian emergencies', but the word 'humanitarian' carries certain dangers. One is the implication that the solution lies with humanitarian relief (rather than with tackling underlying human rights abuses, for example). Another is that the word may prejudge the motives of interveners as altruistic (when they may be much more complicated).[3] Another title might have been 'civil wars', but 'complex emergencies' is again preferred – in part because the book looks in detail at aid interventions. A second reason is that the term 'civil wars' tends to obscure the international element in many conflicts;[4] a third is that the book includes some analysis of the global 'war on terror'; most importantly, labelling diverse crises (including genocide) as 'civil war' has proven very damaging when it comes to interventions. The classic case of this was the 1994 Rwandan genocide. Key members of the UN Security Council used the term 'civil war' during the early stages of the Rwandan genocide and this allowed the UK, the US and France to argue that a major peace-keeping operation was inappropriate in such a context – effectively giving Rwandan extremists free rein for their mass killing.[5] More generally, the term 'civil war' can prejudice our understanding of the complex fault-lines of conflict and the complex manipulation of violence for a wide variety of purposes, whereas the label 'complex emergency' draws attention to complexity and embodies a useful degree of vagueness about the *nature* of a violent conflict.[6]

The full version of OCHA's definition of a complex emergency is that it it is 'a humanitarian crisis in a country, region or society where there is total or considerable breakdown of authority resulting from internal or external conflict and which requires an international response that goes beyond the mandate or capacity of any single agency and/or the ongoing United Nations country program'.[7] OCHA adds that complex emergencies are typically characterized by, first, 'extensive violence and loss of life; massive displacements of people; widespread damage to societies and economies'. A second characteristic is 'the need for large-scale, multi-faceted humanitarian assistance'. A third is 'the hindrance or prevention of humanitarian assistance by political and military constraints', and a fourth is the existence of 'significant security risks for humanitarian relief workers in some areas'.[8]

The recognition of the role of violence in many emergencies was an important advance, as was the realization that decentralized violence is a factor and the acknowledgement of the likelihood of obstruction. These phenomena had been damagingly neglected in the 1980s, as Cold War allegiances combined with a near reverence for 'national sovereignty' within the United Nations in particular. Experience of a variety of crises – notably in Ethiopia, Sudan, Somalia, Angola, Bosnia and Rwanda – helped to prompt a better awareness of the importance of violence in emergencies, though this has generally been both belated and incomplete.

Two potential problems with OCHA's definition are worth stressing, and they are linked with continuing shortcomings in international interventions. The first difficulty arises from defining a complex emergency in terms of a 'breakdown of authority'. At the time of the 1994 Rwandan genocide, UN Secretary General Boutros Boutros-Ghali damagingly claimed that authority in Rwanda had collapsed. Yet the problem was not so much that authority had broken down; rather, it was being imposed with ruthless and vicious efficiency.[9] Even in Sudan, where poverty and geography have created major obstacles to imposing state authority, a discussion centred on the 'breakdown of authority' risks endorsing the dubious alibi of governments in

Khartoum that have cleverly manipulated and exacerbated ethnic tensions for more than twenty years.[10]

A second problem arises from the statement that a complex emergency 'requires an international response that goes beyond the mandate or capacity of any single agency and/or the ongoing United National country program'. For one thing, is there really *any* emergency that can be properly handled by a single agency? More worryingly, defining the emergency in terms of the required response has at least the potential for muddling up problem and solution (not an aid to clear thinking) and for serving as a tool for bureaucratic in-fighting. The definition hints at possible 'turf battles' within the UN itself – in particular between OCHA and UNDP (in charge of the normal country programmes).

While this book focuses on emergencies linked to violent conflict, it does not entirely ignore natural disasters. One consideration here is that if we are to understand famines that are linked to violent conflict, we need to understand the mechanisms of famine more generally – for example, the role of markets, asset-transfers and disease. Thus, the chapter on famine includes some brief discussion of drought- and flood-driven famines. Second, we need to understand that violent conflict and natural disaster may interact. Third, interventions have often been hampered by treating complex emergencies as if they were natural disasters.[11] We need to understand the profound differences that armed conflict can make. Fourth, even though we are distinguishing natural disasters from complex emergencies on the grounds of the absence of large-scale conflict, there is always a politics to any disaster, and there will be elements of conflict and even outright coercion in a natural disaster (to which brief reference is made in chapter 5). In this sense (among others), no emergency is simple. Fifth, natural disasters are likely to become more frequent and intense with global warming (which is itself largely a human-made rather than a natural process).[12] Resultant resource scarcities can be expected to feed into armed conflict, moreover. Analysing such scenarios would mean writing a different book, however, and the focus here remains on violence-linked emergencies that have already occurred and on what we can learn from them.

Violence as 'Evil'

Where atrocities are seen as a kind of moral collapse, they are usually portrayed as the work of particularly bad (or evil) individuals. This is a central theme in the so-called 'war on terror', for example, where a key working assumption – perhaps not working very well – has been that if the evil embodied in al-Qaida or Hizbollah can be eliminated (and if their state backers can be disposed of), then security will follow.

After the May 2003 bombings of housing compounds in Riyadh, Saudi Arabia, US Vice-President Dick Cheney advised an audience in Washington 'to recognize the fact that the only way to deal with this threat ultimately is to destroy it. There's no treaty can solve this problem, there's no peace agreement, no policy of containment . . . we have to go find the terrorists.'[13] George W. Bush himself said that 'our responsibility to history is already clear: to answer these attacks and rid the world of evil'.[14] Like Israel, Bush has had a rogue's gallery of wanted terrorists, crossing them off as they are killed or captured.[15]

Johan Galtung contrasts his own 'peace approach' (based on mapping legitimate goals and bridging them) with a much more dominant 'security approach' that is underpinned by 'a hard, absolutist reading of the Abrahamitic regions [Christianity, Judaism and Islam]' and that involves 'construction of the Other as evil, with no legitimate goal, driven by lust, greed or envy, somebody with whom one would never negotiate since there is no grievance and no basis for any solution'. This 'security approach' demands a response based on 'strength, to defeat or deter the evil party'.[16]

Violent groups that have recently been condemned as evil or mad or both include not only al-Qaida and Hizbollah but also the Revolutionary United Front in Sierra Leone and the Lord's Resistance Army in Uganda. Underpinning such portrayals – apart from an understandable revulsion at atrocities themselves – is a belief that there is a strong disjuncture between, on the one hand, these reviled groups and individuals and, on the other hand, the category of 'normal people'. In the Sierra Leonean context, this theme underpinned a trenchant 1997 article by Sierra Leonean analyst Yusuf Bangura, who portrayed RUF rebels as a small minority of bitter and war-drugged individuals.[17] Diana Lary, in her study of warfare in early twentieth-century China, noted that a common explanation among the Chinese for atrocities was that these were manifestations of evil, while the soldiers' motives were seen as essentially incoherent.[18] Indeed, Chinese armies were seen as behaving badly precisely because they attracted those of bad character. Some theorists (like Theodor Adorno) have argued that fascist organizations have similarly attracted individuals with particular psychological traits and problems.[19]

Of course, violence does attract plenty of individuals who are attracted to violence! But condemning evil or disturbed individuals does not get us very far at a societal level. In fact, from a social science perspective, 'evil' (like 'chaos' and 'mindless violence') is not so much an explanation of violence as a confession that one has been unable to explain it and that one has few ideas (at least in the secular sphere) about how to prevent it.

One way into this topic is to unpack the term 'evil' a little more. Suppose something bad happens, something terrible. How are you going to explain it and make sense of it? Religious interpretations of calamity have tended to run into a difficult problem: if the supernatural power is seen as fundamentally benevolent, how is it possible for that being to allow such terrible things to happen?

Within the Judaeo-Christian tradition, two main explanations have been advanced. The first is that suffering is punishment for human sins. We can see this, for example, in the Judaic and Christian belief that calamities were God's punishment for human sins. A second (more or less competing) explanation is that this suffering is actually the work of malevolent forces. Peter Stanford argues in his interesting book *The Devil: A Biography* that the Devil was invented to preserve the image of God in the face of mass suffering, including the forced exile of the Jews recounted in the Old Testament. This can be seen as an example of 'splitting': preserving the image of the good by attributing everything bad to some demonic force.[20]

Moving beyond the label of evil – and beyond the simple and unequivocal condemnation of violence – is an uncomfortable position. In fact, attempts to explain violence have often been seen as coming dangerously close to excusing it. One fear here is that explanations may erode any sense of personal responsibility (or free will) on the part of the violent, and certainly there is always a risk of accepting too readily the 'explanations' and rationalizations that are offered after violence occurs – with perpetrators perhaps trying to justify the unjustifiable, not least to themselves.[21] An important step forward in explaining violence comes from realizing that killers often see themselves as *victims* (chapters 3 and 4);[22] yet if we take seriously killers' perception of themselves as victims, to what extent are we reinforcing a 'victim ideology' – perhaps one being whipped up and sustained by manipulative politicians – which itself energizes and legitimizes extreme violence?

The tight-rope between explaining and excusing is one that has been walked by anyone trying to explain or understand the attacks on New York and Washington on September 11 2001, and similar hazards have applied in civil wars. Many people in Sierra Leone, for example, have emphasized that grievances themselves are hardly an adequate justification for violence. Olu Gordon, a leading light in the radical newspaper *For Di People*, referred to the amputations by the rebel RUF and added indignantly: 'I was beaten up by thugs in 1977 under [President Siaka] Stevens. I've been arrested eight times. So why don't I take up a machete and start chopping off people's hands?' One man who had been held hostage in July 2000 by a rogue army faction known as the 'West Side Boys' told me: 'Some civilians who have really suffered will react very strongly against you if you seem to be justifying what they have suffered.'

A second reason why moving beyond condemnation of atrocities towards explanation is uncomfortable is that it diminishes the distance between 'them' (who cannot so easily be labelled as evil or mad) and 'us' (who conversely cannot so readily reassure ourselves that we are, by contrast, good and sane).[23] If we accept the existence of the psychoanalytical concept of projection, part of the point of condemning the 'barbarism' of others may be precisely to ward off discomfort with our own aggressive or even sexual drives. Yet significant evidence (drawn from studies in psychology as well as from the record of history) points to the existence of a disconcerting truth: there is not necessarily a huge disjuncture between the perpetrators of violence and the rest of us, and in special social circumstances even normal human motivations can feed into the perpetration of atrocities (chapters 3 and 4).

The dichotomy between the sane and benevolent 'us' and the evil and crazy 'them' has frequently had a paternalist and racist dimension. Within this framework, ethnicity is something that happens to other people. An emphasis on (fractious) ethnicity has been part of an enduring ideology of empire: the myth of the 'civilizing mission', the imperial power as a pacifier who keeps the 'primitive tribes' from one another's throats. In her study of war in the former Yugoslavia, Susan Woodward noted that even those outraged by war often adopted a language of barbarism which implicitly drew a line between the region and more 'civilized' peoples to the west.[24] In the wake of the 2003 invasion of Iraq, the US-led occupying force has often been portrayed as the only thing keeping Iraq's Sunnis and Shi'ites from full-scale war with each other.

Chapter 1 looks critically at the concept and practice of war. In particular, it explores the idea that civil war is better understood as a *system* than a *contest*. The same goes for the 'war on terror', a significant (though not principal) focus in the book. The chapter stresses that the 'fault-lines' of war should not be taken at face value (for example, 'government' versus 'rebels'). Rather, we need to be aware of a range of other conflicts that may shape a war. Significantly, these other conflicts may flourish under the cover of a declared war against a particular named enemy.

Chapter 2 looks at the relationship between trade and complex emergencies, stressing the way rebellions have been nurtured by profitable international trading links and the way 'counter-insurgency' operations have frequently been ineffective when poorly paid and poorly motivated soldiers are sent to confront rebels in resource-rich areas. The chapter emphasizes the importance of 'sell-game' (that is, collusion between ostensibly rival parties) in many civil wars, questioning the sincerity of official definitions of 'the enemy'. This pattern of conflict can be understood to some extent through a 'rational actor' framework: 'sell-game' reflects a rational interest in making money and a rational interest in staying alive. The chapter looks critically at the work of Paul Collier in particular, emphasizing the need to understand the role of grievances (and their relationship to trade), the interaction of 'greed' and grievance, and the importance of looking not just at rebels but at the state too.

If chapters 1 and 2 emphasize that we should not take the fault-lines of conflict at face value, chapters 3 and 4 try to develop this line of thought by deconstructing the process by which enemies are chosen and defined. Chapter 3 focuses on the perspectives and grievances of combatants (and notably on how civilians may come to be defined by combatants as part of the enemy), while chapter 4 looks at wider political processes, including the way elites have manipulated both ethnic conflict and soldiers' grievances and including also the processes by which ethnic conflict may be embraced by non-elite groups. It is stressed that identifying an 'ethnic' enemy inevitably implicates civilians within the 'enemy' category.

There is something about extreme violence that is not adequately explained within a 'rational actor' framework. In particular, this framework deals very poorly with the strong emotions that are frequently harboured by the perpetrators of extreme violence. This does not mean, however, that violence has to be dismissed as totally irrational or incomprehensible. Chapter 4 suggests that atrocity is not just the breakdown of morality, or simply a manifestation of anarchy or evil, or even a breakdown of discipline and authority; there is a degree of predictability in atrocity, it is argued, and atrocities proliferate in particular environments.

Understanding the role of emotions tends to involve a shift of focus from 'greed' to 'grievance' (including the grievances of soldiers) and from economic functions to those we may call *psychological*. To take one particularly important example, certain kinds of military structures with high levels of institutionalized abuse seem to produce a marked incidence of extreme violence.

Understanding emotional factors will usually involve an exploration of the moral frameworks to which perpetrators adhere, their sense of right and wrong, justice and injustice. Of course, even to talk of a 'moral framework' in relation to the perpetrators of atrocities will be anathema to many people. However, if we are to move beyond the (often counterproductive) tactics of condemnation and elimination (not least in the so-called 'war on terror), then some more sophisticated understanding of atrocity is urgently required.

Several chapters analyse the interaction of 'greed' and 'grievance' – including the relationships between abusive, 'greed-based' war systems, on the one hand, and antipathy between fighters and civilians, on the other. Chapter 3 draws particularly on work in Sierra Leone. My book *Conflict and Collusion in Sierra Leone* has sometimes been seen as a challenge to Paul Collier's emphasis on greed as the key driver of civil wars;[25] however, the book tries to show how 'greed' and 'grievance' interact and is in many ways an extension of my earlier work on this interaction in Sudan in particular.[26] Although Collier cited the Sudan study – *The Benefits of Famine* – in a 1995 article dealing with private portfolios (as evidence that wartime profits could be significant),[27] subsequent citations in the voluminous output by Collier/Hoeffler on 'greed' from 1998 generally neglect the broad body of work on the political economy of war that was developed in the 1990s and that encouraged the UN to take on the political economy of war through various Panels of Experts and targeted sanctions (including key texts by Mark Duffield, Alex de Waal and William Reno).[28]

Chapter 5 introduces major theories of famine and explains how important groups may benefit both from famine and from relief 'failures'. It highlights the importance of understanding *strategies*: the strategies of those suffering from famine and of other parties who are in a position to help or hinder those who are suffering.

Chapter 6 looks at humanitarian aid and asks whether it has offered a solution to complex emergencies or whether it has been part of the 'problem' – for example, by fuelling war economies, by propping up abusive governments or by distracting from the international community's failure to act on other fronts (for instance, military or diplomatic). The chapter seeks a way forward from the sometimes paralysing debate between those 'attacking' and those 'defending' humanitarian aid.

Chapter 7 looks at information – the information systems in the humanitarian world and in the media that surround and infuse complex emergencies. Drawing on work by Michel Foucault and Noam Chomsky in particular, it analyses the silences within these information systems, the way that language can constrain thought and action, and the functions of particular 'blinkered' ways of looking at disasters. The chapter argues that the political and economic interests that help to generate complex emergencies also tend to generate rather constrained and distorted patterns of information which routinely perpetuate or deepen these emergencies.

The failings of the international humanitarian system are typically accommodated with relatively little introspection or accountability: in line with pioneering (but often neglected) analysis by Edward Clay and Bernard Schaffer, failings are routinely attributed to 'problems of implementation' rather than to faulty design of policy.[29] In many respects, an image of success (of functioning bureaucracies and flourishing careers) has existed alongside a marked 'failure' to meet humanitarian needs. This is part of the system that the book will seek to analyse: the bureaucratic and political interests of donor governments and aid organizations are part of the focus here. More generally, the tendency to explain unwelcome phenomena (disasters, relief inadequacy, terrorism) as the result of *extrinsic* factors ('drought', 'evil', 'chaos', 'tribal violence', 'problems of implementation') serves a function in removing responsibility from society as a whole (including key actors in the West), thereby narrowing what Clay and Schaffer would call the 'room for manoeuvre' towards more helpful policies. This focus on extrinsic factors can be seen as another form of 'splitting', where the image of the good is preserved by locating all the bad things in a separate entity.

Chapter 8 looks at how abusive war systems may mutate into various kinds of peace and at the kinds of violence, corruption and exploitation that may be embodied within this 'peace'. The chapter suggests that peace frequently involves difficult trade-offs: for example, some element of 'justice' may need to be set aside if combatants and warlords are to agree to peace in the first place. Continuities between war and peace are emphasized, and it is suggested that these continuities need to be understood if we are to understand transitions from war to peace, and peace to war. The chapter suggests that interventions need to take account of both the vested interests in a conflict and the emotional factors (anger, fear, and so on) which also inform violence; otherwise, these interventions can very easily be counterproductive. Without adequate attention to the functions of *disasters*, even well-meaning interventions are susceptible to being hijacked, and they can easily promote calamitous political and military backlashes.

Finally, the conclusion sums up the overall themes and arguments. The conclusions are not definitive, and the analysis of such a broad topic as complex emergencies is never going to be comprehensive. Nor do I wish to claim that 'if I were in charge', the practical response would run smoothly: someone who has difficulty organizing his own desk is not necessarily in a position to lecture those with years of operational experience in complex emergencies! My aims here are in many ways more modest (but actually not *that* modest!): to try to think clearly about recent disasters, to shake up some common assumptions, and to provide a set of tools for those seeking to deepen their understanding or improve their interventions.

1

War

A common-sense view is that development and peace are good, and famine and war are bad. War is conceptualized as very violent and peace, not unnaturally, as very peaceful. More specifically, war has been portrayed (particularly within the aid world) as disrupting the economy, as an interruption in a (mostly benevolent) process of development which must be resumed when the war is over.

One problem with this common-sense model is that it tells us very little about the causes of violence and famine or the relationship between war and peace. In many portrayals of the development process, conflict and hunger seem to come out of nowhere. Rwanda, for example, was generally depicted by aid donors prior to the 1994 genocide as a great success story of development.[1] Yet we need to ask: what is it about the process of development in particular countries that has fed into conflict; and what has been the hidden violence in development that may feed into the more overt violence of civil conflict?[2]

The view of war and peace as opposites has obvious appeal for the media. Journalists (and I was one myself) are primarily interested in change: theirs is a world of news (what is *new*), of events, discontinuities and drama; and what could be more dramatic than the change from one thing into its opposite, especially a change from a good and peaceful world into an evil and violent one? Historians, by contrast, are often interested in continuities, and this approach can usually take us further. What do war and peace have in common? Answering this question will be particularly important if we hope to understand *transitions*: the transition from peace to war and the transition from war to peace. Perhaps we can take a cue here from the natural sciences: how can one thing change into another – a bulb into a plant, or a liquid into a gas – unless it has already begun to resemble it?

The view of war as an incomprehensible other is often reinforced when human rights reports or NGOs or journalists concentrate on condemning violence rather than explaining it. Even describing extreme violence is actually very difficult without resorting to words like 'savage', 'brutal', 'inhuman' and 'inhumane' – words that may subtly or not so subtly dehumanize the perpetrators of violence, marginalizing the possibility that the perpetrators' motives may be those that a great many people share, and taking violence away from the sphere of the human and the comprehensible.

Of course, the political, military and economic costs of mass violence are all too obvious. Genocides and mass persecutions represent (apart from anything else) a huge loss of labour and productive potential.[3] Civil wars wreak mass destruction of infrastructure and livelihoods as well as lives. Yet the habitual (and natural) emphasis on war and other kinds of mass violence as negative phenomena should perhaps induce in us some sense of puzzlement: how is it that phenomena so universally disastrous could be allowed, and indeed *made*, to happen – and very often, in the case of civil wars in particular, to persist over years or even decades? Mark Duffield has written, paradoxically, of 'permanent emergencies'.[4]

This book argues that significant (and very often politically significant) sectors of society may benefit from war and other disasters, and that we are unlikely to find out why wars happen (and are made to happen) unless we understand what these benefits are. At the same time, it is important to keep in mind that even a vicious war is unlikely to represent *total* violence; indeed, a priority for those waging war may be *limiting* violence in various ways (not least their own exposure to it). To a degree, there is violence in peacetime and order in wartime. We should not let the words 'war' and 'peace' seduce us into believing that neither has elements (or seeds) of the other. The primary focus here is on civil wars (though these often have an important international dimension, as noted); particularly in chapter 4, we also discuss the global 'war on terror', notably in terms of how enemies have been defined and redefined and how violence has been legitimized.[5]

The traditional idea of war is as a *contest between two sides*, each of which is trying to defeat the enemy and win. This idea owed a good deal to the work of Prussian General and military analyst Carl von Clausewitz, who famously stated that war was 'a continuation of politics by other means', adding that it was 'an act of violence to compel the enemy to fulfil your will'.[6] Although Clausewitz's main focus was inter-state war, civil wars have usually been analysed through this lens and have historically been seen as an ideological, political or perhaps religious contest for control of the state, usually between the government and a rebel group. Civilians have typically been seen as caught in the cross-fire of this contest, with casualties among civilians presented as a by-product of war.

The idea of a war between 'sides' (usually two, often 'ethnic') is easy to grasp; it helps to make complex events digestible and (apparently) comprehensible. James Fallows has suggested that the US media have tended to cover US politics as if they were covering sport.[7] Who is going to win? Who is ahead in the polls? What are the tactics? Other questions (like 'What are the policy issues?') are hard to answer and easy to neglect. One could say the same for much contemporary coverage of violent conflict. Who is it between? Who is going to win? What are the tactics? And (if we are being really sophisticated) who are the goodies and baddies? Again, we may be left with little idea – in this parade of warring initials, warring factions or warring tribes – of the issues behind the conflict.

Contemporary civil conflicts are particularly confusing as well as appalling. Ideology has often been hard to spot, especially with the thawing Cold War translating into a loss of confidence and support for socialist or communist movements. There has often been a proliferation of factions and much-publicized atrocities. The displacement of civilians has frequently been a *goal* of conflict (as in ethnic cleansing) rather than just a by-product. And civilians have often been key targets of violence (and arguably key *perpetrators*, for example as members of *ad hoc* and unpaid militias).[8]

Insofar as war has not conformed to the traditional idea of a contest between two sides, this has tended to deepen the perception of war as a kind of *breakdown*. Recall from the introduction that the very definition of a complex emergency by the UN's Office for the Coordination of Humanitarian Assistance (OCHA) has consistently included the notion of a 'breakdown of authority'. Contemporary conflict has repeatedly been depicted, notably in much of the media, as mindless violence, tribalism, chaos, or some combination of these. But it is not always clear whether it is the violence that is mindless, or the analysis. We should keep in mind that war may be *intended* to be confusing.[9] Nor is it always evident that the tribalism is embedded in the society under discussion rather than in the attitude of the author (for example, the view that 'we' in the West are civilized whilst 'they' are savage, tribal and fractious). While it is tempting to attach the label of 'chaos' to many violent contexts, chaos is really a kind of *non-explanation* – a confession of bafflement. Yet the secret weapon of those who advance the 'explanation' of chaos and anarchy is that the more incompetent their attempts to explain what is going on, the more convincing their explanation – that it is all anarchy – becomes.[10] Meanwhile, the label of 'chaos' may serve as effective cover for all kinds of political and economic manipulation.

Explanations centring on ethnicity also have a dangerous allure. Those who are ready to use easy labels and to accept the inevitability of ethnic violence may actually play into the hands of local or international actors seeking to bolster their own power and privileges by forcing politics along ethnic lines.[11] At the national level, stirring up violence between ethnic groups may represent a cheap way of waging war for financially strapped governments and even for rebel movements, whilst simultaneously confusing the international community (and perhaps many local people) about who is responsible for the violence. Certainly, this was the case in Sudan in the late 1980s when the US in particular tended to blame government-sponsored militia raids on ancient tribal enmities.

Yet, as David Turton has convincingly argued, ethnicity should not be regarded simply as an explanation; it is something which itself needs to be explained. Further, ethnic allegiances may be a *product* of conflict as much as a cause of it.[12] At the global level, this had been a key problem with Samuel Huntington's analysis in *The Clash of Civilizations* (1993 article, 1996 book): Huntington posited civilizational tensions as an explanation for violent conflict but was largely blind to how underlying tensions come into existence (or indeed the role of this kind of analysis in contributing to the process).

If chaos and ethnicity are often dangerous and inadequate 'explanations', can we offer any more helpful tools for understanding contemporary conflict? One way into the problem is to suggest that wars – like ethnicity and (as we shall see) like famines – need to be explained as *positive* phenomena, that is, as phenomena that have *functions* as well as causes and effects.[13]

French philosopher and historian Michel Foucault gave some advice to those who might wish to understand the internment of dissidents – which he referred to as the Gulag – in the former Soviet Union. He emphasized the importance of:

> Refusing to restrict one's questioning to the level of causes. If one begins by asking for the 'cause' of the Gulag (Russia's retarded development, the transformation of the party into a bureaucracy, the specific economic difficulties of the USSR), one makes the Gulag appear as a sort of disease or abscess, an infection, degeneration or involution. This is to think of the Gulag only negatively, a dysfunctioning to be rectified – a maternity illness of the country which is painfully giving birth to socialism. The Gulag question has to be posed in positive terms.[14] The problem of causes must not be dissociated from that of function: what use is the Gulag, what functions does it assure, in what strategies is it integrated?[15]

Rather than listing the causes of war or famine and rather than portraying war as fundamentally irrational or as an aberration or interruption, it would be more helpful to investigate how violence is generated by particular patterns of development, by particular political economies which violence in turn modifies (but does not destroy). Indeed, part of the problem in much existing analysis is that conflict is regarded as, simply, a breakdown in a particular system, rather than as the emergence of another, alternative system of profit, power and even protection. Yet events, however horrible and catastrophic, are actually *produced*, they are made to happen by a diverse and complicated set of actors who may well be achieving their objectives in the midst of what looks like failure and breakdown.[16]

In addition to understanding the system of benefits that may emerge in a war (or, as we shall see, a famine), we also need to try to deconstruct the discussions that surround these damaging political and economic systems. Following Foucault again, it is important to look at how truth is constructed, who has the right to speak what counts as the truth, and whose interpretations of reality are ignored, marginalized, forgotten or disqualified as anecdotal or unscientific. Part of this relates to the portrayal of humanitarian operations as helpful even when they have not been. Foucault stressed that particular systems of social intervention (of whatever kind) tend to generate the data that in turn legitimize and sustain them, and this insight can help us to understand shortcomings in humanitarian interventions (see chapter 7).

While conflict is an undeniable reality in many countries, we need to keep a very open mind about the *nature* of that conflict. Who has been given the right to speak what counts as the truth about a given conflict? Whose interpretations have been marginalized and disqualified? And what practical purposes are served – and reinforced – by the definitions adopted? The fault-lines of conflict should not be taken at face value. What are the systems of collusion obscured by 'war'? And what are the hidden conflicts (for example, class conflict, conflict between armed and unarmed groups, conflict between men and women, between young and old) that are obscured when officials and journalists portray civil war as a battle between two or more armed groups? During the Cold War, presenting war as ideological had obvious advantages for factions seeking support from one of the two superpowers.[17] More generally, Stathis Kalyvas finds an 'urban bias' in academic and media discussions of civil wars, leading to a neglect of local agendas, an overemphasis on ideological motivations and on fixed identities among the warring parties, and an adoption of overly rigid distinctions between combatants and non-combatants.[18] In my own fieldwork, I have found that, while 'both sides' in a war may stress that the conflict is a battle between 'us' and 'them', civilians (if one takes the trouble to ask) will frequently point to motivations that have very little to do with 'winning' and perhaps also to systems of collusion.

Connections between war and peace also become clearer when seen through this lens. We may discern how systems of exclusion and violence in peacetime are modified and exaggerated in wartime. Often, an ethnic group will fall partially below the protection of the law in peacetime and then, once a rebellion takes place, members of that ethnic group are further stigmatized and exploited under the cover of 'war'. A somewhat similar process has also taken a toll on other social groups, including women, children and 'youths',[19] particularly (but not only) where these categories overlap with a stigmatized ethnic group. Continuities may also extend in the other direction: for example, in a peace agreement, violence and corruption are likely to be institutionalized to some extent. In fact, peace may not be possible without this. It is important to look at who is being excluded from a peace agreement and what forms of collusion and violence are continuing into 'peacetime'. This will be difficult if we stick too rigidly to a rigid conception of war and peace as opposites.

What are the forms of violence that flourish, half-concealed and perhaps legitimized, under the general label of a war against this or that? In Sierra Leone and Uganda, a number of groups (often government-affiliated) have benefited from the impunity created by declared wars against demonized enemies (the Revolutionary United Front and Lord's Resistance Army, respectively).[20] In the international area, the enemy – the source of 'evil' – has been continually redefined. After the 'war on communism', there was the 'war on drugs', and now the 'war on terror'. Each war has carried the need to win allies and with it the (whispered) implication that abuses by these allies will be tolerated. The war against communism gave valuable leeway to the Sudan government, for example, in waging war against southern Sudanese rebels and civilians in the 1980s. The war against drugs has allowed brutal counterinsurgency in Colombia to launder its own abuses and to delegitimize its enemies as 'narco-guerrillas'. Most recently, the war on terrorism has presented abundant opportunities for autocrats like Pakistan's Pervez Musharraf to pose as a pillar of freedom, for Russian President Vladimir Putin to present the Russian threat to Chechnya or Georgia within the framework of anti-terrorism,[21] for the Philippine and Indonesian governments to present separatism in Mindanao and Aceh as terrorism, for Israel to present its own abuses against Palestinians and Lebanese as part of a joint worldwide struggle against terrorism, for the Chinese government to suppress Uighur rebels in Xinj Lang, and for the Sudanese government to pursue mass killing in Darfur whilst getting credit

for sharing information on extremists with the US.[22] Sudan's cooperation
with the US increased dramatically after 9/11 and has included: giving
access to banking and other details relating to bin Laden, who lived in
Sudan from 1991 to 1996, and other al-Qaida operatives; detaining militants
on their way to join the Iraqi insurgency; and acting as the 'eyes and ears'
of the CIA in relation to Islamist groups in Somalia. Sudan intelligence chief
Major General Salah Gosh, accused by US Congress members of directing
military attacks against civilians in Darfur, was flown to the US in an executive jet by the CIA to further what US officials have publicly hailed as
increased cooperation in the 'war on terror'.[23]

The legitimacy or otherwise of these various struggles and 'wars' –
whether civil or global – can be debated. But we need to be aware of the
hidden (or partially hidden) conflicts and oppressions that may go unaddressed in the middle of an officially sanctioned 'consensus' on the nature
of the threat and the identity of the enemy, whether this is in the context
of a global war, a civil war, or some combination of the two.[24]

It may be useful to categorize some key aims in a war that depart from
the normally emphasized aim of 'winning'. One is a concern with *limiting
violence* (especially one's own exposure to it or that of a key political constituency). A second is the desire for *immediate gain* (perhaps economic gain,
improved safety or some psychological benefit) through violence.[25] A third
is the concern with *weakening political opposition*. Importantly, all of these
aims may not only compete with the priority of winning but may also be
actively counterproductive from a military point of view.

Consider, first, the aim of *limiting violence*. Frequently, governments in
war-affected societies have tried to 'farm out' violence and its adverse consequences to ethnic militias, motivated in part by a desire to avoid the political unpopularity that may be associated with a large conscripted army. The
strategy may have important drawbacks from a military point of view, particularly when such militias (perhaps for economic reasons) engage in
attacks on civilians with minimal allegiance to rebel groups, thereby predictably radicalizing them. In Sudan, for example, northern Sudanese
militia raiding on a variety of groups preceded and helped to create their
affiliation with the rebel Sudan People's Liberation Army (SPLA).[26] Today
in Darfur, government-supported militias have increasingly preferred to
attack civilians rather than attacking armed rebels, again predictably radicalizing civilians.[27] Risks to a core constituency have sometimes been
minimized by turning a victim group against itself. In Sudan, southern
rebels and now western rebels have both split, in large part along ethnic
lines – with encouragement from Khartoum. Other examples include the

Guatemalan government recruiting Mayans into its abusive 'civil defence' units[28] and Russia's attempt to 'Chechenize' the conflict in Chechnya.[29]

Another way of limiting one's own exposure to violence is to avoid direct confrontation with an armed enemy. Within civil conflicts, cooperation between armed groups has often been significant. Pitched battles have seemingly been the exception rather than the rule, and civilians have typically borne the brunt of the violence. Sierra Leone is a paradigmatic case of this, but there are many others. Fear of taking on rebels directly can lead to an emphasis on razing civilian villages and using starvation as a weapon, as with the under-equipped and poorly trained forces of the Burmese army who face Karen National Union guerrilla tactics honed by almost six decades of resistance.[30] One military expert in Guatemala told me the army was often afraid of the guerrillas during that country's civil war, which lasted from 1960 to 1996 and was most bloody in the early 1980s:

> They were sometimes more interested in attacking civilians than armed rebels. . . . Despite being very desirable to attack a guerrilla concentration, it was very costly and particularly when going against well-trained troops who'd been perfecting military strategies for a long time, using traps, holes in the ground, mines. They could lose a whole thirty people.[31]

After war resumed in Angola in 1992, there were reports of trading and fraternizing between UNITA and government forces.[32] In Liberia, faction leaders were reported drinking together in Monrovia while violence raged upcountry; pitched battles between armed groups were relatively rare, with civilians consistently targeted for violence.[33] In Algeria, the government cancelled elections in January 1992 after the Islamic Salvation Front (FIS) had won a near-landslide in the first round; worried by 'Islamic fundamentalism', US and France were quick to offer their support, and Algerian veterans of Afghanistan and other radical Islamists quickly chose armed resistance. For its part, the Algerian army pursued a policy of torture and assassinations against opposition groups, with soldiers raiding mosques and rounding up thousands of suspects into internment camps in the Sahara.[34] According to Habib Souaidia, a former officer in the Algerian army, soldiers would sometimes disguise themselves as Islamist militants before embarking on massacres that were later attributed to the Armed Islamic Group (GIA).[35]

Rather than being confined to civil wars or poor countries, a reluctance to engage the enemy has often been notable at the international level. During the Cold War, although the two superpowers were sometimes sucked in directly (the US in Vietnam, the Soviet Union in Afghanistan), they most often conducted their ideological struggle by means of proxies (in Guatemala, El Salvador, Mozambique, Angola, and so on). Noticeably absent during the Cold War were direct (and almost certainly suicidal) attacks by the superpowers on one another. So this was in many ways a system for limiting conflict and for ensuring that it happened to other people: the majority of casualties were effectively 'exported' to the developing world. For all the obscenity of large nuclear arsenals, only two nuclear weapons have so far been detonated in combat – at Hiroshima and Nagasaki – and these were unleashed against civilians within a nation that was known to be unable to strike back. Reinforcing the impression that the Cold War was a *system* as well as a *contest* was the use of Cold War enmities to legitimize military-industrial complexes on 'both sides' as well as to legitimize the suppression of internal dissent (a process that went to horrific extremes in the Soviet Union and was not insignificant in the US, notably during the McCarthyite witch-hunts of the 1950s).

When industrialized countries *have* opted to go to war, this has generally been against much weaker countries or regions where there is a reasonable certainty of winning (Britain versus Argentina; the US versus Panama, Grenada or Libya). A special category consists of targets where this optimism has proven largely misplaced (Vietnam, Chechnya, Afghanistan – whether in the Soviet- or US-led invasions – and Iraq), but the perception of one's own superior strength was nevertheless important in the decision to resort to war. When it comes to keeping Western soldiers safe, popular options in contemporary conflicts have included high-altitude bombings (transferring risks to the civilian population on the ground),[36] the use of private military companies,[37] and the use of regional peacekeeping operations such as ECOMOG (Economic Community of West African States Monitoring Group) in West Africa.[38]

A second set of concerns that goes well beyond a preoccupation with 'winning war' centres on the *local and immediate functions of violence*. In discussions of war, abuses against civilians have usually been portrayed as an unfortunate deviation from humanitarian law (as embodied particularly in the Geneva Conventions), or as a means to a military or political victory. However, such abuses may confer benefits that have little or nothing to do with winning the war (and may actively impede this endeavour). The point of war may lie precisely in the legitimacy which it confers on these abuses – in other words, the legitimacy it confers on actions that in peacetime would be punishable as 'crimes'. The aim may not be to change the law but to break it.

Whereas analysts have tended to assume that war is the 'end' and abuses the 'means', it is important to consider the opposite possibility: that the 'end' is to engage in abuses or crimes that bring immediate rewards, whilst the 'means' is war and the perpetuation of war. In war (whether civil or global), some groups of people will effectively fall below the protection of the law, while some groups will in effect be elevated above the law. We can expect the latter to abuse the former, and 'winning the war' may not be their only (or even their overriding) aim in so doing. Where conflict has elevated some groups above the law, they may be reluctant to let go of that new status – a significant motive for keeping conflict going in some form.

Some of the immediate functions of violence are *economic*. While these are considered in more detail in chapter 2, the way these may actively interfere with 'winning' is worth stressing here. We have seen how raiding in Sudan (often with significant economic motivations) has predictably both radicalized its civilian victims and encouraged support for the rebels. In Sierra Leone, attacks on civilians by the rebel Revolutionary United Front (RUF) – again often with economic motivations – also predictably alienated the very civilians that the rebels said they were trying to recruit and represent; meanwhile, Sierra Leonean government soldiers' looting of civilians (and forced evacuations from resource-rich areas) impeded government efforts to win hearts and minds in the war against the RUF – once more, a foreseeable outcome.[39] A particularly paradoxical phenomenon – especially if we see war as 'all about winning' – has been the practice (noted in the Democratic Republic of Congo, the Philippines and Chechnya as well as Sierra Leone) of selling arms to the other side.

Another local and immediate function of violence may lie in enhancing your *security*. Even ethnic cleansing may be done in the pursuit of security (chapter 4). Moreover, from the individual's point of view, warfare that consists primarily of violence directed at civilians may mean that it is safer to be inside an armed band than outside one.[40] In Sierra Leone, youths were always at risk of being accused of collaborating with 'the other side', giving them a particular incentive for joining one military faction or another. Their often precarious legal protection in peacetime (particularly in relation to local chiefs)[41] became still more precarious in wartime, reflecting the possibility of denunciation as a 'rebel' by local chiefs in particular.[42]

As for the immediate *psychological* functions of violence, these may include the satisfactions of revenge, of reversing previous or present power inequalities and humiliations through the barrel of a gun (chapter 3), and even of the perverse cognitive satisfaction that may come from making your chosen enemy resemble your own propaganda (chapter 4). In Sierra

Leone, accusing someone of rebel sympathies was often a vehicle for personal ambitions and jealousies – a process echoed in many other conflicts, including Zimbabwe in the 1970s and Kashmir in recent years.[43] Some of this jealousy and finger-pointing has been reminiscent of Arthur Miller's play *The Crucible*, which showed how accusing someone of witchcraft could serve as a vehicle for a wide range of economic ambitions, sexual jealousies and other personal agendas: 'Old scores could be settled on a plane of heavenly combat between Lucifer and the Lord,' Miller wrote, 'suspicions and the envy of the miserable toward the happy could and did burst out in the general revenge.'[44]

It is important to note that violence in a war is not confined to the warring parties and that there may be connections between systems of violence operating at different levels.[45] The links between warfare and domestic violence are complicated, but Chris Dolan's important study of war and displacement in northern Uganda showed how war may undermine men's ability to provide for their families and may sometimes lead them to seek more violent and abusive interpretations of their own masculinity, including domestic violence and military recruitment.[46] Such dynamics can interact damagingly with ethnic tensions and prejudices. After Judith Zur described how Mayan communities provided recruits for abusive civil defence patrols that the government used for 'counterinsurgency' from around 1981, she observed:

> The humiliation of not being able to protect and provide for their families – the traditional practice of providing economic and labour support for widowed kin was abandoned as men were forced to concentrate on their immediate interests – led to anger and resentment, which some men took out on their wives. These factors contributed to a loss of identity as a male, Indian agriculturalist associated with locality. Having set in motion the conditions to create patrollers' feelings of alienation, the army and its local cohorts proceeded to manipulate them, promoting the patrols, with their emphasis on violence, as a new space for the reassertion of male dominance. The military dictatorship also offered its (voluntary and forcibly enrolled) followers a new, tenuous identity through identification with the Guatemalan state and an equally suspect self-respect through its ideology of the superior, military/ladino race.[47]

A third goal beyond 'winning' is *political*: a key aim in a war may be to weaken actual or potential opposition by suppressing, dividing or delegitimizing it, and conflict may be manipulated and even prolonged as a tool for political survival. This helps to explain the (surprisingly common) adoption of tactics that predictably strengthen the enemy. Indeed, *both* 'sides' in a war may find some political advantages in strengthening or radicalizing the other (chapter 4). The concepts of 'rebel', 'subversive' or 'terrorist' may be kept conveniently vague and fluid.

Looking back on the long civil war in Guatemala (1960–96), some analysts felt that the army (given sufficient resolve) could have destroyed a not very numerous guerrilla movement, but that the army actually found the rebels' continued existence useful – in legitimizing both the army's own economic enterprises and the suppression of human rights and pro-democracy forces. The officially defined enemy was communism. But the war was also an occasion for intimidatory violence against a wide range of pro-democracy, union and human rights groups. Once civil war broke out in Guatemala, villages could be dubbed a 'guerrilla village' not because guerrillas were present but because of villagers' progressive politics.[48] In fact, a significant element of the counterinsurgency was the attempt to deter an indigenous political awakening in a country where racism was underpinning profoundly exploitative economic relations. These fears were stoked by the Sandinistas' seizure of power in Nicaragua in 1979: as one experienced Guatemalan analyst said of his country: 'It's a society with a strong racist element, a traditional fear of an indigenous uprising, and it was inflated by 1979 in Nicaragua and the idea that this was contagious in Central America.'[49]

In Cambodia in the 1990s, opponents of the government were easily tarred as Khmer Rouge sympathizers.[50] In Algeria during the same period, suppressing Islamist extremists legitimized the army's rule and its suppression of 'subversives' more generally. In Nepal, conflict has been used to narrow the space for democratic opposition. As Isabel Hilton put it in May 2005: 'The king has tried to reduce Nepal's three-way power struggle – monarchy, Maoists and political parties – to a simple military struggle between the monarchy and the Maoists, and has challenged international opinion to make its choice. Under this scenario, the legitimate political parties are out of the picture.'[51] In Pakistan, the military have used the conflict with India (notably, the nuclear stand-off and the conflict over Kashmir) to justify their continued interference in politics and a large military budget.[52]

Elites have frequently sought to deflect political threats by inciting violence along ethnic lines, whether this takes the form of war, genocide, or some combination of the two (chapter 4). Where such incitement is a key strategy, a state of emergency may sometimes be more useful than a victory. In Sudan, members of the ruling National Congress Party (NCP) – successor to the National Islamic Front (NIF), which took power in a military coup in 1989 – appear to recognize that elections which the 2005 Comprehensive Peace Agreement has scheduled for 2009 would probably eject them from power, and many within the ruling elite fear that the planned self-determination referendum in the south will lead to the loss of the south (and its oil). Already in July 2005, the International Crisis Group was noting, 'There are signs the NCP seeks to undercut implementation [of the north–south agreement] through its use of the militias (the South Sudan Defence Forces, SSDF), bribery, and through the tactics of divide and rule.'[53] Even more alarmingly, maintaining a prolonged emergency in Darfur could also help in delaying national elections and could thereby help to preserve NCP rule and to protect the economic interests of the influential government security agencies, which are making profits from the booming oil and construction sectors as well as from the service sector.[54] Ruling groups may also find it advantageous to maintain (or at least tolerate) a degree of conflict within ethnic groups that are seen as troublesome or potentially so. There is some evidence that this way of thinking has contributed to prolonged conflict in Acholi areas of northern Uganda and that it contributed, during Sierra Leone's civil war, to the neglect and even exacerbation of violence among the Mende in the south and east of the country.[55]

Weakening and dividing potential sources of opposition may also mean keeping the military weak – an obvious impediment to military victory if there is a rebellion of some kind. In Sierra Leone, fear of military coups encouraged an intentional neglect of the army alongside the nurturing of a special force under Presidential control, known as the SSD (Special Security Division).[56] In Zaïre (Democratic Republic of Congo), Mobutu maintained privileged paramilitary forces (often from his own Ngbandi ethnic group), while the army was left in such a neglected state – with corrupt officers appropriating soldiers' pay and supplies – that extortion by the military became rife and Laurent Kabila's rebels were able to advance easily to take the capital in 1997.[57] In Sudan, Sadiq el-Mahdi (Prime Minister from 1986 to 1989) did not trust the Sudanese army and built up the Arab *murahaleen* militias as a counter-weight. His successor as head of state, President Omar el-Beshir, created the paramilitary Popular Defence Forces (drawing on the Arab *murahaleen*), again seeking a counter-weight to the army. The sizeable Darfuri contingent in the Sudanese army has raised doubts about the army's loyalty in the crisis there – again feeding into the use of militias.[58]

In an important analysis, Sciences Po lecturer Thorniké Gordadze noted the Russian failure to quell resistance in Chechnya despite two costly wars and highlighted the importance of internal problems within the Russian military machine:

> [T]he units belonging to various ministries and departments act independently. This extreme compartmentalisation is partly motivated by rivalry between security services seeking to monopolise 'administrative resources' but it is also founded on the Kremlin's traditional suspicion of political power in the hands of security organisations. The Russian government has not forgotten the threat of Bonapartism exemplified by General Alexander Lebed (a signatory to the agreement terminating the first Chechen war who then pursued a promising political career until his death in a helicopter accident), and is afraid of entrusting command of all the armies in Chechnya to a single general.[59]

Those manipulating conflict for political power may include not only ethnic nationalists, warlords and autocrats but also democratic leaders or quasi-democratic leaders who find that war boosts their popularity. In Russia, Putin rode to the Presidency in 2000 on the back of war-fever over Chechen 'terrorists', and there are serious worries over possible involvement by Russian oligarchs linked to Putin in the Moscow and Volgodonsk apartment bombings of August–September 1999 that served as a justification for renewed Russian forces' attacks in Chechnya from September 1999.[60] In the US the 'war on terror' dramatically boosted George W. Bush's popularity – at least until victory in Iraq turned sour. We return to the various functions of the 'war on terror' in chapter 4. Before that, we focus on some of the economic functions of war – and on the interaction of so-called 'greed' and 'grievance'.

3 goals beyond winning

- liminting violence.
- local and immediate functions of violence
- political

2

'Greed'

Economic Agendas

This chapter looks at the role of economic agendas in complex emergencies. It argues that these agendas have helped to shape the nature of these emergencies, including the definition of the enemy – both at the level of rhetoric (who is declared to be the enemy) and at the level of reality (who is actually attacked). One aim in this discussion is to 'rescue' the study of economic agendas – already well established in the 1990s – from a rather extreme interpretation emanating from the World Bank at the end of the 1990s, an interpretation focused overwhelmingly on 'rebel greed'. This relatively recent and econometric strand of the literature – associated with Paul Collier in particular – can be seen as another example of 'splitting' – or perhaps 'othering' – in which the most fundamental problems are said to lie with an abusive 'other' (whether motivated by greed, evil or blind hatred), whilst broader societal problems are largely ignored. To some extent at least, the emphasis on 'rebel greed' has chimed with an emerging 'anti-terror' agenda: for example, reports of links between Sierra Leonean RUF rebels and al-Qaida money-laundering activities gave urgency to international efforts to rein in the support that the RUF was getting from President Charles Taylor in neighbouring Liberia.[1] George W. Bush likes to refer to 'the forces of terrorism and extremism', while the US Institute of Peace refers to the 'illicit power structures' that appear to stand in the way of freedom and democracy, a conceptualization that implicitly brackets terrorism and rebellion. [2] The prevailing approach to security is neatly summarized by one of its leading critics, Mark Duffield: 'Once violent, corrupt and criminal leaders are neutralised or removed, liberal peace, in alliance with the poor, can once again resume normal development.'[3]

The most commonly expressed opinion (at least until recently) has been that war is very bad for trade, and trade is very bad for war. Thus, war has been seen as undermining trade by disrupting production, distribution and purchasing power; meanwhile, trade has often been presented as making war unlikely – because it creates prosperity and because (according to the free trade school and the likes of British manufacturer and activist Richard

Cobden in the nineteenth century, for example) a flourishing and free trade would mean that countries and businesses acquired such an interest in peaceful conditions that war would become unlikely or impossible.

War does indeed disrupt many kinds of trade and financial flows, while trade and commerce do sometimes create vested interests in favour of peace.[4] But trade has also fed strongly into conflict. This has come to the fore with the end of the Cold War, a landmark that spelled the end of one ready explanation for civil conflict and encouraged greater attention to the *internal* dynamics that might perpetuate armed conflicts.[5] With warring factions tending to receive less funding from alliances with Cold War super-powers, violence does seems to have become more 'self-funding' – and it has been financed in large part by international trade.

In this context, particular attention has recently been given to 'war economies'. A war economy is taken here to include all the economic activities (legal and illegal) during a war. Profits may arise from pillage, protection money and ransoms, controlling trade, exploiting labour, gaining access to land or appropriating aid. Salaries and corrupt benefits accruing to military personnel may also be important.[6] International trading frequently fuels these profits. A war economy may also involve income emanating from an émigré community allied to one group or another.[7]

Economic activities in wartime can be placed in the following three categories:

1 Some activities – the majority – are *impeded* by war. This includes most kinds of industrial and agricultural production, and most services. Activities particularly impeded will include those requiring high levels of organization and infrastructure and those aimed at local demand. Tourism tends to be very badly hit by war.

2 Some economic activities are *consistent* with war. This includes the exploitation of low-tech, high-value commodities like alluvial diamonds. Offshore oil can be exploited while conflict is raging (as in Angola), as can inland oil that is either far from the locus of conflict (as in the deserts of Algeria) or well protected by military forces (as in Colombia).

3 Some economic activities are actually *more profitable* in conditions of conflict. Those profiting are likely to be a small minority of the population, but perhaps a very influential and often well-armed minority. Artificially high prices may make food trading very profitable for a few merchants. Conflict will boosts demand for arms. Though agricultural production will typically suffer in a war, some kinds of agricultural production may be facilitated by the cheap labour of displaced people. Exploiting natural

resources may be easier when conflict minimizes state control or environmental restrictions. The drugs trade may also be more profitable in the absence of government interference. Various estimates have put the illegal drugs trade at between £250 and £400 billion a year – perhaps a little under 10 per cent of world trade. Frequently, the military has become involved in the drugs trade.

Within a 'rational actor' framework that focuses to a large extent on the individual, bizarre and militarily counterproductive atrocities against civilians may begin to look less incomprehensible (though no less abhorrent). In Sierra Leone, for example, notorious atrocities sometimes served an economic function in depopulating resource-rich areas with minimal military resources;[8] it was common to find that one person had been spared in a massacre and told to go and tell others about the atrocities as part of a tactic of manipulating fear and rumour.[9] Atrocities directed at civilians may also be part of a system in which fighters (in some sense rationally) avoid confrontation with other armed groups.

One Khmer Rouge commander told Philippe Le Billon: 'The big problem with getting our funding from business [rather than China] was to prevent an explosion of the movement because everybody likes to do business and soldiers risked doing more business than fighting'.[10] Le Billon suggested that a combination of ideological indoctrination, harsh sanctions and forced recruitment (especially of children) had served to counter the resulting tendency to fragmentation.[11]

Paul Collier's Approach: Some Problems

In a widely cited and influential article published in 2000, Paul Collier argued that recent conflicts have been driven overwhelmingly by 'greed' rather than by 'grievance'.[12] Collier – who also produced several papers on the topic with Anke Hoeffler and then with Hoeffler and Dominic Rohner [13] – identified a number of proxies – or stand-ins – for economically motivated violence (for example, heavy reliance on exports of primary products, low education levels) and a number of proxies for grievance (for example, economic inequality), and then found that the first set of proxies were much more closely correlated with the occurrence of civil wars than the second set.

Concluding that 'greed' was much more important than 'grievance' in causing civil wars, Collier explained the apparent absence of a link between grievances and rebellions as arising from a 'collective action' problem: participating in a grievance-led rebellion, particularly in the early stages, carried a lot of personal risks and few immediate benefits, he stressed; it would generally be tempting to let others take these risks and to hope to share in the long-term benefits if the rebellion were successfully to overturn a particular political system. By contrast, where violence brought immediate benefits (such as access to valuable resources), this collective action problem could be more readily overcome.[14]

In a modification of his earlier position, Collier argued in 2006 that civil wars occur when they are *feasible* (with exploitable resources being one factor) and that there is no need to have reference to motivation at all. In other words, where rebellion is materially possible, it will occur. Collier, Hoeffler and Rohner suggested that feasibility can also be proxied by a high proportion of young men in a society, by population size, by the existence of mountains, and by being a former French colony in sub-Saharan Africa.

Economic agendas have certainly been important in civil war, as we have seen, and the collective action problem is not to be dismissed. At a practical level, Collier's work added impetus to important initiatives designed to rein in illegal commodity flows. However, Collier took the political economy of war in a very particular (and potentially damaging) direction; four criticisms of his work are articulated in this chapter. The discussion focuses primarily on Collier's emphasis on greed, since this is the position for which he is best known. Some reference is also made to the new emphasis on feasibility, however.

The first main problem is that Collier's conclusions have rested on a rather dubious selection of proxies. Why, for example, should low literacy levels be taken as a proxy for 'greed' (as they were by Collier) rather than as a proxy for 'grievance'? The case of Sierra Leone shows that deficiencies in education can be a major grievance. Where proxies are allocated to 'greed' or 'grievance' in a rather arbitrary way, the scientific quality of the study will be more apparent than real.

The same criticism goes for the new emphasis on feasibility – a case of jumping out of the frying pan and into the fire. Collier, Hoeffler and Rohner state that proxies for feasibility have a substantial impact on the likelihood of civil war, and 'are far easier to interpret than any of the variables that were previously thought to be significant'.[15] They explain, 'The Francophone security guarantee made rebellion more dangerous and less likely to succeed. Mountainous terrain provides an obvious safe haven for rebel forces, and the proportion of young men in the society is a good proxy for the proportion of the population predisposed to violence.'[16] In addition, population size and primary commodity exports are defended as proxies for feasibility: 'Population size probably proxies the scale economies in security provision. Primary commodity exports probably proxy the scope for rebel financial predation.'[17]

But are these variables really so 'easy' to interpret? A high proportion of young men, for example, might equally be taken as a proxy for grievance (in circumstances where numbers of young men may outstrip employment). Population size as a proxy for security provision is quite a leap. The apparent Francophone connection might have many explanations. There is also a problem with where all this might be leading. If mountains are a problem, what is the policy implication? This latest work seems to point in the direction of levelling the mountains, not to mention bringing back the French; one suspects that neither option would go down well in most of Africa.

A second problem with Collier's analysis is that the political goals of rebellions cannot be so easily dismissed. Grievances have not gone away or become unimportant just because ideological conflicts are less easy to spot or because resource-acquisition has been shown to be a major goal in many conflicts.[18] In 2000, Collier went so far as to say that it was pointless asking a rebel group about their grievances since rebels will always emphasize grievances even when their motivation is greed. Here, it was almost as if economics was trying to abolish politics, sociology and anthropology, and to declare: no more listening required! Collier's latest formulation – that motivation is *irrelevant* – is hardly a step forward. If we follow his approach we may be left with a lot of numbers and very little real understanding of conflicts. Conflict resolution *demands* listening,[19] and as Mark Duffield has observed, the Collier approach has tended to delegitimize violent protest in general.[20] The fact that Collier's research has emanated from the World Bank has added to the suspicion that it might serve as a way to obliterate or ignore the grievances of anyone unhappy with the national or global status quo. The long colonial tradition of dismissing rebellion as criminal is hardly an encouraging precedent in this respect.

The case of Sierra Leone illustrates some of the practical problems that may result from a heavy international focus on 'greed' (especially on the role of diamonds in the war).[21] This focus seems to have distracted attention in the post-war period from very fundamental grievances (particularly in relation to governance) that helped fuel the rebellion (see chapter 3 in particular). A key grievance today, as at the start of the war, is that Sierra Leone's valuable resources (including diamonds) have been draining away over a long period and have yielded remarkably few developmental benefits. In other countries, different resource endowments have fed into different kinds of grievance. For example, the discovery of oil has often spurred violent separatist movements in oil-rich areas where people feel they are not benefiting sufficiently. In one interesting study, Michael Ross concluded that resource endowments requiring complex and stable systems for their extraction (like oil or liquid gas) have tended to encourage rebellions with separatist goals (Biafra/Nigeria, Sudan, Aceh/Indonesia), while resource endowments that can be relatively easily exploited (like the alluvial diamonds in Sierra Leone) have tended to encourage rebellions focusing on more immediate economic agendas as well as encouraging significant discipline problems within government forces.[22] However, even these latter rebellions may be powerfully motivated by grievances, and many of these are likely to reflect the treasury's difficulty in taxing a lootable resource and thereby harnessing it for development.

A third and related problem with the Collier approach is that we really need to understand how 'greed' and grievance *interact*.[23] Again, this is helped neither by focusing only on greed nor by ignoring motivation altogether. To give one example of the interaction of greed and grievance, elite economic agendas may fuel grievances and hence rebellion, creating a (spurious) legitimacy for the intensified exploitation of a group associated with rebellion (which has, in effect, fallen still further below the protection of the law). Mechanistic, economistic analysis that highlights 'greed' actually begs a large number of vital questions. If economic goals are important, under what circumstances are they pursued through violence? What is the role of institutions in influencing these decisions? To the extent that violence is seen as rational, what were the conditions that *led* violence to be seen as rational? Where predatory activities are prominent, are these an end in themselves or merely a means to some kind of military objective (perhaps one ultimately inspired by grievance)?[24] To what extent are people merely struggling to survive (rather than being 'greedy'), and sometimes using violent means to do so; and how does this choice relate to their grievances?[25] Where selfish and ruthless behaviour becomes prominent, what are the causes of this selfishness and ruthlessness? And what, conversely, can rein in this behaviour? In Sierra Leone, one local aid worker explained how he secured his food-store and prevented his store guards from defecting to the rebels or the government army: he said he did it by paying a small wage but also providing some medical care and food and by spending time with them, knowing their names: 'Trust and confidence – it's not much money they want. But when they know you have no trust or care for them, all they want to do is make money on the side.' A problem with a great deal of economic analysis (though this is beginning to change) is that it tends to assume selfish behaviour – and indeed to call it 'rational' – thus instantly marginalizing a range of questions about the origins or extent of selfishness. As with 'ethnicity' (another important variable that has been used to 'explain' conflict), greed is not so much an explanation as something that needs to be explained. If violent accumulation becomes commonplace, why do many people still choose another path? How do we explain apparently gratuitous atrocities that seem to have little or no economic or political function, and how do we explain the manifest fear and anger among rebel groups or other fighters? What differences can be discerned between the motivations of leaders and of ordinary fighters, particularly in factions (like the RUF in Sierra Leone) where the most important material benefits have gone to the leadership?[26]

A fourth problem with Collier's analysis provides the focus for the rest of this chapter. This is the lack of attention to the state, whether this is the state within a crisis-affected country or the state as an international actor.

States within the crisis-affected country

In his influential 2000 chapter in *Greed and Grievance*, Collier touched on the state only extremely briefly; assessing the causes of civil wars, he focused almost exclusively on the rebels. His 2006 analysis briefly discusses the state in terms of whether it can deter rebellion or not (with the French 'security umbrella' said to be a key factor). But this is quite inadequate. The reality is that governments and government forces – from within and beyond a crisis-affected country – may do at least as much as rebels to propel and deepen civil conflict, and this dimension has gone missing. It takes two hands to clap, and blaming rebels is sometimes much too easy. Blindness to abuses by government actors creates conditions of impunity, and sometimes also a sense among rebels that they are being unfairly singled out for criticism, something that can itself stand in the way of peace and reconciliation. A key problem in Sierra Leone's war, for example, was precisely the overwhelming focus on rebel abuses, while government soldiers' abuses went virtually unaddressed. A similar bias has clouded discussions (and interventions) in northern Uganda.[27] We have noted how the manipulation of conflict may include the incitement of ethnic conflict and even genocide by elites who are threatened by democracy (see also chapter 4); a focus on 'rebel greed' does little or nothing to illuminate these processes.

Consider first the role of government actors *within* an affected country. Again, the case of Sierra Leone is instructive.

Perhaps 150 insurgents associated with the rebel RUF came across from Liberia into Sierra Leone in March 1991. Despite these small numbers and significant oscillations in the strength of support from Charles Taylor (the Liberian rebel who became President of Liberia in 1997), the RUF rebels had managed to displace about half of Sierra Leone's population of some 4 million people within around four years. In part, this was because so many Sierra Leoneans were harbouring a variety of grievances, including grievances against the abuse of power by local chiefs.[28] Another factor was the rebels' cunning and ruthless use of terror to promote fear and displacement, as with the use of amputations and the sending of letters announcing impending attack to maximize terror. However, rebels' atrocities – and their evident interest in looting and diamond mining – tended to destroy any sympathy with the rebellion.

What sustained the rebellion more than anything seems to have been the role of the Sierra Leone army. In a bizarre pattern, government soldiers in the early and mid-1990s were observed attacking civilians, engaging in illegal diamond mining, dressing up as rebels, selling arms to rebels, and coordinating movements with rebels so as to minimize clashes and maximize the exploitation of civilians. In an Orwellian twist, it was logically 'impossible' for government soldiers to abuse civilians, since those who did so were quickly labelled deserters or rebels.

Chapter 1 discussed the (misleading) notion that conflict is analogous to a sporting contest between two rival teams. But recent betting scandals in football and cricket should remind us that when we think we know what 'game' is being played, we may sometimes be surprised. In Sierra Leone, some local people took to labelling collaboration by government soldiers as 'sell-game' – a reference to a bent football match.[29] The image of war as a contest between two sides seemed to serve as a smoke-screen for the emergence of a wartime political economy from which rebels and even government-affiliated groups were benefiting.

Government soldiers were typically under-trained and under-paid; they were often also under-aged. These soldiers tended to share with the rebels a similar hostility to the educated and to established and often corrupt politicians, and increasingly these young soldiers tried to use the war as a chance to rise above the lowly opportunities that peace had offered them. Under slightly different circumstances, many of the rural recruits to the army might equally have joined the rebels. Sending this kind of rag-tag army into diamond-rich areas in order to suppress a rebellion was a recipe for disaster.

One clue to the role of state actors in recent conflicts is that war expenditure has not always been as high as one might expect.[30] A major part of the reason is predatory behaviour of various kinds. This can produce a bizarre situation where a government looks good precisely because it is waging an abusive and predatory war. Sierra Leone achieved strangely low rates of inflation under the predatory military government of 1992–6. Donors and the World Bank noted how impressed they were by the 'financial magicians' of the military government.

In peace negotiations just before the hand-over to democratic rule in 1996, witnesses reported something distasteful in the warmth with which allegedly opposing commanders embraced each other. The army and the rebels both resisted the advent of democracy, with both groups fearing a loss of economic opportunities and prosecution for what they had done to civilians in the war. These joint concerns culminated in what was effectively a joint military coup in May 1997, when the covert cooperation upcountry came out into the open and arrived in the capital, Freetown. Once democratic government was restored in 1998, some of the worst state abuses were gradually reined in, but problems remained. In particular, Sierra Leone's civil defence forces – now receiving significant support from the state – were themselves drawn into abuses and violence aimed at securing diamond windfalls.[31]

Significantly, the pattern of 'sell-game' during civil war in Sierra Leone was a variation on a peacetime phenomenon. Collaborative conflict was in many ways a mutation of peacetime corruption, particularly in relation to the diamond economy. Prior to the outbreak of war in 1991, state officials had repeatedly participated in the smuggling they were supposed to be suppressing. The state was actively participating in the informal economy, and anti-corruption drives proved again and again to be a fertile ground for extending corruption. Meanwhile, the corruption of government officials helped to ensure, first, a lack of genuine development in Sierra Leone (including a collapse in education) and, second, a lack of treasury revenue to suppress either smuggling or the growing discontent encouraged by precisely this lack of development.

If Sierra Leone shows how peacetime processes may sometimes resemble wartime processes and how a weak state can encourage and shape conflict, this is by no means an isolated example. In her 1991 study of Zaïre (later the Democratic Republic of Congo, DRC), Janet MacGaffey suggested that the country's 'real economy' might have been as much as three times its recorded GDP. Subsequent events in the DRC showed how widespread smuggling and a bankrupt treasury had encouraged a collapsing and corrupt army, feeding in turn into wars with prominent external players and economic agendas. In Sierra Leone, Zaïre/DRC and elsewhere, the state proved unable to clamp down on the informal economy *or* on wars with economic agendas, and this 'failure' was intimately linked with the participation of the wealthy and powerful in these related phenomena.[32] Continuities between war and peace are further underlined by the fact that rebel financing may emerge from the actions of state officials, and that trading networks built up by rebel groups may also corrupt government structures when peace is agreed upon; Liberia illustrated both processes.[33]

It was partly the role of weak states in shaping contemporary conflict that led Martin Van Creveld to suggest that there has been a return to patterns of conflict in the Middle Ages, when weak states were the norm. Diana Lary's discussion of warlords in early twentieth-century China brings out the fluidity of conflict at that time, with soldiers selling arms to bandits and 'defeating' bandits by absorbing them.[34] The work by Van Creveld, Lary, Dominique Jacquin-Berdal and Mats Berdal shows that many of the phenomena identified by Mary Kaldor as characteristic of 'new wars' are not particularly new.[35]

Also in the early and mid-1990s, another kind of 'sell-game' was going on in Cambodia. After the Paris peace agreement of 1991, exporting timber and gems through Thailand helped the Khmer Rouge to resist UN pressures for disarmament. At the same time, Cambodian government officials and especially the armed forces had become heavily involved in the logging business, helping to strip Cambodia's forests. In 1994, the Defence Ministry was awarded the sole right to license timber exports and to all the revenue received from those exports. All this gave the armed forces, particularly senior officers, a powerful interest in not eliminating the Khmer Rouge altogether, and the army in fact winked at timber concessions in areas they knew would provide funding for the Khmer Rouge. Between 1994 and 1997, elements of the army came to arrangements with the Khmer Rouge over the control of economic resources in respective areas of influence, and actually cooperated in exporting, and in getting the best prices for, some commodities. Some soldiers were even reported to be selling armaments to the Khmer Rouge.[36]

In northern Uganda, a strong suspicion has grown up among many actors that government forces are not particularly interested in ending a conflict from which many have been benefiting.[37] The persistent failure to defeat a movement drawing heavily on children has been matched by aggressive government actions seen by many to be calculated to undermine successive peace initiatives.[38] Military involvement in the cattle trade may be one economic factor, and the aid economy another. In addition, significant profits have accrued to senior officers in the Ugandan army from the supply (and non-supply) of provisions to troops in northern Uganda.[39] Corrupt activities included obtaining very large payments for brokering the acquisition of substandard equipment, including helicopters from Belarus.[40] Aid workers reported that senior Ugandan army officers were even selling supplies to the Lord's Resistance Army, including army uniforms, and that many officers profited by inflating the number of soldiers in their units, pocketing the pay of these so-called 'ghost soldiers'.[41]

During war in Angola, the rebel group UNITA received most of the international criticism – particularly in the 1990s, when the end of the Cold War and the demise of apartheid removed the sense that UNITA was a valuable Western ally against 'communism'. Meanwhile, senior Angolan politicians and army officers were able to use the country's civil war for a variety of purposes, notably warding off any genuine democracy and free speech whilst simultaneously making huge profits from diamond mining, from weapons procurement and most of all from offshore oil (with large kickbacks reportedly going direct to the Presidency rather than the national budget). While the rebel UNITA movement raised money on the basis of diamond deposits, the government repeatedly raised loans on the basis of oil deposits.[42] Provincial leaders operating within the ruling MPLA party showed signs of 'warlordism', using state repression to shore up corruption and to underpin the exploitation of wartime shortages. Elements of collusion were noted in chapter 1, and the military leadership of the MPLA – as well as the UNITA leadership – were for a long time opposed to the demobilization that would undermine their profits, status and position.[43] Pointing to the existence of a corrupt 'oiligarchy' in Angola, the London-based NGO Global Witness called for the oil industry to join with international financial institutions and together insist that the Angolan government become accountable to its people, adding that banks should stop making loans (advanced against future oil revenues) that are used for buying weapons.[44]

In June 2001, it seems the Philippine army had the chance virtually to destroy the entire leadership of the radical Islamic Abu Sayyaf faction that was based in the island of Basilan, where the army had displaced more than 150,000 people in attempts to crack down on this and other organizations of the Moro Muslims in the Philippines. But the rebels escaped when the army pulled its troops away from the building that was housing the insurgents. According to a detailed article in Foreign Affairs, money from one of the hostages, a businessman, was used not only to secure his release by the rebels but also to pay off the local government and military officials who let the rebels escape.[45] Two years later, Naomi Klein reported in the Guardian that mutinous soldiers in the Philippines had accused senior military officials and the government of inflating the terrorist threat from Mindanao, of selling weapons to the Mindanao rebels, of helping prisoners accused of terrorist crimes to escape from jail, and even of carrying out their own terror bombings (notably at Davao airport). The accusations were supported by local newspapers and some senior military figures, Klein added. Frustrated soldiers suggested that the purpose of such bizarre actions was to secure US military intervention and increased US aid, both of which have been duly forthcoming.[46]

Lesley McCulloch, who was arrested and kept in an Aceh jail for five months during her research, reported that elements of the Indonesian military were involved in illegal logging, the drugs economy, and in providing lucrative 'protection' for oil palm plantations, oil and gas companies, and other businesses. Seizing land on behalf of plantations has also been profitable for the military. Fishermen and coffee farmers have been forced to sell their yields at below market rates, and local restaurants have regularly provided free food. Individual soldiers sold weapons to the rebel Aceh Sumatra National Liberation Front (ASNLF) and key military personnel provided a reliable supply line for ammunition and specific weapons. Economic interests have led to tension between the military and the police. The military's economic activities have themselves deepened grievances in the region, a case of greed leading to grievance.[47] It is not only in Aceh that the Indonesian military has funded itself (and lined its own pockets) through business activities.[48]

In an interesting study of the last years of the civil war in Peru, veteran journalist John Simpson observed that the beneficiaries of continued conflict included army officers stationed in areas where they were supposed to be suppressing both the drugs trade and the Shining Path rebels. In the coca region of Huallaga Valley, the army tolerated and taxed drug shipments; and army officers repeatedly released captured guerrillas (for a ransom), apparently seeking to perpetuate low-level conflict – thereby legitimizing their continued, and highly profitable, presence in drug-production areas.[49] Of course, such interests are not always an overwhelming factor in warfare: in Peru, an alliance between the state and a peasant-based civil defence did eventually bring defeat to the Shining Path;[50] the capture of Shining Path leader Abimael Guzman in Lima in 1992 (after a car-bombing campaign brought terror to Lima's richest neighbourhoods) represented a turning point.

The war in Colombia has seen guerrillas negotiating cease-fires and bribing army units in areas of key economic activity.[51] The counterinsurgency has been undermined by complex agendas, many of them economic. For one thing, the Colombian military has often been more interested in consolidating economic benefits (salaries, pensions, involvement in the drugs trade) than in military confrontation with the guerrillas.[52] In a revealing analysis, Francisco Gutierrez Sanin compares the unsuccessful counterinsurgency in Colombia with the (eventually) successful counterinsurgency in Peru. Whereas the Peruvian counterinsurgency saw a civil defence mobilized in association with the state against the Shining Path rebels, in Colombia there was no genuine alliance between the army and the peasantry; the Colombian counterinsurgency was waged in large part through paramilitaries that were themselves deeply involved in narcotics and liable to 'play their own game' rather than defeating the FARC (Revolutionary Armed Forces of Colombia, the main rebel group) or building political alliances against it. To compensate for its heavy reliance on paramilitaries that were involved in narcotics (and, more particularly, to maintain US support), the Colombian state took a very hawkish line on destroying illegal crops, something that further disaffected the peasantry and local officials.[53]

A vital and often neglected issue is that of 'ghost soldiers' (already noted in relation to Uganda). Military commanders have frequently made large profits – and have acquired an interest in continued conflict – by pocketing the difference between recorded numbers of soldiers and the (lower) actual numbers.

Consider the DRC. At the start of the peace transition in 2002, President Joseph Kabila claimed he had 120,000 troops in his FAC army (Congolese Armed Forces), yet around half may have existed only on pay rosters. At Sun City, South Africa, in 2002, Congolese belligerents declared their collective forces were 220,000, but this rose to 340,000 when the time came to put soldiers on the pay-roll; this was revised down to 240,000 by the Superior Defence Council. But most observers – and a South African-led counting process – put the true number at 130,000 or fewer. Inflating numbers bolsters the claim to political power and (in line with a well-established practice in Zaïre/DRC) allows the pocketing of salaries allocated to 'ghost soldiers'. In this way, as much as $100 million of soldiers' salaries may have been embezzled over the last few years.[54]

Following the 1996 peace agreement in Guatemala, military spending actually rose. Many observers said the numbers of soldiers on the pay-roll had been cut significantly, but the official figure had been kept high, with the difference going into the pockets of officers.[55]

In post-war Guatemala, members of the Guatemalan security sector have often been involved in organized crime.[56] (The army's attempts to secure finance from various kinds of relationships with organized crime – including drugs and kidnapping – goes back even to the 1970s.[57]) In addition to the immediate benefits from criminal activity, this involvement may serve a function in reinforcing the very phenomenon that does most to justify the budgets of counterinsurgency structures.

There have been versions of 'sell-game' even in industrialized countries. Commenting on war in Chechya in a 2004 publication, Thorniké Gordadze observed:

> Evidence suggests that the federal forces are behind the supply of arms to Chechen independence fighters . . . the Chechens are equipped with the same types of weapons as the federal forces. Since the rebels do not have any aircraft, the army has no need of anti-aircraft weapons in Chechnya, so the rebels cannot obtain them. . . . While ordinary soldiers may trade a grenade or a box of bullets for vodka or hashish, the officers deal in shells, mortars, rockets, information on their colleagues, and even the liberation of imprisoned rebels.[58]

In addition, Russian soldiers have made money from the small oil refineries (more than 1,500) in Chechnya, from smuggling, from 'protection' of aid workers and journalists, from arbitrary arrest and ransom payments, from theft, and from payments for leaving certain villages or districts alone (sometimes the well-known refuges of rebel leaders). On top of this, militarily counterproductive tactics have included freeing rebels and brutality against civilians (including heavy bombing): 'The inhumanity of federal troops maintains the rebellion's strength.'[59] More generally, the conflict strengthens the army, despite the heavy losses.[60] Chechens recruited into the Russian repressive apparatus have also captured alleged rebels and held them for ransom.[61]

Serious suspicions over state officials' involvement in explosions in Moscow and Volgodonsk have been mentioned in the previous chapter. Referring to the Chechen siege of a Moscow theatre in October 2002, Gordadze observed: 'The security apparatus maintains an impressive presence in Moscow and pursues the government policy of hunting down Caucasians, but proved incapable of intercepting – in the centre of the country's capital – a group of over forty heavily armed commandos or of thwarting an attack that had been meticulously prepared months in advance.'[62] He added that the police and security services 'seem to pass most of their time extorting money from people of Caucasian origin by means of intimidation, arbitrary arrests and torture. Corruption is so rampant that anyone with money can obtain a pass signed by the security authorities or vehicle licence plates reserved for officials.'[63]

Meanwhile, within Chechnya, the illegal financial activities of the Russian forces have fed into internal rivalries:

> Confrontations frequently break out between, for example, the FSB [federal security service, formerly KGB] and the army, or interior ministry troops and paratroopers. These confrontations sometimes end in pitched battles: serious fighting between Russian units broke out in Grozny in March 2001 following the arrest of a Chechen leader. One unit tried to free the rebel leader because it had received money from him to ignore his presence in the city.[64]

As in Sierra Leone, the elements of 'sell-game' and profiteering in Chechnya can be seen as a logical outcome of processes of corruption and state collapse in Russian society more generally. In his book *End of Millenium*, Manuel Castells argued that the new criminal networks in Russia were formed in the 1987–93 period for the sake of proceeding with the pillage of Russian oil, other minerals, weapons and other assets; much of this was done through a corrupt process of privatization. There was a wild competition to grab state assets.[65] The partial criminalization of business in Russia has been linked to the transition from a command economy to a market economy operated without the institutions (banks, accounting systems, means of enforcing contracts) that organize and regulate markets. The process has been accelerated by the collapse of state agencies, which became unable or unwilling to control this criminalization. In Russia, weak institutions for enforcing market transactions have fed into violence and a demand for private security, with some criminal organizations making businesses the proverbial 'offer they cannot refuse'.[66] At the same time, poor pay and redundancies in the state security sector have created an abundant supply of people ready to exercise various kinds of force on behalf of private clients. Seen from the other side, organized crime like drug trafficking demands some kind of penetration of the state, notably by intimidating and bribing politician, judges, officials and journalists.[67] Meanwhile, Chechens have sometimes been singled out as a key element in organized crime – effectively scapegoated for a process of criminalization that has benefited a political and criminal elite at the expense of ordinary Russians.

(Events in Russia find echoes in other countries, and indeed in the global system. As Mark Duffield and Federico Varese show, unregulated and illicit global markets tend to create a demand for private protection and for weaponry.[68] The thawing of the Cold War created a large supply of weapons and security personnel looking for a market. In South Africa, the

end of apartheid also left a legacy of a substantial, partially redundant security apparatus. The wars in Angola and Sierra Leone offered an outlet, and
the South African mercenary company Executive Outcomes became
involved in the fighting in both countries. In Angola, Executive Outcomes
fought on both sides, though admittedly not at the same time. Although
mercenaries helped government forces in Sierra Leone, some were also
seen helping rebels. The reluctance to risk Western lives in peacekeeping
operations has apparently encouraged Western governments to wink at
mercenary involvement.[69])

If government actors' economic agendas may lead to various kinds of
collaboration with rebels and criminals, economic motivations can also
make violence more indiscriminate, something that in turn tends to boost
rebel strength. One example – noted in chapter 1 – is raiding of civilians that
predictably radicalizes them. Another is indiscriminate attacks that are
fuelled by incentive structures within military bureaucracies.

After serving in the Indian army during counterinsurgency operations in
Kashmir, Gopal Mitra noted that senior commanders give out monthly 'kill
targets' in the manner of insurance salesmen handing out monthly sales
targets. He added that 'Sharing of intelligence information which should be
done routinely is often withheld for the fear that neighbouring units will
get better kill numbers.'[70]

Again, this is not particularly new. During the Vietnam war, some US
officers became obsessed by 'kill ratios' and 'body counts'. In her book
Stiffed, Susan Faludi compared these individuals to middle-tier corporate
managers pursuing the advancement of their careers.[71] One relevant
opportunity was the chance to pass off civilians as rebels, as made clear by
Faludi's interview with Michael Bernhardt (who resisted participation in
the infamous My Lai massacre of perhaps some 500 Vietnamese villagers
by US troops in 1968):

> In every encounter with a Vietnamese, he said, you could decide whether
> 'the person is a threat to the security of yourself and your unit, or not a
> threat. The person is a threat and you decide to kill the person and that's
> a correct action. . . . Or the person is not a threat, and you can kill the
> person. The trouble is, the outcome looks the same as the correct action.
> It doesn't look any different, and it's not scored any differently. And you
> need the score. The individual soldier needs the score, the commanding
> officer needs the score, the battalion commander and the division com-
> manders need the score. So what else is going to happen?'[72]

Neighbouring states

Consider now the role of states neighbouring the crisis-affected country.

Liberia played a destabilizing role in Sierra Leone's civil war. Although Charles Taylor originally supported Sierra Leone's rebels when he himself was a rebel, he won an election in July 1997 and thereafter delivered his support as head of state. We have seen how the belated (and constructive) pressure on Taylor was linked to reports of a connection with al-Qaida.

The role of neighbouring states has perhaps been most damaging in the case of the DRC. In August 1998, Rwanda and Uganda backed a rebellion against their former ally, President Laurent Kabila, who in turn was defended by troops from Angola, Zimbabwe, Namibia, Chad and Sudan. The resulting war was devastating for civilians, particularly in the east of the country, and, according to the International Rescue Committee, between 1998 and 2004 some 3.9 million people were killed as a result of the conflict.[73] The final report of the UN Panel of Experts on the DRC notes that while Rwanda claimed to have stayed in the Congo to hunt the Hutu *interahamwe* militia responsible for the 1994 Rwandan genocide, in fact this served as cover for the Rwandan army's desire to strip minerals.

In fact, the Rwandan President Paul Kagame's government described its military activities in the Congo as 'self-financing'.[74] Fabienne Hara of the International Crisis Group noted: 'About half of Rwanda's oversized army is now reliant on occupied territory to survive. A formal peace agreement and withdrawal from Congo would mean demobilising huge numbers of men into a tiny, poor country.'[75] The *Observer* newspaper also made an investigation and found many diplomats, fighters, aid workers and refugees reporting that Rwandan soldiers were cynically prolonging their stay in the Congo and collaborating with their supposed enemies. Tactics appear to have included stalling on the disarmament of the *interahamwe*, exaggerating the numbers of *interahamwe* in the Congo who took part in the genocide, persistently making little effort to engage the *interahamwe* in battle, and even selling arms to the *interahamwe*.[76] One Rwandan-trained rebel fighter said his orders were no longer to pursue the *interahamwe*: 'Rwanda came here to fight the Interahamwe but its objectives have changed. These days, we only pretend to fight them – it's all politics.'[77] Here one gets a very sinister picture – not entirely dissimilar to the dynamic in Sierra Leone, where the RUF was sometimes apparently maintained as a useful threat that justified abuses by parties other than the RUF. Rwanda's biggest ally and backer has been Britain, which has given a lot of aid money to Rwanda and has said very little in public about these abuses.

Uganda's troops also became heavily involved in mineral resource extraction from the Congo. The UN Panel of Experts report provided evidence of Ugandan commanders inciting violence between rebel groups, apparently so as to remain in regions rich in gold and coltan (used in mobile phones).

Yet Uganda was attracting particularly favourable comment from international financial institutions (or IFIs). Uganda agreed with the IFIs to limit defence spending to 2 per cent of GDP. Meanwhile, donors were praising Uganda for increasing its tax revenues, much of which was actually coming from taxing logging coming out of conflict zones in the Congo.[78] Donors, whilst providing roughly a half of Uganda's budgetary support, have been extremely slow to challenge military corruption within Uganda[79] – often seen as a 'golden boy' in a much larger field of unsavoury regimes.

In an important article, Tangri and Mwenda have carefully documented widespread corruption among senior officers in the Ugandan army – many of them close to President Museveni. Profits from supplying (or withholding) provisions have been made in relation to Ugandan troops in the DRC as well as in northern Uganda.[80] Conflict in the DRC – ostensibly to clear rebel forces trying to destabilize the Ugandan government – proved intensely profitable for a small number of senior officers, who became involved in smuggling gold, diamonds, timber and coffee from the DRC to Uganda, sometimes paying for these supplies with the salaries that had been intended for ordinary Ugandan soldiers fighting (and dying) in the DRC. This corruption gave rise to serious political opposition to Museveni, which he countered partly through intimidation and accusations of undermining the 'good order' of the army.[81]

Zimbabwe was also meddling in the DRC. Zimbabwe lowered its defence budget at the very time when its troops were entrenching themselves in the Congo.[82] Large profits from the cobalt, copper and diamond mines in Congo are thought to have gone to members of the Zimbabwean government and army. Zimbabwean officials also benefited from defence contracts to supply the Congolese army. (In fact, Zimbabwean commercial interests seem to have advanced significant sums to Laurent Kabila for his rebellion.[83]) More generally, the UN Panel of Experts on the DRC observed that the number of conventional battles between rival armies had been decreasing, with increased attention and energy being directed towards economic exploitation.[84] Where there was conflict, it was mostly in areas rich in cobalt, copper or diamonds.

The destabilizing role of neighbouring states has also been clear in Afghanistan. Here, the *mujahadeen* forced the withdrawal of Soviet forces in 1989, but with the end of the Cold War, the Afghan government found itself unable to pay for its militias, leading to the breakdown of government in 1992 and a period of more or less rampant warlordism in 1992–6, when a variety of warlords used their trading connections with neighbouring countries (Uzbekistan, Tajikistan, Pakistan, Iran) to pay their militiamen and fund their violence. After the advent of the Taliban, Russia and Iran backed the anti-Taliban coalition; both were interested in preventing the construction of a pipeline that would take oil and gas from the Caspian sea region across Afghanistan to Pakistan. That route was favoured not only by Pakistan, which supported the Taliban, but also by the United States.[85]

States beyond the region

The role of states beyond the region can also get neglected in the focus on 'rebel greed'.

Chapter 8 includes an extended discussion of the damaging role of Western powers and international financial institutions in many complex emergencies. This negative impact receives scant attention in Collier's research or other research emanating from the World Bank, an institution that bears its own share of responsibility. As Mark Duffield has noted, power does not like to analyse itself.[86]

China has propped up the abusive regime in Sudan through its oil purchases and arms sales. It has also supplied military equipment and interest-free loans to Robert Mugabe in Zimbabwe; it has even provided a radio jammer to help silence opposition broadcasts. In return it gets access to Zimbabwean gold and platinum and to Zimbabwean markets for its manufactured goods.[87] Potentially, China's interest may offer African governments a chance to carve out a sphere of relative autonomy (in contrast to the history of various kinds of subordination to the West).[88] Nevertheless, China's role in supporting abusive governments remains very worrying.

States in richer countries have been reluctant to rein in profitable commodity flows, even when these are clearly fuelling war economies. In Cambodia, Burma, Liberia and Sierra Leone, violence has been fuelled by foreign interest in timber and valuable minerals. For example, De Beers fuelled diamond smuggling from Sierra Leone – including smuggling by rebels during wartime – by buying within countries that have a minimal production base, such as Liberia and Ivory Coast.[89] In 1998, Belgium recorded imports from Liberia totalling 2.56 million carats; yet even the highest estimates of Liberian production capacity were not above 150,000 carats per year.[90]

While progress has been made in regulating 'conflict diamonds', regulation is impeded by the fear of lost business. For example, London and Antwerp worry about driving business to Tel Aviv and Bombay. Companies involved in war economies may also be protected from accountability, including possible legal action. In an October 2003 UN Panel of Experts report on DRC, forty-two companies that had been named as breaching OECD Guidelines (in the October 2002 Panel of Experts report) were classified as 'resolved' with 'no outstanding issues'; however, there was no information on why individual companies had been granted this status.[91] The strong suspicion is that diplomatic pressure was brought to bear.[92] Of twelve British companies named as breaching OECD Guidelines, the British government was investigating only one, Das Air.[93]

One specialized problem is when companies actually fund rebel groups in the hope of obtaining favourable mineral concessions. Foreign mining interests quickly deserted Mobutu and started funding Laurent Kabila's rebels when they realized that Mobutu's fall was imminent.[94] The UN's Panel of Experts on the Congo noted in 2001 that every time one company gets a major concession in alliance with one military faction, there are other sidelined companies anxious to guarantee their presence in the region.

States in developed countries have also been slow to rein in flows of corruptly or violently obtained funding from poor countries into richer countries' banks. The role of Swiss banks in the Nazi war economy has recently been highlighted (as has foot-dragging by these banks when it came to returning stolen money and money remaining in the accounts of Holocaust victims);[95] but the role of banks as havens for stolen goods cannot be conveniently consigned to 'the past'. For example, Singapore – which in many ways shares the Swiss reputation for cleanliness – has been involved in its own 'dirty money' scandal, banking the proceeds of Burma's destructive opium trade as well as supplying the Burmese military and lobbying on the government's behalf within the UN and the regional group of states known as ASEAN.

The problem is not simply that banks may fuel war economies; by accepting corruptly obtained funds, they fuel corruption and autocratic rule in many countries around the world. Some of the statistics on covert banking are amazing. For example, in 2000 some £400 billion – roughly half of Britain's GDP – was being held in the UK's tiny offshore islands, where around 90,000 anonymously owned companies were registered; around £100 billion was being held in Jersey alone. A huge amount has also been invested in Caribbean offshore centres, most of them UK Overseas Territories. Millions of dollars of IMF loans to Russia were laundered through the London branch of the Bank of New York, a manoeuvre made easier by the UK's banking secrecy.[96] Luxembourg and Austria have been among the main centres for money-laundering. Lebanon's status as a key financial centre was battered by its own civil war, but has been restored, partly by making sure that the banking system offers extreme privacy for its clients and, by extension, a refuge for money that may be tainted.[97] Cyprus has also benefited in this way.[98] This state of affairs persists because, as with restrictions on commodity flows, banking regulation is often seen as a threat to the domestic economy. Moves to tighten financial controls in the UK, for example, produced a split in Tony Blair's cabinet, with some ministers expressing the fear that the country would lose out to rivals like Switzerland.[99]

When major corporations give bribes to win contracts, this bolsters corruption and autocratic rule in poorer countries. Defence contracts have a particularly bad record here: Susan Hawley reported in 2000 that half the bribery complaints received by the US Commerce Department concerned defence contracts.[100]

That brings us to the arms trade, another powerful contributor to complex emergencies whose role is rather obscured by a discourse of 'rebel greed'. Arms exports have fed wars around the world. Nick Stockton, formerly head of emergencies at Oxfam, tells how when he was in Goma on the Zaïre/Rwanda border, commercial crews hired to bring in food aid by air said they could predict where this kind of business would arise since food aid typically followed shipments of guns, a business in which they were also profitably involved.

Four points are worth stressing here. First, a huge vested interest has grown up in the continuation of an industry that absorbs an obscene quantity of resources that could be far better spent elsewhere. The five permanent members of the Security Council – the US, Britain, France, Russia and China – account for over four-fifths of the weapons exported to developing countries.[101] For every dollar that the US allocates to peacekeeping, it allocates $200–300 to US defence.[102] A huge military-industrial complex has come to depend on the arms trade, particularly in the US. Arms, like drugs, tend to create their own demand: the supplies are addictive for abusive governments; and the more you sell, the greater the demand. The best way to stop the flow of small arms or any other kind of arms is to stop making them.

Second, while the official line in Britain and the US is that exports are only to responsible governments, the export of arms to so-called 'friendly' governments is extremely problematic. Many loopholes exist. A major loophole is that national laws generally do not cover the activities of arms brokers.[103] The British company Mil-tec supplied arms to the genocidal government of Rwanda both before and during the genocide (including small arms and millions of rounds of ammunition).[104] Traffickers have rarely faced any legal consequences, though there has been some small progress here.[105] Moreover, if favoured governments are so responsible, why do they need all those arms? Crucially, arms also tend to build a wall between governments and their own people. In the 1970s and 1980s, US supplies of arms to Liberia, Somalia, Sudan and Zaïre and French support to Rwanda helped to consolidate authoritarian regimes, stoking up resentment in these countries. These arms have then been used in conflicts arising, in part, from this resentment. Arms sold to particular governments have frequently ended up distributed among rival factions, often on ethnic or clan lines. Civil conflict in Somalia is a prime example. The arming of *mujahadeen* rebels in Afghanistan during the 1980s struggle against Soviet occupation – notably by the US and Pakistan – subsequently fuelled factional warfare inside Afghanistan. In Angola, large-scale and covert US military aid to UNITA in the 1980s strengthened the rebel organization, and helped it to ignore the 1992 election results and re-start a highly destructive war. Once arms have been sold, it is difficult or impossible to control how they are re-sold or re-exported at a later date. Moreover, arms sales tend to stimulate arms acquisition in neighbouring or rival countries.

Third, the proliferation of arms encourages economic violence and often leads to weak chains of command. This means it is very hard to rein in violence: a peace settlement may be declared, but will ordinary fighters follow their leaders? As Sharon Hutchinson shows in her book on the Nuer of Sudan, guns make it much harder to trace accountability for violence and to enforce traditional mechanisms for conflict resolution.[106] Long-standing disputes and tensions become much more destructive.

Fourth, the end of the Cold War created very particular problems which have been poorly addressed. Existing military industries are looking for new markets – a very important effect of cuts in official military spending in the former Soviet Union and Eastern Europe. There were huge stockpiles of armaments in newly created countries facing an acute lack of revenue. The devastating effects of Eastern bloc arsenals on parts of West Africa are dramatically depicted in the film *Lord of War*, starring Nicolas Cage. Although a fictionalized account, the film has been endorsed by Amnesty International and in many ways complements more sober accounts of this process (notably, in UN Panel of Experts reports). Michael Klare notes how the Soviet Union and Warsaw Pact black market (involving the state and privatized firms) sourced a lot of the weapons that were used in Bosnia. When Mil-tec, based on the Isle of Man, supplied arms to Hutu extremists in Goma during the Rwandan genocide, the shipment came from Albania.[107] Moreover, Ukraine has supplied weapons to embargoed rebels in Sierra Leone and the embargoed government in Liberia.[108] Meanwhile, the smuggling of nuclear materials has sometimes been too hard to resist for underpaid workers in Russia's nuclear industry. The NGO Human Rights Watch has noted:

> Many Central and Eastern European countries have huge stockpiles of aging Soviet-standard military equipment they no longer need. This is particularly true for candidates for NATO membership, as well as members admitted in 1999, who are modernizing their armed forces in line with NATO guidelines. The discarded weapons are sold off to clients that can afford little else, usually unaccountable armed forces in areas of violent conflict in Africa and Asia. The proceeds from such sales help finance purchases of newer weapons, often obtained from European or North American suppliers.[109]

States have frequently exerted great influence via international financial institutions, with the US particularly influential in the World Bank and the IMF. IFIs' role in conflicts is discussed in more detail in chapter 8, but it is worth noting at this point that IFIs have frequently played a major part in eroding state institutions and in setting the stage for complex emergencies. My research in Sierra Leone suggested that policies of liberalization pushed through by the IFIs had actually fuelled conflict in four main ways: first, by encouraging inflation, drastic devaluation, and the creation of private oligopolies when state enterprises were privatized; second, by reducing key state services such as education and health, and thereby fuelling grievances; third, by fuelling corruption as real state salaries were cut, corruption that eventually included soldiers' collaboration with rebels; and, fourth, by taking attention away from soldiers' abuses under the military government of 1992–6, a government that, as noted, was actually praised and rewarded for its 'financial orthodoxy' and liberalization agenda.[110]

Again, the discourse of 'rebel greed' does not get us very far in understanding these complex processes and tends to let the West off the hook when it comes to allocating responsibility.

Conclusion

The international impunity over DRC interventions that was enjoyed for a crucial period by Uganda and Rwanda in particular suggests dangers not only in blaming 'rebel greed' but also in the increasing fashion for 'picking winners' when allocating aid resources – that is, picking countries that seem to have good governance (at least within their own borders) and a plausible anti-poverty programme, it is not only people in the 'loser' countries who may suffer. The tendency to favour states with 'good governance' seems only to have been encouraged by the 'war on terror': it is notable that Rwanda and Uganda were among the select 'coalition of the willing' who supported the invasion of Iraq.[111]

The analysis in this chapter underlines the danger of simplistically dividing the world into good and evil, those who are 'with us' and those who are 'against us', the 'good guys' and the 'greedy rebels'. The world is much more complex than this, and violence – whether we approve of it or not – happens for a reason. A lesson from several civil wars – and increasingly from the global 'war on terror' too – is that the initial legitimacy of a particular struggle provides space, opportunity and impunity for abuses which may not be acknowledged, denounced or corrected. We know from actions by Israel and Rwanda that 'legitimate self-defence' after a genocide can be a fertile climate for abuse.

One way into the problem of mass violence is to examine the structures of incentives and punishments within which perpetrators are operating – in other words, a 'rational actor' framework. Such an examination should include consideration of the resources that violence may permit them to extract from their victims or from the natural environment as well as the 'career benefits' that may also accrue. We have suggested that war may often be best conceptualized not as a *contest* or a *collapse* but as a *system*, and this chapter has focused on war as an *economic system*. The degree to which violence is or is not punished – the extent of impunity – will also be a critical variable. But 'rational actor' analysis should not distract attention from grievances or to their complex interaction with economic agendas in civil wars.

The longevity of many armed conflicts is particularly baffling if we ignore state actors. Mark Duffield suggests that Africa is usually regarded as facing a problem of development and Eastern Europe and Russia as facing a problem of transition. Both are seen as progressing, haltingly, towards a liberal democratic future. Complex emergencies themselves are often seen as a temporary deviation from normality, a substantial hiccup on the road to development and peace.[112] But certain kinds of contemporary disorder are proving extremely durable, and this reflects in large measure the fact that various kind of illicit global trade are often successfully confronting states that lack the ability or will to control such trading. These states are not only in war-affected countries but also in neighbouring countries where the profits from smuggling may defeat and corrupt any government attempt to rein in a transnational war economy. Collapsing states have sometimes created space for new kinds of transnational conflict, with foreign countries backing factions within the collapsed state, and often getting an economic return. Examples include Congo/Zaïre and Afghanistan. These strategies have political as well as economic dimensions.

Again, an investigation of war systems needs to get beyond a focus on the rebels or a condemnation and simplification of their motives. The following chapter attempts to contribute to a broader picture by examining the complex motives of a variety of combatants – both in wartime and in the fragile peace that often ensues.

3
Combatants and Their Grievances

Chapter 1 stressed the dangers in taking the fault-lines of conflict at face value and chapter 2 showed how these fault-lines may be profoundly influenced by economic agendas. Chapters 3 and 4 examine how emotional and political factors have affected these fault-lines, helping to shape how enemies are defined and re-defined. This involves a shift of focus from a 'rational actor' framework to one that is more informed by psychology, sociology and history. It also involves an intensified focus on 'grievance' rather than 'greed'. The current chapter focuses on *combatants'* grievances, distinguishing between pre-war grievances, wartime grievances and post-war grievances, and drawing particularly on my research in Sierra Leone. Chapter 4 goes on to examine how some wider political forces and vested interests have shaped the choice of enemy and the fault-lines of various conflicts; it looks particularly at factors that have channelled politics and conflict along ethnic lines.

One of the most important roots of violence is a sense of having been *humiliated.*[1] Combatants have frequently harboured some sense of humiliation, whether arising from wartime or peacetime, and this can feed into their own violence. The classic case is perhaps Adolf Hitler. A decorated soldier in the First World War, Hitler seems to have carried with him his own personal sense of humiliation not only arising from the hated Versailles treaty but also at the hands of the Jews who he said had 'laughed' at him as a struggling artist in Vienna after the war. In his Reichstag speech of January 1939, Hitler proclaimed: 'During the time of my struggle for power it was in the first instance the Jewish race which only received my prophesies with laughter when I said that I would take over the leadership of the state . . . I think that for some time now they have been laughing on the other side of their face.'[2]

Violence in wartime has often been designed to humiliate the victims, and this offers a significant clue to understanding the importance of humiliation in *producing* (or at least contributing to) that violence. The work of psychiatrist James Gilligan is particularly helpful in understanding the role of humiliation. In his book *Violence: Reflections on Our Deadliest Epidemic*, Gilligan observed that his experience of working with and listening to some of America's most violent criminals convinced him that these individuals' past experiences had given them a heightened sensitivity to feelings of shame and humiliation, and that when these feelings were strongly aroused or reawakened, the individuals had sometimes attacked or even killed the person who was arousing these feelings – even though the current 'disrespect' might have been slight or imagined and even though this unfortunate person was not usually responsible for the initial humiliation.[3] Gilligan argued that the desire to eliminate a source of shame and thereby keep a sense of personal worth was often a more powerful motivation even than self-preservation, leading violent criminals into self-destructive behaviour as well as the abuse of others. One intriguing implication of this argument is that our most immoral actions may stem precisely from our moral impulses, since without these we would have no sense of shame in the first place. While moving from criminology to war studies is not without its hazards, the moral frameworks of combatants turn out to be just as important as the moral frameworks of individual criminals.

Pre-war Grievances

When old ideological and political models for explaining civil wars began to look increasingly inappropriate with the end of the Cold War, two models that gained increased exposure and credence were the 'greed' model (chapters 1 and 2) and the model of war as 'chaos' and 'breakdown' (chapter 1). These contrasting models seemed happily to co-exist in discussions of war in Sierra Leone, where violence was presented as simultaneously 'diamond-fuelled' and 'mindless'. In both parts of this schizophrenic discourse, the role of pre-war grievances tended to be squeezed out of the analysis.

An important exception was *Fighting for the Rain Forest* by British anthropologist Paul Richards. Challenging the 're-primitivization' of Africa by Western commentators such as Robert Kaplan,[4] Richards argued that the violence of Sierra Leone's rebel Revolutionary United Front (RUF), so far from being 'mindless', 'random' or driven simply by 'greed', was an attempt to articulate and dramatize the grievances of those floundering at the margins of both an exploitative world economy and a 'patrimonial' state that was no longer able to extend even minimal services to much of the population. Richards saw the extremity of the rebels' violence as a plea for attention: as if the rebels wished to say to the world, 'Look what you have driven us to!'[5]

Ironically, Richards' challenge to the racist overtones in Kaplan's so-called 'new barbarism' was to expose him to the accusation of lending legitimacy to actions that many Sierra Leoneans felt *deserved* the label 'barbaric'. Richards' harshest critic here was Yusuf Bangura, who stressed the hostility of civilians towards the RUF and the strong strain of banditry, hedonism, and drugs-consumption among the rebels.[6]

If Richards' attempt to find a political rationale in even the most bizarre and extreme acts of violence did not go down well with many observers, his book was nevertheless important in putting grievances on the map. My own research in Sierra Leone focused on how 'greed' and 'grievance' *interacted*. A range of informants spoke of the widespread anger among Sierra Leonean youth, particularly males, at collapsing public services (especially education), and at youths' perceived low status in a society offering them few opportunities to advance or to perform a meaningful role.[7] Equally striking was that this anger generally did not find a coherent political expression. The RUF's political ideology was poorly articulated, impeded by low levels of education and by a widespread suspicion of educated people (not least on the part of RUF leader Foday Sankoh); the educated were often regarded as having collaborated with the longstanding appropriation of the country's resources.[8] Youths often sought revenge against chiefs and elders who had excluded and exploited them in a system that was inherited from the indirect rule of the British colonialists and that conformed quite closely to what Mahmood Mamdani has described as 'decentralized despotism'.[9] One Sierra Leonean student who had worked with demobilized soldiers (many of them children) told me: 'The feeling seemed to be: "Let's destabilize everything and try to look forward to a new order. We might as well participate in the total destruction of the state because people have been destroying it for a long time."'

Significantly, violence was often intended to be profoundly humiliating. Frequently, there were attempts to compel 'approval' of, or indifference towards, atrocities from the relatives of those directly abused – as if the rebels were staging a bizarre drama with a script that made them, for once, look like 'big men'. In some instances, chiefs were made to dance naked, to plant swamp rice, to crawl about on the floor, or to act as 'waiter' to the rebel invaders.[10] There were echoes here of the way Cambodia's Khmer Rouge – on a far greater and more systematic scale – had forced privileged urban populations to farm; one gets a similar sense of the revenge of the excluded and exploited.[11] Another echo of Cambodia was the replacement of old structures, on occasion, by farcical child-chiefs.[12] One local worker with Catholic Relief Services emphasized that violence in Sierra Leone could somehow reverse a loss of face, including that associated with drop-ping out of school:

> A lot drop out of school early and these do not have fair job opportuni-ties and, having gone to [secondary] school, they do not want to go back to their villages and till the land. They feel they are a little too enlightened to go back and till the soil! They feel their friends will laugh at them, and say you're still farming even though you went off to school. They saw that being a rebel you can loot at will, then you have a sway over your former master, who used to lord it over you, or the others who might have laughed.

In Sierra Leone's war, status and visibility were violently inverted. Those who were poor and poorly regarded could become 'big men', and those who were ignored and forgotten could become front-page news. Sam 'Mosquito' Bockarie, a one-time diamond-miner and professional disco-dancer who became the RUF's acting commander, said, 'I never wanted myself to be overlooked by my fellow men. I think I am at a stage where I am satisfied. I have heard my name all over, I have become famous.'[13] RUF leader Foday Sankoh boasted that because he had taken to the bush, he had arrived at the position were he could receive a phone call from the President of the United States (at that time, Bill Clinton).

Various factions tried to coerce 'respect'. One man taken hostage in 2000 by the West Side Boys (a rogue army faction) linked their violence against civilians and their 'greed' to more fundamental motivation: 'They have the gun and they've seen a way how people of their ranks can mobilize and get some worth and some money. Without money, they don't have self-worth. And when they have the gun, whether you like it or not, you must respect them . . . .' To a significant extent, both rebels and soldiers of the National Provisional Ruling Council (NPRC) military regime (1992–6) were con-cerned to 'turn the tables' on elites who had dominated under the one-party rule of the All People's Congress (APC) during the 1970s and 1980s; fre-quently the aim was to invert the social pyramid so that rebels and soldiers could experience what it was like to be rich or powerful. These processes bring to mind Eric Hobsbawm's insights in his brief history of bandits and rebels. Hobsbawm wrote, 'Killing and torture is the most primitive and per-sonal assertion of ultimate power, and the weaker the rebel feels himself to be at bottom, the greater, we may suppose, the temptation to assert it.'[14] In a passage that resonates with global conflict as well as inside Sierra Leone, Hobsbawm's wide-ranging study also referred to a category of bandits – labelled by him as 'the avengers' – who carried out spectacular acts of terror, often but not always against the powerful, and who proved, he observed, that 'even the poor and weak can be terrible'.[15]

If the case of Sierra Leone shows how peacetime grievances may find expression in atrocities that restore a sense of power in the here and now, it is by no means an isolated example. In her study of China in the early twentieth century, Diana Lary mentions ordinary Chinese soldiers' 'lust for revenge against a world in which they had been impotent as civilians, even before they went into the army'.[16] In Guatemala, participation in abusive counterinsurgency militias (known, misleadingly, as 'civil defence') seems to have offered a chance for respect to some who were accustomed to discrimination on racial or ethnic lines. Commenting on the leaders of these militias in her insightful study *Violent Memories*, Judith Zur wrote:

> Power is sought by and granted to the frustrated, to men who crave authority and are willing to venerate hierarchic authority in order to obtain it: the immediate power of the rifle and the ability to evoke fear in fellow villagers is a more than satisfactory compensation for all the years of disrespect.[17]

In a related observation, Betty Bigombe – in her reflections on trying to broker peace in northern Uganda as a government representative in 1994 – noted that the Ugandan army officers who seemed most unhappy with the peace initiative were themselves Acholi (the group that had not only been most devastated by war but also frequently blamed for the war and for the rebel LRA): 'The senior Acholi army commanders were more hostile to me than other army commanders. Perhaps it is the psychology of people who feel they are marginalized.'[18]

Wartime Grievances

Compounding peacetime grievances in Sierra Leone were those arising more immediately from the war itself. Naturally, wartime attacks created a desire for revenge. More interestingly, grievances were often harboured in relation to one's own faction or military structure. For combatants, war threw up contrasting experiences: an experience of *powerlessness* (to some extent in relation to the enemy and to some extent in relation to one's own commanders) and at the same time an experience of *power* (in relation to groups of unarmed civilians). In combination with economic agendas, this fed strongly into violence against the unarmed civilians. As René Girard has noted: 'When unappeased, violence seeks and always finds a surrogate victim. The creature that excited its fury is abruptly replaced by another, chosen only because it is vulnerable and close at hand.'[19] When civilians reacted angrily, the fault-line between armed groups and civilians was reinforced. While the initial victims of violence were often local notables vilified by RUF rebels, over time the violence in Sierra Leone seems to have become more indiscriminate.

With corruption depriving front-line soldiers of essential supplies, these men were left to face a clever and elusive enemy. This fed into the exercise of power over relatively powerless civilians. With the IMF pushing for reduced spending on the security sector, 1997 saw cuts in the size of the rations of the Sierra Leonean army as well as the departure of mercenary outfit Executive Outcomes. Unfortunately, in the absence of a UN peacekeeping presence, these measures paved the way for a military coup in May 1997 by disgruntled junior officers, who joined with the rebel RUF to form a highly abusive government.[20]

Some members of the abusive rogue army faction known as the West Side Boys had direct experience of the Sierra Leonean army, and seem to have been embittered by it; indeed, grievances within the army had often exacerbated a prior sense of grievance. The former hostage of the West Side Boys told me:

> They were angry with the system – politically, and the economic effect it had. Truly there has been misrule with those at the top amassing wealth and using the young people, like in elections when youths were sometimes recruited to intimidate voters and opponents. After elections, some were abandoned and some turned to crime. Some who were lucky found themselves going into the army. One way they tried to compensate some people was to put them in the military. And even within the army, they feel they are not treated fairly, not receiving sacks of rice, and feel they are being used or bullied. . . . When they find themselves in the bush, they inflict the same injustice on those under them that they are complaining about. . . . They're finding worth, attention and respect, and they think one way is by bullying those under them. They want to be powerful. They want to control people. It's some kind of normal human tendency, picking on those less strong than themselves . . . .

Rebels' abuse of civilians was also related to their own experience of abuse. Many recruits had been forced into attacking their own families and communities, something that (in addition to outright intimidation by rebel leaders) made it risky to leave the rebels and return home.[21] David Lord, former head of the NGO Conciliation Resources, commented in 2000:

> The RUF's horrific human rights abuses are often (perhaps even mainly) committed by abducted children. Those who command the movement

(and perhaps order the atrocities) are themselves the product of earlier cycles of abduction. Now in their late teens or early twenties, these leading fighters are the human rights abusing products of human rights abuses. The original leadership is mainly dead or disappeared.[22]

If part of the impetus for atrocities in Sierra Leone's civil war was resentment at neglect and abuse (and a concomitant desire for respect, however forced), then another seems to have been a perception within various fighting groups that civilians had somehow 'turned against' or 'betrayed' them.

Recognition from civilians seemed to be strangely prized, even as atrocities were driving them away. In the 1995 pamphlet *Footpaths to Democracy*, apparently emanating from the RUF rebels, it was stated: 'The rebel NPRC behaves as if we are despicable aliens from another planet and not Sierra Leoneans.'[23] A local aid worker said of the rebels and rogue soldiers who staged a joint coup in 1997: 'They felt that the civilians had gone against them, so they started killing the civilians indiscriminately. They thought they were unimportant in the eyes of the civilians. So they were finding every way to find recognition.' Significantly, after the May 1997 coup, the RUF broadcast an 'Apology to the Nation'. It included the statement: 'We did not take to the bush because we wanted to be barbarians, not because we wanted to be inhuman, but because we wanted to state our humanhood . . . .'[24]

The RUF's 'Apology to the Nation' in particular is reminiscent of the famous speech by Shakespeare's Shylock in *The Merchant of Venice*. While the speech is normally interpreted as a protest against anti-Semitism, it seems to be more besides. Shylock explains his seemingly inhuman desire to mutilate Antonio (who owes him money) precisely as a manifestation of his own humanity:

> He hath disgraced me . . . laughed at my losses . . . and what's his reason? I am a Jew. Hath not a Jew eyes? Hath not a Jew hands, organs, dimensions, senses, affections, passions? . . . If you prick us, do we not bleed? If you tickle us, do we not laugh? If you poison us, do we not die? And if you wrong us, shall we not revenge? . . . The villainy you teach me I will execute, and it shall go hard but I will better the instruction.[25]

Whilst presenting his violence as a manifestation of his humanity, Shylock is also ready to adopt the inhuman persona he has been saddled with: 'Thou call'dst me dog before thou hadst a cause; But, since I am a dog, beware my fangs.'[26] Compare this sentiment with the words of a man who survived among the mixed group of RUF rebels and rogue government soldiers invading the Freetown area in December 1998 to January 1999: 'You don't want to treat these people as animals. There has to be some respect. I think that was one of the reasons I survived [in Waterloo] for all that time.' Being taken seriously as moral actors seems to have been important to at least some of the attackers. The survivor commented:

> They still don't want to accept that their philosophy does not appeal, so they want to do it by force. . . . They unleash punishment, which makes the civilians shy away or treat them as enemies. At the same time, they want some kind of recognition from the civilians because they have some kind of ideology and beliefs.

Recognition

The invaders (often drunk or drugged) were hypersensitive to betrayal and rejection:

> They worry about betrayal to the army or the kamajors [civil defence]. One wrong move would have meant death or amputation for me and my family. . . . By running away from him, this is going to make things worse. Hence the [rebel] slogan: 'Why are you running from us, and you don't run away from ECOMOG [the West African peacekeepers ranged against the attackers]? What do you see in us that you don't see in them?' So sometimes running away is going to exacerbate more cruelty. You have to say, 'OK, I'm with you. I support you. There's nothing wrong with you.' I was able to use this tool to survive.

Civilians were an easy target after military reversals, and were quickly accused of betrayal or passing information to 'the other side'. One young man with several friends in the RUF rebel group said, 'The RUF at first used to interact with civilians, but then found the military was gaining success, so started casting aspersions on civilians.' A local journalist told me: 'In the RUF, there was anger at civilians, and fear. . . . When government soldiers fought back, rebels attributed their loss to the civilians.' Significantly, most of the worst violence in early 1999 – both in Freetown and upcountry – came when rebels had been forced to retreat by the West African peace-keeping forces.

Many young fighters had been subjected to propaganda suggesting they would secure quick victories and easy pickings. When these hopes were blocked, the temptation to turn on civilians was all the greater. Within the rogue army faction known as the West Side Boys, military setbacks report-edly led to the execution of six women associated with the group, who were accused of being witches and undermining the war effort.

Particularly where violence was related to a desire for recognition, the condemnation and rejection following rebel cruelty only deepened the rebels' sense of alienation – a vicious circle that appears to have significantly deepened the violence in Sierra Leone. As one human rights worker put it,

'When we realized it was a war against civilians, the rebels became our enemies. And because the civilians now condemned them, they actually turned [all the more] on the civilians.'[27]

Some of these dynamics were echoed within the army, where there was a sense that soldiers were being stigmatized as greedy 'sobels' (soldiers by day, rebels by night), and that the efforts of loyal soldiers in defending civilians were not being recognized. Even where abuses are carried out by a relatively small group, they may set off a process of alienation (civilian disgust, fighters' perception of civilian ingratitude) that encourages abuses by a much larger group.[28]

Mixed in with the feeling of betrayal, very often, was the fighter's fear of the civilian. The phrase is a bizarre one: how can one speak of the soldier's fear of the civilian in a context where, on any reasonable view of the facts, it is civilians who should be fearing the soldiers?

Whilst fear of the innocent is a counterintuitive concept, there are sometimes reasons why the innocent may be *particularly* feared. First, they may be used by the other side precisely because they are not usually suspected of involvement in conflict – as in the use of women and children as spies.[29] Rebels and civilians were frequently hard to distinguish, and government soldiers complained that while they themselves wore uniforms, rebels did not. Second, the importance of flows of information means that it was not only the armed or the physically strong who could hurt you; pointing a finger, or passing a secret, might be just as deadly. Third, there is the possibility of judicial procedures spearheaded by angry civilians – a particular concern in Sierra Leone. Fourth, only those who appear benign can actually betray: those who are unambiguously enemies might kill you but they could not betray you since you never trusted them in the first place; it is natural, in some ways, to fear the 'unknown quantity'.[30] Fifth, the perceived importance of the spiritual sphere in relation to conflict – in terms of witchcraft, charms, prayer, and so on – meant that even the apparently weak and unarmed could be seen as a threat: you did not have to be armed to exert spiritual power. Sixth, the innocent may eventually rise up and defend themselves, as happened with the civil defence movement in Sierra Leone. At this point, they may become a military threat to existing armed factions.

Collaboration between armed groups was encouraged not only by economic agendas and the desire for safety but also by some degree of shared ideology and shared grievances between the various factions. In particular, young men from various fighting factions frequently blamed politicians for inciting a war without putting themselves on the front-line, and for profiting from the violence. Older people were sometimes seen as having ruined the country through peacetime corruption, as having invited young people into violence, and then as failing to support them or even actually condemning them. Senior commanders were also sometimes accused of exploitation. The fact that young recruits on opposing sides frequently came from similarly humble backgrounds also fed into collaboration.

Fear of, or anger at, civilian 'betrayal' that proved so important in Sierra Leone finds many echoes elsewhere. In Liberia's civil war, Bishop William Nah Dixon of the Pentecostal Church said of abusive government soldiers in 1992: 'Incapable of facing the enemy on the battlefield, [they] turned against innocent civilians . . ., killing them on suspicion of abetting and hiding the rebels.'[31] Discussing increasing abuses by the rebel Rwandan Patriotic Front in northern Rwanda in the early 1990s, Mahmood Mamdani wrote, 'From recognizing that peasants distrusted them to a distrust of peasants, a sort of mutual distrust, was but a short step.'[32] Commenting on the intense violence in Algeria during the 1990s, Chawki Amari noted, 'Terrorists exhorted helpless civilians to choose sides or face "punishment" for their lack of commitment to the struggle against the state.'[33] These attacks reached a peak in 1997 during peace negotiations between the army and the AIS (Armée Islamique de Salut, the armed wing of the FIS [Islamic Salvation Front]). In Cambodia, the Khmer Rouge's hostility towards civilians was fed by fear that spies were providing the US government with valuable information on which areas to bomb. Peasants fleeing to the capital Phnom Penh were seen as having chosen sides while the revolutionaries were bombed to pieces, convincing some Khmer Rouge leaders that these civilians should be punished; these fears and resentments seem to have compounded a longstanding rural resentment of traders and urban populations.[34] Anger at civilians (and their accessibility) was also important in the 1998–9 Kosovo crisis. Serb forces' attacks on Kosovar civilians escalated during a NATO air campaign that was supposed to deter them. The Independent International Commission on Kosovo commented, 'The FRY [Federal Republic of Yugoslavia] forces could not hit NATO, but they could hit the Albanians who had asked for NATO's support and intervention.'[35]

Antonius Robben has argued that in Argentina's 'Dirty War' of 1976–83 both the military and the guerillas had a kind of fear of the neutral; indeed, those who refused to take sides were often attacked, verbally or physically. Robben noted that indifference was a conceptual and moral threat to the prevailing and officially favoured partisan mentality; indifference showed, firstly, that violence was not inevitable and, secondly, that battle-lines could be questioned.[36]

There are also many examples of combatants' powerlessness feeding into the abusive exertion of power over civilians. This might be powerlessness in relation to the enemy. During renewed warfare in Angola 1998–2002, the rebel UNITA forces – faced with international sanctions and military reversals – stepped up their exploitation of civilians in areas they controlled, including through pillage, extortion and forced recruitment of men and children. The increased levels of cruelty included resort to mutilations.[37]

Recalling his experience in the Vietnam war, former American GI Greg Olsen told Susan Faludi: 'We did a lot of walking in the jungle, but never once did we have a confrontation with a mass enemy that we could see.'[38] In their American Division, more than 90 per cent of casualties that year were the result of booby traps and land mines. Lt. William Calley, who played a prominent role in ordering the My Lai massacre, wrote later:

> My duty in our whole area was to find, to close with, and to destroy the VC [Vietcong]. I had now found the VC. Everyone there was VC. The old men, the children – the babies were all VC or would be VC in about three years. And inside of VC women, I guess there were a thousand little VC now.[39]

Faludi commented perceptively, 'The killing of civilians was not simply a primal rampage in an out-of-control realm; it was also an attempt to reimpose an expected framework, no matter how ridiculous the fit. . . . The men would have their mission, one way or another.'[40]

A sense of powerlessness *in relation to one's own commanders* has strongly fuelled abuse in many wars. In Vietnam, levels of anger among American troops reflected a growing hostility towards US political and even military authorities. The sense of vulnerability in the face of the enemy was compounded by a sense of abandonment. Commenting on the experiences and perceptions of US soldiers in Vietnam, Faludi noted:

> The way that vast numbers of GIs came to see it, the invisible men in the control ships had left the troops to die on the ground while they buzzed back for hot showers, martinis and movies in their air-conditioned suites at base camp. 'We felt abandoned,' [Sergeant Michael] Bernhardt said, using a verb commonly invoked by Vietnam vets. 'We felt abandoned,' he amended, pointing skyward, 'by all the men up there.' Men in the field were often meant to be the ambushable 'bait,' put there to attract enemy fire so that the air force could swoop down and claim a fat body count.[41]

By the late 1960s and early 1970s, whole platoons and even companies were beginning to mutiny.[42] By 1971, there were some 89,000 deserters.[43]

Thorniké Gordadze has painted a grim picture of life for young Russian soldiers in Chechnya:

> Conflicts between officers and men, discrimination against young con-
> scripts, physical and even sexual violence practiced by the older soldiers,
> and a high rate of alcoholism and drug abuse all take their toll. Several
> hundred young conscripts die every year in senselessly violent initiation
> ceremonies, fights, or the settling of personal grudges.[44]

This in turn affected soldiers' behaviour towards the Chechens. As Gordadze observed, 'Humiliated, beaten and starved, Russian soldiers avenge their miserable existence on Chechen civilians by subjecting them to even worse treatment in order to regain a sense of superiority.'[45]

In Angola, a combination of impunity and poor pay and supplies fed into abuses by government forces at the expense of civilians.[46] Back in early twentieth-century China, soldiers in the armies of the various warlords were routinely subjected to beatings and terrible disease-inducing condi-tions. In Diana Lary's view, Chinese soldiers' abuses against civilians sprang partly from their sense of powerlessness; part of the problem was simply imitation of their commanders.[47]

Human beings' violent reactions to humiliation have actually been exploited and institutionalized within numerous military organizations. Japanese historian Saburo Ienaga observed of Japanese military training during the Second World War: 'Individuals whose own dignity and manhood had been so cruelly violated would hardly refrain from doing the same to defenceless persons under their control.'[48] Somewhat similarly, a psychiatric study of Vietnam veterans concluded:

> Behavior in war is patterned on the drill field. There, the training officer
> treats the trainee in the same way that he wants the soldier to treat the
> enemy in battle. To escape the low and painful status of victim and target
> of aggression, the mantle of the aggressor is assumed with more or less
> guilt. In so far as this identification with the aggressor is successfully
> maintained . . . the soldier's activity in war, all the shooting, maiming and
> killing, is perceived as moral, legitimate and meaningful.[49]

Post-war

In any war-to-peace transition, ex-combatants are potentially an important destabilizing agent. Their grievances can feed strongly into various kinds of violence, including political repression, organized crime, terrorism, renewed warfare at home, military adventures abroad, and even genocide.

The following discussion moves swiftly between examples and time periods, but is designed to show the variety of post-war violence and the links with ex-combatants.

Statistical evidence suggests that when countries have recently experienced a civil war, they are at particular risk of suffering another one.[50] The way one confict can feed into a subsequent conflict – even after a significant interval – is illustrated by the case of Zimbabwe, where Robert Mugabe has recently been able to draw on the grievances of guerrilla soldiers (notably in relation to land) when intimidating the political opposition and sponsoring the occupation of white-owned farms; many of those mobilized were too young to be 'war veterans', but acquired the label nonetheless.[51] Large and unbudgeted payments to war veterans in August 1997 played a role in destabilizing Zimbabwe's finances and precipitating political crisis.[52] The possibility of renewed warfare was also shown in West Africa, which also illustrates the dangers of wider regional warfare when war in one country draws to a close. The adequacy or otherwise of schemes of Disarmament, Demobilization and Reintegration (DDR) can make a big difference to subsequent patterns of conflict. For example, in Liberia, DDR was a notable failure in 1997 (particularly in terms of encouraging reintegration into agriculture), and these failings facilitated the re-recruitment of fighters into the groups that devastated the country in 1999–2003. DDR subsequently remained underfunded with demobilization programmes and reintegration particularly neglected, again facilitating re-recruitment.[53] Weak DDR was seen by combatants as a broken promise.[54] Many went to fight in neighbouring countries.[55] DDR was also neglected in Sierra Leone through the 1990s. Persistent problems with the 'reintegration' element fed into regional instability, and corruption of the DDR was a serious problem; many demobilized Sierra Leonean fighters became involved in violence in Liberia, Guinea and Ivory Coast.[56] Meanwhile, perhaps only between 2 and 10 per cent of the arms were collected, with many leaking over the borders into Guinea and Liberia.[57] One DDR specialist went so far as to say 'The best disarmament initiative in Sierra Leone has been [continued fighting in] Liberia and Ivory Coast.'[58]

Consider, also, a much earlier example of soldiers fuelling regional warfare at the end of a conflict. After the first English civil war of 1642–6, Parliament lacked a military force of its own, but was very suspicious of the army that had secured victory on its behalf over the royalists.[59] Conrad Russell stresses the folly of leading Parliamentarians in their attitude to the army:

For [Denzil] Holles [a leading Parliamentarian] . . . the army were the
'meanest of men, the basest and vilest of the nation, the lowest of the
people', and he was too frightened of them to consider the possibility that
they might have legitimate grievances: to give concessions to such dangerous revolutionaries was only to encourage them. In fact, the army's
demands at first were extremely moderate. The first essential was their
arrears of pay: 1647–9 were years of a serious slump, drastic price rises,
and heavy unemployment, and to be turned loose penniless and without
a job was an uninviting prospect. . . . Since they were not paid, the army
were forced to live at free quarter [free lodging], and thus Parliament
could force them to make themselves more unpopular.[60]

Important in defusing the internal threat from soldiers at the end of the
English civil war was the tactic of diverting soldiers' discontent abroad. In
April 1647, Parliament offered to disband part of the army, paying their
arrears, and to send the rest to Ireland to suppress a continuing Catholic pro-
royalist revolt.[61] (There had been a rebellion in Ireland in 1641, with many
Protestant settlers killed.) In 1649, Cromwell did send a large force to Ireland,
where some 10,000 war-hardened troops engaged in widespread crop-
burning and induced large-scale starvation, with an estimated 600,000 to 1.4
million people dying as a result.[62] Depending on which number is adopted,
this represents somewhat less than the 1994 Rwandan genocide, or significantly more. The mass expulsions and killings were linked to a new plantation scheme centred on the east of Ireland, with English settlers displacing
large numbers of the Irish to the more infertile lands of the west.[63] Tristram
Hunt notes that 'a large part of the New Model Army funding had been
secured from the City on the promise of Irish land. The City institutions were
now calling in their debts.'[64] Commercial investors, as well as Parliamentary
soldiers, took up the best estates.[65] Arguably, England's New Model Army
was tamed – and ultimately paid – at the expense of mass suffering in Ireland.

In terms of combatants' role in *genocidal processes*, the cases of Germany
and Rwanda are salutary.[66] In both, a military setback led to a search (including by major elements of the military) for internal enemies who had undermined national strength – a search that gathered force in Germany with the
massive economic crisis of the late 1920s and 1930s.

Particularly in the German context, the historian Omer Bartov has made
a contribution to our understanding of how enemies have been defined and
redefined. Part of Bartov's argument was that the search for the 'real'
enemy at the end of the First World War fed into the subsequent Nazi
Holocaust: the mass destruction of soldiers turned into a mass destruction
of civilians. Bartov described how enemies were redefined as the First

World War drew to a close, a process driven in part by the human need to both glorify and explain suffering:

> The 'real' enemy was . . . to be found in the rear, among the staff officers, the noncombatants, the politicians and industrialists, even the workers in the factories, all those who were perceived as having shirked the fighting and thus having excluded themselves from that community of battle increasingly celebrated by the fighting troops. The search for those guilty of the massacre in the trenches, the 'real' enemy, began in Germany even before the deteriorating military situation at the front and its ultimate collapse made for open accusations of subversion against those least capable of defending themselves. The legend of the 'stab in the back' (*Dolchstosslegende*) was preceded by the notorious 'Jew count' (*Judenzahlung*) of 1916, an official inquiry aimed at gauging the alleged underrepresentation of Jews in the army.[67]

If Hitler was shaken by the 'humiliation' of Versailles and desperate to reverse it, he was by no means the only one. Klaus Theweleit made a study of the often-disturbed members of the Freikorps – the volunteer armies of former soldiers who battled against revolutionaries after the First World War and went on to form an important part of the Nazi machinery of violence, most notably in Hitler's SA stormtroopers. In an argument related to Arendt's and Bartov's, Theweleit stressed that some of the origins of Nazism lay in a hostility among German soldiers in particular to some very diverse forces and people – broadly, 'women', 'revolution', 'Jews', 'corruption' – that were seen as undermining the strength, masculinity, pride and purity of Germany. Theweleit also highlighted a loss of faith in a German patriarchy that was seen as having brought the nation to defeat. Identities forged in war were not easily shed, and one member of the Freikorps (who had been 16 when he began fighting in the First World War) commented:

> People told us that the War was over. That made us laugh. We ourselves are the War. Its flame burns strongly in us. It envelops our whole being and fascinates us with the enticing urge to destroy. We obeyed . . . and marched onto the battle fields of the postwar world just as we had gone into battle on the Western Front; singing, reckless and filled with the joy of adventure as we marched to the attack; silent, deadly, remorseless in battle.[68]

If the Nazi genocide was fed in part by a sense of betrayal and a search for purity, these themes re-emerged with devastating effect in the context of the Rwandan genocide (discussed in more detail in chapter 4). Mahmood Mamdani has analysed how the enemy mutated from the Rwandan Patriotic Front (RPF) fighters (who had successfully advanced into Rwanda from Uganda and had secured a power-sharing agreement) to the 'Tutsi' enemy inside Rwanda itself:

> From confronting the enemy that seemed to advance relentlessly on the battlefield or on the diplomatic frontier, they turned around to face the enemy within . . . the Rwandan military and its paramilitary attachments went on to purify the nation and rid it of all impurities that detracted from its strength . . . the genocide was both a continuation of the civil war and marked a rupture with it.[69]

Following the so-called 'Hutu revolution' in 1959–62, large numbers of Tutsis had fled to Uganda. They were subsequently barred from returning to Rwanda, with the Rwandan government claiming the country was already 'overpopulated'. In October 1990, the RPF had attacked from Uganda. A peace agreement at Arusha in August 1993 promised that the RPF would provide 40 per cent of the army's soldiers and 50 per cent of its officers. This was like serving notice to young army recruits – and unemployment was already very high.[70] With many soldiers mutinying, President Juvenal Habyarimana declared the August 1993 Arusha Accords to be no more than 'a scrap of paper'.[71] Mamdani noted that the army's leadership

> held the political opposition responsible for dressing up defeat as power sharing and disguising national betrayal as democratic opposition. . . . The hour had struck for the most ardent champions of Hutu Power – for those whose patriotic zeal knew no limits – to call the nation to arms against those they considered to have betrayed it. The enemy within were the Tutsi and their objective accomplices, the Hutu political opposition . . . .[72]

In Rwanda, the army had a key role in the 1994 genocide, promoting fear and hatred of Tutsis, arguing that the 'ethnic problem' was being neglected in favour of a politics of rich and poor, carrying out its own massacres, often commanding the *interahamwe* militias, leading the way in attacks on civilians, and attacking the Hutu opposition. Sometimes, as in Butare, it was relatively junior officers who had the strongest hatred of Tutsis as well as the greatest access to personal guards; those sent to Butare from the war-front (especially those who had been wounded) were reportedly among the most ruthless in the genocide.[73]

We need to understand how key elements of the army saw the prospect of peace and democracy. Human Rights Watch noted:

> By the time serious talks with the RPF began in 1992, the Rwandan army had grown to some 30,000 soldiers. An important number of them opposed the negotiations, not just because they did not want to give up the fight, but also because they dreaded demobilization. The thousands of

troops who had been recruited since the start of the war had become accustomed to the advantages of military life. The MRND [Mouvement Révolutionaire pour le Développement, Habyarimana's party] and the CDR [Coalition pour la défense de la République, an extreme anti-Tutsi breakaway group that was strong in the army and the government but excluded from Parliament under the 1993 Arusha agreement] fed their fears by spreading rumours that soldiers would be thrown out into a dis-integrating economy without hope of finding work. The prime minister, Dismas Nsengiyaremye of the MDR [Mouvement Démocratique Républicain, a leading opposition party], attempted to reassure the troops by talking of using demobilized soldiers in economic development pro-jects, such as draining marshes to obtain new land for cultivation. This proposal incensed the soldiers further; it was just such menial labour that they thought they had left behind in their new military careers.[74]

The case of Afghanistan shows how ex-combatants' grievances can feed into *terrorism* as well as into war in other countries. The terrorism by extreme Islamist groups in the 1990s and in the early twenty-first century has strong roots in the Afghan jihad against the Soviet Union in the 1980s – not least in the exhilaration of victory and the sense of betrayal at sudden Western disengagement.

Together with the Saudis, the US government supported the Afghan mujahadeen resistance against Soviet occupation in the 1980s. Helping to mediate the Saudi assistance (with CIA encouragement) was the Saudi billionaire Osama bin Laden.[75] After a long and costly campaign, the Soviets withdrew from Afghanistan in 1989. The Soviet defeat there was a key con-tributor to the demise of the Soviet Union and the demise of communism in general – in many ways a dramatic foreign policy success for the US.[76] But this very success encouraged a drastic curtailment of support for the victorious rebels, with the US also citing soldiers' involvement in the heroin trade as a factor. At this point, Afghanistan descended into warlordism and many of the mujahadeen took their new-found confidence and their sense of betrayal to other countries and conflicts. Anger at the US was greatly compounded by the use of US bases in Saudi Arabia for attacks on Iraq after Saddam Hussein had invaded Kuwait in 1990. Kepel noted:

> The jihad intensified in 1992 in Bosnia, Algeria, and Egypt, as soon as vet-erans of the Afghan war began arriving home from Peshawar [Pakistan, near the Afghan border]. . . . The dispersal all over the world, after 1992, of the [jihadists] formerly concentrated in Kabul and Peshawar, more than anything else, explains the sudden, lightning expansion of radical Islamism in Muslim countries and the West.[77]

The way soldiers' grievances can feed into *organized crime* can be illustrated with the case of Guatemala. The end of a long and bitter civil war in 1996 did not mean the end of pervasive violence in Guatemala. In fact, the peace agreement seems to have induced a sense of disorientation and betrayal within significant elements of the security sector, and this in turn has fed into criminal activity as well as the continued persecution of 'subversives', including human rights groups.

Many senior officers took the view that the war went on, peace or no peace.[78] The peacetime enemy was defined as criminals and subversives, a transition that was perhaps smoother than it might appear, since the rebels had also been referred to as criminals and subversives.[79] The continuing struggles against criminals and subversives have been linked, with clandestine intelligence organizations being used to combat human rights organizations as well as organized crime. Many of these human rights organizations have been involved in gathering information to enable the prosecution of key perpetrators, notably in the army. Security organizations have also been deployed in extreme violence against youthful 'delinquents' – ostensibly to combat youth gangs but also apparently in an attempt to intimidate and discourage political participation.

Some analysts stressed that during the war the Guatemalan army had effectively been invited into violence (specifically, into an anti-communist struggle) by the private sector and by the United States. However, in an era of thawing Cold War tensions when human rights concerns had (at least on the face of it) taken precedence over Cold War struggles, both the Guatemalan private sector and the US had tended to retreat from their support of the army and had increasingly condemned precisely the people who were previously invited into violence. The sense of betrayal and loss of mission within the military has been a major factor in peacetime violence. This seems to be an important explanation for the large-scale deviation of the Guatemalan military into criminal activities and their apparent symbiosis with organized crime (at once a financial opportunity and a new, legitimizing source of 'threat'). The discontents of former combatants have been channelled towards the intimidation of those seeking various kinds of political and socio-economic reforms, while leaders have been concerned to protect their own budget and privileges.[80] The US government's suspension of trade privileges in 1993 had led to business pressure on the Guatemalan government,[81] and one source very close to the army told me in 2002:

Those depending on the army came to see it as an obstacle – their repressive tactics were stopping markets in the US and vacations in Miami and

> whatever. Now there's a huge protest in the officers' corps against the
> moneyed classes because they feel betrayed. They were doing their dirty
> work and then their backers decided they were no longer useful. . . . The
> US cut off all assistance to the army. . . . It is significant enough, the sense
> of betrayal.[82]

Part of the process of the government distancing itself from human rights
abuses was making new appointments at the top of the army, mostly from
the air force and navy. Retired army staff played a key role in the emerging
synergy between military actors and organized crime and many have
also been involved in the intimidation of human rights organizations.
Meanwhile, fear of crime has often heightened the appeal of right-wing
political leaders, including Rios Montt; having presided over some of the
worst massacres in Guatemala's history as head of the 1982–3 military
regime, Montt became head of the national congress after his party, the
Guatemalan Republican Front (FRG), won elections in November 1999. He
even ran for President in 2003.

In South Africa, some ex-combatants have been implicated in criminal
activities, while some have also been drawn into the dubious activities of
mercenary companies – notably Executive Outcomes – beyond South
Africa's borders.[83] One former African National Congress combatant complained, 'The disparities that exist now are not only between ourselves and
our white counterparts but our comrades as well, that have become,
overnight, bourgeousie and they are driving flashy cars and sleeping in
expensive hotels; they fly over our heads'.[84]

Conclusion

If power corrupts, so too does powerlessness; the two together have proven
particularly dangerous. A sense of powerlessness can feed into the assertion
of power through violence; frequently the perpetrator feels powerless in
relation to one set of people but exerts power over a separate and vulnerable group (usually the *unarmed*). This helps explain why the perpetrator frequently *feels like a victim*. In the midst of carnage, morality does not always
or completely collapse; instead, it is typically twisted, distorted, perverted
and even inverted,[85] with attack perhaps redefined as self-defence and
restraint as weakness.

Experience in Sierra Leone and elsewhere suggests that where peacetime
breeds a widespread sense of powerlessness, this can easily feed into
wartime abuses; where wartime conditions compound this sense of powerlessness, the likelihood of atrocity – and abuse of the weak – is even greater.

Power, but also powerlessness, corrupts

humiliation, seeking recognition

One practical conclusion emerges clearly: if people's environment is a large part of the problem in generating atrocities, then changing that environment can be part of the solution. More specifically, if neglect and abuse breed neglect and abuse, then it follows that respect and care (eventually) will have a more positive effect. A good example was the Sierra Leonean aid worker (mentioned in chapter 2) who secured the loyalty of his guards through trust and care. If neglect and powerlessness are feeding abuse, security sector reform is likely to be critical. After the reforms of the army and police that were promoted by the British in Sierra Leone, one young man said he had wanted to get into the army but had been denied because he lacked the right connections. But he was optimistic nonetheless:

> The soldiers now have pride in the job, because they have been given the basic things. The British have done well here. The British are providing bread and tea for the police. They are proud. They have mobile phones. If you deprive him, he will become undisciplined. Civilians have started praising the military. You can be naturally peaceful, but the situation can make you behave like an animal. People can change. The environment is the thing.

The importance of considering soldiers' grievances has been underestimated – not only in explaining important dynamics deepening violence during civil wars, but also in explaining the patterns of violence that emerge in the aftermath of a war. One lesson is that it may be easier to recruit someone into fighting than to control their subsequent definition of the enemy or to rein in the violence that has been instilled in them. Another is the importance of dealing properly with ex-combatants and their potential for various kinds of post-war violence (see chapter 8). We have seen how a sense of betrayal may be important in propelling the redefinition of enemies. Chapter 2 noted that Cold War arms stocks may end up being employed in new and different contexts; the same applies to Cold War soldiers.

While the regime of rewards/punishments and the moral environment can be seen as two separate factors, there is likely to be a connection between them. A far-reaching climate of impunity may end up redefining people's ideas about what is moral and what is immoral. How does an individual know the difference between what is right and what is wrong? A major part of our education in this comes when we learn about which actions are punished and which are not: in other words, it is not simply that bad actions are discouraged through punishment, but that punishment is part of how we learn that they *are* bad. What are the implications for a generation that has grown up in wartime Sierra Leone or Liberia, for example, where violence has frequently been rewarded and where trying to stay aloof from the violence has frequently been an invitation to 'punishment' at the hands of one faction or another? Scarier and more destructive even than a collapse of morality may be a *reversal* of morality, where bad actions become good actions (and vice versa). Further complicating matters is the fact that perceptions of right and wrong (and of incentives and punishments) are likely to be strongly shaped by the information environment in which the perpetrators are operating (see also chapters 4 and 7).

The following chapter continues the exploration of how and why enemies are chosen and defined, focusing on broader political processes – including the manipulation of soldiers' grievances by political elites and, more generally, the manipulation of ethnic conflict.

4

Defining the Enemy

The common view that an evil enemy must be physically eliminated or deterred – what Galtung calls the 'security approach' – has been noted. This view informed the Bush/Blair approach to the 'war on terror', with its lists of the 'most wanted' and its succession of evil leaders – Osama bin Laden, Saddam Hussein, Saddam's sons Uday and Qusay, Abu Musab al-Zarqawi, and so on – whose expulsion, deposition or elimination, it is repeatedly proclaimed, will radically improve security. This approach has also been adopted by the Russian government in Chechnya, for example. 'According to Kremlin propaganda,' Thorniké Gordadze noted in 2004, 'the elimination of the rebel leaders would automatically provoke the collapse of the resistance movement.'[1]

There is a great deal of evidence that the violent and in many respects indiscriminate response to 9/11 is creating terrorists more quickly than it can eliminate them.[2] Nor is the elimination of 'evil' individuals a more promising avenue in civil wars: after rebel-turned-President Charles Taylor had taken refuge in Nigeria in August 2003, a saying in vogue in Monrovia was that he was replaced by '100 small Taylors'.[3] The fantasy of eliminating the evil ones suffers from a lack of any sense of *becoming*: the process by which people become radicalized.

This chapter steps back a little from discussions about what to do with the enemy, asking how the enemy comes to be defined as such in the first place. The chapter stresses a profound fluidity in the way enemies are defined. It also emphasizes that many parties will have an interest (perhaps a material interest) in particular definitions of the enemy. Enemies may broaden from a named military foe to a much larger group of civilians – perhaps an entire ethnic group. Any ethnic definition of enmity implicitly targets civilians, perhaps in acts of terrorism or counterterrorism; at the extreme, targeting an ethnic enemy takes the form of genocide. Genocides have frequently taken place in wartime and may represent an exaggeration of certain tendencies manifest in many wars. These include the redefinition of the enemy from the external to the internal, from an armed group to a particular ethnic group, and from the soldier to the civilian.

What is an ethnic group? The phrase usually refers to some kind of social group bonded together by ties of race, religion, culture or some combination of these. A common media emphasis on 'ethnic conflict' – and on 'ancient ethnic hatreds' – has a close affinity with so-called 'primordialist' academic work, which portrays ethnicity as a biological and historical given. Yet emphasizing 'ancient ethnic hatreds' as the cause of conflict carries the danger of making ethnic conflict seem both inevitable and intractable.

Ethnicity is also something that is *constructed*. To some extent, we construct our own ethnicity, perhaps entertaining several different self-definitions at once and giving different emphasis to different identities at different times.[4] Frederik Barth stressed that the ethnicity of a group is defined in relation to other groups, and that we need to look at the processes by which ethnicity is generated and maintained.[5] As noted in chapter 1, David Turton showed how the emphasis placed on ethnicity may change in response to conflict: ethnicity may be a *result* of conflict as much as a cause of it.[6]

The hardening of ethnic distinctions by conflict can be seen, for example, in accounts of the Nazi Holocaust. Even liberal and Jewish accounts have often made a distinction (and it is not hard to imagine why this might be so) between the Germans, on the one hand, and the Jews, on the other; and yet the Jews in Germany were mostly German too, even though they were stripped of their rights as Germans and separated from the rest of society. In effect, the categories (as well as the people) were separated by violence.[7]

Ethnicity is not just an identity you choose, but also an identity that others may try to choose for you. This relates to a common complaint among some British Asians, for example. A white British person might ask a British Asian, 'Where are you from?', and they may get the answer (perhaps in a strong Midlands accent): 'Birmingham'. But this does not satisfy the questioner, who insists, 'Yes, but where are you from, originally?' And the answer comes again, 'Birmingham'. 'Yes, but where are your parents from?' 'Birmingham', and so on. As William Shakespeare nearly said, some are born into ethnicity, some achieve or choose ethnicity, and some have ethnicity thrust upon them.

When others want to define you in particular ways, this may be to recruit supporters or perhaps to label you as an 'other'. This labelling as 'other' may be part of a process of defining oneself and one's own group and of promoting self-esteem.[8] It may also be part of a programme of discrimination, exploitation and/or scapegoating. Some people may be very anxious to put you in a box, and in extreme cases they may mean this literally.

We need to look not only at the consequences of ethnicity but also at its causes and functions. Ethnicity may be constructed and embraced by both elites and ordinary people for a variety of reasons, including pragmatic ones like economic gain and physical survival. This is in line with the emphasis of 'instrumentalists', who have stressed the function of appeals to ethnicity, particularly by elites. David Turton has stressed that appeals to ethnicity that are made in the service of economic and political goals may be particularly effective since they involve an appeal to a sphere that seems to lie *outside* the realms of mere self-interest.[9]

We need to understand both the manipulation of violence by elites (following section) and the embracing of violence (either more or less reluctantly) by ordinary people (third section). Like combatants, elites and ordinary people may see themselves as victims, even as they participate in acts of violence. Understanding the *interaction* between 'top-down' and 'bottom-up' processes will be important. The final section focuses on an important and rarely discussed aspect of this interaction: the use by elites of what Hannah Arendt called 'action-as-propaganda' to generate spurious legitimacy for particular (often highly ethnicized) definitions of the enemy.[10]

'Top-Down' Processes: Elite Goals

There are many possible motivations when elites manipulate ethnic conflict, and three key goals are set out below.

Establishing colonial rule

Some colonies were subject to significant settlement by conquering powers (such as Kenya and Rhodesia/Zimbabwe and the Spanish and Portuguese colonies in Central and South America); but in most colonies the number of European colonialists was tiny in relation to the colonized population. Everywhere, imposing and sustaining colonial rule inevitably involved an intensive search for collaborators upon whom the colonists felt they could rely.[11] One such case was Iraq, where the British, who invaded Mesopotamia in 1914 and forged Iraq out of the remnants of the Ottoman Empire, relied heavily on the mostly Sunni Arab officers and officials who had earlier held sway under Ottoman rule.[12]

The British in particular relied on 'indirect rule', reinforcing the power of 'tribal leaders' as an instrument of colonialism.[13] Frequently, the power of these allegedly 'traditional' leaders was significantly enhanced by putting the weight of the state behind them.[14] At the same time, as Mahmood Mamdani stressed in his book *Citizen and Subject*, tribal authorities were particularly useful as an instrument of colonial rule because they tended to have some degree of historical legitimacy.

In the case of South Africa, Mamdani showed how the white elite was for a long time able to use tribal distinctions among the black population to forestall a general protest or uprising by what was effectively, within the context of apartheid, an oppressed black *class*. Mamdani argued that the favoured solution to urban unrest in South Africa was, first, reviving Native Authority to try to splinter racial/class awareness into tribalism and to harness the coercive power of chiefs over young people, and, second, to enforce a kind of partial de-urbanization through the apartheid system.[15]

Using one ethnic group to police another was a common imperial tactic. For example, during the gradual imposition of British rule in Sudan from the end of the nineteenth century, elements of the Baggara cattle herders of western Sudan were used to quell southern Sudanese groups who were resisting colonial rule, and the use of southern slaves among the Baggara was tolerated by the British.[16] Since the Baggara were themselves a potential threat (particularly after their role in the 1883 Mahdist uprising), this strategy offered to reinforce colonial rule on two fronts.

In Rwanda, ethnic distinctions were also a tool of colonial rule; indeed the colonial strategy of 'divide and rule' laid some of the groundwork for what was to be the 1994 genocide. Portraying the Hutus and Tutsis as two distinct and opposing 'tribes' is misleading.[17] Both groups have shared the same language; there has been no 'Hutuland' or 'Tutsiland' within Rwanda; and in the nineteenth century, Hutus and Tutsis frequently faced a common enemy in neighbouring kingdoms. It is true that an element of physical difference can sometimes be detected, but intermarriage has substantially blurred the boundaries.[18] In fact, during the genocide of 1994 it was often hard to determine whether individuals were Hutu or Tutsi, and killing was frequently carried out on the basis of an identity card system originally established by Belgian colonists.

Visiting Europeans in the nineteenth century tended to see the Tutsis as tall, elegant and intelligent and during the 1994 genocide the image of Tutsi women as somehow more beautiful as well as arrogant and unavailable seems to have fed into the horrendous levels of sexual violence.[19] Under colonial rule, white anthropologists and other visitors loved to speculate on the origins of this marvellous superior people: some felt they had come from Ethiopia and some from Asia Minor; some felt they were Greek, some saw them as Semitic and some held that they were originally Indian; still other experts believed the Tutsis had come from the Garden of Eden.[20] These fantasies were to feed into the idea that the Tutsis were not really 'Rwandan', something that was later to prove useful for those organizing the 1994 genocide. Narcissistic fantasies about the Tutsis were mirrored in a more overtly racist discussion that stigmatized the Hutus and others as primitive and simple.

Helping to fuel the stereotypes about Tutsis and Hutus was the pragmatic need to find a group of collaborators. The Belgian colonial rulers, who took over from Germany in 1916, went so far as to decree that only Tutsis could be government officials or have access to higher education. In these circumstances, the term 'Tutsi' was not simply a description of a (primordial) ethnic group who were conferred privileges; it also came to be a description of those who (for whatever reasons) had achieved a privileged position (for example, as part of a governing class or as someone with many cattle).

Tutsi notables took advantage of the status given them by colonialists in claiming many onerous duties from the Hutus as 'traditional' when in fact they were far from it.[21] Gerard Prunier has suggested that the veneration of the Tutsis and the bias towards Tutsi officials and Tutsi chiefs inordinately inflated what he called the Tutsi 'cultural ego' and simultaneously gave many Hutu an aggressive 'inferiority complex'.[22] Although the Tutsis were elevated above the Hutu, powerful Tutsi chiefs would sometimes be whipped by Belgian colonists in the presence of their Hutu charges; humiliated, the chiefs sometimes turned on the Hutus after the white official had departed, contributing to underlying resentments. The privileges of the Tutsis helped to spur a 'Hutu' revolution in 1959, prompting an exodus of Tutsis – some of whom later returned from Uganda as the Rwandan Patriotic Front in an incursion that was to precipitate the 1994 genocide.

Shoring up elite power

If colonialism frequently shored up the power of an ethnic elite, processes of decolonization and democratization have often constituted a threat to these elites.

Cold War aid helped to prop up unrepresentative regimes in post-independence Africa and elsewhere.[23] When internal and external pressures for democracy became particularly strong at the end of the Cold War, many of these entrenched elites proved willing to destroy their own countries (most notably by whipping up ethnic rivalries) in defence of these artificially preserved privileges. Elites in the former eastern bloc have not been above the manipulation of ethnicity to ward off threats posed by democratization.

This process may arise at the end of a war. For example, at the end of the First World War – as Omer Bartov has emphasized – the process of scape-goating the Jews served a function for much of the German establishment in derailing 'class' politics. Particularly after the Russian Revolution of 1917 (itself precipitated by the First World War), economic insecurity and the resulting dissatisfactions were reinforcing elites' determination to channel resentment away from economic issues and towards foreign or internal enemies and cultural issues.[24] The Freikorps – privately financed paramili-taries consisting of demobilized soldiers – were deployed against uprisings within Germany. In addition, the Nazis offered the prospect of physically absorbing into their apparatus many of the unemployed youths for whom communism might have some attraction.[25]

The 1994 Rwandan genocide shows very clearly how elites may try to deflect democracy by forcing politics and conflict along ethnic lines. Some 800,000–850,000 people, most of them Tutsis, were killed in the genocide.[26] The UN estimated that between 250,000 and 500,000 women and girls, most of them Tutsis, were raped.[27] Belgian rulers had sponsored a transi-tion to Hutu majority rule in 1959–62, a process accompanied by large-scale violence against the Tutsis, violence that received official encouragment.[28] Many Tutsis fled to Uganda and Tanzania. After a military coup in 1973, the government came to be dominated by a small Hutu clique from north-western Rwanda, who were known as the Akazu. By the end of the 1980s, international donors and many Rwandans were pushing strongly for democracy, and in 1990 the Rwandan Patriotic Front (RPF), consisting largely of Tutsi refugees, crossed into Rwanda from Uganda. In August 1993, the signing of the Arusha accords (with a high level of foreign diplo-matic and head of state involvement) spelled the end of twenty years of autocratic, single-party rule in Rwanda and stipulated a shift to parliamen-tary government as well as the incorporation of the RPF into the army. The Arusha accords were a major success both for the RPF and for the internal Hutu opposition. At this point, there was a clear prospect that the RPF would be able to combine with internal Hutu opposition (notably from the south of the country) to upset the domination of the northwestern Hutu elite. Yet the hardline northwestern Hutus in the government did not go quietly: fomenting ethnic violence against the Tutsis - first in a series of massacres and then in a carefully planned genocide – offered the prospect of sabotaging the peace process, derailing democracy and preventing an alliance of the RPF and the Hutu opposition. As René Lemarchand observed, the wanton killing of Tutsi civilians – beginning with individual massacres and culminating in genocide in April 1994 – was designed to make it unthinkable for the Tutsis and Hutus to agree on anything.[29] Rakiya Omaar's powerful book for African Rights, *Death, Despair and Defiance*, shows how the Rwandan genocide was carefully planned and was much more than an outbreak of tribal hostilities. Significantly, the genocide targeted not only the Tutsis, but also leading members of the Hutu opposition.

The case of Rwanda – a small, highly centralized country with a strong authoritarian tradition – shows how contemporary conflict cannot simply be dismissed as stemming from collapsed states. As noted, the then UN Secretary-General Boutros Boutros-Ghali misread the Rwandan genocide as a collapse in state authority.[30] Compounding this misreading were calls from UN officials, during the genocide, for a cease-fire 'to stop the massacres'. Whilst it is true that the RPF incursion helped to create a climate of paranoia that contributed to the genocide, it was actually the successful advance of the RPF that eventually stopped the genocide, and any halt in this advance would have prolonged the killing.[31]

The case of Rwanda shows some of the dangers of a too rapid and poorly planned democratization.[32] In their more general statistical analysis, Mansfield and Snyder found that during the 170 years from 1811 to 1980, the danger of war (external and internal) was greatest when states were moving rapidly towards democracy.[33] They argued that elites, when threatened by democratic change, have frequently mobilized support through nationalist appeals, and have typically found that once populations have been mobilized, they are difficult to demobilize.[34] Moreover, ethnic nationalists have frequently been able to use their rivals' nationalism to justify internal repression. Roland Paris has also stressed the dangers of an overhasty push for democracy, especially when this push is accompanied by an austerity-inducing programme of structural adjustment (as in Rwanda).[35]

In Sudan, the colonial pattern of 'divide and rule' continues to this day, albeit in modified form. Before and after independence in 1956, riverine groups (notably the Shaiqiyya and Ja'aliyyin) from the central Nilotic areas have tended to dominate, both politically and economically. The second civil war from 1983 saw Khartoum deflecting the discontent of neglected Baggara groups in the west against the still more marginalized southern Sudanese and Nuba in government-backed raiding that led to widespread famine. The Khartoum government also stirred up Nuer/Dinka tensions in the south to weaken the rebel Sudan People's Liberation Army.

If 'religious war', 'ethnic war' and 'ancient ethnic hatreds' have provided convenient smokescreens for economic and political interests in Sudan, ethnic identities have also frequently been strengthened by the war there. For example, many people in the south were attacked because they were Dinka rather than because their Dinka subsection had actually supported the SPLA rebels, and this tended to reinforce their sense of Dinka ethnicity as well as their desire to join the rebellion.[36]

From 2003, a major humanitarian and human rights crisis in Darfur was precipitated when Khartoum allied with other pastoral groups in the west (notably, camel-herders, some of Chadian origin) against ethnic groups (this time fellow Muslims) who were seen as supporting rebellion there.[37] Again, Khartoum has succeeded in stirring up ethnic tensions among the rebels.[38] As noted in chapter 1, an important motive for Khartoum stirring conflict in the west (and perhaps also the south, using remnants of the South Sudan Defence Forces) may well be a desire to derail elections scheduled for 2009.

International attention to Darfur was impeded by a widespread assumption that the key fault-lines in Sudan were between the 'Muslim north' and the 'largely Christian south', and, correspondingly, that a north–south peace agreement would solve the problem. In fact, the north–south peace agreement sparked rebellion in Darfur, where many felt excluded by the SPLA/Khartoum deal and perceived that the SPLA had won a share of power through its violence. (This perception was accurate, though the human cost of war in the south had been catastrophic.)

In Darfur (as for almost two decades in Bahr el Ghazal), Khartoum has tended to deny that it has responsibility for, or control over, aggressive militias. One International Crisis Group report noted of Darfur: 'A tribal militia can wipe out an entire village . . . and the government can plead innocence, even as it creates the conditions for the militias to operate by giving impunity, supplying weapons and ammunition, deploying police who do nothing to stop attacks and co-ordinating between the militias and the state government.'[39] Meanwhile, the discourse of 'ancient ethnic hatreds' has resurfaced.[40] US Deputy Secretary of State Robert Zoellick told an audience at Khartoum University in November 2005: 'It's a tribal war, that has been exacerbated by other conditions, and frankly, I don't think foreign forces ought to get themselves in the middle of a tribal war of Sudanese.'[41] A related version of dismissing the conflict as *essentially local* involves portraying it as farmers versus nomads, usually 'Arab nomads'.[42]

Yet all this lets the Sudanese government conveniently off the hook. As Sudan expert John Ryle wrote in the *New York Review of Books* in August 2004:

In 2002, in northern Bahr-el-Ghazal (to the south of Darfur), after years of international condemnation of the abduction and enslavement of local people by Murahaliin militia groups – and years of denial of official involvement – raids on villages ceased when the United States stepped up diplomatic pressure on the Sudanese government. Claims that the Janjawiid are beyond government control are similarly unconvincing. It is clear that, when it wants, the government can call off the dogs of war.[43]

That process could be re-enacted over Darfur. The International Crisis Group has noted that ever since the military government seized power in 1989, 'when the government has been the target of serious pressure with a specific objective, it has modified its behaviour'.[44]

In a variety of countries, ethnicity has been used to cement elite power even when governments have explicitly rejected ethnicity as an organizing principle (whether in the name of socialism or modernization). In Iraq, Saddam Hussein's strongly nationalist and avowedly socialist ideology did not prevent him from relying heavily on the Sunni minority whose position had been bolstered by both Ottoman and British colonialism; more than that, he relied on a cabal from in and around the town of Tikrit, the area where he was born. After the 2003 US-led invasion and occupation, the army (with its largely Sunni officer corps) was disbanded, and some 50,000 mostly Sunni bureaucrats were fired, stirring Sunni Shi'ite tensions.[45]

Africa too provides revealing examples of ethnic politics thriving under the cover of an ideology that rejects 'ethnicity'. Through most of the 1970s, for instance, the Somali state formally subscribed to socialist ideology and at one point coffins were ritually buried by President Muhammad Siad Barre to symbolize the end of clan politics. But behind the scenes Barre was playing ethnic politics to the hilt, favouring his own Marehan clan and those related to it. This created the conditions for civil war with the fall of Barre in January 1991 as heavily armed Marehan groups turned on weaker groups (often occupying more fertile land). In Liberia, President Samuel Doe, who came to power in a military coup in 1980, relied very heavily on his own Krahn ethnic group, and this helped to fuel the civil war there.[46] In Rwanda, the period after the 1994 genocide has seen the RPF-installed government outlawing the language of ethnicity; however, Tutsis have been given a highly disproportionate share of government and senior military posts.[47]

Turning to the former Yugoslavia, elite manipulation of ethnicity was an important cause of the wars there. Whilst some analysts (like Patrick Moynihan and Robert Kaplan) have suggested that the end of communism effectively 'lifted the lid' on longstanding and underlying ethnic hatreds in the former Yugoslavia,[48] David Turton has pointed out that socialist systems in the eastern bloc actually encouraged ethnic nationalism in many ways, notably by privileging certain groups like Russians and Serbs within their respective political systems. This helped to create the conditions for violence along ethnic lines when these systems began to collapse.[49]

In the former Yugoslavia – with communism collapsing, democracy pending and economic crisis intensifying – the tactic of stirring up ethnic nationalism was one way for the old communist elites to attempt to secure power and legitimacy. IMF-sponsored devaluation and austerity programmes had led to rapidly falling real wages and mass unemployment, and had increased the incentives for Croatia and Slovenia to break away from a crumbling federal structure.[50] Then, in February–March 1992, Bosnians followed suit and opted for independence in a referendum; Bosnian Muslims and Croats voting overwhelmingly for independence whilst most Bosnian Serbs abstained. As in many other contexts where a plural political culture was weak or missing, ethnic mobilization proved the easiest way of securing a political constituency.[51] Serbian leader Slobodan Milošević calculated that if the other republics in Yugoslavia would not agree to Serbian domination, he would incite the Serbian minorities in Kosovo, Croatia and Bosnia-Herzegovina to rise up and demand Serbian protection. This involved major military support from Belgrade for Serbian militias that engaged in what has been called 'ethnic cleansing' (a strange euphemism that has curiously bought into the fascist language of purity and hygiene).[52] Even the international sanctions to which this aggression gave rise seemed to help Milošević – at least, for a significant period – to consolidate his image as the Serbs' protector against a hostile world (see chapter 8). Behind the official discourse of ethnicity, however, a kind of class politics was damagingly played out: whilst a business and government elite grew richer, the middle class virtually disappeared (with many forced abroad) and the poor were further impoverished.[53]

Even as Milošević was stirring tensions, Croatian leaders were making their own appeals to ethnic nationalism, adding to the perception of danger among Serbs in Croatia. Yet ethnicity did not have to be a dominant consideration among groups who were often physically indistinguishable, who were speaking the same language (Serbo-Croat) and who were routinely intermarrying.[54]

In his book *National Deconstruction*, David Campbell argued that insofar as an anti-Western Muslim identity began to be advocated by religious leaders in Bosnia (for example, in hostility to drugs, alcohol and intermarriage and favouring an Islamic curriculum), this was in large part a *reaction* to violence, something that reflected a sense of betrayal by a West that claimed to be supportive of democracy and multiculturalism but had not in practice supported a multicultural Bosnia.[55] Campbell argued that multicultural visions were further marginalized by Western peace plans, including the 1993 Vance–Owen plan, which was based on the idea of an ethnic carve-up.

The techniques of ethnic nationalists – and, by extension, of those promoting a 'war on terror' – include pointing to a threat and rendering it plausible by depicting it as an extension of past violence; this may involve a degree of re-writing history but often contains at least some element of truth.[56] Serbian extremists' calculating use of atrocities in Croatia in 1990–1 was accompanied by extensive fear-mongering in the media, with politicians playing a prominent part.[57] Croats were portrayed as latter-day examples of the Ustashe Croatian fascists who had cooperated with the Nazis against the Serbs in the Second World War, and Croatian extremists had their own dehumanizing propaganda against the Serbs. Serbian propaganda in Bosnia centred on the supposed threat of Islamic fundamentalism as well as on the 'Ustashe' threat.[58]

Psychological functions

A third motive elites may have for stirring up ethnic conflict is that such conflict may offer to resolve personal insecurities surrounding their own ethnic identity. This is not the place for an in-depth examination of that mechanism, but it is striking that some of the most vehement nationalists were not born in the country on whose behalf they were so nationalistic. Stalin was from Georgia, Napoleon was from Corsica, Hitler was from Austria. Many of the Young Turk leaders involved in the massacres of Armenians at the end of the First World War were of non-Turkish ethnic origin.[59] It seems at least plausible that vehement nationalism has served, in part, as a way of overcoming doubts about one's own identity. Of course, we know that Nazi ideology praised the German *Volk* as a tall, blond Aryan race; yet Hitler himself certainly did not conform to this racial stereotype. One problem with dividing discussion into 'top-down' and 'bottom-up' processes (as here) is that we may miss the importance of those who occupy some kind of middle ground – for example, those who use ethnic antipathies to move from a lowly to a more elite status. The classic case of this is perhaps the Mayan Indian *jefes* (chiefs) of the abusive civil patrols in Guatemala, who found an elite status (in alliance with a Latino-based regime) at the cost of contributing to violence against their own people as part of the counterinsurgency forces there.[60]

'Bottom-Up' Processes: Ordinary People's Goals

One of Michel Foucault's central insights was that power is not simply held by the state and wielded over people. Instead, power is exercised, often subtly, at all levels of society; all manner of people collude in, and participate in, the exercise of power at various levels. If we apply this insight to ethnicity – and, at the extreme, to ethnic conflict – we can see the importance of understanding 'bottom-up' as well as 'top-down' processes.

Although the primordialists (including those who emphasize 'ancient ethnic tensions') have received justifiable criticism, ethnic tensions are not purely and simply the result of machinations by elites. Elites cannot simply whip up ethnic hostility from nothing, and very rarely can they simply *impose* their will. If elite manipulation was perhaps more important than non-elite motivations during the Rwandan genocide, this probably reflected the highly centralized nature of a strong government structure within a small and relatively controllable African state. Donald Horowitz noted in his book *Ethnic Groups in Conflict*, 'If elites pursue a policy of deflecting mass antagonisms onto other ethnic groups, such a policy must strike roots in mass sentiments, apprehensions and aspirations in order to succeed.'[61] Even if we believe that ethnicity is fuelled by conflict, we need to recognize (according to the logic of this very argument) that strong ethnic sentiments can predate and help to shape a conflict – if only because they have been created by conflicts in the past.

Ordinary people may sometimes find it desirable to embrace ethnic self-definitions, ethnic politics and even (at the extreme) ethnic violence. Part of this can be understood within an instrumentalist framework that focuses on the practical economic and political functions of ethnicity and ethnic violence. For example, an arbitrary state may encourage a pursuit of trust through ethnic networks.[62] Also significant may be psychological functions – like a sense of belonging – that lie outside the instrumentalist framework.[63]

Fear

A key factor driving ordinary people to participate in ethnic violence may be fear. Nazi propaganda said not simply that the Jews should be destroyed but, as the groundwork for this, that the Jews were trying to destroy Germany. Likewise, before and during the 1994 genocide, Hutus in Rwanda were subjected to a massive propaganda campaign insisting that the Tutsis and the Rwandan Patriotic Front were planning to wipe them out.[64]

A particularly important factor in promoting fear may be any falling away of state protection, either before or during outright conflict. For example, fears among the Serb minority in Croatia were an important factor mobilizing many Serbs into ethnic violence in 1990–1 as Yugoslavia fell apart. These fears were partly due to real factors like the sacking of Serbian policemen and they were partly whipped up by nationalist propaganda.[65] In conditions where state power is being used in a conspicuously partial way, such fear is likely to be intense and may even generate a desire for a new or expanded territory to provide security. During a seminar I attended in Belgrade in 1999, one local policy analyst commented, 'We connect the protection of human rights with taking ground or territory, not as a principle.'[66]

Some people have a vested interest in keeping alive certain societal or historical memories, notably the politicians who manipulate ethnicity to encourage conflict. They are like the worst kind of therapists: they will not let you forget certain historical instances of abuse; their status and economic privileges are underpinned by your inability ever to break free from the past (especially from your self-image as a victim); and they may even encourage you to imagine or articulate instances of abuse that never actually took place. On the other hand, if a politician or anyone else wishes to *obliterate* any memory of particular abuses (as when Tito ordered the bulldozing of the Jasenovac camp, the site of mass killing of Serbs during the Second World War),[67] then that too has its dangers: an experience of group persecution, like an individual's experience of abuse, is not going to go away just because an attempt has been made to bury it. Indeed, a coordinated attempt at forced forgetting may create optimum conditions for the propagandists promoting incendiary versions of 'remembering', particularly where religious and ethnic identities have been to some extent suppressed.[68] In relation to Rwanda before the 1994 genocide, Peter Uvin noted the resounding silences – at least at the level of official and international discourse – that surrounded some rather profound ethnic tensions as well as past episodes of ethnic violence. These silences did not prevent (and may have encouraged) the exploitation of group memories, many of which related to an historical experience of domination by Tutsi elites, and they could still be exploited.[69] As Mamdani noted in *When Victims Become Killers*:

> If it is the struggle for power that explains the motivation of those who crafted the genocide, then it is the combined fear of a return to servitude and of reprisals thereafter that energized the foot soldiers of the genocide . . . the perpetrators of the genocide saw themselves as the true victims of an ongoing political drama, victims of yesterday who may yet be victims again . . . .[70]

Whilst moving from the analysis of individuals to the analysis of societies has many hazards, a striking parallel is American psychiatrist James Gilligan's belief that violent individuals have a heightened sensitivity to humiliation because of their past experience of humiliation.

It seems that fear has often been most intense in contexts where ethnic differences have been small. The former Yugoslavia is one example. Significantly, Nazi propaganda tried to heighten fear of, and hostility towards, the Jews by playing on the fact that, very often, Jews could not be easily distinguished from non-Jews. Dehumanizing language was sometimes linked with the statement, intended to shock and frighten, that 'they' (the Jews) look just like 'us' (the Gentiles). Assimilation was successfully redefined by the Nazis as pollution and infection, and the implication was drawn that the pollutant or infection should be labelled, isolated and ultimately eliminated.[71]

The search for security also seems to be particularly intense in circumstances where 'both sides' see themselves as, in some sense, an embattled minority. This has been the case in Northern Ireland: Catholics have been a minority there, but many Protestants have seen themselves as a potential minority within a united Ireland. In Sri Lanka, the Sinhalese, though the largest ethnic group, have often seen themselves as a threatened minority in relation to the combined Tamil population on the island and in India.

The fear of being or becoming a minority is often related to fear of the fertility or sexual potency of a 'rival' ethnic group. In Northern Ireland, fertility levels have been higher among Catholics, fuelling fears among Protestants that they will eventually be outnumbered. Israeli fears of Palestinian population growth are significant (and informed the withdrawal from Gaza). In the US, the fears among the 'WASPs' (White Anglo-Saxon Protestants) have sometimes centred on the fertility and rising population of Hispanic elements in particular. (Some of this fear was exhibited in Huntington's 2004 book, *Who Are We?*, in which Huntington condemned those Hispanics for being resistant to learning English and appealed for a return to America's 'core' Anglo-Saxon identity.[72]) In India, extremist Hindu groups have drawn on Hindu demographic anxieties (real if largely unsubstantiated) about population growth and higher fertility among Muslims.[73] Again, the Muslims – though a minority in India – are sometimes seen as part of a very large and threatening group, with Hindu nationalists pointing to the 'extraterritorial loyalty' (in Bardhan's phrase) of the Muslims, a reference to pan-Islamic loyalties and to sympathies with Pakistan.[74] Memories of a period of subjugation in the past have again added fuel to these fears: Hindu fears of a return to Mughal rule can be compared with Serb and Croat fears that Muslim rule (as under the Ottomans) was about to be reimposed and with Hutu fears that Tutsi rule (as under colonialism) was about to resume.

The search for physical security also impacts on ethnic conflict at the global level, and writers like Huntington have played to these fears. In *The Clash of Civilizations*, Huntington wanted to emphasize that the war between the West and Islam was already underway. His thesis of 'civilizational' tensions was not entirely without evidence, and he gave an interesting account of culturally and religiously influenced reactions to Iraq's invasion of Kuwait and the conflict in the former Yugoslavia. But Huntington's book was itself a good example of how intolerance works. Even hard-line fascists do not simply say: 'Let's wage war on this group!', but prefer a message on the lines of: 'Conflict is already underway; the war has already begun; the other group is planning our demise; strengthen yourself!' *The Clash of Civilizations* conformed closely to this template.

Significantly, Huntington explicitly excluded the Jews from his list of clashing civilizations, even though he acknowledged that the Jews (with their own religion, language and territorial home) possess most of the essential characteristics of a civilization. Perhaps a prediction that conflict between Jews and 'the West' was inevitable and that 'the West' should prepare itself for this showdown would not be considered acceptable around the dinner table at Harvard?

Not that I wish to doubt the intensity of some of the religious and ethnic conflicts highlighted by Huntington and others. In 1999, I was travelling overnight on a train from Munich to Belgrade. I had a sleeping compartment to myself, but then a big, heavily built and unshaven man entered. We started talking, and it soon turned out he was half-Croatian, half-German and half-drunk. Within a few minutes he had lost any small reserve he had possessed and was busy thumping his fist on my bunk-bed and telling me that 'we' should have let all the Bosnian Muslims (or 'Turks', as he called them) die in Yugoslavia because they were all 'breeding like rabbits', having one child every year, and were preparing to sweep across the West and 'destroy our civilization'. I was not able to check whether he had a copy of *The Clash of Civilizations* in his back pocket, but I was thinking, 'This is just what I need. I'm sharing a sleeping compartment with a genocidal maniac!'

Perhaps surprisingly (and we have seen how even atrocity has a very human aspect), my intemperate intruder had quite a nice side to him. He stopped hammering my bed long enough to reach into his bag and say, 'Can I interest you in a pork sandwich?', which somehow I wasn't expecting.

I quickly accepted, if only to prove I wasn't a Muslim.

Acquiring resources

Non-elite groups may use their ethnicity to try to acquire resources. This can be a relatively peaceful process in which an ethnic group mobilizes to stake a claim to resources that are controlled by the state.[75] It may, however, take a much more violent form. In wartime Sudan, it has not only been the elites who have benefited economically from famine and war. We have seen how ordinary Sudanese – notably among the cattle- and camel-owning groups of the west – have benefited from looting, access to grazing land, and/or the cheap or free labour of famine migrants and captives.

Contributing to violence within the dissolving state of Yugoslavia was the opportunism of ordinary people, whether driven by greed or simply by an instinct for survival. This was documented, for example, by Peter Maass, in his ironically titled book *Love Thy Neighbor*. Ethnic cleansing was accompanied by looting and the occupation of vacated houses.

Even the Nazi genocide yielded benefits for some people in terms of looting and access to jobs during the earlier stages. In Rwanda, the 1994 genocide was fuelled not only by elite manipulation but also by acquisitiveness (and fear) among ordinary Rwandans. There was a significant land shortage in Rwanda, a small country with a rapidly rising population. Both Rakiya Omaar and Gerard Prunier, though stressing top-down manipulation of ethnic violence, acknowledged that land hunger played a role in the genocide.[76] Part of the problem was that official restrictions on migration to towns had tended to confine young people to rural areas. Whilst easing urban overcrowding, this also helped to store up problems and resentments in the countryside; there had even been famine in the south.[77] Although Mamdani argued that ordinary people's fear was more important in propelling the genocide than their greed, he did note that previous massacres had been accompanied by significant acquisition of land.[78] There was also a fear that returning Tutsis might take land away.

One study of 350 Rwandan households found that while middle-sized farmers were relatively unlikely to participate in the Rwandan genocide, there was a much higher level of participation among the two other selected categories: the landless or land-poor; and landlords or employers. The study suggested that '[t]he landlords or employers [overwhelmingly Hutu in the sample] had "something to defend" [from the power-sharing agreement and possible socio-economic reform], meaning their job, their land, their farm or farm output and their overall privileged position in Rwandan society', while the poorest group (again, overwhelmingly Hutu) 'could expect to gain from participation' – in particular, from the land and other property of murdered Tutsis – and were probably susceptible to a genocidal ideology that blamed Tutsi traders for low off-farm income, particularly in the context of collapsing coffee prices. Verwimp draws a parallel between the latter dynamic and evidence that the Nazis' propaganda against Jewish traders and bankers was particularly attractive to farmers lacking substantial land, often indebted and heavily dependent on fluctuating market prices.[79]

Psychological functions

A third set of functions that ethnic violence may serve for ordinary people are psychological in nature. A key motivation may be simple revenge. Beyond this, finding a scapegoat for one's troubles has had an enduring appeal, and this impulse is considered in what follows.

Peter Uvin has noted that the frustrations of development and underdevelopment provided a distraction from the privileges of the Rwandan elite, and that the scapegoating of Tutsis was a factor in the genocide.[80] Following Galtung's lead on the importance of 'structural violence', Uvin examined some of the hidden violence in the apparent 'success story' of rapid growth in Rwanda prior to the 1994 genocide (overseen by the highest concentration of foreign experts in Africa). He analysed the everyday humiliations in the development process there, and the traditions of impunity and extreme inequality. This pernicious system, he argued, created conditions of frustration and anger in which it became possible for certain Hutu elites, themselves threatened by moves towards democracy, to mobilize and orchestrate a genocide.

A particularly rounded and subtle analysis of the appeal of nationalism and extreme ethnic politics was provided by Hannah Arendt in *The Origins of Totalitarianism*. She linked the mass appeal of Nazism to the occurrence of social and economic crisis accompanying the historical transition to modernity. Rapid urbanization in Germany had been followed by hyperinflation in the 1920s and then by a dramatic economic slump from 1929.[81] Arendt referred to 'the dispossessed middle classes, the unemployed, the small rentiers, the pensioners whom events had deprived of social status, the possibility to work, and the right to hold property'.[82] She saw increasingly atomized individuals facing a world they could not control or predict, a world where they lacked the self-respect formerly derived from an acknowledged social function within particular communities.[83] She observed that this predicament had given rise to a 'self-centred bitterness', and added: 'The fact that with monotonous but abstract uniformity the same fate had befallen a mass of individuals did not prevent their judging themselves in terms or individual failure or the world in terms of specific injustice.'[84]

Compounding social and economic crisis had been a sense of humiliation linked to military defeat and the terms of the 1919 Treaty of Versailles (including reparations and loss of territory).[85] This was fertile soil in which to plant the idea that German – and individual – pride could be restored through military aggression and through the elimination of the group that was portrayed as undermining Germany's economy and racial purity as well as the German war effort in the First World War.[86] Focusing on some named enemy and on one's alleged racial superiority could bring a dubious measure of self-respect. Moreover, in Arendt's view, 'men in the midst of communal disintegration and social atomization wanted to belong at any price'.[87] Identifying an enemy – even if the choice was arbitrary – seemed to offer the cognitive satisfaction of certainty in uncertain times. Indeed, Arendt suggested that part of the appeal of fascism was that the identification of a clearly identified enemy – whilst certainly frightening – was less frightening and less disorienting than a world in which the source of insecurity remained obscure. In Germany, the fascist project involved taking those 'enemies' who were 'already amongst us', labelling them, separating them, and eventually eliminating them.

Nazi accusations of Jewish economic dominance have found echoes in many parts of the world. In many countries, ethnic conflict has reflected the tension between local groups and relatively prosperous middlemen minorities (for example, Indians in East Africa, Lebanese in West Africa, Chinese in Southeast Asia and Jews in Europe).[88] Economic imbalances can be particularly incendiary during a process of democratization. Amy Chua has commented: 'When sudden democratisation gives voice to [the] previously silenced majority, opportunistic demagogues can swiftly marshal animosity into powerful ethno-nationalist movements that can subvert both markets and democracy.'[89]

Pranab Bardhan, Andrew Fischer and Amy Chua have all drawn attention to links between mass violence and ethnically-structured economic rivalries.[90] Tensions between Muslim Bangladeshi immigrants and locals in many parts of India have reflected rivalry within the low-skilled job market. In Sri Lanka, meanwhile, violence was fuelled by a perception of the over-representation of Tamils in government jobs.

Resolving insecurities may be relevant for ordinary people, just as for elites, and Sudan would seem to be a case in point. Here, the Baggara cattle-herders of western Sudan have tended to be dark in colour, reflecting a good deal of intermarriage with southern Sudanese. Francis Deng, a prominent Dinka, has argued that many Baggara seem to be anxious to distinguish themselves from a supposedly 'inferior' population to the south, as with the racist use of the word '*abid*', or slave, to describe southern Sudanese.[91] In the very different context of the Guatemalan civil war, we have seen how some Mayans' participation in abusive civil patrols was linked to a desire to be identified with the dominant Latinos.[92] In the former Yugoslavia, too, insecurities could feed into intolerance. Many Serbs seemed keen to embrace the image of a heroic Serbian dynasty (past or present) as an escape from the reality of social and economic backwardness.[93] The Serbs' very similarities with their fellow Yugoslavs (for example, linguistically and often in terms of appearances) may have contributed, in volatile circumstances, to a desire to underline differences through violence: Michael Ignatieff referred to the 'narcissism of minor difference' in this context.[94] Insofar as modernization and urbanization blur cultural distinctions, they may sometimes ignite a desire to re-emphasize them.

Action-as-Propaganda

It is notable that fascistic propaganda in the former Yugoslavia was initially seen by many as ridiculous; however, as one Bosnian woman later explained to me, over time this propaganda could be made to appear more and more plausible. Atrocity was a response to coexistence as much as to hostility; as one analyst noted, 'Sarajevo is an irrefutable rebuttal to the Serbian war refrain that it is impossible to live together. This is why it must be completely ravaged.'[95]

In any kind of conflict – whether international, ethnic or an international conflict with ethnic dimensions – an aura of legitimacy for violence can sometimes be generated by violence itself. Highlighting the importance of 'action-as-propaganda', Hannah Arendt observed, 'The advantages of a propaganda that constantly "adds the power of organization" to the feeble and unreliable voice of argument, and thereby realizes, so to speak, on the spur of the moment, whatever it says, are obvious beyond demonstration.'[96] Or again: 'Not Stalin's and Hitler's skill in the art of lying but the fact that they were able to organize the masses into a collective unit to back up their lies – for example, predictions about dying classes or soon-to-be-extinct races – with impressive magnificence, exerted the fascination.'[97]

One way that violence could serve as propaganda for the violent was by allowing leaders to make their own predictions come true: first, when people came to resemble a distorted and propagandistic image of them (as the seemingly-less-than-human inhabitants of a disease-ridden ghetto, for example); second, when alleged historical laws about the triumph of a particular group or idea were 'revealed' as accurate; and, third, when humanitarian ideals were similarly 'revealed' as an unrealistic irrelevance. Arendt suggested that the masses were 'predisposed to all ideologies because they explain facts as mere examples of laws and eliminate coincidences by inventing an all-embracing omnipotence which is supposed to be at the root of every accident.'[98] An example of how action-as propaganda was intended to work was through the creation of mass Jewish emigration. As Arendt explained: 'The official SS newspaper, the *Schwarze Korps*, stated explicitly in 1938 that if the world was not yet convinced that the Jews were the scum of the earth, it soon would be when unidentifiable beggars, without nationality, without money, and without passports crossed their frontiers.'[99] Arendt argued that mass atrocities and expulsions meant that

> the incredible plight of an ever-growing group of innocent people was like a practical demonstration of the totalitarian movements' cynical claims that no such thing as inalienable human rights existed and that the affirmations of democracies to the contrary were mere prejudice, hypocrisy, and cowardice in the face of the cruel majesty of a new world. The very phrase 'human rights' became for all concerned – victims, persecutors, and onlookers alike – the evidence of hopeless idealism or fumbling feeble-minded hypocrisy.[100]

Apart from making predictions come true, a second reason why action could serve as effective propaganda was that punishment, in many people's eyes, implied guilt. Here, Arendt was drawing attention to what others have subsequently called 'just world thinking',[101] where people in effect assume that punishment implies a crime, and where this assumption serves to protect them from the fear of a totally arbitrary world.[102] Arendt observed in the context of the Nazi Holocaust: 'Common sense reacted to the horrors of Buchenwald and Auschwitz with the plausible argument: "What crime must these people have committed that such things were done to them!"'[103]

The 'war on terror'

We have seen how political leaders have frequently highlighted (even exaggerated) the ethnic element in conflicts, and often for self-interested reasons. The so-called 'war on terror' presents an interesting contrast in the sense that Western leaders have gone to great lengths to stress that this is *not* an ethnic or religious war. Revealing slips have been made, however, as when Bush referred to the 'war on terrorism' as a 'crusade'. Moreover, the indiscriminate nature of terror and counter-terror attacks has tended to move in the direction of an ethnic definition of the enemy.

In some academic circles, the dangerous argument has also been made that Afghan civilians perhaps *deserved* to lose protection because of their alleged support for the Taliban regime.[104] The hazards of this line are underscored when we remember that Mohamed Siddiq Khan, one of the July 2005 London bombers, argued – in a video recorded before the atrocities – that civilians in the West were 'directly responsible' for the deaths of Muslims when they supported democratic governments that perpetrated atrocities.[105]

In the global 'war on terror' (and very often in civil warfare and criminal behaviour), there has been a major disjuncture between problem and solution, between provocation and chosen enemy. Suicide terrorists are difficult to deter or punish: they tend to die in the course of their crime; and since they court death, deterrence has little meaning for them.[106] When the enemy is elusive, more accessible enemies are often found. Recall Girard's view that violence will always find a surrogate victim who is close at hand. The more obscure and elusive the threat, the more intense may be the desire to find an identifiable enemy – perhaps *any* identifiable enemy.[107]

Just after September 11, Bush declared: 'Somebody is going to pay.'[108] He told King Abdullah of Jordan: 'There's a certain amount of blood-lust, but we won't let it drive our reaction. . . . We're steady, clear-eyed and patient, but pretty soon we'll have to start displaying scalps.'[109] This brings to mind the view of James Gilligan, noted earlier, that violent criminals tend to be venting their fury at past humiliations on those who are unfortunate enough to be close at hand and to have somehow reawakened past humiliations.

The focus in the 'war on terror' quickly centred on the alleged 'state backers' of terrorism, but who exactly were these backers? An obvious candidate for retribution was Saudi Arabia. Fifteen of the nineteen hijackers on September 11 were Saudis, after all. Yet we have heard very little suggestion that the US should bomb this key oil-rich ally in retaliation. Instead, the already-weakened state of Afghanistan (an important base for al-Qaida) was selected as the enemy.

The evidence linking Saddam Hussein to 9/11 was non-existent. Yet a poll in February 2003 suggested that 72 per cent of Americans believed it was likely that Saddam was personally involved in the attacks.[110] Given a certain level of trust in – and deference towards – the US government and the US President, guilt could to some extent be inferred from punishment.

Remember Arendt's observation that the horrors of the concentration camps led many to wonder what the Jews had done to deserve that fate. In the case of Iraq, using punishment to imply guilt was never going to be entirely convincing, but it was supplemented by a continuous barrage of propaganda (in the US and UK in particular) about what Saddam was *about to do* (alongside a more limited discourse on what he had done already, notably to the Iraqi Kurds). The US government specifically asserted the right to intervene and override sovereignty where a government supported terrorism (or massacred its own people), and also to attack if there were grounds for thinking that the US was going to be attacked. Washington has invoked a 'right of preventive self-defence'.[111]

Under fire for wavering on major issues, Democratic Presidential candidate John Kerry made a telling comment in one of his pre-election debates with Bush in 2004. 'It's one thing to be certain,' he said, 'but you can be certain and be wrong.' Yet one of Arendt's insights was that for those leaders wishing to attract a mass following, the point was not be right, it was to be certain. We have seen how the very assimilation of Jews in Germany was used by the Nazis to heighten the fears of the Jewish 'menace'. The elusiveness of the terrorist – and the knowledge that he may be already 'amongst us' – has also fed into a desire to find an identifiable target, perhaps a terror 'mastermind' like Bin Laden or al-Zarqawi or a state 'backer' like Iraq or Iran. The search for certainty has fed not only into Bush-style fundamentalism but also into fundamentalism within the Islamic world. As Scilla Elworthy observed in relation to the occupation of Iraq in particular, 'In an atmosphere of chaos and humiliation, fundamentalism offers a firm philosophy which can give the impression of certainty in an uncertain world.'[112]

Arendt's action-as propaganda has been very much at work in other ways. Bush's close adviser Karl Rove said of the war on terrorism: 'Everything will be measured by results. The victor is always right. History ascribes to the victor qualities that may not actually have been there. And similarly to the defeated.'[113] (Hitler expressed a similar sentiment: 'I shall give a propagandist reason for starting the war, no matter whether it is plausible or not. The victor will not be asked afterwards whether he told the truth or not. When starting and waging a war it is not right that matters, but victory.'[114]) Bush himself said:

> I believe in results. . . . I know the world is watching carefully, would be impressed and will be impressed with results achieved . . . we're never going to get people all in agreement about force and the use of force . . . but action – confident action that will yield positive results – provides

kind of a slipstream into which reluctant nations and leaders can get behind . . . .[115]

Relying on 'victory' to generate legitimacy is of course a double-edged sword – as evidenced by a sharp fall in Bush's popularity when victory turned to quagmire in Iraq. But Arendt's analysis remains relevant – particularly her sense of how abusive regimes may take advantage of the desire for predictability and consistency, underlining and bolstering their own power by making their own predictions come true. In Bush's case, there were frequent assertions that the direction of history was on his side.[116] In line with Arendt's analysis, the 'irrelevance' of the rights that were backed by international law was to be demonstrated by a bold use of force. Just after the start of the attack on Iraq, Richard Perle eagerly anticipated: 'As we sift the debris of the war to liberate Iraq, it will be important to preserve, the better to understand, the intellectual wreckage of the liberal conceit of safety through international law administered by international institutions.'[117] (In some sense, NATO intervention over Kosovo had already prepared the ground, with the Independent International Commission on Kosovo concluding that NATO's air campaign was 'illegal but legitimate'.[118]) Attacking Iraq in the absence of evidence linking it to 9/11 only served to underline the weakness and lack of credibility of the UN.[119] Condemning one critical journalist as coming from 'the reality-based community', one senior Bush adviser said in the summer of 2002:

> We're an empire now, and when we act, we create our own reality. And while you're studying that reality – judiciously, as you will – we'll act again, creating other new realities, which you can study too, and that's how things will sort out. We're history's actors . . . and you, all of you, will be left to just study what we do.[120]

Another key aspect of action-as-propaganda should be noted. The 'war on terror' is a classic example of turning 'the other' into a preconceived and negative image that has been entertained (and propagated) by the perpetrators of violence. This applies to both sides of the conflict, since both sides seem to share an interest in nurturing their favourite nightmares and in 'proving' their enemy to be just as brutal as they had always insisted. In civil wars and global wars, violence tends to create the enemies it claims to weaken or eliminate (chapter 1), and thereby generates its own (spurious) legitimacy. In the context of Algeria's war for independence from France, Frantz Fanon understood how terrorists themselves could take advantage of the phenomenon of 'action-as-propaganda' – notably by using violence to bring out the underlying and previously part-hidden brutality of their opponent/oppressor.[121] Bin Laden also seems to understand this. The Arabic word for 'martyr' (*shahid*) can also be translated as 'witness': the martyr is someone who by his or her actions or speech makes a hidden truth clear to an audience.[122]

Counterproductive actions that lead to a proliferation of angry enemies will tend to promote a pervasive climate of fear. But in circumstances where the terrorist has been portrayed as omnipresent and hell-bent on our destruction, such actions at least bring the sponsors and supporters of the 'war on terror' the perverse cognitive satisfaction of knowing: 'Yes we are right, the enemy is indeed as powerful, pervasive and dangerous as we portrayed it; we must redouble our efforts!' It is hard to imagine that Bush and Blair consciously wished to make things worse; even so, they inhabited a world in which mad solutions generated (spurious) legitimacy for themselves. Billed erroneously as a key source of terrorism prior to the war, Iraq has become so – a development that lends spurious credibility to the initial accusation. The propaganda was made to become true. If the Soviet occupation of Afghanistan created an international brigade for Islamic extremists who have proved key figures in subsequent terrorism, the US-led occupation of Iraq has served as a focus and a training ground for a new generation of angry young men.[123] Meanwhile, an October 2006 study in *The Lancet* suggested that some 655,000 had died as a result of the US-led invasion – a careful calculation made by a team from Johns Hopkins University.[124]

In practice if not in theory, the 'war on terror' has repeatedly seen civilians caught up in the definition of the enemy. If Iraq was a readily identifiable enemy, identifying the enemy *within* Iraq was much more complicated. Echoing some of the accounts of US soldiers in Vietnam, US marine Michael Hoffman wrote of his Iraq experience, 'When your enemy is unclear, everyone becomes your enemy.'[125]

If Arendt's analysis reveals some of the links between enemy definition and social and economic processes at home, this is also an important line of inquiry in the 'war on terror'. In his book *What's the Matter with America?* (published in the US as *What's the Matter with Kansas?*), Thomas Frank has provided a revealing case-study of how economic insecurity has fed into support for Bush and for right-wing politicians more generally. Frank argued that in the context of diminishing safety-nets and a declining farming sector, a radical tradition of hostility towards corporations has been displaced onto hostility towards a range of 'out-groups' and towards the forces (science, evolution, secularism, pluralism) that seem to undermine old and comfortable certainties. Frank referred to the 'backlash' politics of the Republican right – a politics that has favoured 'tough' foreign policy whilst stressing a diverse range of mostly cultural issues.[126]

A dramatic military reverse or humiliation can easily add further fuel to this kind of 'backlash' politics, including renewed emphasis on the virtues whose alleged decline facilitated the humiliation. After 9/11, Bush 'worried that the United States had lost its edge'.[127] Referring to Clinton's response to the 1998 US embassy bombings in Africa, Bush said:

> The antiseptic notion of launching a cruise missile into some guy's, you know, tent, really is a joke. I mean, people viewed that as the impotent America . . . a flaccid, you know, kind of technologically competent but not very tough country that was willing to launch a cruise missile out of a submarine and that'd be it. I do believe there is the image of America out there that we are so materialistic, that we're almost hedonistic, that we don't have values, and that when struck, we wouldn't fight back. It was clear that bin Laden felt emboldened and didn't feel threatened by the United States.[128]

Regaining strength to revive deterrence implies that the enemy is highly centralized, an approach also underpinned by routine references to terror 'masterminds' and by Bush's notorious list of the 'most wanted'. But putting too much faith in the elimination of evil individuals encouraged great naïvety in relation to Iraq, which has paid heavily for the US government's tendency to reduce every problem to the evil of Saddam and his fellow Ba'athists. The hierarchical organization that is the US military has tended to imagine the enemy in its own image – that is, as a hierarchical organization which will be fatally weakened by the elimination of key leaders. In late 1993, military strategist Jon Arquilla said of the hunt for Saddam in Iraq: 'We are a hierarchy and we like to fight hierarchies. We think if we cut off the head, we can end this.'[129] A key error was sacking the entire Iraqi army (of 400,000) and the entire senior civil service. The sacked soldiers in particular have been a key component in the Iraqi insurgency/resistance.[130]

Keith Thomas noted in his classic study *Religion and the Decline of Magic* that when suffering is not explicable within existing frameworks, human beings have tended to resort to magical thinking. The limits of medical knowledge in the sixteenth and seventeenth centuries, for example, created a powerful impulse to explain illness through 'witchcraft'. It may be that, in the face of the 'disease' of contemporary terrorism, the evident shortcomings in academic frameworks – a militaristic 'war studies', a state-centric international relations, and a statistically obsessed political science – have helped to create political and intellectual space for explanations that are once more leading us into the realms of the superstitious and the persecutory.

As with earlier witch-hunts, the focus is on 'evil intentions' rather than actual deeds. It is the victim's weakness (the *lack* of weapons of mass destruction, for example) that offers an attractive choice for collective persecution. A confession is once more highly prized, as when Bush said Saddam's only way to avoid war was to give a 'full and complete' declaration of the WMD he did not in fact possess. Meanwhile, opposing the dubious persecutions may once again bring the accusation that you too have joined the ranks of the demons. Finally, as in the unhappy days of Salem in seventeenth-century Massachusetts, the lack of causal connection between problem and favoured solution (and the evident persistence of terror after the named 'evil' has been removed) serves merely to reinforce the search for new victims (in this case, for new backers of terrorism, whether in Iraq, Iran, Syria, Lebanon, Somalia or Afghanistan).

If the desire to restore respect is a central aim in projects designed to eliminate external (and perhaps internal) enemies, it follows that the leaders in this persecutory project must keep from consciousness any views that would undermine this self-respect. Given that the US/UK 'war on terror' has been both violent and counterproductive, it is unsurprising that many people have spoken out against it – both within the West and beyond it. Critics then risk the ire of these leaders, as shame is warded off with a progressively wider definition of the enemy.[131]

Conclusion

While 'rational actor' explanations have often been contrasted with accounts stressing the 'irrationality' of violence, there is no reason why instrumental and emotional factors should not operate in tandem. A classic case is when grievances are manipulated by the greedy. Fear, too, may be manipulated by the powerful; as Bob Dylan saw, a brain can be mismanaged with considerable skill.[132]

Whilst our major case-study of action-as-propaganda has been the so-called 'war on terror', a more general point can be made. An aura of legitimacy for oppression may come in large part from the changes and reactions it engenders, and sometimes the deepening of ethnic violence works in the following way. First, there is oppression (violence, exploitation, neglect). The victim groups fall partially below the protection of the law. This may still be called 'peace'. Second, there is a reaction to oppression (which may include rebellion, terrorism, various kinds of atrocity, acts of 'savagery', a defensive emphasis on your own ethnicity). Third, the reaction is used to legitimize and deepen oppression – and the labelling of groups prone to violence as evil, greedy or barbaric may in turn add a sense of alienation, intensifying the violence. Both war and famine may reflect a deepening of existing processes of exploitation, and victim groups are likely to fall further below the law's protection. In terms of the greed/grievance framework, one could speak of greed generating grievance, which in turn legitimizes more greed.

We have seen how making rigid ethnic distinctions can easily become a self-fulfilling prophecy. War has a tendency to become the way it is described and mis-described – underlining the importance of questioning simplistic descriptions of the fault-lines in a conflict (or who it is 'between'). These dangers are replicated at the global level: Huntington's potentially self-fulfilling prophecy has been mentioned and his book can be seen as feeding into antipathy to so-called 'non-Western cultures'. Since some of the sources cited by Huntington on the strength of the Islamic threat are precisely US military personnel, there is a notable circularity about his argument.

Drawing principally on Guatemala, it is worth mentioning five additional mechanisms by which action may serve as propaganda. We have noted that a good deal of violence and intimidation during the civil war there was directed at the political opposition and not simply at the rebels. This violence had a polarizing effect and served propagandistic functions as well as the more obvious function in weakening the opposition. In particular, it seems to have helped dominant groups to redefine the enemy: the enemy was no longer *the left* (which might have had significant legitimacy and support) but an *extreme* (and demonized) left. As one Guatemalan analyst put it to me in 2002:

> In 1996–97, there was a huge debate on who won the war. It was often said that the army won the military war while the guerrillas won the political war. . . . But people miss that the battle won was the ideological war, by the counterinsurgent state, the army and private interests. The ideology triumphed not officially but in the minds of the people. The peace accords were not extremely revolutionary either. The Guatemalan people came to perceive the left as evil and unpatriotic and so forth – even those people who actually resent the private sector. The reasons were, first, the big success of the state's ideological campaign and, second, the democratic left were killed or in exile or silent, and that opened the field to the extreme left in the context of a huge propaganda war.

A second form of action-as-propaganda in Guatemala was that when civilians were punished for the presence of guerrillas, the left got much of the blame. As the same analyst put it, 'The far left was not very successful in protecting the population. In areas with massive violations of human rights, the majority voted for Rios Montt [that is, for his party, the FRG, in 1999].' (The FRG took a 'law-and-order' stand; as a coup-maker, Montt himself was constitutionally barred from standing for President. A third form of action-as-propaganda was relocating shame to the victim community. Sources reported that many victims blamed themselves for the violence afflicting them: lacking knowledge about the counterinsurgency as a whole, they sometimes asked what they had done to bring an attack on their particular village.[133] Meanwhile, kindling violence among the Mayans helped to offload (in a sense, to decentralize) the blame (and much the same could be said about Khartoum stirring up violence among the southern Sudanese and Moscow organizing violence among the Chechens.)

The reference to Montt reminds us of a fourth mechanism: at some level, violence 'demonstrates' that only the violent can save or protect us. This seems to have been part of Milošević's calculation in the former Yugoslavia. In some instances, violence may make not only human rights seem like an irrelevance but even God himself. When rebels attacked one community in Sierra Leone, a Christian preacher pleaded, 'Please God, spare my life!', but the rebels replied, 'There is no God here. We are God. Because if there is a God, he would have saved you by now.'[134] Whatever morality was underpinned by peacetime punishments and rewards may be dramatically challenged by the 'new rules' that violence ushers in. Paul Richards observed in a perceptive paper: '[T]he rebels in Sierra Leone have reduced a country they presumed rotten to the core to ruins. Through their actions, the country has become in reality the wasteland they always supposed it to be.'[135]

A fifth mechanism is the suppression of memory. Drawing on his experience of censorship in Pakistan in particular, Salman Rushdie wrote in 1983:

> Where there is no debate, it is hard to go on remembering, every day, that there is a suppressed side to every argument. It becomes almost impossible to conceive of what the suppressed things might be. It becomes easy to think what has been suppressed was valueless anyway or so dangerous that it needed to be suppressed. And then the victory of the censor is total.[136]

If this book's introduction emphasized the shortcomings of 'evil' as an explanation for atrocity, examining the process by which enemies are defined suggests that very often it is not 'evil' that creates atrocity but the category of 'evil' and the use of 'evil' as a key explanatory framework. This process is integral to the demonization of certain groups. In other words, part of the moral force for atrocity lies precisely in the business of explaining previous atrocities. Solzhenitsyn wrote in *The Gulag Archipelago*: 'If only it were all so simple! If only there were evil people somewhere insidiously committing evil deeds, and it were necessary only to separate them from the rest of us and destroy them. But the line dividing good and evil cuts through the heart of every human being.'[137]

The widening search for enemies in a (counterproductive) 'war on terror' can be compared with widening searches for *internal* enemies. As with the 'war on terror', the misery accompanying ineffective policies does not necessarily undermine the persecution. In their interesting book *Political Paranoia*, Robert Robins and Jerrold Post noted that Khmer Rouge leaders in the 1970s interpreted the country's distress as requiring the destruction of a demonized group (basically non-ethnic Khmer). A millenarian future was promised upon the annihilation of the demons. However, policies based on these beliefs (including forcible de-urbanization) actually brought a deepening of misery and even outright starvation. After that, in Robins and Post's more general formulation:

> The leader rationalizes the failure of these policies in terms of the alleged continuation of demon-group values and conspiracies. The ideologically correct but discredited policies are therefore redoubled, and the hunt for the 'conspirators' and 'saboteurs' gains strength, destroying many innocent persons. In reaction to these policies, hostility and suspicion . . . actual conspiracies and sabotage against the regime, begin to develop.[138]

The analysis in this chapter underlines the importance of how enemies have come to be defined and how this may change over time.[139] Challenging this process requires acts of collective memory. The short-term horizons of the media, as we shall see in chapter 7, are often unhelpful here. Some of the policy implications of this chapter's analysis of 'top-down' and bottom-up' processes are considered in chapter 7 (information) and chapter 8 (peace). But first, we consider a central element in complex emergencies – the nature, causes and functions of famine (chapter 5) – after which we examine humanitarian aid (chapter 6).

5

Famine

What are the processes driving famine, and what causes deaths during a famine? This chapter looks at both peacetime and wartime famines, and at various theories underpinning different approaches to relief. Michel Foucault set himself the task of 'eventalization', something he defined as 'rediscovering the connections, encounters, supports, blockages, plays of forces, strategies and so on which at a given moment establish what counts as being self-evident, universal and necessary'. He stressed the importance of 'shaking [the] false self-evidence' of particular practices.[1] Changing theories about famine relief illustrate his point quite well.

The 'common-sense' view of famine can be represented roughly like this: famine is a shortage of food causing large numbers of people to starve to death; the remedy is to give people food. However, many theorists both in the past and today have rejected – in whole or in part – this apparently common-sense view. Consider Thomas Malthus. Certainly, this influential Anglican clergyman agreed broadly with this 'common-sense' view of what famine was. In his *Essay on the Principle of Population*, first published in 1798, Malthus famously argued that population will inevitably outstrip food supply: population tended to rise in a geometrical progression, whilst food production – impeded by a limited supply of land, for example – would rise at best in an arithmetical progression. However, he rejected the 'common-sense' remedy of giving people food. Malthus was writing partly in opposition to systems, set up in England just after the French Revolution, that linked poor relief to the price of bread and the number of children. He suggested this would only deepen poverty by encouraging fertility. He added that famine was 'the last and most dreadful mode by which nature represses a redundant population'.[2] This was verging on seeing famine as a kind of perverse solution to the imbalance of population.

A major challenge to the emphasis on inadequate food supplies came with the work of Amartya Sen. Returning to our 'common-sense' view of famine, Sen rejected the definition – famine as a shortage of food – and at least partially rejected the obvious remedy of giving food, emphasizing – particularly

in his collaboration with Jean Dreze – the importance of supporting entitlements through cash distributions and work schemes.

In his 1981 book *Poverty and Famines*, Sen famously suggested that '[s]tar-
vation is the characteristic of some people not having enough food to eat.
It is not the characteristic of there not being enough food to eat. While the
latter can be a cause of the former, it is but one of many possible causes.' [3]
The critical thing was not the total food in a given society or area but
whether individuals could stake a claim to an adequate quantity of this
food. What determined whether individuals could stake such a claim was
the *network of entitlements* that operated in a given society. This referred to
the range of means by which individuals could legitimately and legally
obtain commodities, including through production, trade, selling labour,
inheritance or obtaining social security. In other words, Sen wanted to look
not simply at what food existed, but at who could command what through
the legal means available. Where trade and selling labour were important
means of obtaining commodities, then the ability to obtain them would
clearly depend not just on the commodities (including labour-power) that
a person owned, but also on the prevailing market conditions. These could
change very rapidly, and these changes were seen by Sen as one of the principal causes (and probably the most important cause) of famines.

One of Sen's case-studies was the Bangladeshi famine of 1974, which was
precipitated by severe floods. Sen noted that rice production in the year preceding the famine was, paradoxically, the highest in the 1971–5 period. That
observation led him to wonder whether the cause of famine was a problem
of food availability within particular regions of Bangladesh. But he found
that this was not the case. Sen noted that Bangladesh's three most famine-
affected districts – Mymensingh, Rangpur and Sylhet – all experienced a
substantial *increase* in their rice output from 1973 to the famine year of
1974. Remarkably, a ranking of Bangladesh's nineteen districts in terms of
absolute availability of food grains per head (with 1 representing the greatest availability) revealed that the three most famine-affected districts had
some of the highest availability – at numbers 2, 3 and 5.

At the same time, Sen went on to explain, these three districts also experienced the most drastic decline in the rice-buying power of wage labour.
Floods greatly reduced employment opportunities during the normally
peak labour time of June to August, bringing down wages and reducing the
opportunities for employment. Labourers and petty traders were among
the hardest hit. The natural disaster of severe flooding had translated into
famine via very human constructions like markets.[4] In the longer term,
from the late 1960s to the mid-1970s, while the proportion of people below

the poverty line had probably fallen, the proportion in extreme poverty had risen sharply, creating vulnerability to famine among this group.

Sen also discussed the Great Bengal Famine of 1943, which killed perhaps 3 million people at a time when India was still ruled by the British. There was, again, no major fall in total food-availability prior to the Bengal famine. However, there was a damaging boom (related to the Second World War) alongside escalating public expenditure, notably on the military effort. This fuelled rapid inflation, as did widespread speculation by traders and panic hoarding by consumers.

Sen noted that there was protection for some groups in Bengal, notably through public distributions in Calcutta at subsidized prices. But this only added to inflationary pressures on those living in rural areas as food was drawn into the city through requisitioning as well as the superior purchasing power of those in Calcutta. As a result, millions – particularly in rural areas – could not afford whatever food was in the market.

The view that poverty and market forces lie at the root of famine has been widely accepted, and aid agencies have taken up Sen's insight that famine is likely to affect the poorest in any society and that these people should be targeted with relief. Sen's insights have also been applied to inequalities between men and women (and girls and boys). For example, in her book *The Story of an African Famine* (1987), Megan Vaughan described how, during famine in Malawi in 1949, women were frequently unable to stake a claim either to marketed food or to relief – partly because the colonial administration would not recognize women who had been deserted by their men as heads of household.

Sen's *Poverty and Famines* is fundamentally an economic analysis. In their 1989 publication, *Hunger and Public Action*, Dreze and Sen explicitly turned their attention to the political sphere, and to the potential role of public policy in protecting entitlements. They suggested that where entitlements collapse and states fail to take measures to protect entitlements, famines are likely. If we go back again to the 'obvious' remedy of giving people food, Dreze and Sen stressed that while transporting food to a food-scarce area might have a useful role (notably in bringing down food prices), another important tool is direct entitlement protection – for example, through cash relief or employment schemes. Particular types of state (lacking democratic forms of government or a free press) were seen as likely to be especially neglectful of famine relief; indeed, effective relief could be prevented by what Dreze and Sen, in a significantly negative form of words, called the 'negligence or smugness or callousness on the part of the non-responding authorities'.[5]

However, this would seem to be a rather inadequate conception of the connection between politics and famine. For one thing, there was remarkably little room in Dreze and Sen's work for the very profound role of violence in famines. Dreze and Sen asserted that '[i]t would be, particularly, a mistake to relate the causation of famines to violations of legality . . . the millions that die in a famine typically die in an astonishingly "legal" and "orderly" way'.[6] Yet this was inaccurate, notably in view of the profound relationship between violence and famines in contemporary Africa in particular. The possibility that states and politically powerful groups may actively promote famine and actively obstruct relief for rational purposes of their own was not addressed.[7] This is important because it appears to have fed into (or at least has done nothing to counter) a tendency in the international humanitarian system to treat complex emergencies as technical problems (or as natural disasters with a bit of violence added in to make things more 'complex'), whilst giving insufficient attention to underlying human rights abuses or to the predictable political problems with targeting that arise in the context of mass disenfranchisement and ruthless counterinsurgency.

As Jenny Edkins has stressed in a perceptive article, Sen's very definition of entitlements – in terms of what commodities people could command through legal means – tended to marginalize violence from the discussion.[8] Edkins suggested that for Sen the key to famines did not lie in the study of relationships between people (and who did what) so much as in the relationship of people to commodities.

The dangers of downplaying the politics of famine were highlighted by the 1983–5 famine in Ethiopia, which eventually precipitated a major relief operation (in part because of Bob Geldof's Band-Aid project).[9] Even though most explanations emanating from aid organizations and the Ethiopian government stressed that the famine arose from some combination of drought, environmental decline and overpopulation, the causes of this famine were closely linked to its *functions*. At least as important as drought or environmental crisis in creating the famine were the government policies of sponsoring raids (by militias and the army) on rural areas where rebel support was strong, and of blocking relief to these areas. Revealingly, the region of Tigray, with around one-third of Ethiopia's famine-affected population, received around one-twentieth of the total relief food. Significant quantities of relief ended up with government soldiers and militias,[10] and President Haile Mariam Mengistu's abusive government was able to triple its foreign currency reserves by ensuring that aid workers and journalists converted their money to the local currency at a rate that was highly favourable to the government.[11] Meanwhile, relief operations were manipulated to encourage population shifts away from rural Tigray and Eritrea towards government towns and so-called 'protected' villages in those provinces, and towards provinces further south, where workers were needed on state farms. In fact, relief was used as bait to lure people to holding centres in the north, from where they were taken by plane to the south. According to Alex de Waal, the numbers killed in the resettlement operation – estimated at between 80,000 and 100,000 – may have matched the numbers saved by emergency relief.[12]

Dreze and Sen stressed that, although there is likely to be some dispute about the division of the benefits, 'public action for social security is in some sense beneficial for all groups'.[13] However, this sense of shared interest is often hard to find, particularly in the middle of a civil war. The delivery of relief is likely to be impeded not just by the 'indifference' and 'callousness' that Dreze and Sen discern in autocratic governments, but also (and more fundamentally) by a range of rational reasons for withholding relief from particular groups of people. (As with Foucault's use of the term 'positive', this use of the term 'rational' is not intended to convey any sense of approval; it is used to indicate an efficient means to a given end.) These interests in withholding relief may be military, political and/or economic; they may be at work in a democracy just as in an autocracy.[14] In either context, targeting relief to those who need it is likely to be a difficult process with important political obstacles.

Military rationales include attempts to starve populations in either rebel-held or government-held areas and are discussed more fully in chapter 6. *Political* rationales might include the use (and withholding) of food aid to get votes, as in Zimbabwe in elections in 2005,[15] or the withholding of relief in order to deter or expel famine migrants from particular areas because of fears of their impact on the health of local people.[16]

Economic rationales for withholding relief can be discussed in a bit more detail. As far back as 1349, England's Statute of Labourers threatened the imprisonment of anyone providing charity to beggars who were capable of work; part of the context was the desperation of landowners seeking to secure labour supplies in the aftermath of the Black Death plague.[17] Restricting relief so as to encourage the poor to work remained a pressing concern right through to Victorian England and beyond, spilling over into colonial officials' Malthusian preoccupation with the 'demoralizing' effects of gratuitous relief in Britain's imperial outposts from India to Sudan to southern Africa.

To understand the economic functions of famine (and, by extension, of withholding relief), we have to go back to price changes. While Sen emphasized that price movements could lead to famine, these price movements may be part of the *function* of famine, and since famine itself leads to price movements (for example, through distress sales and purchases), taking steps that create or exacerbate a famine will contribute to price movements that are likely to be advantageous for significant groups of people.

It was Indian sociologist and activist Amrita Rangasami who first directed systematic attention towards the beneficiaries of famine, notably in an important 1985 article for *Economic and Political Weekly*. In contrast to Sen, Rangasami stressed that famines had not been eradicated from India, despite the democratic forms of government that have prevailed since independence. She examined both colonial and recent famines, and made three key points.[18] First, drawing on local understandings of famine in India (and also on studies of famine in the Netherlands under Nazi occupation), she argued that famine is typically a long process, a process of progressive impoverishment and loss of assets, which might or might not culminate in death. Her main focus was on famines linked to natural disasters like drought and floods; even so, she argued that some combination of economic, military, political, social and psychological pressure was habitually exerted on victims over a period of time.

Second, Rangasami argued that this process had beneficiaries. In famines, grain prices typically rocketed, while labour, land and livestock prices plummeted as people were desperate to sell their assets to get food. Rangasami emphasized that important groups stood to gain as desperate people sold their labour, land and other assets cheaply in a famine, whilst at the same time buying grain at an inflated price. Going back to the 'common-sense' definition of famine, Rangasami rejected the view of famine as a *shortage* and stressed that it was more fundamentally a *transfer*.

Third, the state – and here Rangasami was thinking primarily but not exclusively of India – has intervened only in the final stages of famine, when economic processes (notably, asset-transfers) had run their course. In nineteenth-century India, the aimless wandering of the distressed was taken as a warning of *impending* famine, whereas it actually only occurred during the final stages of famine.

While Rangasami's main focus has been India, many other famines also reveal the importance of her view of famine as essentially a competitive process. The Great Famine in Ireland – which peaked in 1847–8 – was precipitated by a failure of the potato crop. In this sense, it was a natural disaster; but it was also profoundly political.[19] At the time, all of Ireland was politically a part of Britain. The Irish famine appears to have conferred significant benefits on some landlords – themselves under significant economic pressures – by clearing large sections of the peasantry and tenant farmers from the land through evictions, emigration and outright mortality. This allowed the consolidation of larger landholdings, and at the same time created a significant group of landless people willing to work as day labourers. For many years before the famine, landlords had used assisted emigration in an attempt to solve what they saw as the overpopulation of their estates. These emigration schemes – and still more the famine itself – facilitated the widespread replacement of agricultural tillage with livestock rearing, helping landlords to meet a growing market for animal products in an increasingly urban England.[20] Local landlords played down the severity of the potato disease appearing in 1845; later, the British reliance on the local organization of relief foundered on landlord indifference. Inadequate relief also helped landlords to save money.

Some benefits from famine were also anticipated in London, where the Assistant Secretary at the Treasury and chief famine administrator, Charles Trevelyan, interpreted the famine as a God-sent opportunity to rid Ireland of an idle and unproductive peasantry, replacing it with educated landlord proprietors on the English model. An influential British government adviser and Oxford professor called Nassau Senior was heard to say that he feared the famine of 1847–8 in Ireland would not kill more than a million people, and that this was scarcely enough to do much good. Under the notorious Quarter Acre Clause of 1847, no relief was allowed to those with more than a quarter acre of land unless they gave it up. In this way, relief itself became an instrument of dispossession. The legacy of bitterness from this famine reminds us that while conflict can create famine, famine can help to create enduring conflict.

Ireland's Great Famine also raises the disturbing possibility that famine may sometimes be seen as an instrument of development – and this is not an isolated case. In the early 1930s, some hard-line Soviet officials saw famine in Ukraine as useful in helping to destroy the 'reactionary' class of kulaks who were regarded as standing in the way of socialism and industrial progress.[21] In Ethiopia in the 1980s, the government sometimes presented the famine-affected areas of the north as non-viable and outmigration as a developmental process, not least in populating government farms in the south.[22] In Sudan, some aid donors said mass migration from the south had a positive aspect in speeding the south's transition from a 'backward' pastoral society, in providing labour on agricultural schemes in the transition zone between north and south, and in avoiding the creation of 'dependency'.[23] We are familiar with the idea of a 'war to end all wars'. Famines, too, have been pursued in the name of a war against famine.

If we link famine too readily with poverty, we may miss the vulnerability of richer groups and of the most economically productive regions. Early warning systems sometimes use satellite images showing varying vegetation; but where fertile land and other rural assets are being coveted by violent groups, a 'green' area may indicate a vulnerable area. In Mozambique, the area of Zambezia, known as the country's 'breadbasket', was devastated by fighting. In the Somali famine that peaked in 1991–2, the three groups that were hardest hit were the Rahanweyn, the Digil and the Bantu. These groups had all tended to be politically marginalized in comparison to dominant and heavily armed pastoral groups, but the Rahanweyn in particular were occupying some of Somalia's most fertile land along the Juba and Shebelle rivers and had already been subject to some quasi-legal dispossession in the 1980s (that is, before the war).[24]

If Rangasami's view of famine as transfer rather than shortage thus receives considerable support, Alex de Waal's important book *Famine That Kills* also challenges 'common sense'. De Waal rejected the 'common-sense' definition of famine (famine resulting from food shortage) and came to be very sceptical about the remedy (give people food). Drawing on local perceptions of famine in Darfur, in western Sudan, in the mid-1980s, he suggested that 'famine' should be understood to mean the disruption of a way of life, involving hunger, destitution (including loss of assets) and *perhaps* death: so there were 'famines' and 'famines that kill'.[25]

De Waal emphasized that proper relief was a matter of providing not simply food, but also water, medical services and help with the economic strategies that local people have long employed in the face of famine; these strategies, he argued, contributed considerably more to survival in Darfur in the mid-1980s than did the small and unreliable quantities of relief food received.

De Waal also put forward two contrasting models of famine mortality. In the first, destitution leads to starvation, which in turn leads to death, usually as a result of the diseases induced by malnutrition. In the second, drought and social disruption and economic crisis combine to create a public health crisis, leading to increased mortality through increased exposure to infection. De Waal stressed that in Darfur in 1984–5, famine mortality arose primarily from an increased *exposure* to infection (due to health crisis) rather than an increased *susceptibility* to infection (due to food crisis and malnutrition). Since infection, especially diarrhoea, can create an inability to retain food, it is possible that a malnourished child such as those seen on television is thin because he or she is ill, rather than ill because he or she is thin. This means we should not assume that food is the most pressing problem, even though photographs would appear to make this self-evident. (The complex interaction of HIV/AIDS and malnutrition has also become of major importance.[26])

There were two main components in the health crisis in Darfur in 1984–5. The first was the unusual concentration of people and of animals because of migration, increasing exposure to infection. The second was the deterioration in the quantity and quality of water (especially well-water) due to drought, which increased the concentration of germs in the water. De Waal observed that mortality was not correlated with indicators of poverty and destitution, either for individuals or for communities. This suggested, contrary to Sen, that it was not poverty and destitution that were causing the famine deaths in Darfur. What was critical was not so much how rich you were but *where* you were. De Waal also argued that while severe malnutrition creates susceptibility to disease and death, moderate and mild malnutrition do not, and he went on to suggest that severe malnutrition was actually rather rare during the 1984–5 Darfur famine. In famines where severe malnutrition *is* more prevalent, de Waal argued, the starvation and health crisis mortality models will both be relevant, with mortality being driven by increased susceptibility to infection as well as increased exposure.

De Waal's analysis has important implications for relief. First, aid should be geared to people's own survival strategies. De Waal saw an important role for food and/or cash distributions in allowing people to stay in their villages – or to move back to them. Bulk distribution of relief before the rains could allow people to plan ahead and to work their own fields during the rains. Also important may be looking at ways of helping people to hold on to their livestock, for example through schemes for purchase and then re-sale, through the provision of veterinary services, and through the provision of fodder.

Second, to prevent deaths in a famine, there should be proper attention to reducing the health crisis. Part of this is helping people to stay in their home areas and avoid crowded and unsanitary urban or camp conditions. Also important are: the provision of water, for example in protecting wells; improving sanitation; giving priority to immunization against key diseases such as measles; making contingency plans for cholera and typhus; and guarding against malaria, for example through better sanitation.

While some of the more unimaginative approaches to needs-assessment focus on what people *lack*, an approach that is in many ways more promising focuses on what people are seeking to *do*, and seeks to assist them in those endeavours. De Waal's work here is complemented by the work of Ken Wilson and Barbara Harrell-Bond, who have stressed that helping refugees should involve removing the constraints on their own enterprise.[27] Important measures here include improving local infrastructure (such as roads), providing cash, and removing trading restrictions (including restrictions on trading relief food itself). Insofar as aid interventions focus on facilitating coping strategies, the often rigid distinction between 'relief' and 'development' tends to dissolve.

The analyses of famine by Sen, Rangasami and de Waal were all developed in relation to famines not directly linked with civil wars, but they all have important implications for reducing famine in the context of a civil war. Although Dreze and Sen underestimated the role of violence in famines, the entitlement framework turns out to be extremely helpful in tracing the mechanisms through which war may translate into famine: that is, through its impact on direct entitlements, or production, and market entitlements. De Waal's 1989 analysis of the health crises associated the large-scale migration and concentration of people proves highly relevant in the context of mass displacement associated with armed conflict. His analysis also underlines that we may need to *expect* local opposition to the provision of relief – if only because relief may attract migrants and associated health crises. Finally, his analysis points to the dangers in any restrictions on people's ability to move freely and pursue their own economic strategies – restrictions that have proven to be abundant and deadly in complex emergencies. For her part, Rangasami drew attention to famine as a competitive process in which force was integral. This turns out to be particularly pertinent in wartime famines, and this is best illustrated with a case-study from southwestern Sudan.

Case-Study: Sudan

If we substitute the word 'famine' for the word 'Gulag' in the Foucault passage quoted in chapter 1, we get 'what use is the famine, what functions does it assure, in what strategies is it integrated?'

Although famines depicted in the media often seem to come 'out of nowhere', the case of Sudan illustrates how famine tends to be rooted in the politics of uneven development. It also highlights some key characteristics of contemporary warfare in poor countries. The focus of this section is on famine in southwestern Sudan in 1986–8, but parallels are drawn with the current crisis in Darfur (discussed further in chapters 6 and 8).

A pivotal problem has been the systematic neglect of development outside of the central Nilotic areas. This has left western, eastern and southern

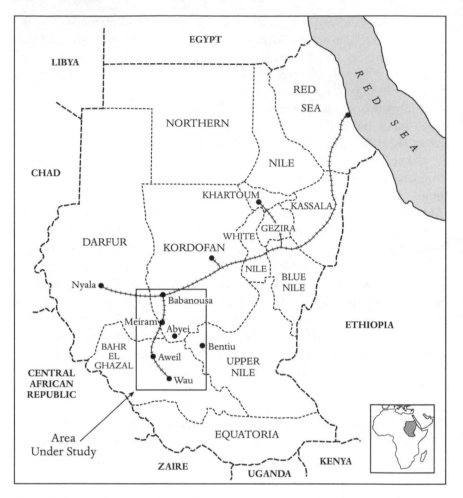

Map: Sudan, with area under study

Sudan in an extreme state of underdevelopment, a key reason for rebellion (starting in the south but more recently spreading to the west and, to a limited extent, the east).

Much of the development that *has* taken place in Sudan has taken the form of a rapid expansion of semi-mechanized farming (with finance from the World Bank and the newly oil-rich Middle East).[28] This expansion proved to be a threat to many Arab pastoralists in the west (often known as 'Baggara') as well as to other groups like the Nuba (living in the Nuba Mountains in the centre of the country). The prospect of quick profits, together with the neglect of fertilizers and the practice of continuous cultivation, meant that

semi-mechanized farming could eat up land very rapidly. Leases for mechanized farms went overwhelmingly to well-connected civil servants, traders,
officers and absentee landlords, and not to the local 'small farmers' who were
supposed to be favoured under World Bank guidelines. As under British rule,
the government in Khartoum used the granting of cheap leases (and privileged access to cheap inputs) as a key strategy in winning political support.
Little or no compensation was paid to the previous users, and the position of
pastoralists worsened during the 1984–5 famine, when relief distributions
frequently discriminated against pastoralist groups.[29]

Even prior to the outbreak of Sudan's second civil war in 1983, many
non-Arab groups considered themselves to be outside the protection of the
government. Thus, one Nuba man analysed conflict in the Nuba Mountains
area, an area that was to become the focus of genocidal violence in the early
1990s, as follows: '[O]ur big problem in the late 1970s and early '80s was the
Government of Sudan policy of taking fertile land for mechanized farms.
They drove the local people off. . . . When our youth in Khartoum and the
northern towns saw these things, they began to know that the Sudan
Government is not our government.'[30] This was a case where victimized
groups fell partially below the protection of the law in peacetime and still
further below its protection in wartime.

Apart from the forcible expropriation of land in Sudan, another part of
the violence of development were the monopolistic profits for Arab traders
bringing cattle out of the south, a trade that increasingly attracted attacks
from southern Sudanese. Significantly, army personnel began to acquire an
increasing interest in this trade in the late 1970s and early 1980s, as they
were bribed into giving special protection to northern merchants. This was
part of the beginnings of an alliance between army officers and merchants
geared towards using more widespread and deeper violence to extract
resources from the south when Sudan's second civil war broke out in 1983
following a near-mutiny by southern Sudanese in the government army.

Unable to afford a large and salaried army, the Sudan government
resorted to a strategy of turning the dissatisfaction of economically marginalized Baggara against the southern Sudanese Dinka and Nuer. This was
doubly 'functional' since the rebel Sudan People's Liberation Army (SPLA)
was itself attempting to recruit Baggara elements. The arming and encouragement of Baggara militias (and some Nuer militias in Upper Nile in the
south) seemed to offer central government a cheap way of dividing and
weakening opposition (though at some cost in terms of radicalizing the
civilians who were attacked). Partly through inducing man-made famine as
crops were stolen and destroyed and livestock was raided, the strategy

offered the prospect of depopulating oil-rich lands and decimating the Dinka, seen as the principal supporters of the rebel SPLA. It also offered an opportunity to confuse the international community and to deflect recriminations from the Sudan government.[31]

Some Baggara militias had already been created to protect large landholdings and oil installations owned by Chevron. The government provided militias with immunity to prosecution for theft, killings and other violations of the law. Militias were encouraged to attack the Dinka in particular and also elements of the southern Sudanese Nuer. Significantly, it was the democratically elected government of Oxford-educated Sadiq el Mahdi, drawing important political support from the western Sudanese Baggara, which engineered much of the worst militia raiding and presided over a devastating famine.

Increasingly through the 1980s, the rebellion came to be used by a coalition of politicians, traders, soldiers and discontented Baggara to portray the Dinka, the Nuba and other non-Arab groups as rebels and as people who could therefore legitimately be attacked and exploited. Exploitative arrangements had fuelled resistance, which in turn provided increased opportunities (and a degree of perceived legitimacy) for heightened exploitation, further fuelling resistance.

Elements of the Baggara sought access to grazing land, stolen cattle and cheap labour. The fact that the late 1985 raids south of the Bahr el Arab river came some two years before a major SPLA presence in the area suggested that the strictly economic motive for the raiding was more important, at least initially, than any counterinsurgency motive. It also highlights the *militarily counterproductive* nature of much of the raiding, which tended to 'spread' rebellion from one geographical area to another.

The role of conflict over oil in underpinning the war was critical. The oil in the south was the government's best hope of meeting its mounting international debt payments, and legislation in 1983 stipulated that oil revenues would go to Khartoum and not the southern regional administration – helping to precipitate rebellion in that year. Following the discovery of oil in 1978, the idea of a 'Unity Region' had been proposed in government circles: the region would embrace the major oil-rich areas of Bentiu and Gogrial area councils in the south and Abyei area council (where additional oil deposits had been discovered) and some other parts of southern Kordofan. Precisely these areas (together with the garrison towns of Aweil and Wau, which served as a refuge for those displaced by militia attacks) were the most severely affected by famine in 1986–8. This was more than a coincidence. The Bentiu area, with the richest oil reserves, was where the initial raiding had been concentrated and where both government and SPLA troops continued to be stationed in the greatest numbers. This area continued to be subject to some of the worst deprivation and blocking of relief until the signing of the January 2005 north–south peace accords. Government manipulation ensured that the limited relief that was delivered in the late 1980s ended up, overwhelmingly, in government-controlled areas on the edge of zones – rich in oil and grazing land – that the government and allied groups wished to depopulate. The zones being depopulated were also areas of rebel strength.

Also significant in driving the famine were a variety of market transactions distorted by various kinds of force. Indeed, 'forced markets' might be said to have played a more significant role in driving famine than 'market forces'. Force played a key role in creating high grain prices, which in turn helped to create famine. In part, the cutting off of southern garrison towns – and the persistence of very high grain prices within Bahr el Ghazal – was due to the SPLA, which attempted to place government-held garrison towns like Aweil and Wau under siege. But another major problem was the manipulation of supply by a variety of northern Sudanese interests profiting from exploitative trading. This strategy was facilitated by the south's dependence on northern grain. One of the main groups to benefit from high grain prices in the south were army officers. In many parts of the south, officers worked together with merchants to shape grain markets and restrict grain movements to their mutual advantage. Both merchants and army officers were involved in delivering commercial goods to Aweil by train, for example, and they were able to maintain high prices by restricting the quantities delivered. The composition of the trains from Babanousa was decided by a combination of local merchants, the town councils in Babanousa and Muglad, and the army.

Meanwhile, movements of famine migrants were being severely restricted in a context where migrants were often seen as a security threat, a health threat and (by some very low-income groups) an economic threat. In effect, a range of more or less violent and exploitative constraints were helping to concentrate the famine and to prevent high grain prices from rippling outwards.[32] Importantly, restrictions on movement helped to concentrate famine migrants in famine camps, something that tended to increase their exposure to diseases associated with population concentrations and unsanitary conditions. Restrictions on movement also interfered with access to wild foods and to relatives as well as impeding other coping strategies.[33]

Livestock markets were also powerfully influenced by the use of force.

The grain-purchasing power of those with cattle was a remarkable twenty-seven times better in El Obeid than in Abyei further south. Significantly, some of the chief beneficiaries of livestock price changes had contributed to the raiding that underpinned these changes, as some livestock traders provided finance for the Baggara militia raids. For example, merchants in Ed Daien – one of the two biggest cattle markets in Darfur region in the far west and an important market for stolen cattle – provided money for guns and ammunition for Baggara militias.

The situation was a dramatic and tragic illustration of Rangasami's point that price movements contributing to famine also confer benefits. One can also see that whilst some benefits were incidental, many beneficiaries were able actively to shape these price movements. Another part of the system of benefits were those arising from relief operations, which were subject to large-scale appropriation, both *en route* and once relief had been delivered.[34] Just a few miles from Meiram famine camp (the site of some of the worst famine mortality figures ever recorded), a feast was prepared for aid workers, traders and local officials. Every kind of culinary delicacy was on offer. The host was a northern merchant involved in famine relief, who told me the famine had been sent to him by God.

Many Dinka were subjected to some form of slavery,[35] with wartime violence effectively shaping not only the price at which commodities were sold but also prevailing conceptions of what might legitimately count as a 'commodity'. Captured Dinka were used for a variety of unpaid herding, farming and domestic work. Often, they were subjected to violence and sexual abuse, including castration of men and boys and rape of women and girls. Southern Sudanese famine migrants were living in fear in areas controlled by hostile northern militias and government officials. One young man said he and other Dinka were being treated 'like dogs' and 'had no rights'. Branding of Dinka captives with cattle irons was common.

All these abuses make it very clear that the absence of political rights was very extreme – notwithstanding the existence of a formally democratic government. Importantly, the people most affected by famine were severely underrepresented, both locally and in Khartoum – partly because war impeded elections in the south, partly because southern politicians tended to be marginalized and discriminated against, and partly because famine migrants displaced into the north were not part of the constituency of local officials and political representatives. In a significant sense, it had not been the poverty of southern Sudanese that exposed them to famine but their wealth (and in particular their wealth of natural resources and cattle) in a context where they lacked representation within the organs of the

Sudanese state.[36] Even *within* the Dinka, wealth could be an important additional source of vulnerability to attack.[37]

For those familiar with this famine (and subsequent famine in Bahr el Ghazal in 1998, for example), the current crisis in Darfur is a horrific case of *déjà vu*. One major *difference*, particularly in comparison to 1988, is that much more of the emergency relief *has got through*, helping to prevent mass mortality from starvation and disease among displaced people. But the similarities are nevertheless sobering. Again, neglect has fed into rebellion. Again, the Sudan government has used militias in a massive and highly indiscriminate overreaction, this time working with the *janjaweed* militias (drawn from Darfurian and Chadian Arab-speaking tribes) to attack civilians and rebel groups, with aerial bombing to support the attacks and the provision (again) of effective legal impunity.[38] Again, a violent process of asset transfer has driven famine forwards and has promised important economic benefits for some groups, including access to fertile land that has been vacated as well as 'protection' payments extracted by militias.[39] The looting of livestock in Darfur seems to have been well organized and even premeditated (often with military involvement).[40] Whilst the current political economy of relief has not been extensively analysed, local purchase of grain for relief has certainly been profitable for Nile Valley merchants and large-scale grain farmers, with both of these groups being key constituents of the Khartoum regime.[41] Even oil should not be discounted as a possible factor in this more recent large-scale displacement: areas coveted by Japan, China and American-turned-British businessman Friedhelm Eronat include parts of northern, western and southern Darfur devastated by the Sudan government and allied *janjaweed* militias.[42]

Famine, then, needs to be understood as resulting from the interaction of diverse *strategies* and not simply as a technical 'deficit' with a technical solution. This focus on strategies is now developed further, as we turn to international humanitarian aid and the interaction of geopolitical strategies, national strategies and, finally, the strategies of international aid organizations.

6

Aid

In discussing humanitarian aid in complex emergencies, it is tempting to start with the imperative of providing relief and then proceed to label anyone impeding this relief as evil or greedy, or both; the story of more or less benevolent intentions undermined by malevolent actors fits well with the much-favoured template of 'good versus evil' (and frequently injects it with distinctly paternalist, even racist, overtones). This chapter takes a rather different approach and examines the various reasons that different groups might have for contributing to an unhelpful outcome in relief operations, whether through blocking relief, through not providing it in the first place, or through not providing it in a form that is useful for the recipients. As with the approach to understanding wars, the chapter looks at the complex interaction of agendas leading to particular outcomes, and it avoids the assumption that human suffering (in this case, the suffering caused by inadequate relief) means that key actors have 'failed' (in the sense of failing in their main goal or goals). The chapter examines the priorities of international governments (first section), the priorities of powerful actors within the affected society (second section), and the priorities of aid organizations (third section). This puts us in a position to assess the degree to which 'failure' is actually *functional*. The fourth section focuses on policy implications and dilemmas. This chapter focuses primarily on emergency food aid rather than the provision of health services, shelter, and so on (though these are evidently also important).

Priorities of International Governments

Understanding the inadequacy of humanitarian interventions is impossible without understanding the complicated functions of 'humanitarianism' for donor governments and the extent to which these are consistent with *not providing relief to needy groups*. One function of 'humanitarianism' is strategic. During the Cold War, US relief and humanitarian assistance was integrated into counterinsurgency operations in Vietnam and again in the

US-backed counterinsurgency in Guatemala from the 1960s. When it came to famine in communist Ethiopia in the mid-1980s, major Western donors proved reluctant to give relief at all – until mass media coverage of famine in late 1984 produced a dramatic about-turn in policy.[1] In Sudan in the 1990s, geopolitics played out rather differently. Cold War concerns encouraged the courting of the Sudan government as an ostensibly friendly and democratic buffer state between socialist Libya and Ethiopia. This – together with the lure of oil – was the context for donors' emphasis on 'tribal' violence and their reluctance to highlight Khartoum's manipulation of ethnic violence and its obstruction of relief.

After the thawing of the Cold War, international political priorities continued powerfully to shape emergency responses. The subordination of aid to geopolitics was dramatically manifest in Afghanistan at the end of 2001 when the US was distributing food during sustained aerial attacks and President Bush memorably suggested, 'Can we have the first bombs we drop be food?'[2] In the ongoing crisis in Darfur, Sudan, a concern to get support from Khartoum in the 'war on terror' – together with a focus on achieving peace in the south – encouraged international 'soft-pedalling' in relation to escalating abuses in the region. Aid agency workers in Darfur have found themselves in a position reminiscent of the 1980s: as Prunier puts it, they have been 'first in the line of fire with no political back-up'.[3] In North Korea, humanitarian aid has been used in an attempt to prevent political collapse, to minimize mass migration into China (or even South Korea), and to put pressure on the government in relation to peace negotiations with South Korea and in relation to the inspection of nuclear weapons and the control of trade in nuclear materials. These geopolitical priorities seem to have led to a tolerance for very high levels of diversion (and poor monitoring) that would be considered unacceptable in most contexts.[4] Significantly, North Korea's inclusion in George W. Bush's 'Axis of Evil' led to a major drop in US food donations.[5] Geopolitical concerns have also affected humanitarian aid during renewed conflict in Liberia from 1999, particularly after press reports of links between al-Qaida and Sierra Leone's rebels (backed by Liberian President Charles Taylor). By July 2002, UN agencies in Liberia had received only $3.9 million of the $15 million requested at the start of the year; yet in the same period, UN agencies in Sierra Leone had received $58.8 million, and in Guinea, $37.7 million.[6]

In several recent crises, the provision of humanitarian aid has encouraged and legitimized international political inaction. Very often, media coverage has demanded some kind of action, whilst other considerations – including a desire to keep favour with host governments and a concern with avoiding the deployment of UN peacekeepers – have simultaneously encouraged political inaction; humanitarian aid can serve a function in resolving this dilemma. Mark Duffield has drawn attention to a withdrawal of diplomatic interest from many parts of the world in the 1990s, something stimulated by the thawing of the Cold War and then further encouraged by the ill-fated US/UN intervention in Somalia in 1992–3.[7] In Sierra Leone for much of the 1990s, aid served as a substitute for vigorous diplomatic engagement; particularly damaging was the international community's virtual silence on human rights abuses by government soldiers. Eventually, malnutrition in some areas did become a major problem, but as an English aid worker in Sierra Leone told me in 1995: 'It's not really a food emergency at heart. It's treated as one because this is what aid agencies do.'[8]

The 'humanitarian' response to war in the former Yugoslavia contributed to the emergence in international policy circles of the phrase 'the well-fed dead', and in his book on war in the former Yugoslavia (with the ironic title of *Love Thy Neighbor*), Peter Maass expressed a common sense of betrayal arising from the neglect of fundamental security issues: 'What, [the Bosnians] asked, was the point in feeding us but not protecting us? So we can die on a full stomach? There was much truth to this: the main humanitarian problem in Sarajevo was not a lack of decent food but a surplus of incoming shells.'[9] Significantly, international willingness to use force against the Serbian forces seems to have been tempered by a felt need to protect aid operations. This included fears that air strikes would hit aid workers – a concern that the Bosnian Serbs sometimes exploited by positioning military forces close to aid operations. Traditional, more consensual peacekeeping (including the protection of humanitarian aid) did not mix well with peace enforcement and outright war.[10]

The story of Rwanda in 1994, as set out in chapter 8, was one of diplomatic inaction and withdrawal.[11] By contrast, the humanitarian aid operation for those who fled from Rwanda to Zaïre and Tanzania was one of the largest in history. A major Danish-led evaluation of interventions in Rwanda concluded that the provision of large-scale humanitarian aid to the (predominantly Hutu) refugees in Zaïre and Tanzania served to disguise the international inaction in relation to the preceding 1994 genocide.

That pattern has been replicated in Darfur more recently, where humanitarianism continues to serve as cover for weak political pressures and for a failure to use the economic leverage that the international community possesses in relation to the Sudan government. The International Crisis Group noted in 2004, 'The U.S. is still fixated on getting humanitarian workers into

Darfur, a worthy but insufficient objective.'[12] Subsequently, the international focus on AMIS (African Union Mission in Sudan) peacekeeping efforts seems to have reduced political pressure on the Khartoum government; the international humanitarian community's claims of providing 'protection by presence' seem to have had a similar effect whilst at the same time only very limited protection on the ground has been provided. Inhibiting factors here have included a desire to keep aid workers (especially international aid workers) *away* from the most dangerous areas, the frequent use of relatively inexperienced field officers, a reluctance to work alongside government actors (with the ICRC being an exception) and, most importantly, the willingness of the Sudanese government to sponsor widespread attacks on civilians despite the large-scale presence of aid workers in the area.[13]

Another important function of 'humanitarianism' for major donors has been limiting population flows. The Western initiative of setting up a 'safe haven' for Iraqi Kurds in northern Iraq was shaped, in part, by the desire to minimize (and reverse) potentially destabilizing flows, notably towards Turkey (a key NATO ally).[14] Limiting population flows also proved an important consideration in the former Yugoslavia. During the early years of the war there, Germany had been receiving large numbers of refugees from former Yugoslavia, while Britain and France were virtually closing their doors. Figures from July 1993 show that Germany had 340,200 such refugees and that Austria had managed to take 89,739; by contrast, Britain had received only 8,640 and France just 5,524.[15] From July 1992, Germany began putting strong pressure on other European countries to increase their intake of refugees. Increasing the strength of the UNHCR (Office of the UN High Commissioner for Refugees) and the size of the humanitarian effort at this time was in large part an attempt to keep those displaced by war from becoming refugees. The British proposal for safe areas within Bosnia (on the lines of the safe haven set up in northern Iraq in 1991) also seems to have been linked to the German pressure to accept more refugees, as well as to a desire to find alternatives to the policy of air strikes and lifting the arms embargo – a policy being proposed, on and off, by the US government at the time.[16] These Bosnian 'safe areas' were to prove tragically unsafe, notably in the case of Srebrenica. Susan Woodward summarizes Western policy towards Bosnia as 'containment with charity'.[17]

Alongside a concern with containing population flows has been a growing concern amongst the international community with those who have been displaced within national borders. During the Cold War, some refugee flows were welcomed as evidence that ordinary people were 'voting with their feet' against a communist regime or a left-wing rebel movement. Relief to internally displaced persons (IDPs) and rebel-held areas was typically neglected amidst an expressed concern with the 'sovereignty' of nation states.[18] Indeed, those who managed to cross international borders and become refugees usually received far better assistance than those who were internally displaced (the latter having no specific treaty or organization to protect them).

After the Cold War ended, there was increasing concern with improving assistance to the internally displaced. In addition to the 'safe haven' initiatives in northern Iraq and Bosnia, the 1990s saw aid operations that involved negotiating access to rebel areas not only in Sudan but also in Ethiopia and Angola.[19] In part, this reflected media coverage of almost unrelieved disasters. But many analysts have expressed concerns that the new attention to the internally displaced serves as a kind of 'Trojan horse' for a more covert agenda: the neglect of responsibilities under international law to provide asylum for refugees, whether in countries that border a disaster-affected country or further afield.[20] During the Bosnian conflict, some European politicians even argued that granting asylum to victims of human rights violations would be contrary to their so-called 'right to remain';[21] assisting or preparing for a refugee influx was sometimes represented as complicity in ethnic cleansing.[22] Where the international community has given the impression that security could be guaranteed within states (for example, through 'safe areas'), this in itself could encourage countries of asylum to ask why they should be receiving or retaining refugees from that 'protected' country.[23] Many Western nations have placed increasing restrictions on asylum and entry – for example, by using detention as a deterrent, by imposing visa requirements on asylum-seekers, and by imposing sanctions on carriers who transport asylum-seekers.[24] In April 2006, UNHCR Commissioner Antonio Guterres warned that since September 11, 2001, many states around the world had invoked security concerns to justify new restrictions on those seeking to enter.[25] Alarmingly, the right to asylum for those with a well-founded fear of persecution can lead potential recipient countries to minimize the persecution that is taking place. For example, UK Home Office reports have sometimes seriously underplayed the threats to returned asylum-seekers, apparently selecting evidence with a view to rejecting asylum-seekers.[26] As evidence of the Nazis' persecution of the Jews accumulated in the Second World War, Swiss officials and aid workers were playing down the human rights abuses in Germany – influenced, among other considerations, by the Swiss authorities' fear of having to accept a major refugee influx.[27]

Priorities of Powerful Actors within the Affected Society

The priorities of powerful local actors have often undermined the helpfulness of relief operations. As Vivian Lee has shown, it has proved tempting for aid officials to dismiss this as a shocking manifestation of callousness or evil, whereas what is needed is to try to understand the diverse motivations and pressures at play.[28] In line with analysis developed by Clay and Schaffer (discussed more fully in chapter 7), these considerations could then be taken into account in the design of policy, rather than noted in retrospect – perhaps under the heading of 'lack of political will' – as a reason why the 'good intentions' of policy-makers did not work out in practice.

A routine practice in international relief operations, whether in wartime or peacetime, has been to focus on the 'poorest and neediest' group, to 'target' relief at this group, and then to dispatch a quantity of relief deemed sufficient for the group's needs, usually with relatively few resources allocated to monitoring the fate of relief and rather little consideration of how to secure the cooperation of local authorities or even transporters for passing that relief to the most needy. However, the most needy groups will tend to be unable to stake a claim to relief for precisely the same reasons that they were exposed to famine and violence in the first place – because they lack political clout within the institutions of their own society.

This applies even in natural disasters. My research on the drought-driven famine in Darfur in 1984–5 showed that relief operations discriminated strongly against rural dwellers, migrants and pastoralists – groups particularly hard-hit by the famine.[29] The lack of political clout of disaster victims recently 'came home' to many in the US when Hurricane Katrina brought flooding to New Orleans in August 2005. The (mostly black) residents of low-lying areas proved gravely lacking in political muscle within relevant US authorities. One manifestation of this was that whilst city residents with cars could simply drive away, insufficient public buses were provided for those in flood-prone areas (who were known to be the least mobile). The government agency responsible for disaster response, the Federal Emergency Management Agency (FEMA), had been run down by President George W. Bush almost as soon as he arrived in office. Significantly, FEMA was part of the Department of Homeland Security, and in the run-up to the disaster nearly 75 per cent of federal funds to local and state disaster units had been earmarked for dealing with terrorism.[30]

If disaster victims lack political clout in peacetime, this is all the more applicable in wartime – particularly where needy groups are being targeted for attacks by their own government.

When we examine the diversions and manipulation of relief by politically influential groups, three sets of agendas stand out. The first (which applies strongly in natural disasters as well as complex emergencies) is the priority given to protecting *resident* populations rather than migrants. The second is the economic agendas of powerful groups (again, an influence in natural disasters as well as complex emergencies). The third set of agendas (by definition restricted to complex emergencies) is military in nature. Apart from depriving victims of aid, the economic and military manipulation of aid can feed into violence. In general, the worse the targeting of aid and the higher the rates of diversion to those not suffering from famine, the more aid is likely to act as an incentive for violence.

Protecting resident populations

The obstruction of relief may be linked to *the protection of resident populations*. Those fleeing famine or war have routinely been seen as a threat by local populations and by local authorities. Significantly, a refugee or an internally displaced person will generally not constitute part of the political constituency of politicians and officials with responsibility for an area of influx. The principal mechanism highlighted by Sen and Dreze as preventing famine – the existence of democratic government – will not necessarily help *migrants*.

Apart from the possibility of bringing disease (chapter 5), famine migrants have often been seen as an economic liability (taking up land, damaging the environment, bringing down wages and / or boosting prices); the threat of high prices, for example, is implicit in Peter Cutler's model of high grain prices spreading out from the 'epicentre' of famine as people move away and grain moves in.[31] Those who flee famine or war may also be seen as a security threat – perhaps a source of crime or a vehicle for rebel infiltration. Such worries may not be unfounded: one factor facilitating the spread of war from Liberia to Sierra Leone in 1991 was that Liberian refugees unwittingly provided 'cover' for rebels (backed by Charles Taylor) to move into Sierra Leone; in 2000–1, Liberian and Sierra Leonean refugees in Guinea proved something of a magnet for violence from armed groups across the respective borders.

Local fears about displaced people are of long standing and should not come as a surprise. A widespread fear of migrants in medieval Europe has been documented by Michel Mollat in *The Poor in the Middle Ages*. Mollat contrasted the charitable attitude to the 'true pauper', who was known to his or her fellow-villagers, with a widespread suspicion of the 'transient pauper', or 'vagabond': 'Next to nothing was known about the men and women who lived as vagabonds. Since they had fled their rightful place in society, might they not be rebels? Or disease carriers? . . . Hospices prudently offered shelter to "transient paupers" for only a limited period, and in times of alarm access to the city was denied.'[32] The restriction of hospice relief here is significant. Today, too, hostility towards migrants can encourage the withholding of relief. This was clearly the case during the drought-famine in western Sudan in 1984–5, as Save the Children Fund field reports demonstrate.[33] In the subsequent war-driven crisis with its epicentre in the south, these fears were redoubled: the late 1980s saw local authorities in northern Sudan frequently withholding relief from southern Sudanese migrants amidst concerns that they constituted a security threat as well as a health threat. Thus, alongside the attempt to gain resources from raiding and the attempt to eject people from certain areas of the south, there was a simultaneous unwillingness to receive them in the north. Together, the implications were *genocidal*, though it would appear that many of those contributing to this process did not have a specific intention of wiping out an ethnic group. Studies of other catastrophes – including even the Nazi Holocaust[34] – have shown that they may occur in stages through the interaction and unfolding of complex agendas.[35]

If fear of migrants may encourage a withholding of relief from them, it should also be recognized that such fears can encourage *provision* of relief in the areas of most intense outmigration. Indeed, responses to natural and human-made disasters (at the national or international level) have sometimes been most vigorous when a problem 'for them' becomes a problem 'for us' (notably as a result of migration).[36]

Economic agendas

Three possible economic benefits of manipulating relief apply in peacetime and wartime. First, relief may be withheld in order to maximize profitable price movements associated with war and famine.[37] Second, relief (or the lack of it) may serve as an instrument for securing resources in areas that are being depopulated; in such circumstances, military and economic purposes may be quite difficult to disentangle.

Third, diversion may be profitable in itself. Appropriation of relief by powerful local actors would seem to be a factor in all disasters.[38] Again, purely economic purposes will be hard to separate from military goals. In

Mozambique in the late 1980s, the rebel group Renamo would frequently attack government Frelimo towns shortly after aid had been delivered there. In the Somali capital of Mogadishu, the prospect of gaining access to aid channelled through the city in the early 1990s was an important cause of inter-factional fighting.[39] Moreover, faction leaders benefited from their status as the principal intermediaries with whom the UN chose to deal.[40] Negotiating with warlords for aid access can strengthen the warlords' legitimacy and their ability to command the loyalty of their 'followers'. Significant profits were made from the protection of aid vehicles.[41] The potential spoils of an aid-dependent, centralized state were a major spur to violence. Conversely, the withdrawal in March 1995 of resources and contracts under UNOSOM (United Nations Operation in Somalia) seems to have had the effect of undermining the patronage systems of Mogadishu-based faction leaders' patronage systems.[42]

Aid may also encourage attacks when these attacks become part of a system that keeps aid flowing into the hands of the attackers or groups colluding with them in some way. This seems to have happened in Somalia.[43] The lure of aid may also encourage armed groups to confine 'magnet' populations to particular geographical areas, as Wendy James has shown in relation to southern Sudan.[44] In Sierra Leone, many citizens suspected that elites were inactive in bringing the war to a close in part because of the flourishing 'war economy' in Freetown in particular, where looted goods were flooding in and where rents had been artificially elevated by people fleeing rural areas and by the influx of aid organizations.[45] A key benefit for government actors has often arisen from the manipulation of exchange rates used by aid organizations.[46]

Reconstruction aid may also be manipulated with a view to resource control. In the wake of the devastating Indian Ocean Tsunami of December 2004, survivors' and fishermen's groups in Thailand and Sri Lanka registered alarm that the evacuation of coastal areas was opening the way for large-scale commercial exploitation of the coastland – for example, for hotels, casinos and shrimp farms.[47] In one assessment, Scott Leckie, head of the Centre on Housing Rights and Evictions, observed that 'the tsunami provided a pretext for evictions, land grabs . . . and other measures designed to prevent homeless residents from returning to their original homes and lands'. India, too, has been affected. In Sri Lanka, fishing communities and others have been ousted from shorelands by a prohibition on building within 100–200 metres of the sea.[48]

The process of 'reconstruction' after Hurricane Katrina is also instructive. According to some estimates, some 80 per cent of New Orleans' black population (the strong majority in low-lying areas) may never return. The government's failure to fund the mending of broken levees – and insurance companies' reluctance to insure new buildings without this work – has helped to stall reconstruction. Some local people have suggested that city authorities and corporate interests favour a 'whitening' of New Orleans.[49]

Military agendas

Forcible depopulation may serve military as well as economic purposes. Again, manipulation of relief is central to such strategies, whether it is governments trying to starve out rural populations or rebels trying to starve out government garrison towns. Chapter 5 noted, first, that those areas of Sudan and Ethiopia that were most in need of relief in major 1980s famines actually received only a tiny proportion of overall relief and, second, that these were areas of relative rebel strength. Meanwhile, respective government forces benefited from relief: for example, in Sudan in the 1980s and 1990s, international aid consistently helped to sustain the government's control of the garrison town of Juba in southern Sudan. In Mozambique and Angola, areas of rebel strength were also deprived of relief. In the former Yugoslavia in the early 1990s, aid crossing Bosnian Serb territory provided a substantial injection of resources for Serbian military forces.[50]

In the Darfur famine from 2003, as earlier in southern Sudan, government obstruction has significantly curtailed deliveries to areas of rebel strength. As UN Special Envoy Tom Vraalsen acknowledged in December 2003: 'Delivery of humanitarian assistance is hampered by systematically denied access. Khartoum authorities claim there is unimpeded access but they greatly restrict access to the areas under their control while imposing blanket denial to all rebel-held areas.'[51] The internally displaced people in the most desperate situation have been those caught behind rebel lines.[52] Meanwhile, humanitarian aid to camps in Darfur (while essential) has sometimes 'locked in' the forcible displacement effected by the Sudan government and its *janjaweed* allies.

One specialized way in which aid can be subordinated to local military objectives is the use of aid as 'cover' for military operations. In Darfur, Sudan Liberation Army (SLA) rebels, not to be confused with the SPLA, threatened to block relief coming from government areas, citing concerns that relief was being manipulated for military purposes.[53] Back in the 1980s, both the Sudanese and Ethiopian governments used aid shipments to channel arms to vulnerable garrisons, adding to the incentive for rebels to attack these shipments. In the oil-rich Bentiu area of Sudan, the presence of aid agencies was used to deter attacks on strategic Sudan government positions.[54] Meanwhile, the rebel SPLA would sometimes try to protect its military installations by assembling civilians in the area.[55] All these manipulations impede the channelling of relief to the most needy. During Nigeria's civil war in 1967–70, the Nigerian government tried to starve out the Biafran rebels; partly to secure relief and partly for military reasons, the rebel Biafran administration mixed relief flights with those bringing in military supplies and insisted on night-flights to impede Nigerian government interceptions.[56]

The history of aid to refugees shows how aid has been repeatedly manipulated by powerful local actors. Refugees have often become pawns in military games, helping to provide cover, legitimacy and material resources that help to sustain a military effort.[57] International aid may play a part here: it may be consumed by fighters or by their dependants; it may be sold for arms; it may attract new recruits, and so on. The military functions of refugees were evident on the Thai–Cambodian border in the 1980s. At this time, massive Western assistance to Cambodian refugees in Thailand helped to revive the Khmer Rouge (responsible for some of the worst mass killings in history). Khmer Rouge fighters lived among and controlled civilian villagers.[58] Entire settlements would move backwards and forwards across the border with Cambodia, depending on the level of hostilities with the Vietnamese-backed forces inside Cambodia. In the context of the Cold War, Western powers were more hostile to the Vietnamese-backed regime in Cambodia than to their Khmer Rouge opponents.

Another warrior-refugee community was that inside Pakistan on the Afghan border in the 1980s. This community was largely controlled by the Afghan *mujahadeen*, who at the time were waging war (with Western support) on a Soviet-controlled regime in Kabul. Relief for these refugees played a part in building up the strength of the *mujahadeen*. While rebel *mujahadeen* trained in military camps, UNHCR found itself supporting their dependants.

Emergency aid to Hutu refugees in Zaïre was notoriously manipulated by militia fighters who had participated in the 1994 Rwandan genocide, something that helped them to rebuild their strength after fleeing the advancing Tutsi-dominated Rwandan Patriotic Front (RPF). Food aid and other relief supplies were diverted from the intended beneficiaries and were used to help the Hutu extremists to recover and rearm. Prunier noted that numbers were inflated by local extremists so as to get more aid, and that a great deal of relief was sold for cash to finance political and military projects.[59] Former government soldiers and *interahamwe* Hutu militias were also able to recruit new members from the refugees. In addition, Hutu extremists seemed to be using refugees as protection against being arrested and as the basis for consolidating a mini-Hutuland that allowed incursions into Rwanda and that could perhaps facilitate a restoration of Hutu supremacy in Rwanda.[60] That meant intimidating those who tried to return to Rwanda, and the Hutu extremist leadership played on fears of Tutsi retaliation within Rwanda to convince Hutu refugees that return was too dangerous. Meanwhile, Zaïrean troops were helping to prevent Hutu refugees from leaving the camps, despite a serious outbreak of cholera.[61] The international community missed the opportunity to send a multinational force to separate and disarm the Hutu extremists, thereby putting aid agencies in an impossible position.[62] Kisangani Emizet notes that since the extremists had committed genocide, the international community actually had an *obligation* to separate them from *bona fide* refugees.[63]

Priorities of Aid Organizations

Another reason for the inadequacy of relief is that the interests and priorities of aid organizations are often at odds with the interests and priorities of those suffering from disasters. A fundamental problem is that organizational health (and individual careers) may sometimes be better served by satisfying donors and host governments than by satisfying the ostensible beneficiaries. This problem can interact damagingly with the agendas of powerful local actors.

Camps

Part of the critique of aid organizations has centred on relief camps. In her pathbreaking book *Imposing Aid*, Barbara Harrell-Bond took some of her inspiration from the work on asylums by Erving Goffman[64] and from the film about a mental institution *One Flew over the Cuckoo's Nest*. She argued that the favoured solution to refugees' problems (providing aid in camps) was actually part of the problem: it constrained the economic strategies of refugees and tended to deepen their trauma by exacerbating feelings of loss of control. Harrell-Bond, the founding director of the Refugee Studies Programme in Oxford, saw camps as tending to induce in refugees a sense of powerlessness and despair which aid organizations would then routinely turn around and condemn as 'dependency' and 'laziness'. Paradoxically, as Allen and Turton later emphasized, even refugees' ingenious attempts to get around the constraints of camp life – such as multiple registration for relief and the practice of selling ration cards or relief goods – have often been interpreted by donors as signs of a 'dependency culture' in which aid has 'morally corrupted' the recipient (a longstanding concern among British officials, for example, both at home in the Victorian era and in the empire).[65] So the danger is that the victim becomes the culprit, and shame is redistributed away from powerful actors who reproduce a damaging system and towards the allegedly 'lazy' or 'deceitful' refugee.

De Waal's work on the 1984–5 Darfur famine showed that the heavy reliance on camps had had two damaging effects. First, the concentrations of people had increased people's exposure to infection. Second, confining people to relatively small geographical areas had imposed severe restrictions on their ability to pursue their economic strategies. De Waal showed that these were people's primary insurance against the famine process and he urged the importance of helping people to sustain their livelihoods in rural areas. While this Darfur famine was drought-driven (rather than a complex emergency involving widespread violence), camps have often been *particularly* favoured (and particularly restrictive) during conflict, when they can provide a means of controlling 'dangerous' populations and a source of legitimacy and resources for military endeavours.

Whilst sexual and gender-based violence can take place anywhere, rape has been a common occurrence in camps; so too have prostitution, the exchange of sexual favours in return for various benefits, and domestic violence more generally. The full extent of rape and other sexual violence is particularly hard to know since these crimes are very frequently under-reported – for example, because of fear of recriminations or fear of social stigma. But Agnes Callamard observed that many of the Somali women who had suffered rape in Kenyan camps had already fled similar experiences in Somalia. Kenyan police ignored their request for protection; some were themselves involved in the criminal acts. Meanwhile, the local structures of representation for refugees tended to be male-dominated. Callamard noted that UNHCR itself sometimes seemed reluctant to bring complaints before the relevant authorities. She also stressed the importance of practical steps like proper lighting and proper locks on sleeping accommodation.[66] In her study of assistance to refugees in Guinea from the early 1990s until 2001, Vivian Lee showed that the inadequacy of relief reaching woman and children was forcing many to resort to damaging strategies in the search for food and income, including the granting of sexual favours.[67] Such strategies may also include journeying long distances in order to get food or water or fuel (and thereby risking attack). Rape of women collecting firewood has been common in the most recent crisis in Darfur.

The hardships and insecurities associated with the refugee experience may themselves fuel the intensity of anger as well as a desire to wage war on whatever regime or group is seen as precipitating these hardships; again, camps can be part of the problem here. Zolberg et al. observed that '[i]ndividuals in exile may find that the most socially meaningful and economically rewarding activity is to join the militants. For many children growing up in camps and knowing nothing but a dependent, degrading, and fundamentally insecure existence, joining the battle is the only relevant future.'[68] The miseries of Palestinian refugees have clearly fed into conflict in the region; and in Afghanistan, the Taliban emerged from the hardships of Afghan refugees in Pakistan.[69] The uncertainty and insecurity of camp life may compound earlier traumas and encourage aggressive ideologies that themselves provide a sense of certainty and an explanation for suffering.[70] The anthropologist Liisa Malkki studied two groups of Burundi Hutu refugees in Tanzania, one in a refugee camp and one in a city nearby. Those in the camp tended to see themselves as Hutu who were forever opposed to the 'evil' Tutsi; but those in the city identified themselves as Burundians or Tanzanians and had little time for the racist imagery of the Hutu–Tutsi conflict.[71]

Restrictive treatment of refugees played a part in the origins of the humanitarian crisis in neighbouring Rwanda. When a Hutu-dominated government took over in Rwanda in 1959, political violence in 1959–63 caused thousands of Tutsis to flee to surrounding countries (including Uganda). Initially, many were confined to camps; many were re-confined under Ugandan President Milton Obote in the early 1980s when they were seen as a threat because of their previous support for Idi Amin. Meanwhile, the Rwandan government was denying them a chance to return, claiming that Rwanda was already overpopulated. In 1986, Rwandan refugees in Uganda helped Museveni to take power in Uganda; encouraged by Museveni, they launched an attack on Rwanda in 1990 with the aim of deposing the Habyarimana regime there, an attack that culminated in genocide. Of course, camps have been favoured for local political reasons and are not simply the work of international organizations. Even so, the minimal international pressure on Uganda and Rwanda to implement their obligations in relation to these refugees does seem to have fed into conflict in the region.

Harrell-Bond argued that while relief camps were for the most part dysfunctional for refugees, they nevertheless served important functions for relief agencies – for example, camps could be relatively easily organized and monitored, any improvements in nutritional status could readily be measured and reported, and visiting journalists could come to publicize the good work of the agency.[72] Randolph Kent and Ken Wilson have both stressed how a concern with organizational health and growth can create a bias towards measurable and visible solutions to measurable and visible problems, including a bias towards shifting physical commodities to people once they have become thin in environments that can be easily monitored and publicized.[73] This is connected with a persistent tendency to give insufficient attention to livelihoods. A report on relief to Somalia, Ethiopia and Kenya during drought in 2004–6 showed that livelihood support (for example, provision of water sources, fodder relief, veterinary programmes, livestock purchase) continued to be weak in comparison to food aid – a longstanding bias that has reflected the existence at various times of surplus food stocks (notably in the US) as well as the view that food aid demands less expertise and is less complicated to organize.[74] Distribution of cash – which directly protects livelihoods and empowers people to move – has tended to be neglected, with some significant exceptions.[75]

In complex emergencies, aid agencies' bias towards providing assistance in camps can play into the hands of governments who are rounding up populations into camps for their own reasons, perhaps as part of a military strategy or because of the fears of resident populations.[76]

A variation on the relief camp is the 'peace village'. This, too, may represent a dubious accommodation to host government priorities. A major independent evaluation of relief in the 1990s under Operation Lifeline Sudan noted that the Sudan government had established a number of so-called 'peace villages' as part of its strategy of promoting development, weaning people from relief, and achieving what the government called 'peace from within'.[77] The UN Development Programme (UNDP) adopted the term 'peace villages', and the UNDP, World Food Programme (WFP) and United Nations Children's Fund (UNICEF) all supported them. Yet these villages were essentially mechanisms for controlling displaced southern Sudanese and Nuba people, and for exploiting their labour on farms owned by northern Sudanese. Rebel-held areas of the Nuba Mountains were being systematically deprived of relief, and reduced rations more generally were helping to propel people into exploitative labour on commercial farms. The UNDP said it was aiming to 'resettle [returnees] in peace villages and then promote agricultural development to strengthen their attachment to land'.[78] Since the Nuba had been forcibly deprived of their land by the Sudanese government, the plan suggested an alarming degree of ignorance and witting or unwitting collusion in this dispossession.[79]

Silence and access

Like Harrell-Bond, Wilson and Kent, de Waal examined aid agencies as economic players, highlighting their economic interests and their concern with the pursuit of funding. In a sense, this strand of analysis can be regarded as part of a wider examination of economic interests during conflict. Without funding, of course, aid agencies cannot do any good. But de Waal focused particularly on the dangers of silence in contexts of massive human rights abuses, arguing that aid agencies have repeatedly kept quiet in order to ensure their presence (often a lucrative presence) in disaster zones. De Waal suggested that the UN's Operation Lifeline in Sudan from 1989 became an end in itself, more important than addressing the underlying human rights abuses, and that this preoccupation with securing access for relief gave the Sudan government important leverage internationally.[80]

The paradigmatic case of 'maintaining access' came during the Second World War. In the early 1940s, the International Committee of the Red Cross (ICRC) was receiving important information from local representatives about massacres of Jews in Nazi-occupied Europe. Yet, as William Shawcross notes in his book *The Quality of Mercy*:

> By the autumn of 1942 about two million Jews had been murdered and so many reports had been received that the ICRC felt compelled to consider whether it should make its information public. An official drafted a bland statement that said merely that civilians should be humanely treated . . . even the bland draft was rejected – on the grounds that it might be seen as a violation of the organization's neutrality.[81]

Responding in 1948 to charges that the aid agency should have spoken out on the basis of its extensive knowledge of Nazi persecution and deportation of the Jews, a 1948 ICRC booklet noted:

> Protest? The International Committee did protest – to the responsible authorities. . . . A whole department of the Committee's work was to make one long series of protests: countless improvements in the camps [that is, the concentration camps], for example, were due to steps of this kind. . . . Every man to his job, every man to his vocation. That of the Red Cross is to nurse the wounded where it can with the means at its disposal. For the Committee to protest publicly would have been not only to outstep its functions, but also to lose thereby all chance of pursuing them, by creating an immediate breach with the government concerned.[82]

The dangers of this approach are all too obvious. They are all the greater when we consider Swiss government pressure on the ICRC to keep quiet amidst fears that Switzerland would be overwhelmed by Jewish refugees.[83] Further muddying the waters were Switzerland's role in providing armaments to Nazi Germany, its fear of an imminent German invasion, and its economic windfall in the form of Jewish resources (including looted resources) that flowed into Swiss bank accounts.[84] During the Nigerian civil war of 1967–70, a Red Cross doctor named Bernard Kouchner became so frustrated with what he saw as the silence of the ICRC on Nigerian abuses (including the blocking of aid) that in 1971 he helped to found a new humanitarian organization called Médecins Sans Frontières (MSF) with an explicit intention of bearing witness during emergencies. ICRC behaviour in the Second World War in particular has been subject to considerable soul-searching within the organization, and on rare occasions the ICRC will make public statements denouncing abuses. However, the dangers of silent compromise by NGOs and UN agencies – prioritizing access, not wishing to offend host governments – remain.

It is not difficult to find examples of UN agencies soft-pedalling on abuses. Part of the mandate of the UN's Office for the Coordination of Humanitarian Affairs (OCHA) is 'to advocate for the rights of people in need'.[85] Yet OCHA's public statements are often very cautious. In Sudan, it has often been oddly 'even-handed' in attributing blame to Khartoum and the Darfur rebels. The idea that disasters might be functional still finds little room: thus, in Sudan, bureaucratic obstacles to relief are described as 'inane' and OCHA adds that 'the people who lose the most are the Sudanese themselves', a strangely aggregated statement.[86] Over Darfur, the various UN agencies have lacked a common advocacy strategy, as earlier; political analysis has generally been weak; and the increased discussion of the need for 'protection' has run up against the reality that providing protection by mere presence, as noted, is often unworkable.[87]

On the faltering reconstruction in Chechnya as massive violence abated somewhat, Gordadze observed in 2004: 'By refusing any confrontation with Russia, UN agencies are complicit in the Kremlin's game by maintaining the illusion of a return to "normality"'.[88] The UN was projecting optimism that the situation was improving. But torture remained widespread and aid reaching the Chechen population was 'derisory' and subject to widespread appropriation.[89]

The Angolan government tried to demonstrate a 'normalization' of the recent war by relocating internally displaced persons to areas other than their area of origin. Christine Messiant noted that this was 'sometimes by force or with the lure of false promises'. She added, 'The vast majority of relief agencies collaborated in this further "positive development", arguing that it was better for the populations to be out of the squalid camps.'[90]

In Sierra Leone, UN agencies contributed very little worthwhile analysis of the conflict. Frustration with UNICEF was high, particularly given its brief for children's welfare. One Irish priest and long-time resident told me in 1995: 'UNICEF are talking about iodized salt when the whole place is burning.' An analysis of interventions in Liberia by Jean-Hervé Jézéquel concluded that UNICEF had gone to considerable lengths to trumpet its 'Child-Friendly Spaces' – solid buildings inside Liberian camps – but had kept quiet on the recruitment of child soldiers, an issue where speaking out would have been seen as questioning the Liberian authorities effectively running the camps.[91]

Agencies sometimes defend the 'division of responsibilities' between human rights organizations and those focusing on relief. But some senior UN officials will privately admit that this is not producing a good result. A greater impact on the crisis – and a greater degree of protection – might come from jointly speaking up together.

Feeding into the silences on major political issues and into a kind of depoliticized 'humanitarianism' has been a tendency, noted by Derek Summerfield, to 'medicalize' suffering. Like Harrell-Bond, Summerfield explored the connections between distress among refugees / IDPs and the nature of the 'assistance' that is offered. He emphasized the dangers in medicalizing social problems (as notably with the label of 'post-traumatic stress disorder' or PTSD). He stressed that this risked deflecting attention from national and international responsibilities to put social problems right. He added that 'for the vast majority of survivors, "traumatisation" is a pseudo-condition; distress or suffering *per se* is not psychological disturbance. . . Much of the distress experienced and communicated by victims is normal, even adaptive.'[92] Suffering could be compounded if the individual was encouraged to think of him- or herself as a passive victim or as 'going crazy'. After working with internally displaced people in Eritrea, Astier Almedom noted that practical measures like keeping village units together in a camp setting could play a major role in social cohesion, and were often more useful than disease- or trauma-centred approaches.[93] Sara Gibbs noted that in Mozambique, local people linked reconstruction and recovery with individual and community *actions* rather than with individual discussions about the traumas of war.[94] A PTSD label tends to place trauma in the past, perhaps distracting attention from *current* difficulties arising from camp life, mistreatment in the country of asylum, or fear of repatriation.[95] Some degree of forgetting could be actively functional.[96]

Chasing the funding

A concern with organizational growth can encourage a concentration of NGO efforts on high-profile crises and even on those parts of crisis-affected areas that are easily accessible to the media. Over half of global humanitarian funding (as of mid-2005) was for Sudan.[97] A common tendency is for aid organizations to 'bite off more than they can chew'. While diplomatic disengagement created opportunities for NGOs to propose a role for themselves in 'conflict resolution', the ability of NGOs to resolve conflicts was easily exaggerated; NGOs may even have a 'comparative disadvantage' when it comes to influencing the behaviour of top government officials.[98] Duffield observed that humanitarian agencies were encouraged to step into the vacuum left by this diplomatic withdrawal and some aid workers saw themselves as *legitimizing* this withdrawal.[99]

A 2006 evaluation of interventions in Darfur found that some aid agencies had 'staked a claim' to areas where they had failed to deliver; moreover, the search for innovative methods was frequently crowding out more tried-and-tested approaches.[100] Publicizing one's own efforts may also be problematic for the recipient. Criticizing the prevalence of NGO T-shirts in one camp, a Kenyan aid worker told me: 'In my culture, if you have done something for someone, you do not advertise it – or you are humiliating them further.'

Donors have fads and fashions, and local and international NGOs may be quick to learn and adapt. One senior official at CIDA (the Canadian government's development arm) complained to me that NGOs were coming to CIDA and asking what these officials were ready to fund and how the NGOs should frame their proposals.[101] The Canadian official had hoped that NGOs would come with projects whose nature was determined by the intended beneficiaries. One analyst said of the United States Agency for International Development, or USAID: '[It] resembles the flame that attracts and may consume a moth that finds its light irresistible.'[102] A skilled NGO can pick up on the 'buzzwords' fashionable with donors – sustainability, rights, empowerment, and so on – and frame proposals accordingly.[103] Sara Pantuliano and Sorcha O'Callaghan have noted that in Darfur 'There is a general perception that some organisations have been re-fashioning their traditional assistance programmes in protection language because they have detected that protection is a new funding fashion.'[104]

Governmental pressures may be exerted by a roundabout route. In 2003, Save the Children UK was told by Save the Children US (which gets around 60 per cent of its funding from the US government) to retract accusations that coalition forces occupying Iraq had breached the Geneva Conventions by blocking a relief plane from landing in northern Iraq; SC-UK stood by its statement, but reportedly toned down some later statements.[105] SC-US also objected to an SC-UK statement demanding the immediate lifting of an Israeli blockade on Gaza.[106] In 2004, CARE USA was receiving 75 per cent of its annual £320 million from the US government. In these circumstances, can it really claim to be an NGO? The organization's security in Iraq (where local director Margaret Hassan was abducted in October 2004 and later killed) will have been compromised by its close association with the US government.[107] Corporate funding also carries dangers of censorship and self-censorship.

Undermining state accountability?

If donor government funding has represented one (hazardous) opportunity for NGOs, the whittling away of the state in crisis-affected countries has represented another. Mark Duffield referred to 'the internationalization of public welfare', suggesting that programmes of structural adjustment and economic liberalization in the 1980s had proven to be a major institutional opportunity for NGOs.[108] As the state retreated from responsibilities for the provision of basic services such as health, agricultural extension and food rations, NGOs were ready to step into the breach.

In line with the argument outlined by Jean Dreze and Amartya Sen, Alex de Waal argued in his book *Famine Crimes* that the best protection against famine lies with accountable forms of government, rather than with the vagaries of international relief. He suggested that famine is not simply prevented; it is deterred by mechanisms for getting rid of politicians who fail either to prevent it or to respond to it. Yet humanitarian aid had frequently helped undermine governments' accountability to their own people.

De Waal stressed that humanitarian operations have often bypassed governmental structures in damaging ways, luring away skilled staff and reducing the sense of responsibility that is felt by governments for ensuring welfare. This argument has also been made in relation to Mozambique by Joseph Hanlon.[109] Some aid agency staff, too, have been very concerned about this, and one senior aid worker in Holland (Jan Birket-Smith of IBIS) told me: 'We see a very dangerous tendency in international NGOs and bilateral donors to push aside public institutions. You can't develop the concept of democracy by bypassing legal and democratic institutions. It's contradictory.'[110]

According to Birket-Smith, international NGOs' desire to bypass cumbersome official procedures had contributed to the bypassing of legitimate

state institutions in Mozambique, thereby moving much of the critical deci-
sion-making out of accountable institutions.[111]

De Waal saw humanitarian aid as frequently propping up rogue regimes,
warlords and unrepresentative rebel movements – an argument that in many
ways mirrored an earlier critique of aid by Peter Bauer.[112] De Waal stressed
that humanitarian aid contributed resources for repression whilst tending to
insulate leaders from the displeasure of their own people. One example –
not discussed by him – is the way humanitarian aid helped to support the
abusive military government in Sierra Leone from 1992 to 1996.[113]

Squaring the circle

Aid workers routinely have to 'square the circle' between massive need and
inadequate funding. This runs the risk of a dishonest discourse that lets
powerful governments off the hook and gives a false impression that an
effective response is being mounted. In this context, the high turnover of
staff in the aid world, the short-term contracts and the frequent inability to
learn the lessons of experience can be seen as in some sense functional.
Mark Duffield has referred to 'functional ignorance'.[114] 'Blinkered' ways of
looking at disasters themselves have functions.

The case of Sierra Leone shows how needs were squared with resources.
Although the severity of the conflict there tended to increase over time, the
level of the ration was actually reduced – from 350 grammes of cereal per
person per day in 1992, to 300 in 1993 and again to 200 in 1994 and 1995.
The WFP was facing a major funding crisis in the region; with the catastrophes in former Yugoslavia and Rwanda taking attention and resources
away, donors were supplying only a fraction of what they had pledged.[115]
Global shipments of cereal food aid plummeted from about 15 million tons
in 1992/3 to about 5 million four years later.[116] Refugees in neighbouring
Guinea were also suffering. A MSF report concluded: 'There has been sustained pressure to reduce quantities of food aid since 1992. Every year since
1992, there has been an increase in the number of refugees, but there has
been a yearly decrease in the amount of food aid distributed.'[117]

How could these low rations be justified? If the response could not be
brought into line with the assessed needs, it was tempting to bring the
assessed needs into line with the actual response. There was an emphasis
on the coping strategies of the Sierra Leoneans and a simultaneous emphasis on the importance of avoiding dependency. Ration reductions, it was
said, would boost these coping strategies. A shift 'from relief to development' was seen as possible even in the midst of conflict.[118] Duffield has

stressed that situations that a decade ago were regarded as warranting a relief intervention were by the 1990s coming to be seen as an opportunity for rehabilitation and development.[119]

Melissa Leach has shown how the failure to supply significant relief to Liberian refugees in Sierra Leone was rationalized, after the event, as 'a policy of integration' that cleverly absorbed Liberians into Sierra Leonean communities, something that ignored the social and economic strains caused by this absorption.[120] Although some refugees in the Sierra Leone/Liberia/Guinea region had good access to land, the presumption of access to land and associated coping strategies was falsely generalized not only to refugees across the region but also to internally displaced people in urban areas. Relief to Sierra Leonean refugees in Guinea and Liberia appears to have been phased out prematurely on the assumption that they had become 'self-sufficient'. Many returned to conditions of considerable danger in Sierra Leone as a result.[121]

Meanwhile, inadequate relief was also blamed on security obstacles. They were considerable, but they were not always as immutable as they were made to appear. Although the Sierra Leonean government and UN organizations tended to attribute attacks on aid convoys to the rebels, many of these attacks were carried out by government soldiers, often the same soldiers who were supposed to be protecting the convoys. Lorry drivers repeatedly called for Nigerian and Guinean ECOMOG troops to escort convoys, but these requests were ignored. The fact that other kinds of violence were usually being blamed on the rebels made it particularly difficult for the UN system to envisage – or move towards – a solution for the more remediable security constraints on relief supplies.

As in several crises in Sudan, systematically exposing impediments to the actual receipt of relief would have required an investigation and discussion of many facets of the emergency – the abuses by government forces and the emergence of economic interests in continued conflict – that major donors (notably within the UN system) seemed anxious to ignore or to dismiss.

Zoë Marriage has argued that aid aganecies err when they express implausible universalist goals such as 'we will reach the needy'; in reality, the number of people reached with humanitarian aid in conflict zones has usually been severely constrained (for example, by resource limitations and by aid agencies' sensitivity to insecurity). The broken promise of humanitarian assistance, she suggested, is particularly provocative when it comes in the context of other broken promises – such as the promise of state or international protection. Marriage urges that it would be better for NGOs to commit to limited but doable tasks than to express universalist aims that perpetually founder. Meanwhile, some measure of 'respectability' within this dysfunctional system is maintained by the way interventions are discussed. Drawing on sociologist Stanley Cohen's work in particular, Marriage suggests that aid workers have found a number of mechanisms that feed into the denial of aid's ineffectiveness. For example, when budgets are tight, 'targeting' helps square the circle, implying that significant impact is possible with insignificant contributions. Inadequate aid has been excused on the grounds that this at least avoids creating 'dependency'.[122]

Particularly within a context where the 1945 UN Charter guarantees economic and social rights, it has often been relatively simple for development organizations to re-label what they are already doing as 'human rights'.[123] Making humanitarian aid conditional on human rights observance can give the appearance of 'tough action' and can save resources. It is very unlikely to help the victims, however.

Mark Duffield points out that with emergency aid increasingly being phased out in favour of development aid, it becomes easier for donors to threaten or carry out a total or near-total cut-off of aid even to countries undergoing severe conflict. In Somalia in 1995, even emergency relief was made conditional to some extent on warlords' behaviour, with particular objections being raised by donors to the use of Islamic *sharia* punishments. In Afghanistan too, even humanitarian aid was linked to human rights observance by the Taliban. Duffield accused donors of hypocritically championing the rights of women in Afghanistan so that former commitments regarding unconditional humanitarian aid could be quietly dropped.[124] Aid was selectively provided to opposition-held areas of Serbia in 1999.[125] In Sierra Leone in 1997–8, international trade sanctions on the military junta were extended in practice to humanitarian aid.[126] Under pressure from NGOs to clarify that humanitarian aid would not be affected by the sanctions, UK Minister for Development Clare Short said, 'We must be sure that the aid will not be delivered or used in such a way as to prolong the current crisis.'[127] In theory, the international sanctions imposed on the junta exempted humanitarian aid; yet in practice food aid dried up and high rates of malnutrition and mortality began to emerge.[128] In Angola, UN agencies confined support to the government side while sanctions were placed on UNITA. Messiant observed: 'For over three years (from the end of 1998 to the beginning of 2002), hundreds of thousands of Angolans were unable to request or receive assistance: more than 3 million were estimated to be beyond reach in 1999, with an additional million at the time of the [April 2002] ceasefire.'[129]

Joanna Macrae has commented that placing conditions on humanitarian assistance was 'not just the result of "bad" foreign policy guys trying to manipulate humanitarian aid, but follows from the logic of integrating developmental and conflict management objectives also advocated by NGOs and the UN.'[130]

Repatriation

UNHCR has increasingly adopted the priority of repatriation to country of origin, a policy that chimes rather disturbingly with the far right's emphasis on repatriation of immigrants.[131] Indeed, the organization declared the 1990s to be the decade of repatriation.[132] In line with major donors' priorities, UNHCR assumed a 'preventive' protection responsibility inside the former Yugoslavia, without having the number of staff or the influence over armed groups to fulfil this task; meanwhile, it went along with major donors' increasing distaste for major resettlement schemes.[133] In a context where it has uncertain funding and relies heavily on the US in particular, UNHCR has found it difficult to adopt a firm defence of the principles in the 1951 Refugee Convention, including the principle that no refugee should be expelled against their will to a country where they fear persecution (the principle of 'non-refoulement').[134] In 1991 Kurds fleeing towards Turkey were quickly lured back from the mountainous borderlands by promises of security that the international community was ill-prepared to meet.[135] During the 1990s, UNHCR's adoption of categories like 'temporary protection', whilst appeasing governments reluctant to welcome large numbers of refugees, posed a significant threat to the institution of asylum.[136] UNHCR helped in the involuntary return of half a million Rwandan refugees from Tanzania in 1996, announcing that all refugees were expected to return home by the end of that year and that economic and agricultural activities in the Tanzanian camps would be suspended. Tanzanian troops forced refugees fleeing *away from* Rwanda to turn back towards the border. UNHCR was mindful of the possibility of Rwandan attacks on Tanzanian camps, where many genocidaires had taken refuge, attacks that had just occurred across Rwanda's border with Zaïre/DRC. But the organization was also mindful of the declining availability of funding for Rwandan refugee programmes, with diminished support from the US particularly notable.[137] As Michael Barnett pointed out, UNHCR's commitment to genuinely voluntary repatriation has been substantially eroded, and the right to decide has been decisively relocated from the refugee to UNHCR itself.[138] At the turn of the century, speedy repatriation of Kosovar Albanians led to the exodus of some 200,000 Serbs and Roma from Kosovo.[139] After the Taliban was overthrown and an Afghanistan

Interim Authority was set up in December 2001, over 1.7 million refugees were encouraged to return from Pakistan and Iran, often to conditions worse than those in the countries to which they had fled.[140] The move also diverted limited funds available for reconstruction. UNHCR spoke of a 'facilitated return', a term it has used when it does not regard the situation as suitable for a 'promoted' return. Turton and Marsden suggest this may be a 'semantic device' to allow international community to put pressure on refugees without appearing to breach agreed norms of voluntary repatriation.[141]

Policy Implications and Dilemmas

Critique of the critique

Analysing the manipulation and shortcomings of humanitarian aid is one thing; knowing what to do about it is another. A key problem is that any 'solution' is likely to run into its own set of problems and manipulations, which must in turn be analysed and incorporated into policy decisions. A worrying example – particularly for those like the current author who have in the past contributed to researching the 'political economy' of war and aid – is the way critiques of aid have been harnessed to projects of inaction and penny-pinching. There is always a danger that critiques of aid will be used to justify the denial of relief to people who need it.[142]

Nick Stockton has argued that critics who emphasized the medium- and long-term dangers of emergency relief actually helped – in practice if not in intent – to legitimize a contraction in relief-giving and an increasing international tolerance of other people's malnutrition and general suffering. Stockton highlighted the meagre international response to crisis in the remaining Hutu refugee camps in eastern former Zaïre and those fleeing west in early 1997, when death rates reportedly reached 300 per 10,000 people per day (the highest figure ever reported anywhere).[143] The fact that this population was tainted by association with genocide, together with fears of a Hutu extremist revival, contributed at some level to this weak international response.

Pottier questioned what he called a widely received 'fairy-tale' – the idea that Hutu refugees were 'liberated' by attacks from groups in Zaïre, freeing them up to return voluntarily to Rwanda in November 1996. Food aid was actually being cut off, and there were concerted military attacks on refugee camps by armed elements of the Banyamulenge – of Tutsi origin but long-established in the Congo – in alliance with the Rwandan government.[144]

(Meanwhile, the Tanzanian army was using force to repatriate Hutu refugees there back to Rwanda, with UNHCR accused of complicity in this, partly because of a joint statement it made with the Tanzanian government calling for repatriation within a month.)

Pottier argued that a fear of Western casualties fed into the preference for an 'African solution to an African problem' and that this preference was in effect embraced by UNHCR. In the UK and the US, the dismantling of Zairean camps and the repatriation to Rwanda were hailed as a triumph. But there were hidden victims. The massacres that followed killed about 232,000 Rwandan refugees, according to Emizet's calculations.[145] Faced only with Mobutu's crumbling army, the Rwandan-backed forces (now in alliance with Laurent Kabila from northern Katanga and known as the Alliance of the Democratic Forces for the Liberation of Congo) pushed on to take the capital city of Kinshasa in May 1997 – seven months after attacking the refugee camps. Some Hutu refugees were tracked down and killed at the opposite end of the huge country of Congo/Zaïre, when Kabila's victory was already assured. Meanwhile, hundreds of thousands of Hutu refugees were denied humanitarian assistance, with the Rwandan argument arguing that the mass repatriation meant international humanitarian intervention was no longer necessary. Where aid was provided, it appears sometimes to have been used by the forces of rebel leader Kabila to get refugees to assemble, after which aid agency access would be cut off and killings would be carried out. Emizet's verdict was a damning one: 'There was little in the way of public protest in the West, and the silence that greeted the massacre of refugees was overwhelming.'[146] Part of the reason was that the Rwandan government, collaborating with Kabila at this time, enjoyed a privileged moral status as victims of the 1994 genocide.

[Hugo Slim] an academic and policy analyst with a background in Save the Children Fund and the UN, acknowledged that de Waal's arguments were important, but suggested that it was dangerous to withhold a definite good or benefit for the sake of an unknowable future good. Slim distinguished 'deontologists' from 'consequentialists' (a category in which he placed de Waal). Deontologists believe that some actions are simply good in themselves, and so one has a duty to do them regardless of the consequences. In an aid context, a deontologist might believe that it is always good, and therefore a duty, to heal a person's wounds if one can. The International Committee of the Red Cross adopts a position quite close to this. However, according to consequentialist ethics, actions must be measured as good or bad according to their wider consequences. Thus, Slim suggested, an adherent to this system might believe that it is not good to heal some people's wounds if it means they will return to battle and kill children. Slim observed that: 'Ethics for consequentialists becomes the complicated and uncertain process of anticipating wider outcomes and holding oneself responsible for events well beyond the present time.'[147] Slim neatly encapsulated some elements of the debate when he wrote:

> A minimalist duty-based approach to the ethics of relief programming will invite the wrath of consequentialist critics whose stinging rebukes will harangue such agencies for their naivety and irresponsibility. A more maximalist approach which tries to take account of consequences will be plagued with uncertainty, speculation and endless calculation about possible outcomes, as well as the temptation (to which the western liberal conscience is already too susceptible) to feel personally responsible for every terrible thing that happens in one's theatre of operations.[148]

On the basis of his case-studies, Slim leant towards the deontological position. For example, he argued that to have withheld relief from Rwandan refugees in eastern Zaïre in the hope that the Hutu regime in exile would not be able to regroup and might not choose violence again would have meant working on the principle of doing evil so that good may come – a position consistently rejected in Christian moral theology. Slim also gave weight to the danger that speaking out will lead to reprisals against an aid agency or its staff.

A related concern with de Waal's argument centres on procedure: how are the kinds of difficult decisions advocated by de Waal actually to be taken? Traditional humanitarian action has at least the merit of possessing a relatively straightforward and comprehensible goal: the immediate saving of lives. If relief is sometimes to be withheld because providing it risks fuelling a war, who would make such a difficult decision, and what mechanisms of representation might give that decision legitimacy?[149]

Emergency aid is only one part of the political economy of war – the system of economic benefits which arises from (and often prolongs) conflict. Many wars have been fuelled by struggles over natural resources and trading profits (notably drugs) more than by emergency aid itself.[150] It is notable that much of the the critique of emergency aid was developed in relation to countries – Sudan, Ethiopia and Mozambique – that lack easily exploitable high-value commodities. The relative economic and strategic importance of aid is much lower in countries with a substantial drugs trade (such as Burma, Afghanistan and Colombia) or a substantial trade in diamonds (such as Angola and Sierra Leone).[151]

One might also doubt whether the withdrawal of emergency aid from a crisis-torn country is really likely to foster the emergence of a famine-preventing political contract on the lines advocated by de Waal. A much stronger case can be made that long-term assistance supports abusive regimes (see chapter 8). As de Waal points out, promising reconstruction efforts in Somaliland show what can sometimes be done even without large-scale international assistance.

When it comes to avoiding the creation of camps, the most desirable course may not always be the most feasible. In the face of the various criticisms of refugee camps, Jeff Crisp (of UNHCR) and Karen Jacobsen have suggested that, for a refugee, a camp might be safer and materially more secure than self-settlement. They noted that refugees and their leaders may actually organize themselves into camp-like settings even before UNHCR or other agencies turn up. They also noted that camps may not actually mean confinement, and that what they call the 'anti-camp' argument 'tends to ignore the fact that local populations in countries of asylum also have rights – including the right not to be dispossessed of their land'.[152]

Crisp and Jacobsen went on to suggest that UNHCR's policy was actually to avoid establishment of camps if there were viable alternatives. It is often host governments that insist on camps, perhaps to prevent local integration of exiled populations, to facilitate early repatriation, and/or to attract international assistance. Amnesty International has noted that large numbers of migrants have often been granted refugee status in neighbouring African countries only so long as they confine themselves to camps. Crisp and Jacobsen also make a tactical argument: given the difficulty of getting countries to accept refugees in the first place, demanding that refugees be free to settle where they want may encourage host governments not to admit refugees at all.

Pushing relief through

In complex emergencies, the hijacking of emergency aid for geopolitical and/or local political purposes would seem to be more the rule than the exception; but this is not an argument against emergency aid *per se*. The best way forward would be to retain the humanitarian ideal of providing relief and protection to those most in need but to adopt a more politically informed approach that will both facilitate this humanitarianism project and highlight that emergency aid can never be sufficient on its own.

When it comes to pushing relief through to those who need it most, one practical step (paradoxically) is to move beyond the focus on the 'target group'. If aid is to reach its designated target, there is a need to take account of those with an economic, political or military interest in blocking it. Trying to overcome this may involve: widespread distributions (to minimize envy and incentives for robbery); close monitoring and political/diplomatic pressures as problems arise; and support from major governments and multilateral organisations for NGOs when they come into conflict with those impeding relief. Too often, the misappropriation of aid has been dismissed as a so-called 'problem of implementation' – and in particular a problem for implementing NGOs – which is therefore not the responsibility of the major donors (who may fund the programme but may be reluctant to use their leverage to make sure the programme works).

The *type* of aid may also be important. |Paul Richards |has written of the need for 'smart aid', aid that is likely to get through political structures and roadblocks. He mentions information as one such item.[153] Relief can be stolen after it has been distributed, and one way of miminizing this has been through distribution of cooked food, a practice used extensively by the ICRC in Somalia during the 1991–2 famine. At the same time, the ICRC's use of multiple entry points and the wide geographical distribution helped reduce incentives for plundering aid shipments; this kind of plunder was commonplace when aid was shipped through the capital of Mogadishu.[154] The emphasis on minimizing warehouse storage time and effecting quick distributions also reduced the opportunities for plunder.

A variation on the idea of widespread distributions is the idea of aid policies that help an entire area, both local people and those who have been displaced. Again, this is different from simply targeting the most needy. Spreading assistance in this way can help to make assistance to the displaced more locally acceptable. It can reduce local conflict, and can make an influx of refugees more acceptable. Practical steps include developing markets and infrastructure.[155]

Another idea that may help in pushing relief through to the most needy is the adoption by aid agencies of various standards and codes of practice. This carries at least the potential of professionalizing assistance and getting away from the idea that relief is a charitable act whose recipients should be grateful for anything they get. Codes of practice can also seek to guard against fuelling a war economy. Relevant projects here include the Providence principles (in the US) and the Sphere project (arising in large part from a major evaluation of responses to the Rwandan genocide).[156]

These initiatives are not uncontroversial, however. MSF has not embraced the Sphere project. Indeed, MSF staff have expressed concern that the Sphere project could further encourage an existing trend where NGOs are seen as technical agents of the donors, with donors using the standards to exert control over NGOs.[157] MSF staff also fear that inability to adhere to the minimum standards could lead to inaction by some agencies, who may prefer easier tasks. These fears are not without foundation. A 2006 UN report on relief to Darfur noted that aid agencies' attempts 'had the unintended consequence of discouraging some actors from undertaking activities, which they knew could not reasonably meet the minimum standards, even if doing so would have filled a critical gap'.[158] There is also a danger that targets and standards might discourage activities (like protection) that are relatively hard to measure.[159] Other projects aimed at increasing accountability include the Code of Conduct, ALNAP (Active Learning Network for Accountability and Performance in Humanitarian Action) and the Humanitarian Accountability Partnership–International.

Another innovation came in Liberia in 1996 when NGOs implemented a Joint Policy of Operation after massive looting of relief resources in Monrovia. NGOs made it clear that they were not prepared to put up with repeated looting; they limited activities to essential life-saving tasks; and they tried to ensure that they were not played off against each other by local warlords. Phillippa Atkinson and Nicholas Leader observed that cooperation between humanitarian agencies at this time helped put civilian protection on the agenda, feeding into a peace process in combination with a range of more diplomatic and legal pressures.[160]

Another possibility is for major donors to give more flexibility to major relief organizations like the WFP and UNHCR in how funding is allocated between regions. In many ways, the trend has been in the opposite direction, with donors tending to keep an increasingly tight rein on the destination of funding. Humanitarian aid could be improved if donors decided to reward needs-assessments that gave due weight to political obstacles and how these might be overcome, as well rewarding evaluations that gave an honest and detailed assessment of what went badly as well as what went well.

Certainly, there is a tension between those who suggest that humanitarians should be prioritizing the delivery of relief to the needy and those who wish to take a broader and longer-term view of the political impact of aid. However, the two positions are not always as contradictory as they appear. Where serious attempts are made to push relief through to the needy in the face of military and political obstacles, there may be important political as well as humanitarian benefits. In fact, precisely because shortage and famine are manipulated for military and economic purposes, pushing relief through to reduce shortages becomes more than simply a humanitarian act; it becomes a radical political act that challenges power structures and exploitation. In particular, confronting – rather than disguising or ignoring – the blocking of relief leads donors and NGOs towards an analysis of the political forces that may be trying to produce a disaster. For example, paying closer attention to the diversion of relief in Sierra Leone would inevitably have highlighted government soldiers' role in stealing relief, bringing greater attention to the army's role in more direct forms of violence against civilians.

Although the crisis in Darfur has again seen silence in effect traded for access, speaking out can sometimes *improve* access. As one very senior UN official said in 2004, 'For 14–15 months, there *was* no access [in Darfur]. It wasn't a question of compromising access. It was a question of winning access' (my emphasis). Large-scale access was granted only in May 2004 (as the rainy season was about to begin).[161]

Emergency aid that is genuinely focused on the needy may encourage the presence of both aid personnel and journalists in areas where they can witness and publicize acts of violence; and this mechanism may be of increasing importance, given the apparent diminution of diplomatic interest in many parts of the world that are deemed to lack strategic importance. Hugo Slim has suggested that a kind of division of responsibilities between relief agencies (with some choosing to speak out and risk expulsion) may be the best option in these situations.[162]

Another radical effect of pushing relief through – if it can be done – is that it tends to reduce asset transfers. Thus, humanitarian aid is also an economic intervention. Rangasami's analysis of 'desperation' sales and purchases during a famine demonstrates that, if more humanitarian aid can be successfully channelled to those who need it, then price movements driving famine can be mitigated.[163] Those buying staple foods at artificially high prices will become less desperate to buy, and this will reduce the price of the staple foods. Those selling livestock and other assets (including labour) at artificially low prices will become less desperate to sell, and this will increase the price at which these assets are sold. Reducing 'desperation' sales and purchases means pushing through relief to people who still have some assets and who are still in their home areas. This, it should be noted, is a different task from simply targeting the poorest. Indeed, targeting the absolutely poor (once they have lost all their assets and perhaps even the ability to work) may be play into the hands of those who benefit from desperation sales and purchases.

Pushing relief through to the needy in the face of political obstacles can also have the beneficial effect of supporting a just political cause. The classic case here was humanitarian aid to Tigray and Eritrea, where relief amounted to a form of solidarity with a rebel war effort that was eventually successful. Humanitarian aid to southern Sudan has also helped to sustain a war effort that many regard as just. Of course, it could be argued that the advantages of sustaining a righteous struggle are outweighed by the disadvantages of sustaining a destructive war, but cutting off aid to the needy in the hope that this will bring war to an end is extremely optimistic as well as morally untenable.

Another case where aid has served as a source of solidarity is northern Iraq. After the 1991 Gulf War, international assistance helped to sustain Kurdish autonomy in the face of intense hostility from Saddam Hussein's regime. Additional aid would have been more helpful still, and the very slow progress in reviving the Kurdish economy and supporting the Kurdish administration had the effect of encouraging intra-Kurdish disputes, allowing Saddam Hussein to forge alliances with elements of the Kurds (notably the Kurdish Democratic Party). This culminated in an incursion by Iraqi troops into the major Kurdish city of Erbil in 1997.[164]

Pushing relief through can also include an effort to channel resources to representative institutions (for example, traditional elders, self-defence groups, women's organizations), even if these can only be found at the local level, as advocated by Mark Bradbury for example.[165] This is likely to help such institutions in the battle for the allegiance of civilians, including those who might otherwise be recruited as fighters.

Insofar as aid impacts on conflict, not all of this is negative. The *lack* of relief during famine in western Sudan in 1983–5 was one factor feeding into the impoverishment of the Baggara pastoralists and their subsequent raiding of the south.[166] Even aid that is stolen can help reduce market prices and prevent people from turning to violence in order to sustain themselves, as experience from Somalia suggests.[167] During civil war in Sierra Leone, aid workers reported that weak delivery of relief was contributing to a dangerous sense of exclusion, with displaced people in particular often facing a stark choice between joining armed bands or joining the ranks of the destitute and starving. Aid in the form of Disarmament, Demobilization and Reintegration is often vital in smoothing the path to peace.

Providing relief and providing security may be complementary. One promising initiative in Darfur has been the distribution of fuel in an attempt to minimize women's and girls' exposure to rape during wood-fetching,[168] though many women have still been relying on fetching wood for income, highlighting the importance of also looking at livelihoods. At one extreme, aid workers have sometimes used humanitarian supplies as a bargaining tool for sexual favours; while dismissing these workers is a good idea, a more fundamental intervention – as Lee demonstrates – would be to tackle the ideological and material and political environment (inadequate rations, inadequate representation for refugees) that encourages abuse.[169]

Stressing the continued relevance of the humanitarian ideal, Geoff Loane, a very experienced aid worker with the ICRC, advised aid workers at a workshop to: 'Know the politics, so you can negotiate the minefield.' Important questions, he stressed, included: How are people manipulating you, what is the level of diversion and what is diverted aid being used for? How does assistance match up to the need and what is the geographical distribution of both? Humanitarian workers and other interested citizens also need to challenge the discourse that says or implies there can be a purely humanitarian solution to a human rights crisis. They should challenge the discourse when it falsely implies that responsibility for a crisis lies equally with 'both sides' or with 'tribal rivalries' or with 'the collapse of authority', even though these descriptions may be particularly convenient for those (notably, UN agencies) who do not wish to offend national governments. It will always be important to put politicians on the spot and to try to embarrass them into prioritizing the protection of human rights (especially the right to life) over the other political and diplomatic games they may seek to play. Too often, the humanitarian world has allowed itself to be manipulated into letting politicians off the hook. Perhaps the key way to make humanitarian aid more effective would be to focus not simply on *deficits* and *needs* but also on *strategies* – facilitating the (non-damaging) strategies of disaster victims and counteracting the strategies of those who manipulate disasters for personal or political gain.

7

Information

Among those who are victims of conflict, flows of information are sometimes seen as more important than the more commonly discussed flows of
grain. After Sudan's first civil war, Acueng Deng, a Dinka elder from Abyei
(an area adjoining the south), noted the importance for the Dinka of building a road to the north so that Abyei would remain accessible during the
rains: 'When the flow of words is broken with the breakdown of commu-
nications in the summer, the man with the power of Government becomes
wild. He takes the thing of the man without a tongue to sustain himself.
And in the dry season, all that is dodged to the other side of the mouth.
That, we hate.'[1] In other words, when people were unable to articulate their
grievances, they were vulnerable to exploitation without redress. These
were conditions of impunity. Of course, it is not just the rains that can block
the flow of words out of a disaster zone; the Dinka's ability to obtain
redress from Khartoum had long been very limited.

To the extent that the voices of victims are publicly heard, there is at least
the possibility for pressures on policy-makers (nationally or internationally)
to remedy the disaster. This underpins the emphasis placed by Dreze and
Sen on the importance of a free press in preventing and relieving disasters.[2]
In practice, people are often silenced by a direct threat of violence, so that
violence may create the conditions for its own continuation. The silencing
effect of violence is often compounded by the international system (including the international humanitarian system), which can add a further layer of
muffling and censorship to the voices of the victims of disasters. This more
subtle process of silencing the victims of disasters is related partly to money
and power, but also – as Foucault's and Chomsky's analysis would both lead
us to suspect – to perceptions, language and belief systems. Of course, these
factors frequently interact, as when people's belief systems, prejudices and
preconceptions are manipulated for a variety of political or economic ends.

Information emerging at the time of the worst disasters may represent the
collision of one set of fictions (for example, deliberate falsehoods and confu-
sions put about by abusive local governments)[3] with another set of distortions

propagated by the international media. The latter include the conventions and 'fables' highlighted by Jonathan Benthall as well as the psychologically seductive 'fear of the other' whipped up by Robert Kaplan, Samuel Huntington et al.[4] International governments and multilateral institutions may add their own layers of distortion and muffling. The idea that rebels' grievances are not worth listening to is not a very helpful starting point.

Shaping the Debate

We tend fondly to imagine that we as human beings react to new and surprising information by changing our views. However, humans have a strong tendency to make new information conform to *existing* views – by dismissing this information as inaccurate, by explaining it away, or by otherwise accommodating it within an existing belief system.[5]

One example was touched on in the discussion of enemies. Let us say we believe that a policy of forcible regime change is a valuable response to 9/11. When we hear that anger is deepening in the Muslim world and decentralized terror attacks are proliferating, we may not wish radically to change our view or admit that we were wrong. Instead, we may call for a deepening of the 'war on terror' and the inclusion of new targets (for example, Somalia, Lebanon or Iran). The war, we may conclude, has simply not been pursued with sufficient vigour. Information we receive about the counterproductive effects of, say, invading Iraq will be unwelcome in at least two senses: first, it is bad news; second, it threatens an entrenched belief system that we may be reluctant to abandon. (Of course, these characteristics are not confined to the political right. Suppose that we believe the 'war on terror' is a *bad* thing. We may be psychologically predisposed to dismiss or explain away any 'good news': for example, Libya's decision to scrap plans for weapons of mass destruction.)

Language also encourages certain rigidities. It tends to channel our thinking in particular directions. So too, by extension, does the production and consumption of certain kinds of information as a result of organizational norms and procedures.[6]

While words are tools of thought, they can also destroy thoughts, particularly when they seem to embody a set of benevolent practices to which no reasonable person would object. Noam Chomsky, a leading critic of US foreign policy, has contributed important work in this area. Part of Chomsky's interest has been the way that language, rather than simply being the outcome of thought, actually *structures* thought. In his political writings, Chomsky pointed to the example of US intervention in Vietnam:

while just as much an invasion as the Soviet intervention in Afghanistan, the US intervention was rarely if ever called an invasion. Chomsky suggested that those (like himself) who attempt to articulate a critique of received wisdom are likely to be met not just with disagreement but with incomprehension. Illusions and self-deception form a framework for debate, and for those who do not take part in those illusions and self-deceptions, what they say is incomprehensible.[7]

Chomsky suggested, further, that good propaganda tends to involve slogans that nobody is going to oppose and that will not encourage people to think. Thus, 'Support our troops!' works well; 'Support our policy!' does not work so well.[8] We might think here of the fierce arguments that have raged over abortion, with the 'Pro-Life' lobby pitted against the 'Pro-Choice' lobby. Who could not be in favour of life? And who, for that matter, could not be in favour of choice?[9] Another seductive and apparently unobjectionable slogan is 'Never again!', something frequently heard in relation to the Nazi holocaust. Who could argue with this sentiment? But at another level, it can reasonably be asked: what other subsequent genocides – in Sudan, Rwanda and Zaïre/Congo, for example – have been subtly dismissed, even obliterated, when we proclaim 'Never again!' in relation to the Nazi Holocaust? What blindness and complacency is mixed in with our fine sentiments and good intentions? In a major speech after September 11, 2001, British Prime Minister Tony Blair invoked the horrors of the Rwandan genocide and underlined precisely this message of 'never again'. Yet this rhetoric proved in practice to be perfectly compatible with the rapidly deepening suffering in neighbouring Congo, where some 3.3 million people had died in the war by 2002[10] and where the conflict continued in large part because of Rwandan government interference and intransigence – an abuse largely uncriticized by Britain, Rwanda's biggest aid donor.[11]

The very term 'war' can seduce us into thinking that events conform to something we understand, often in very misleading ways. Chapter 1 noted that the term 'war' can be used to legitimize crime and exploitation against particular groups; it can also be used to legitimize one-sided international attacks, and this has been discussed in an interesting way by the perceptive (and sometimes incomprehensible) French writer Jean Baudrillard.

In January 1991, a little more than a month after the UN Security Council had authorized the use of force over Iraq's invasion of Kuwait, Baudrillard published an article called 'The Gulf War Will Not Take Place'. Undeterred by the outbreak of hostilities, he then published an article called 'The Gulf War: Is It Really Taking Place?' Perhaps there were signs of a slight failure of nerve in the question mark here, but by the end of hostilities at the end of February 1991, Baudrillard was back to his confident best, asserting 'The Gulf War Did Not Take Place'.[12]

Baudrillard seems to have meant many things by this rather cryptic set of statements. Most significantly, he stressed that this was not really a war; it was a one-sided attack against a country that hardly fought back. In the absence of any real battles between aircraft, it was a kind of highly destructive international policing operation (including air attacks on retreating Iraqi soldiers), and a policing operation which continued after the so-called 'war' was over. In some circumstances, calling a particular set of violent acts a 'war' is rather akin to calling bullfights a sport: it implies the presence of a contest (and hence a degree of legitimacy) when perhaps there is no contest. As Tim Allen has stressed, 'war' is in part a way of conferring status and legitimacy on violence.[13]

Human rights outrage has been highly selective. Chomsky has noted that information vacuums have been particularly notable when it comes to human rights abuses within countries that have been allied with major Western powers (especially the US).[14] If a government perpetrating abuses is a major trading partner (especially a major oil producer or arms purchaser), this silence tends to be all the more marked. Saudi Arabia's status as a key US ally, arms purchaser and oil exporter has undoubtedly protected an abusive Saudi regime from criticism. In his 1994 study, Said Aburish noted that he could not find a single public statement by a Western leader about Saudi Arabia's atrocious human rights record.[15] This favoured status survived even September 11, when fifteen of the nineteen hijackers were Saudis. Other examples are legion. In the context of friendly relations during the Cold War and US arms sales, Indonesia's take-over of East Timor in 1975 was met with conspicuous silence on the part of the US government. During the 1980s, Iraqi President Saddam Hussein received little criticism from the West; in the context of the 1980–8 Iran–Iraq war, he was seen as an ally against the fundamentalist regime in Iran. His gas attacks against the Iraqi Kurds did eventually prompt increased Western criticism, but much less was heard about the abuse of Kurdish citizens by the Turkish government – a key Western ally. This imbalance led some to suggest that a one-eyed international community somehow imagined that there were 'good Kurds' (in Iraq) and 'bad Kurds' (in Turkey).[16]

Chomsky referred to the 'manufacture of consent'[17] by politicians, business and the media, stressing the selective memory in the US in particular:

> How many Vietnamese casualties would you estimate that there were during the Vietnam war? The average response on the part of Americans

today is about 100,000. The official figure is two million. The actual figure is probably three to four million.[18] The people who conducted the study [a University of Massachusetts study of the media, the 1991 Gulf War and US interventions] raised an appropriate question: what would we think about German political culture if, when you asked people today how many Jews died in the holocaust, they estimated about 300,000. What would that tell us about German political culture?[19]

In wartime, international censorship and agenda-shaping have often been particularly intense. It is true that media coverage of the Vietnam war helped spur a powerful anti-war movement; but this very example encouraged an intensification of the control of journalists in many recent wars. Part of this has been the increasingly popular practice of 'embedding' journalists with Western troops – for example, in the 1991 Gulf War and the 2003 attack on Iraq.

In his 2001 book *Debating War and Peace*, Jonathan Mermin discussed media coverage of US intervention in Grenada in 1983 and Panama in 1989, as well as the build-up to the 1991 Gulf War. He showed that the range of US media debate on any given crisis was very closely tied to the degree of criticism coming from politicians in the Democratic Party (in opposition to a Republican administration throughout this period): where there was little Congressional criticism, there was little debate. Mermin argued that polls showing public support for an aggressive military line had a circular quality, since limited media coverage had powerfully shaped the public opinion that was then polled.[20] The build-ups to war in Afghanistan in 2001 and Iraq in 2002–3 were fuelled by a remarkably constrained 'debate'.[21]

Shaking the 'False Self-Evidence' of Policy: Foucault

Michel Foucault argued that any set of social practices will have an accompanying system of knowledge that creates, reinforces and legitimizes it; at the same time, the social practices will themselves help to generate that system of knowledge.[22] Fashions might change over time, and in particular the aim and focus of interventions might alter. Foucault gave the example of French penal practices at the beginning of the nineteenth century, when there was a fairly dramatic switch in the mode of punishment for criminals. Suddenly, almost every crime became punishable with prison. There was a feeling that public torture and executions – much favoured previously – were inciting riots as the public frequently came to see the executioner as a criminal and to regard the criminal, however briefly, as a kind of hero or an object of pity. Increasingly, the aim was not to punish the body, but to reform the mind.[23]

Foucault invited his readers to apply a critical and sceptical eye to present practices as well as those of the past, to look at how it is that some things come to seem unobjectionable at particular points in time. In other words, he stressed the importance of 'shaking the false self-evidence' of particular practices.[24] Among the key questions which his analysis highlighted were: what is the proper sphere of interventions (for example, in the case of a criminal justice system, is it the body or the mind)?; what is the aim of the intervention?; what kinds of information count as scientific and relevant in any particular time and place?; and, perhaps most importantly, who has the right to speak what counts as true and relevant?

Foucault's point here can be illustrated by Antoine de Saint-Exupéry's classic story *The Little Prince*. In this story, an astronomer attended an international conference, donning a traditional Turkish costume to present his discovery of an asteroid, but no-one believed him. Years later, a 'Turkish dictator'[25] made a law that everyone must wear European costume; at another conference, the astronomer presented his findings dressed in a suit and tie, 'and this time everybody accepted his report'.[26] The process here is reminiscent of a true story in Barbara Harrell-Bond's classic study of Ugandan refugees in southern Sudan, *Imposing Aid*: the principal demand made by one refugee was not for emergency food or medicines but for a neck-tie; he said this would enable him to be treated like a human being and not a statue.

Foucault's rather elaborate and flowery writing style was in many ways intentional: by adopting a self-consciously elaborate and even literary style, he wanted to assist his own deconstruction of supposed sciences and to put as much distance as possible between himself and those who might wish to pretend, through a plodding, technical and seemingly objective style, that they were communicating some kind of 'science'.[27]

Information Flows in the Aid World: Clay and Schaffer

In their important edited collection *Room for Manoeuvre*, Edward Clay and Bernard Schaffer stressed that the shaping of agendas is not always an active, calculating process on the part of officials; while officials may manipulate data and definitions, the existing data and prevailing definitions may in some sense manipulate officials. Geoff Wood suggested that labels for given sectors of the population often encourage a focus on 'cases' rather than on people with stories: for example, a focus on 'the landless' in Bangladesh might appear uncontroversial and benevolent, but risks ignoring the processes through which people lose their land, an omission that would not be encouraged by the use of a word like 'dispossessed'.[28] Contributions to Clay and Schaffer's *Room for Manoeuvre* reflected Foucault's interest not only in the way power shapes the production of truth and language but also in the way truth and language simultaneously shape the production of power. While the focus of the analysis was on development aid, the insights can be applied equally well to humanitarian aid.

In the book's most important chapter, Schaffer pointed to an important connection between the way policies are discussed and the perpetuation of policies that are unhelpful.[29] The most common way of depicting social interventions is as a shared attempt to remedy poverty, disease, underdevelopment, famine or whatever. If such benevolent policies 'fail' (for example, if aid interventions fail to make a dent in the poverty of the intended beneficiaries), then according to what Schaffer called this 'main-stream' approach, it is likely to be because 'policy' was thwarted by a variety of 'obstacles to implementation'.

An alternative perspective rejects the assumption that policy aims are necessarily benevolent, and questions the usefulness of this idea of 'policy failure'. As Schaffer put it: 'The . . . important question is not why public policy "fails". It does not always necessarily or completely do so. The for-mulation expresses an odd reification. Public policy is, after all, what it does. The point is to explain what that is, and then see if that explanation can itself be an instrument for change and improvement . . . .'[30] Thus, even as policy-makers 'failed' to achieve stated goals, it was quite possible that they were achieving other, unstated goals. Just as a disaster does not necessarily imply a local policy failure (that is, it might be a *policy success*), so also the appar-ent failure of an external intervention does not necessarily mean that all those contributing to the intervention have failed in their most important goals. Again, we can see here the influence of Foucault, who regarded prisons, for example, as failing to prevent crime, but at the same time as serving hidden functions, for example in producing a class of criminals who could be easily monitored by the police.[31]

One of the reasons why 'policy failures' should not be taken at face value is that policy outcomes may be actively and successfully shaped by groups with goals that differ from those expressed by policy-makers 'at the top'. Of course, this creates problems for these top-level policy-makers. When their expressed goals do not work out in practice, Schaffer asked, by what means can this turn of events be accommodated? One way that policy-makers could escape responsibility for poor policy outcomes was through a rigid distinction between 'policy' and (subsequent) 'implementation'. When things turned out badly in practice, they could blame 'implementation'. Schaffer said this common distinction tended to prevent improvements in policy: lists of 'obstacles to implementation' (perhaps including a 'lack of political will' among the would-be implementers) were likely to discourage adequate thought about what decision-makers might have done differently, what they might do differently in the future, or how the varied goals of those who had been able to shape policy outcomes might have been allowed for in advance. More generally, maintaining an appearance of good policy routinely militated against achieving good outcomes in practice.

Schaffer and his co-editor Edward Clay also stressed that only a limited range of issues, and a limited range of data, were likely to be considered by policy-makers. Given the issues considered, and given the data taken into consideration, policy could be presented as remarkably 'unobjectionable'. To the extent that the existence of alternatives could be suppressed, to the extent that decisions could be presented as springing automatically from the data available, then few opportunities for blame would arise. As Schaffer put it, 'Paradoxically enough it always tends to appear that "there was no choice" while, at the same time, what is done conveniently seems both therapeutic and axiomatic.'[32] Clay and Schaffer stressed that there always are choices to be made; there are always other possible issues and agendas, other data that might be taken into consideration. They advocated a method of inquiry which sought to highlight these choices, and to consider what 'room for manoeuvre' there might be to do things differently.[33]

Apart from blaming 'implementation', a key way of escaping responsibility for poor outcomes, Schaffer suggested, had been a lack of openness and a lack of proper evaluation of policy outcomes, including a frequent failure to consult the intended beneficiaries.[34] Another way to avoid blame was through defining goals very narrowly (and perhaps redefining them after the event).

Information Flows and Humanitarian Aid

Needs assessment and evaluation

The analysis developed by Foucault – and by Clay and Schaffer – proves helpful in understanding the relationship between humanitarian aid and flows of information. NGOs – whether local or international – are often seen as transmitting needs and information 'upwards' from needy people and transmitting resources 'downwards'. These channels are usually conceptualized as separate and complementary. However, in practice the two channels have no firm barrier between them; in particular, the flow of resources 'downwards' tends to contaminate and disrupt the flow of information 'upwards'. Efficient relief of suffering depends on bringing a response into line with evolving needs (and securing good information on these); however, the success of an aid organization (and of individuals within it) may depend on presenting an image of success, perhaps bringing the portrayal of a crisis into line with the favoured response or massaging the way that the response is portrayed.[35]

In his book *Anatomy of Disaster Relief*, Randolph Kent noted that accepting substantial resources from governmental donors may compromise an NGO's independence. Robinson suggested that with the rise in government funding of British NGOs in the 1980s, NGOs became more muted in their criticism of the British government's aid arm, then known as the Overseas Development Administration.[36] Legal constraints may also be significant: for example, Britain's charity laws impose restrictions on political activity by NGOs.

We have seen that organizations' desire to do things that can be measured can lead to an emphasis on curative interventions in controlled environments rather than on prevention and empowerment.

For NGOs, accountability is often more upwards to donors than downwards to beneficiaries. In large part because of a concern to attract future funding, NGOs and UN agencies typically put a positive gloss on the impact of their own operations. One Dutch study found that out of some thirty-five Dutch NGO relief self-evaluations, none came up with a predominantly negative assessment. In a culture where success is habitually claimed, even admitting a small failing may be seen as implying a large one.[37]

Occasionally, the pressures to come up with a positive evaluation are quite blatant, and they may include a pressure to falsify figures. For example, aid staff at Save the Children Fund complained that the European Community's aid coordinator in Sudan had told them to produce a report indicating the large-scale distribution of European grain within western Sudan in 1986, when the reality was that most of the grain was still sitting in warehouses. European grain was old and much of it was unfit for human consumption; in general, local government officials preferred to distribute United States grain. However, without such a misleadingly positive report, Save the Children staff had been told, the NGO's funding would be threatened not just in Sudan but also in Mozambique and elsewhere.[38]

It is important to note that the process of presenting a positive image of aid does not usually imply outright lying, but rather a selective (and sometimes unconsciously selective) use of information. Often, the procedures involved in producing this information become so routine that participating individuals may be only dimly aware of all the different kinds of information that are not being generated, or are being suppressed.

What is particularly striking in the evaluation of aid in particular is the neglect of the question of *impact*. John Seaman, formerly of Save the Children Fund, observed in 1991 that the system has tended to measure the aid process itself – for example, the quantity of food that has been shifted – rather than the actual impact of this aid on the region in question.[39]

Within this broader heading of not considering impact, eleven common *failings* in evaluations – whether of humanitarian or development aid – can be detected.[40] Of course, evaluation is difficult, especially in wartime; it is nevertheless useful to keep some idea of an ideal evaluation and to consider how much a given practice resembles it. In line with Foucault (and Clay and Schaffer), such an approach helps to clarify the way that discussions may be limited – the way agendas may be shaped within a given discourse that perhaps seems to be more 'scientific' or objective than it actually is.

A first common failing is not looking at the impact on political and economic processes. Instead of just looking at the aid operation itself, it is important to look at political and economic processes (for example, degrees of protection for vulnerable groups, market price changes), and then at the impact of the aid on them. This applies to evaluations, but should also be borne in mind in needs assessments.

A second common failing in evaluations – as in the original formulation of interventions – is not spelling out the aims of the programme. Possible aims in a relief programme include keeping people alive, reducing malnutrition, preventing people's exposure to a disease environment, protecting people's livelihoods and assets, improving their security, offering an economic alternative to economic violence, and so on.

A third common weakness is that there is little attempt at establishing the baseline: the circumstances of the targeted population before the aid intervention. A fourth common weakness is not considering the situation of those who did not receive aid; this may include those who were not intended to receive aid, and those who *were* intended to receive it. Considering – and perhaps addressing – the views of those not receiving aid will usually be important in securing the political space in which particular groups can be effectively targeted and protected from violence. For example, envy towards groups receiving aid may be an important cause of violence.

A fifth common failing in evaluations is the lack of attention to *causation*: for example, to what has been driving mortality in a famine process. One hazard is that improvements may be attributed to aid when other factors (like a harvest or improved security) have been more important. A sixth and related problem with evaluations may be called 'the doomsday fallacy': the common tendency for aid agencies to exaggerate the likely mortality in a crisis (notably, to encourage a vigorous response from donors) and then subsequently to attribute a lower actual mortality rate to their own aid operations.

A seventh problem is neglecting long-term impact. There are usually a lot of unanswered questions about the long-term impact of aid, for example in drawing skilled staff away from government structures or in changing the incentives for agricultural production. An eighth problem is not consulting the end-user. The voice of the victim only rarely comes through in evaluations. Calling victims or end-users 'beneficiaries' tends to pre-empt the crucial question or whether they have indeed benefited.

A ninth common failing in evaluations is not asking sensible or sensitive questions. Anthropologist Jok Madut Jok, a Dinka from southern Sudan and author of *War and Slavery in Sudan* , points to what he calls 'assessment fatigue', a weariness on the part of end-users who are constantly being asked foolish and perhaps intrusive questions by visiting aid workers, creating the temptation of offering foolish or misleading answers.[41]

A tenth problem centres on timing. Insofar as evaluations are carried out at the end of a project (whether this is development or relief), there will be few opportunities for putting right problems as they arise. The temptation is for funders to take minimal responsibility for implementation problems (for example, through political pressure) and simply to decide at the end whether the implementing partners performed well or badly (which in turn is a disincentive to self-criticism by these partners). A final (related) problem with evaluations centres on who is evaluating whom. Some aid workers have stressed that a proper evaluation should be a 'two-way street': there should be opportunities for recipients to evaluate donors as well as the other way round.[42]

On the face of it, measuring impact has now become a higher priority. However, Mark Duffield has argued persuasively that an increased emphasis on evaluation may serve as a tool for donor governments to extend their control over NGOs and, by extension, over many poor countries.[43]

Case-Study: Sudan

The history of humanitarian aid to Sudan represents an extreme example of local manipulation interacting damagingly with wilful international blindness – very much on the lines that Clay and Schaffer would anticipate. Consider the efforts to relieve devastating famine in the south in the late 1980s. If we analyse donors' behaviour and discourse, we notice a number of 'blinkers' or 'blind-spots'.

For the most part, donors adopted a technocratic and seemingly benevolent language behind which exploitation could take place with considerable impunity. In practice, the framework used by major donors to describe the evolving disaster helped to dry up what the Dinka elder called the 'flow of words' from Abyei and other famine areas. This helped to expose southern Sudanese to some of the worst forms of exploitation imaginable. How was this done?

First, there was a *temporal* blinker. By effectively equating famine with the final stage of severe nutritional crisis, a point when people had lost most of their assets and had been forcibly displaced into northern Sudan or Ethiopia, governments giving aid created the impression of a prompt response to a measurable crisis. Targeting the poorest displaced people looked benevolent, but it ignored the process by which groups lacking a political voice had been forcibly impoverished. As with the common national and international focus on another 'target group' – the evil enemies targeted for destruction in civil or global warfare – an essentially *ahistorical* approach marginalized processes of *becoming* .

Second, interventions in Sudan suffered from a *spatial* blinker. Donors' focus was on northern Sudan and, to a lesser extent, government garrison towns in the south. Those in most of southern Sudan were deemed to be 'unreachable';[44] yet in reality rebel hostility to relief shipments in the south reflected the fact that they were being directed at government garrison towns, a bias made worse by the use of relief operations as 'cover' for channelling military supplies to these garrisons.

The level of humanitarian need in southern Sudan was played down by a variety of techniques.[45] USAID asserted that people in southern Sudan needed only two-thirds the quantity of grain required by northern Sudanese; this was based on the assumption that southern Sudanese had access to cattle, but of course a key process in the war had been precisely the devastating raiding of cattle in southern Sudan by northern militiamen. Donors sometimes claimed that the situation in the south was 'unknowable'; but people who had recently been forced out of the south were camped out within miles of the donors' offices in the capital, Khartoum. Reports of atrocities were dismissed as 'anecdotal', and entire areas of the south were dismissed as 'empty areas'. Foucault's injunction to analyse which discourses are taken seriously (and which neglected) proved all too relevant: 'What types of knowledge do you want to disqualify in the very instant of your demand: "Is it a science?" Which speaking, discoursing subjects – which subjects of experience and knowledge – do you want to "diminish" when you say: "I who conduct this discourse am conducting a scientific discourse . . .?" '[46]

That analysis relates also to a third blinker: namely that the very *symbols and words* used to describe the evolving famine helped to shape the inadequate response in powerful ways. The information that was demanded and produced centred largely on numbers not words, on consequences and not causes, on deficits not strategies, on needs not grievances, and on flows of grain rather than flows of words. In practice, this meant an overwhelming focus on the number of displaced people in particular areas and the number of tonnes of grain they would need, alongside an unrealistic optimism about their prospects of getting it. Clearly, there is a legitimate role for numbers in aid interventions and other social interventions; indeed a proper assessment of needs, baselines and impacts *requires* the deployment of numbers, whilst some numbers can be very politically damning. However, it is at least arguable that numbers have acquired an almost magical status in the West in particular; it is as if numbers denote 'science' and as if, by putting a figure on a given phenomenon, that phenomenon can somehow be understood, controlled and even defused. The question of which numbers are seen to be relevant is also significant.[47]

Humanitarian aid is habitually based on needs assessments and early-warning systems that are themselves based on systems of counting – on measurements of thinness, rainfall, production, numbers of displaced people, and so on. Such number-based systems may miss most of the important things that are going on in a particular society. The danger is that they will provide an apparently unobjectionable, technological screen behind which ethnic manipulation and economic exploitation can proceed unhindered.[48] Many of these variables came to prominence in relation to natural disasters.[49]

Among the political variables that might usefully be monitored are media propaganda, arms flows and attempts to replace government officials from one ethnic group with officials from another group. This would take famine monitoring and early warning closer to intelligence work. In fact, some USAID workers have complained that Famine Early-Warning Systems do not allow proper consideration of political factors, since these are seen as the province of the intelligence services.

In Sudan, the focus on numbers combined with TV images to create a double discrimination against words. This left little room for any sense of history, even the history of the previous few years, and little possibility for wondering what was politically possible in the light of this history. Donors, like TV viewers, seemed to be trapped within a perpetual present, responding to snapshots of the current situation, rather than to processes as they evolved. Most damagingly, the government-sponsored raiding that underpinned the famine (just as it has done in Darfur from 2003) – was not publicly discussed or condemned by major donors or the UN. In effect, the government was allowed to get away with its own self-serving definitions of the violence as 'self-defence' or ethnic conflict.

In Sudan in the late 1980s, a fourth set of blinkers was manifested in a *focus on policy*, and an *impulse to separate policy from implementation*. This was also very damaging. There was little ongoing evaluation of how relief was progressing and of the many political obstacles to effective relief that were created by a central government trying to promote famine and by local authorities trying to discourage migration to their areas. Nor was there much diplomatic support for NGOs (who were charged with implementing relief operations) when they ran into all kinds of official obstruction. Major donors tended to regard evaluation as the business of assessing which NGOs had done well and which had not. In these circumstances, as Clay and Schaffer have emphasized in their general discussion of the aid process, the question of one's own responsibility as a donor for poor policy outcomes could be neatly avoided.[50]

The Media

A rounded understanding of the complexity of conflict is necessary for at least two reasons. First, it helps in the design of international interventions that will help (and not harm). Second, it makes it less likely that information will encourage its recipients (including those in richer countries) into actively contributing to violence that is fuelled by over-simplistic definitions of the enemy; skewed information can make even the most irrational violence look 'rational' to the perpetrators.

International interventions

Consider the international interventions first. International media coverage can certainly spur humanitarian action, as in Ethiopia in the mid-1980s, and Sudan in 1988, 1998 and 2004.[51] A free press, as noted, was identified by Dreze and Sen in *Hunger and Public Action* as a key factor preventing famine, and this analysis was echoed by de Waal in *Famine Crimes*, where he stressed that a free press and democracy can help to deter politicians from allowing or promoting famine. De Waal noted that in India, the nationalists' condemnation of colonial responses to famine helped to create a political climate in which famine (but not necessarily other suffering) was strongly perceived as illegitimate and as a threat to the position of elected politicians. Media coverage can also create valuable pressure for an end to military activities (classically, during the Vietnam war).[52] Susan Sontag contrasted the 'reality' of the Vietnam war with the 'unreality' of the more or less unphotographed Gulag system in the Soviet Union.[53]

However, there are certain characteristics of international media coverage which tend to undermine its ability to prompt the amelioration of suffering. In fact, the local political economy of war may interact very damagingly with the international political economy of news.

When it comes to coverage of disasters, a key problem is television's tendency to provide 'snapshots' of the current situation rather than a sense of the underlying processes.[54] Television is better at consequences than causes, not least because you can photograph a consequence more easily than a cause. Television often panders to short attention spans with an emphasis on updates rather than understanding. The limitations of television and photography more generally can encourage reports that focus on the final, visible stage of famine, and that emphasize (as in Ethiopia in 1984–5) the existence of highly visible drought rather than what may be more politically sensitive and harder-to-photograph problems like government-sponsored violence and forced resettlement. De Waal argued in *Famine Crimes* that journalists and NGOs have a kind of mutual dependence that prioritizes last-minute assistance at the expense of political solutions. The problem is compounded by the sheer difficulty of getting poor countries' news into richer countries' media, a difficulty that itself encourages sensationalism by journalists seeking space or airtime. Nicholas Kristof notes, 'In June 2005, the combined networks of CNN, Fox News, NBC, MSNBC, ABC and CBS ran 55 times as many stories about the trial of Michael Jackson as they did about the genocide in Darfur.'[55] George Monbiot notes that despite globalization and the increasing interconnectedness of the world, the UK has seen falling coverage of serious issues in poor countries (though plenty of programmes about Britons making idiots of themselves in far-away places). Referring to 9/11, he adds, 'Our understanding diminishes correspondingly, until all we know of foreigners is that, for no reason that we can discern, they suddenly attack us.'[56]

Jonathan Benthall examined the hidden 'narratives' in media coverage of disasters. He suggested that sometimes, in a sense, 'the story' had already been written even before the journalist began writing or filming: that is, there were certain fables or templates to which stories needed to conform if they were to be easily comprehensible and digestible. Benthall suggested that in the context of relief operations, we frequently find the fable of the heroic aid worker confronting evil with the application of medical technology, often with a Princess (like the UK's Anne or Diana) somewhere in the background. Meanwhile, the ever-popular image of the passive starving child has acquired an almost iconic status, drawing attention to important problems but also tending to confirm a Western self-image as powerful and generous whilst taking attention away from the strategies of famine victims.[57]

The story of the West as saviour has often been highlighted to the exclusion of other crucial processes. When the media cover a humanitarian intervention, it will also be important to ask about the interventions that have taken place *before the aid ever arrives*. It is as if we usually only observe the tip of the iceberg (with aid flowing into a 'disaster zone'), whilst beneath the surface are other, often more substantial resource flows (including long-term aid and arms flowing to abusive governments, and natural resources flowing out of a disaster zone).

An example of trying to make news digestible came when one British television channel promised, 'All the news you want – the way you want it – next on Channel 5.' This was moving towards a conception of news as a kind of food, as something to be consumed with pleasure – a very different idea from the conception of news as a happening that you may or may not like. To the extent that the coverage even of disasters is shaped by a desire for ratings and a concern that news be digestible, is there a distinction between news and entertainment? What does the proliferation of peak-viewing documentaries depicting 'real-life' crimes and minor disasters suggest about the future of (and motives for) coverage of large-scale disasters? In the UK, viewers have been treated to a popular and long-running TV show called *Police, Camera, Action* – not much more than a collection of traffic accidents set to music.

One recurring 'myth' (not without some basis in reality) is the story of the heroic journalist. Journalists often like to turn themselves into the story and to portray parts of the world as irredeemably dangerous. Phillip Knightley notes the prevalence of what he calls 'I was there' coverage during the Vietnam war: correspondents were usually more interested in being seen to be at the heart of the action than in understanding its causes. This mode remains very strong today. Images may help in raising awareness of a crisis, but at same time may tend to confirm every stereotype about the so-called Third World – starving, violent, dirty, chaotic.[58] The incomprehensible – because it has not been understood in terms of normal human motivations – remains reassuringly *other*. Yet this can be as depressing as it is disempowering: if watching the news suggests no solutions, people may prefer simply not to watch.[59] One local television slogan in the US proclaimed, 'If it bleeds, it leads'; has US TV news in particular become so violent that the rest of the world must be depicted as violent mayhem to preserve any semblance of the superiority of the American way of life?

Another popular narrative framework is that of a sporting contest. Chapter 1 noted that US politics has often been covered as if it were sport, and that this mode of coverage finds echoes in the common portrayal of war as a kind of sporting contest between 'government' and 'rebels' or between two ethnic groups. Damage has been done when international journalists take divisions between government forces and rebels as a given, rather than investigating the violent and exploitative processes which this discourse may facilitate. Also damaging is journalists' habit of taking ethnic divisions as an immutable given, rather than questioning how ethnicity has come to be important, and how this process has been manipulated. Rakiya Omaar, among others, has argued that media depictions of the Rwandan genocide as 'tribal violence' made it easy for the UN to withdraw, a departure that helped the genocide to proceed virtually unchecked.[60] One problem was that many newspapers had just one correspondent covering the whole of Africa. Philippa Atkinson has argued that when the media depicts war as 'chaos' or 'collapsing states', this tends to encourage defeatism among international actors and leads to a neglect of the opportunities for building on what remains of the state.[61] Commenting on the war in Bosnia, BBC journalist Martin Bell noted a tendency for reporters, holed up in Sarajevo's Holiday Inn while it was bombarded by Serb forces, to ask with disbelief how the Serbs could do such terrible things; the question, Bell pointed out, foreclosed the chances of an interesting or helpful answer. In Bell's view, even the consequences of the Bosnian war were not adequately covered; he objected to what he saw as the BBC's sanitizing of violence there.[62]

Mobilizing violence

Consider now the role of information in mobilizing violence. Local media may play a role in inducing a sense that it is 'us against them', and, at the extreme, that 'unless we kill them, they will kill us'. One common technique is for politically biased media to emphasize abuses by 'the other side' (perhaps another ethnic group), whilst minimizing abuses by one's own group. There may be very limited space and airtime for those seeking to argue that there is more to politics than a clash between two ethnic groups, or between government and rebel forces. At the extreme, we may define one group not only as 'non-kin' but even as 'non-human', a key step towards preparing the ground for ethnic cleansing or genocide. In a sense, humans are often defined out of existence before they are physically 'eliminated' (as in Rwanda and Nazi-occupied Europe, for example).

The most notorious example of the media inciting ethnic violence was the role of state-controlled radio in Rwanda in stirring up the genocide, notably by dehumanizing the Tutsis and by insisting that the Tutsis and the Rwandan Patriotic Front posed an immediate threat to the lives of Hutus.[63] The possibility of jamming Rwandan radio was neglected. The former Yugoslavia was another striking example of media incitement, with significant elements of the Serbian and Croatian media generating a powerful sense of threat and even of impending genocide against Serbs and Croats, respectively.[64] As massacres by Bosnian Serb forces began to escalate, the Serbian press played them down or ignored them completely. In the former Yugoslavia, the systematic capture and destruction of transmitters proved how much store the warring sides set by the electronic media.[65] When sanctions were imposed on Milošević from 1992, he was able to use his control over the media (especially television) to reinforce a strong historical sense among many Serbs that 'the world is against them'.[66]

At the local or national level, the middle ground may become dangerously constricted in wartime. Croatian writer Dubravka Ugrešić notes that the passion for naming and labelling during ethnic conflicts can put pressure on a writer to abandon his or her sense of ambiguity and multiple truths; suddenly there is an army of petty informers (often with petty jealousies) who are ready to point the finger at those who reject this new passion for labelling.[67] Turkish dissident Yasar Kemal observed in 1998 that when the army burned villages, the government blamed this on the rebel PKK (Kurdistan Workers' Party) – a distortion usually reported uncritically in the Turkish press. Paradoxically, resisting this conspiracy of silence and pursuing an objective truth was seen as taking sides.[68] This has also been the case in Cambodia and Sierra Leone.[69] We have noted the possible function of war in suppressing opposition and free speech. In this context, labelling dissident journalists as rebels may not simply be a *tactic*; it may be part of the *function* of a war. The 'war on terror' has been accompanied in the US by a fashion for singling out 'anti-American' journalists and academics in a manner reminiscent of the witch-hunts of the McCarthy era.[70]

Optical illusions

Photography and moving images have tended to encourage in the viewer the feeling that he or she is witnessing reality very directly. With live television and internet coverage, we have the possibility of seeing things while they are actually happening; and so we seem to be moving even closer to the position of a witness who is physically present as events unfold. Yet the sense of getting direct access to 'reality' can often be an illusion.[71]

Photography's penchant for consequences rather than causes has been mentioned. Another problem is that all news is edited. A CNN advertisement about its own role in the 1991 war over Kuwait claimed, 'We'll tell you the facts. You decide'; the advertisement also made the claim that: 'There was no editing. [CNN] simply reported the news as it occurred.' Yet CNN – like every other media organization – made decisions about whom to hire, where to send them, what to cover, and what to put on air.[72] The text of CNN's advertisement provides an interesting example of a discourse that offers the consumer a feeling of empowerment whilst subtly shaping the debate: 'True, such reporting often puts the facts, the world and all of us to account. [We may note here that this is clearly a good thing.] It may have resolved nothing [a neutral thing]. On the other hand it can provoke informed debate and in that way influence how the world works [a good thing]. Is that good? You decide.' We are thus offered a choice between a favourable interpretation of CNN's role, a neutral interpretation and another favourable interpretation, a good example of how debates may be carefully and covertly constrained.

A second obstacle to directly accessing 'reality' is that the demands of maintaining a round-the-clock supply of news may mean that journalists find it difficult to leave the office and find out what is happening first-hand.[73]

A third problem is that the impact of photographs depends heavily on context.[74] Harold Evans, former editor of *The Times*, noted that in the early stages of the Vietnam war pictures of US soldiers' despair or of abuses on the American side were usually rejected because the war – on a relatively small scale at this time – was viewed favourably.[75] In the case of Rwanda in 1994, even images of bodies floating down a Rwandan river did not prove a catalyst for US or international military intervention. The subsequent humanitarian crisis in Congo/Zaïre was a different matter.[76] This was seen as 'doable' and as playing to the strengths of US logistics capacity. In the prevailing climate of isolationism, the US in particular was anxious to have an 'exit strategy' and military interventions always carried the threat of a Vietnam-style 'quagmire'.

A fourth problem is that the apparently direct access to so much 'reality' can be numbing. Relentless coverage of an endless succession of horrific events can easily produce 'compassion fatigue', the title of an interesting book by Susan Moeller. Susan Sontag, in her book *On Photography*, wrote of image junkies who had become immune to the impact of horrific photographs. The problem is exacerbated by the unimaginative templates that Benthall highlights.

A fifth problem is that spectacular disasters get much more coverage than endemic poverty. When Hurricane Katrina devastated New Orleans, it 'revealed' deep endemic poverty. But if the mainstream media were taken by surprise, many insiders were not: the head of one US food aid organization, Gleaners Food Bank, observed, 'Organizations like ours were feeding the impoverished in the south before the storm; we were feeding them through the storm; and we are feeding them after the storm.'[77]

Conclusion

Improving information flows can play a key role in reducing suffering in complex emergencies. That means trying to remove the blinkers from humanitarian operations and to uncover the 'alternative truths' that can provide the basis for more effective interventions. The example of humanitarian aid in Sudan can be set alongside the example of long-term aid to Rwanda. Uvin asked a stark question in his book *Aiding Violence*: 'Why did those of us who worked there [in Rwanda] have no idea that this was coming? Is there something about our definition of development, and the indicators we use to measure it, that makes us blind to the social, political, and ethnic forces that exist in society?'[78] He also noted that World Bank analyses of Rwanda hardly mentioned ethnicity. The aim of uncovering 'alternative truths' could be furthered if the allocation of aid funds and the promotion of aid personnel were more closely linked to the ability to produce an honest account of successes and failures which showed a genuine understanding of the relationship between aid and society, rather than to an account which says, in effect, 'Didn't we do well?'

Also important would be a concerted attempt to get away from the current tendency for conforming to templates, where 'the story' (an aid deficit, a starving child, a tribal war, a dangerous terrain confronted by heroic journalists) has too often been written, in effect, before the aid worker, consultant or journalist boards the plane. Challenging media stereotypes is also part of challenging the way enemies are defined and demonized, and this means examining the discourse of the 'enemy' circulating within richer countries as well as within the poorer countries that bear the brunt of disasters. Rather than insisting that violence is 'rational' or 'irrational', it may be more helpful to investigate who has the ability to shape the information environment so as to influence what courses of action people *perceive* as rational. Who is able to shape the interpretations that are put on the past? Who has the ability to manipulate the emotions of others (perhaps for self-interested reasons of their own)?

Although the inadequacies of early warning (for conflicts as well as conflict-related famines) have sometimes been attributed to shortages of appropriate information, often the real problem may not be lack of information so much as the fact that relevant political information is not circulating beyond the narrow confines of intelligence organizations and senior government officials in the industrialized world. (One might compare this to Sen's portrayal of famine as poor distribution rather than overall shortage.[79])

The case of France and Rwanda illustrates the problem of information distribution. As a key backer of the pre-genocide Habyarimana regime in Rwanda, France was in a position to track the behaviour of Hutu extremists inside and outside Rwanda, but much of this information went no further than the French intelligence services.[80] France was also well placed to track the flow of arms to these extremists, since it was providing a lot of them itself. Linda Melvern, who studied this relationship in detail, commented:

> France was Rwanda's one great ally and the French must have known of the activities of the extremists – certainly in the army. France provided arms, soldiers, technical advice and expertise to the Rwandan military, even embedding French officers to work side by side with officers and known extremists. Just two weeks before the genocide began, French officers were still serving in the very units that were responsible for carrying out the elimination of the entire political opposition, touring Kigali at dawn with prepared lists.[81]

Neither France nor the US was sharing vital information on preparations for genocide with non-permanent members of the Security Council.[82] Nor was the information shared with Lt-Gen. Romeo Dallaire, the force commander of the peacekeeping mission in Rwanda, UNAMIR. Yet Melvern notes, 'In January 1994 the CIA had given the [US] State Department an analysis which warned that if hostilities resumed, up to half a million people would die.'[83] Even within the UN, warnings existed. Massacres of Tutsis orchestrated by government officials and radio broadcasts had already been reported in an August 1993 report by the UN Commission on Human Rights.[84]

The mere existence of rights under international law has sometimes dis-torted information flows in very damaging ways. We have seen how the fear of having to grant asylum may lead to the downplaying of human rights abuses. Fear of having to intervene to prevent a genocide may lead to the denial that a genocide is taking place.

New technology can change the balance of power. As a means of circu-lating information beyond the constraints of censorship and lazy commer-cial media, the internet is hugely important. The ability of a repressive regime to control the flow of words from within its own borders is now more limited, though this does not prevent regimes from trying. The increasingly wide circulation of video cameras – including videos on mobile phones – also creates difficulties for anyone wanting to monopolize the circulation of moving images: one politically charged example was the video of Los Angeles policemen assaulting a black man, Rodney King – a case of 'Big brother, we're watching you!' Private videos of the allied bomb-ings of Baghdad are another example.

However, the facile temptations of a 'dumbed-down' media – in what-ever format – are not to be underestimated. In her eloquent preface to the book *An Embarrassment of Tyrannies*, Ursula Owen commented:

> Release from tyranny [under communism] turns out not, on the whole, to have led to an upsurge of creativity. We have to concern ourselves with how freedom is used as well as its suppression, and there are certainly freedoms lost by us in the West, 'the spoilt brats of civilization', when we allow ourselves to be dominated by the mediocrity of media moguls and the bottom line.[85]

8

Peace

Peace is a moment of possibility and danger: it brings the possibility of positive political change, but also the danger of further violence (which may include crime, terrorism, totalitarian revolution, the suppression of human rights and progressive politics, genocide, renewed war, or some combination of these). Studying war and peace over the long view suggests that violence is a bit like energy: it may mutate into new forms without actually disappearing.

As Wolfgang Schivelbusch shows, the end of a war (and, more especially, a *defeat*) may be seen as an opportunity to rid oneself of an autocratic regime that led a nation into war.[1] Leon Trotsky famously described war as 'the locomotive of history', and it was the final stages of the First World War that precipitated the Russian Revolution. The potential for change unleashed by *civil* war may be linked to processes of political mobilization during a war (as in Uganda, where wartime mobilization fed into Museveni's developmental initiatives). Moreover, the experience of fighting and migration may open people's eyes to structures of oppression.[2] To give one example among many, Caspar Fithen and Paul Richards, observing the expansion of livelihood associations and small businesses like motorbike taxis in the town of Bo, Sierra Leone, were struck by 'the sense of common purpose among young men fighting each other only a few years earlier, and their recognition they had been manipulated to fight. Their scepticism about "big men", and vertically-linked "ethnic" or locality-based associations is evident. . . . These ex-combatants are not just "fitting into" such a society – they are helping to forge it.'[3] We have seen how these shared grievances had sometimes fuelled collusion in wartime; now they were offering at least the hope of positive change.

If peace is both possibility and danger, this underlines that what is desirable is not just peace *per se* but *the right kind of peace*. The distinction between different kinds of peace has been emphasized by Johan Galtung, for whom 'positive peace' would include love, freedom from exploitation and repression, and the existence of a culture of peace. Galtung distinguished 'structural violence' (arising from social structures) from 'direct violence' (harm that is specifically intended).[4] 'Structural violence', for Galtung, includes exploitation and marginalization – anything that limits human well-being; it contains the seeds for direct violence. Nancy Scheper-Hughes' work on northeastern Brazil reminds us that even in peacetime particular groups (in this case, particularly, young black males) may come to be seen as expendable.[5] Carolyn Nordstrom has drawn attention to widespread sexual violence and sexual exploitation in peacetime Mozambique, noting that the label of 'peace' helped to disguise the existence of this violence.[6] She also stresses that we cannot understand sexual violence in wartime without understanding the degree to which sexual violence was tolerated in the 'peace' that preceded the war.[7] 'Peace' may sometimes involve a relocation of violence from the public to the domestic sphere.[8] Moreover, cases like El Salvador and South Africa suggest that the number of violent deaths can actually be higher in peacetime than in wartime.[9]

The kind of peace that prevails will be linked to the kind of violence that preceded it, and again Galtung's work is helpful. A commonly advocated route to peace – indeed one that, in Foucault's terms, has *been made to function as true* – is what Galtung calls the 'security approach'. The aim here – or at least the *expressed* aim – is to destroy, defeat or deter the enemy. However, there are several problems with this approach. First, the expressed aim may come into conflict with unexpressed aims: chapter 1 noted that violence may have *many* functions and that there may be significant vested interests in perpetuating violence. Second, the 'security approach' is *inherently* violent: while arguments have often been made for violence in the name of peace (and advocates rarely fail to mention the name of Adolf Hitler), we should at least notice the inherent contradiction.

A third (related) problem is that the 'security approach' may be ill-suited to securing a *long-term* peace. Betty Bigombe, a respected Ugandan government mediator in northern Uganda in 1994 and again in 2004, said, 'You cannot have a sustainable peace with a totally military solution.'[10] Without tackling underlying grievances, there will always be new recruits for violence. Even where military conquest is achieved, the enemy will not necessarily melt away. After US-led forces attacked Iraq in 2003, the sacking of the Iraqi army seemed to complete the rout of Saddam Hussein and his supporters. We have seen how many of these soldiers went on to join the Iraqi insurgency (often with support from civil servants dismissed because of their association with Saddam Hussein's Ba'athist regime).

A fourth (again related) problem with the 'security approach' is that violence tends to create enemies more quickly than it eliminates them.

Civilians always fall victim to violence to some extent, and we have seen a number of reasons why civilians have been defined, in practice, as part of the enemy. In any case, the idea of a finite number of evil people is an obvious (if seductive) fantasy: if it were really true, for example, that there exist a finite number of suicidal terrorists who are hell-bent on destruction (including their own), then the problem of suicide terrorism would neatly (if murderously) take care of itself.[11]

A fifth problem with the 'security approach' is that destroying the enemy leadership may make it difficult or impossible to find leaders with whom to negotiate during a peace process.[12] Any emerging leadership may be more radical and more belligerent than the previous leaders.[13]

The analysis so far has suggested some other routes to peace that might work better than the 'security approach', particularly in the medium and long term. One is the attempt to question the definition of the enemy that has been sanctioned and propagated by officialdom (in whatever form) and perhaps also by rebels or terrorists. That questioning will need to include an attempt to deconstruct the process by which a particular enemy came to be *defined* as the enemy (see, particularly, chapter 4). This may sound like an academic exercise but is often pivotal in making peace possible. A second approach is to try to map the various functions of violence for the various parties who have contributed to violence (an approach emphasized in the book as a whole), and then to use this analysis as a way of trying to reduce violent behaviour (see second and third sections of this chapter). This means looking at the incentives and disincentives under which the violent are operating.

This 'mapping' approach has been subject to a very particular (and very narrow) interpretation in the form of analyses and interventions based around the idea of 'rebel greed' (chapter 2). According to this limited perspective, the most useful interventions are those that constrain the money that rebels can make, thereby removing the key cause of civil war and of its perpetuation. But we have seen that any adequate mapping of the functions of violence requires a much broader interpretation. For one thing, it will need to include a mapping of the functions of violence for actors *within the state apparatus*. For another, it will need to include an understanding of the political and psychological functions of violence, going beyond the focus on economic functions. (Suicide terrorists demonstrate very clearly the limits of a narrow focus on economic incentives, but these limits do not only apply to them.) Finally, it will be important to understand the *dynamic interaction* of incentives among the various groups contributing to violence. This involves an understanding of the historical interaction of greed and grievance, including the phenomenon of 'greedy' and powerful actors manipulating the grievances and emotions of others.

Once the many functions of violence have been mapped, external interveners can try to make peace appear a more attractive option than war – both for those who manipulate violence from 'above' and for those who take it up 'from below'. This may be done with a combination of rewards and punishments, incentives and disincentives, and these may be economic, political, judicial or psychological.

Such social engineering has its dangers, however, and the third section examines some of the hazards accompanying the manipulation of the incentives under which violent groups are operating. It is stressed that, while the project of manipulating incentives holds out a good deal of promise, its cruder manifestations can be blinkered, mechanistic, ahistorical, arrogant and even counterproductive. Using the analogy of medicine, we need to understand not just how an intervention may attack a particular disease or infection but how *the body as a whole* will respond to that medicine, and what may be the unanticipated side-effects.

One key problem is that, in focusing on *the violent*, the manipulation of incentives tends to ignore those who have not (or *not yet*) been drawn into participation in violent processes. We have seen how famine interventions, counterinsurgency campaigns and counterterrorism operations have all frequently been impeded by focusing on a particular target group – 'the starving', 'the rebels', 'the terrorists' – whilst virtually ignoring the process by which people have arrived (and perhaps continue to arrive) at that extreme position or situation. Many of the interventions that offer the most promise in relation to those who have already been violent may end up sending the most dangerous signal to those who have so far refrained from violence. Thus, material or political rewards for peaceful behaviour in any given crisis may serve as an incentive for giving up violence, but also as an incentive for *taking it up*, particularly where the benefits of a peace agreement do not percolate much beyond the warring parties. Similarly, an amnesty for warring parties may represent a good way of persuading violent groups to opt for peace, but at the same time it tends to send a dangerous signal: it may not only compound a dangerous sense of impunity among the violent but may also strongly encourage violence on the part of the as-yet-non-violent.

Nor is the problem only one of 'signals': interventions that give priority to 'buying off' violent groups may also institutionalize a corrupt (and in many ways violent) peace that prolongs and deepens societal grievances in such a way that peace is undermined in the medium or long term. In fact, when civilians fall victim to an exclusionary peace agreement that institutionalizes corruption, this may sometimes be an extension of collaborative warfare that targeted and exploited civilians. In other words, war-as-collusion may mutate into peace-as-collusion.[14]

Manipulating the Incentives of the Violent

Economic instruments

Economic sanctions
A promising means of punishing violent behaviour is through some kind of targeted economic sanction. One such is targeting the illegal trade in particular commodities, a tactic that has had some degree of success. A threat by the US Congress to impose sanctions on countries aiding the Khmer Rouge eventually prompted Thailand to close the border with Cambodia in late 1996. This created incentives for Thai officials, military officers and gem and log traders on the ground to deal directly with elements of the Cambodian government, something that in turn encouraged defections by those elements of the Khmer Rouge who had benefited most from doing business with Thai officials.[15]

In January 2001, the US introduced a motion in the UN Security Council to impose sanctions on the Liberian government because of its support both for Sierra Leone's Revolutionary United Front (RUF) rebels and for rebel groups in Guinea. These sanctions included banning Liberian diamond exports, strengthening an existing arms embargo, grounding Liberian-registered aircraft and banning international travel by senior Liberian officials (though pressures were weakened by France and China blocking timber sanctions). The Liberian government was clearly alarmed by the US initiative, and tried to distance itself from acting RUF leader Sam Bockarie and, more generally, from the accusation of fuelling war in Sierra Leone.[16] In combination with Sierra Leone's national diamond certification scheme, pressure on Liberia also appears to have made it harder and less profitable for the RUF to sell diamonds.[17] Together with the military squeeze on the RUF and externally encouraged reforms within the Sierra Leonean military, the pressures on Liberia helped to make peace possible in Sierra Leone.[18]

A promising general initiative on 'conflict diamonds' has been the 'Kimberley process', which formally began in November 2002 and which has involved the major diamond trading countries and companies. Participants agreed to establish controls (certification plus tamper-proof containers) to eliminate conflict diamonds from shipments of rough diamonds coming to or leaving their countries.

Interventions in conflicts in Cambodia and Sierra Leone showed the advantages of a *regional* approach. Sanctions always bring attempts at evasion, and commodity-based sanctions are unlikely to work without systematically pressing for (and providing incentives for) enforcement by a range of regional and global actors.

In 1998, twenty-four years after the Angolan civil war began, the UN banned the purchase of any Angolan diamonds lacking an official government certificate of origin, and the European Union quickly applied similar measures. Unfortunately, the rebel group UNITA found a number of ways of getting round these measures, including continued trade to South Africa and flights to Europe and Israel via Ivory Coast, Morocco and the Central African Republic.[19] One of the problems with sanctions on particular commodities is familiar from the drugs trade: prohibitions may actually *increase* the rewards for those who can successfully bypass them. For example, controls on trade passing from Colombia through the Caribbean to the US had the effect of increasing the rewards for those involved in trading overland from Colombia, including through Guatemala.

Some interventions have targeted the *production* of particular commodities – a method that involves elements of the 'security approach'. This strategy has been applied principally to drugs. Again, the side-effects of the intervention may be very marked. Meanwhile, we have seen how destruction of coca crops in Colombia, though designed to undermine the Revolutionary Armed Forces of Colombia (FARC), ended up strengthening its support. Moves against drugs production in Bolivia and a crack-down on cartels in Colombia seem to have helped the FARC to step into the gap. Often forgotten is the fact that drugs flowing *into* a conflict can exacerbate violence (as in West Africa) and these flows (like those in richer countries) need to be controlled.

Another type of targeted sanction is financial – normally freezing or confiscating the foreign assets of a particular warring party or of particular individuals.[20] The idea is relatively new and presents major difficulties, including the ease with which money can be transferred electronically, the use of false identities, and the use of offshore havens like the Cayman Islands. Nevertheless, the idea is a promising alternative to cruder measures like general sanctions and the use of force. Charles King reported in 1997 that the Colombian government's action in freezing guerrilla bank accounts had probably had more success in weakening rebels than had military action,[21] though international efforts to clamp down on FARC finances later ran into opposition from Switzerland. The technique was also used against UNITA rebels in Angola.[22]

In 1999, the United States, the EU and Switzerland attempted to impose targeted financial sanctions on individual businesspeople and politicians in the Federal Republic of Yugoslavia (FRY) as part of the international pressures over Kosovo. The US's Office of Foreign Asset Control has particular expertise in this area. There was no UN Security Resolution authorizing these measures. Since a range of international pressures on the FRY had been imposed significantly earlier (in 1992), targeted individuals had probably already moved assets to secure locations. Even so, the move was seen as welcome (if belated) by a wide range of intellectuals and activists. The departure from general sanctions was particularly favoured – not only because these had caused a lot suffering but also because they were widely seen as *bolstering* Milošević's abusive government (see later in this chapter). Sources in Belgrade in 1999 reported that targeted sanctions were already having a powerful effect on the elite. 'Psychologically, it's created a lot of problems,' one analyst told me. 'People are understanding they will not have a future. If it continues like this, they can lose all the money they have.' Part of the elites' anxiety was said to be the fear that the list could form the basis for some kind of international criminal tribunal. The list was also seen as a good way of producing incriminating information. As one local analyst put it: 'Those on the list are denouncing others not on the list. It's fantastic for blackmailing, and getting more details on Milošević's bank accounts!'

Much of the potential of targeted commodity and financial sanctions remains unexplored. Freezing individual bank accounts has also been suggested as a way of bringing pressure on Russian leaders over the abuses in Chechnya, but concrete actions to pressure the Russians over Chechnya have been scarce. In Sudan, one key step in tackling abuses in Darfur in particular would be tough and targeted sanctions against those senior government officials who have been most responsible, including sanctions against companies owned and controlled by them.[23] Another step forward over Sudan would be a clear specific threat to the country's oil trade and to future investments in oil production. Yet the UN has consistently held back from trade sanctions, and even targeted sanctions have been weak – sending a correspondingly weak message. In May 2006, the UN did impose sanctions on four Sudanese – two rebels, one government military man and one government-aligned militia *janjaweed* militia leader. Yet no senior political figure in Khartoum was targeted, and the great majority of those fifty-one Sudanese who have been referred to the International Criminal Court over Darfur have not been targeted for sanctions. This weak response inevitably undermines any public stance against the Darfur atrocities from the US or UK, and Khartoum seems reassured by extensive private diplomatic contacts – often centred on cooperation with the US in the 'war on terror' – whilst virtually ignoring critical public statements emerging from the international community.[24] The foot-dragging of the US and UK in particular over 'smart sanctions' for Sudan contrasts with vigorous attempts to stop flows of finances to al-Qaida.[25]

Another promising restriction on resource flows is controlling the arms trade. This is a large topic (which cannot be dealt with adequately here)[26] and a problem from which the focus on 'rebel greed' risks diverting attention. In 2001, Sierra Leone's Peace Commissioner, Dennis Bright, noted how the devastating effect of arms trading has been somehow taken for granted: 'Those who produced and sold the guns also have a case to answer – it's somehow seen as an unavoidable vice, essential to our economy [that is, in the arms-producing countries]. This was the way slavery was seen before. But through the moral and spiritual strength of the church, slavery was abolished.'[27]

Economic rewards

Just as important as targeted economic sanctions may be the provision of economic rewards for peaceful behaviour. These may be extended to elites and to ordinary combatants.

In Mozambique, the 1992 peace agreement was secured, in large part, through institutionalizing corruption – not only through helping Renamo to transform itself into a political movement but also through allowing it to tax businesses in Renamo areas of control, and through a pre-electoral agreement that Renamo leaders be included in the new government.[28]

We have seen how the Cambodian army developed economic relationships with elements of the Khmer Rouge; this seems to have provided the basis for drawing defectors into cooperation with the government in a context where the restrictions on Khmer Rouge trade with Thailand from 1996 encouraged the pursuit of business through government channels.[29] Ieng Sary and his supporters in the Khmer Rouge were offered access to lucrative gem and timber concessions within the Cambodian government system.[30] The links that he had built up with traders, army commanders and the Cambodian government contrasted with the more isolated and ideologically 'pure' world inhabited by Pol Pot himself, and these links seem to have prepared the way for Ieng Sary's defection in 1996.[31] These processes helped to weaken the Khmer Rouge and to make some kind of peace possible, though the resulting government coalition proved very unstable.[32]

Economic rewards for peaceful behaviour may also usefully be extended to ordinary soldiers – in the form of programmes for Disarmament, Demobilization and Reintegration (DDR).

A good DDR programme can lure soldiers away from loyalty to leaders who often have a particularly strong vested interest in continuing conflict and in avoiding the accountability and punishment that peace might bring. Loss of faith in a greedy leadership can be an advantage here, and this was one element that helped facilitate the disarmament of rebels in Sierra Leone.[33] More generally, weak chains of command in modern wars, as well as creating difficulties in enforcing peace agreements, can play a positive role in encouraging belligerents to negotiate.[34]

It has often been assumed that demobilization and disarmament will follow naturally from a peace agreement, especially if a few seeds and tools are provided to ease the soldiers' path back to agricultural life. However, particularly where economic agendas and attacks on civilians are prevalent, DDR is deeply problematic.[35] A lasting disarmament will be particularly difficult in contexts where it is precisely the distinction between the armed and the unarmed that distinguishes the attackers and the attacked, the exploiters and the exploited. All this underlines the need for a properly funded and well-conceived DDR. That means serious attention to supporting agriculture and urban livelihoods.[36] This was not the case in Sierra Leone and Liberia, the inadequacy of whose DDR – and especially reintegration – was noted in chapter 3.

If soldiers were properly cared for at the end of a war, this would significantly reduce the room for manoeuvre for political and commercial interests who have repeatedly harnessed the grievances of combatants and ex-combatants for political and economic purposes of their own – not least to derail the political and socio-economic reforms that tend to loom when military defeat discredits an autocratic regime. Variations on this process played out in post-First World War Germany and in Rwanda in 1993–4. We have seen how fear of unemployment arising from the Arusha accords encouraged many soldiers in the Rwandan army to participate in a genocide designed, in large part, to sabotage those accords.

Cuts in soldiers' employment and pay can be very dangerous, particularly where good DDR structures are not in place. We have seen in chapter 3 how the 1996 peace agreement in Sierra Leone was followed by a strong push from the IMF for major cuts in the size and rations of the Sierra Leonean army (and for a withdrawal of the South African security company, Executive Outcomes), and how these measures fed into a May 1997 coup. The fact that the measures were part of the IMF's 'anti-poverty' programme did not prevent them from greatly exacerbating poverty via renewed civil war.

Encouraging peaceful behaviour may mean encouraging *relatively unabusive* behaviour even while a war is going on. Poor conditions for soldiers represent a powerful incentive (both economic and psychological) for abuse. These poor conditions are often the result, in part, of the diversion of funding to senior officers, a diversion which itself provides an important incentive for military commanders to keep conflict going. We have seen how corruption within the military has frequently provided incentives for continued conflict – for example, in northern Uganda, in Guatemala and in Chechnya.

In the Democratic Republic of Congo (DRC), it has proved extremely difficult to integrate the various military factions into disciplined brigades; they have continued to attack civilians (including widespread sexual violence); and they have retained a degree of loyalty to faction leaders from the 1998–2002 war. These leaders, benefiting from many kinds of illegal deals and international trading, have been helping to block security sector reform.[37] In June 2003, Simon Robinson and Vivienne Watt reported, 'Some Congolese units have split back into their rebel and ethnic parts and turned on one another.' There had been an 'upsurge in rapes, killings and torture by Congo's security forces'.[38] In an important 2006 report, the International Crisis Group noted:

> While donors have supported MONUC [United Nations Mission in the Democratic Republic of Congo] at an operational rate of approximately $1 billion a year to improve the situation in the East, they have balked at the concept of providing basic equipment to the integrated brigades, let alone decent living conditions. . . . The integration centres at Mushaki, Nyaleke and Luberizi were largely unsuitable for human habitation, let alone training, forcing some soldiers to live in straw huts amid outbreaks of disease such as cholera and tuberculosis.[39]

Particularly since the rebellion in 1996, the weakness of the national army has repeatedly exposed the country to interference from foreign powers, who have looked to exploit the country's valuable natural resources. A key problem has been that even the low salaries for soldiers (around US$10 a month) have not actually reached the rank and file, due to corruption higher up the hierarchy. Even a senior officer's official monthly salary is only US$50 (less than one-tenth the salary of a UN driver) – a major incentive for embezzlement.[40] As we saw in chapter 2, corruption in the DRC army has also taken the form of inventing 'ghost soldiers' as a means of lining the pockets of senior military figures. Such abuses arise in part because Zaïre/DRC's army has long lacked effective civilian oversight, and establishing this is a major challenge.[41] Many governmental and multilateral donors are not ready to be seen giving any funding at all to security sectors; however, Britain's Department for International Development has been giving serious attention to security sector reform.[42] Separating the chain of payment from the chain of command is one promising avenue, and EU involvement here is encouraging.[43]

Judicial instruments

One way of influencing the violent is through national or international judicial action. Amnesty International and Human Rights Watch have often emphasized that justice – holding human rights abusers accountable in some way – is necessary for a lasting peace, and one NGO calls itself 'No Peace without Justice'.

The International Criminal Court (ICC) – formally established in 2002 – has opened investigations into Uganda, the DRC and Sudan. Back in 2000, US President Bill Clinton had signed the ICC founding treaty, but under George W. Bush the US government withdrew in May 2002. China and India have not signed the ICC treaty.

In March 2005, the UN Security Council referred the situation in Darfur to the ICC. In April 2005 the United Nations International Commission of Inquiry on Darfur recommended that fifty-one (undisclosed) people be referred to the court. Sources reported major anxiety within the Khartoum government over the referrals. However, subsequent pressure on Khartoum to comply has been weak and disjointed.[44]

In his 2006 study of northern Uganda, Tim Allen reported significant positive reactions to the ICC among those in northern Uganda who know about it, adding that local enthusiasm for traditional justice mediated through chiefs can easily be overstated. Allen argued that people in northern Uganda require the same kinds of conventional legal mechanisms that are demanded by others in modern states, and that those who put faith in traditional methods of healing and reconciliation among northern Uganda's Acholi might actually be underscoring a common prejudice in the capital, Kampala – namely, that the Acholi are somehow not like normal people.[45]

Although most media attention has focused on the ICC, other judicial avenues are also important. Governments, too, can be targeted for judicial proceedings. In December 2005, the International Court of Justice – the

UN's highest judicial body – ordered Uganda to pay reparations to the DRC for the occupation of its eastern regions in 1998–2003, dismissing Uganda's claim that it had acted in self-defence.[46] Extradition procedures by individual countries also have a role. In Colombia, right-wing paramilitary leaders have accepted a large degree of demobilization under President Uribe, apparently keen to avoid extradition to the US for drug-trafficking;[47] these leaders are also worried about the threat of prosecution under Colombia's Justice and Peace Law.[48] Finally, the importance of building up or reviving the *national* justice system is often overlooked: key areas include the police, the prison system, legal training and the physical infrastructure of the courts.[49]

Although it is commonly said that peace and justice are 'indivisible', there are dangers in a rigid policy of punishing abuses in national or international conflicts. To put the matter very starkly: if you are determined to punish everyone who has carried out human rights abuses, how do you expect them to lay down their arms and surrender themselves to your punishments? If peace is to bring immediate justice for all the guilty, how will peace ever be possible? The prospect of legal recriminations may be an incentive to spurn peace negotiations and to renege on commitments during the implementation of peace agreements.[50] After interviews with a range of local actors on the subject of peace and justice in northern Uganda, Andrew Mawson (then with Amnesty International) concluded in 2000: 'Some people want revenge for things Lord's Resistance Army (LRA) soldiers have done to them or their families. However, others, including almost all intellectuals, want to bury the past as the price of peace.'[51] Betty Bigombe has reported that people in the camps in northern Uganda are very ambivalent about the ICC: they want some justice but don't want to wreck the progress towards peace. (Bigombe herself has favoured some kind of judicial procedure, warning that in the absence of justice, local people may take revenge into their own hands.[52]) Supplementing the economic incentives for Ieng Sary and others to defect from the Khmer Rouge was the offer of a pardon.[53] Holding back from certain kinds of prosecutions may also be important in *averting* a civil war: for example, it is doubtful whether South Africa's security services would have accepted the end of apartheid without the prospect of some kind of amnesty, such as the amnesty that was granted (provided there was full disclosure) to those responsible for abuses that could be shown to be politically motivated and 'proportional' to the political objectives.

As with economic instruments, the best hope may lie in a pragmatic combination of sanctions and rewards: the threat of punishment probably needs to be combined with the pragmatic provision of amnesty. Jon Lunn sensibly advocates a 'transitional justice' approach, which includes the use of truth commissions and of material compensation for war victims, whilst keeping the option of judicial action open *in the longer term*, when abusers may have less power to disrupt the peace (perhaps having been disarmed).[54] In Colombia, the government has been reluctant to submit the list of names of ex-combatants to be prosecuted before the demobilizing of the military structure of key paramilitaries.[55] Lunn notes that the political pitfalls of a 'justice' approach created the space for Truth Commissions in South and Central America in the 1980s, but adds that Amnesty International and Human Rights Watch have since then moved in the direction of what he calls 'judicial absolutism', whilst an enthusiasm for 'a potentially endless "war for human rights"' has included the 'buying' of Slobodan Milošević for the Hague Tribunal via a US threat to withdraw aid to Serbia.[56]

Note that even within long-established systems of domestic law, some element of compromise has routinely been operative, as when sentences are reduced for a 'guilty' plea or when charges are dropped in return for the supply of valuable information.

Manipulating the Incentives of the Violent: Some Problems

Focusing only on violent groups (and manipulating their incentives) carries three main dangers: putting power and resources into the hands of violent groups; sending a signal to the wider society that violence 'works'; and neglecting the grievances in the wider society.[57] These are considered below.

Putting power and resources in the hands of violent groups

What looks to some people like realism and pragmatism may look to others like appeasement. Resources accumulated during war may already be considerable; where violent groups are rewarded for adopting peaceful behaviour, this will tend to put state power and additional resources into the hands of groups who have been responsible for violence.[58] This may be an immediate transfer or it may arise from their subsequent control of the state. Power and resources may subsequently be put to damaging or outright destructive use, especially where warring parties draw a lesson that violence pays. Of course, the hope is that violent groups will *change* their behaviour; but this hope may not be fulfilled.

In Somalia and Liberia, civilian organizations have often opposed recognition of armed faction leaders in peace negotiations, arguing that this rewards their violence and boosts their prestige and their ability to attract a following.[59] In Cambodia, one source of instability after the Khmer Rouge was brought inside the government was that endemic corruption was depriving the treasury of revenue.[60] Similar concerns have resurfaced in the DRC. In Sierra Leone, the controversial appointment of RUF leader Foday Sankoh as Vice-President and head of a new mineral resources commission (under the 1999 Lome agreement) was profoundly offensive to many Sierra Leoneans; it looked even more distasteful when the RUF returned to war in 2000.[61]

Antonio Giustozzi has highlighted how Afghan warlords have tried to use peace agreements to become 'respectable' and to consolidate their ill-gotten gains; indeed, this impulse may even help to explain why peace becomes possible.[62] Some analysts suggest that during negotiations over the composition of an interim government (starting in November 2001 in Bonn), the US – together with UN diplomat Lakhdar Brahimi (who also dealt with unsavoury leaders at the end of Lebanon's civil war in 1989) – actually strengthened the morale of, and support for, warlords (some of them described as 'paper tigers') at a moment when they could have been weakened.[63] Subsequently, warlords were able to withhold a great deal of customs revenue from the centre, making reconstruction (and restoring some kind of central authority) more difficult.[64]

In Colombia, the progressive incorporation of demobilizing paramilitaries into organized crime networks may represent an advance over outright war, but it also represents a deeply corrupt and exclusionary peace. When Alavaro Uribe Velez was elected President of Colombia in 2002, he soon produced a peace plan that provided for the demobilization of armed groups from both the left and the right. Most of the early beneficiaries were the far-right paramilitaries. Ivan Roberto Dugue, leader of a major paramilitary force known as the United Self-Defence Forces (AUC), said he wanted to 'legitimize the AUC's power and build it into a big political movement'.[65] Paramilitaries have been looking to control organized crime in food markets and racketeering, and to consolidate their hold on drug trafficking; consolidating their political power will help in this endeavour.[66] Whether they will renounce violence in the long term is unclear.

Sending a signal to the wider society that violence 'works'

A second danger with focusing on incentives for violent groups lies in the signal that is sent out to the wider society. Where amnesties are granted to the violent, this may encourage others to follow the path of violence. Where economic or political benefits are being handed to violent parties, others may conclude that violence is a rational means to achieving their own goals.[67]

In Cambodia, the deal with elements of the Khmer Rouge under Ieng Sary can be seen as sending out potentially damaging signals on the accept-ability of violence and corruption. Certainly, Amnesty International com-plained that the deal contributed to a climate of impunity.[68] A notable danger is that rewarding people for giving up violence (or giving up arms) will serve as an additional incentive to take up violence (or arms) in the first place. Many local people saw Sierra Leone's 1999 Lome agreement – bring-ing the RUF inside the government – as an unfortunate necessity, given the preceding attack on Freetown and the weakness of international protec-tion. Mediators in Sierra Leone also used educational scholarships as an incentive for peace. But if necessity is the mother of concession, what kind of message does this send? An analysis of the various coups and renewed rebellions in Sierra Leone from the 1992 coup onwards suggests that a variety of groups have tried to use violence to force their way inside the existing system of rewards and benefits.[69] A young man working on the demobilization scheme commented in 2001:

> The civilians – I don't know what is being done for them. If you pay much attention to perpetrators without recognizing the civilians or helping them like the ex-combatants, you are sending another signal. There might be another uprising. At the amputees' camp, there is nothing being done for them. Politicians just wanted ex-combatants to forget about waging war against them. What about the victims who have suffered most? In years to come, it's a merry-go-round as I see it. Civilians will get up and say the people who caused this havoc, they are now living big.[70]

In Sudan, a near-exclusive international focus on Khartoum and the rebel SPLA – in line with a binary understanding of a north/south or even a Muslim/Christian divide – has tended to encourage a neglect of the inter-ests of those northerners who oppose the current government in Sudan, some of whom turned to violence in an attempt to win the international recognition (and the place at the negotiating table) that has been accorded to the SPLA, for whom violent resistance seemed at last to have paid dividends.[71]

Neglecting grievances in civil society

A third danger (quite closely related to the other two) is that peace agree-ments geared towards meeting the demands of the violent may end up feeding into the neglect of grievances in civil society; in fact, these grievances may be exacerbated by the spectacle of warring factions rewarding themselves through institutionalized corruption. Tackling grievances in civil society involves seeking *inclusive* peace agreements and taking seriously phenomena like poverty, inequality and uneven development.

Peace agreements: inclusive or exclusive?
The existence of peace begs important questions such as: whose peace?; peace on what terms?; peace in whose interests?; and peace negotiated by which individuals or groups? Sometimes it seems that everybody wants peace; it's just that they want *their* peace.[72] In other words, they want peace on their terms. NGOs have sometimes been criticized for working for peace without giving enough thought to *what kind of peace* they are working towards.[73]

Who is being excluded in a particular peace settlement? To what extent is it an agreement between armed factions to the exclusion of most elements of civil society or most forms of political opposition? What forms of corruption are being institutionalized in a particular peace process? And what exactly is the difference between peace and war in circumstances where war itself involves forms of covert cooperation and tacit non-aggression between ostensibly warring parties, and at the expense of civilians?

While it is likely to be difficult or impossible to exclude warlords and faction leaders from peace negotiations, serious attempts to recognize civilian groups and a wide range of political forces offer a better chance that peace will not simply institutionalize corruption, violence and impunity.[74]

War may feed into peace in quite sinister ways, particularly where war is itself collusive. Groups that have been able to use violence to secure control of production, trade and emergency aid in wartime may be able to carve out for themselves a degree of control over production, trade and development or reconstruction aid after a peace settlement.[75] Faction leaders may find some advantages in the new arrangements: for example, Menkhaus and Prendergast reported that in Somalia mafia-type operations benefited from a degree of order as outright conflict abated somewhat towards the mid-1990s; this limited order assisted trade and minimized turf battles whilst holding out the prospect of attracting foreign donors.[76] Alex de Waal pointed in 1994 to the shared interest that many Somali landlord-elders had in a particular kind of peace, a peace that excluded politically marginalized agriculturalists from land that they used to cultivate before it was taken away by quasi-legal means or simply by force. Outsiders largely failed to engage with this aspect of the transition; as de Waal put it, clan analysis was tending to obscure class analysis.[77]

If agreement between government elites and rebels can exclude civil society, sometimes the rebels themselves have been excluded from a peace process. The 1997 Sudan Peace Agreement was in many ways an agreement between military *allies* – the Sudan government and southern factions (under the United Democratic Salvation Front) with which it was already linked. The rebel SPLA was excluded. The agreement actually coincided with a marked escalation of the war.[78] The January 2005 Comprehensive Peace Agreement (CPA) between Khartoum and the Sudan Peoples Liberation Movement / SPLA – recognized as the sole representative of southern interests – was a much more genuine breakthrough. But this time it was the South Sudan Defence Forces (SSDF, only partially reconciled to the SPLA) that was excluded. The 2005 peace agreement stipulated that only 2 per cent of oil revenues were to go to oil-producing states (where the SSDF is strong), compared to 40 per cent in the 1997 peace agreement that southern militias (precursors of the SSDF) had made with Khartoum.[79] The SSDF have complained that they have not been getting even the allotted share.[80]

Sudan's 2005 Comprehensive Peace Agreement also carries the seeds of major problems in relation to opposition groups in the north. The agreement excluded the opposition National Democratic Alliance, and the CPA allocated only 14 per cent of positions in the national and state executive and legislative branches to the northern opposition (compared to 52 per cent to the National Congress Party and 28 per cent to the SPLM).[81] Opponents of the current regime have included those Muslims who hoped (wrongly as it turned out) that common religion could be a basis for common citizenship; many in the north also fear that they will now have no option but to become part of an Islamic state, particularly if the south secedes.[82] Key grievances in the north include, first, years of neglect by the government and, second, the loss of access to land (by both smallholders and pastoralists) as a result of the expansion of Sudan's large semi-mechanized farms.[83]

Significantly, the 2005 peace agreement is not the first time that a military government in Sudan has made peace in the south and entered into a political alliance with the former rebels at the expense of rival political forces within the north: General Jaafar Nimeiri pursued this tactic via the Addis Ababa agreement at the end of Sudan's first civil war in 1972; part of the reason why that agreement did not last was the continuing discontent of northern groups who had been excluded from power (and whose discontent was eventually redirected against the south by Nimeiri and his successors). In this political context, the eonomic rehabilitation of the south (notably, the cattle stocks) actually served as an incentive for renewed raiding from 1983.

A third problematic peace accord in Sudan was the May 2006 Darfur Peace Agreement. Two of the three rebel delegations did not accept this agreement, and the Khartoum government then set about attacking and intimidating the non-signatories, in alliance with the one faction (under Minni Minawi) that had signed the agreement.

If Sudan has been the focus of this discussion, the question of exclusion from peace agreements has arisen in many other contexts. For example, in Sri Lanka an important limitation of the 2002 ceasefire agreement was that it focused on the government and the secessionist LTTE (Liberation Tigers of Tamil Eelam) but largely excluded southern political elites, non-LTTE Tamil parties and the Muslim community.[84]

Tackling poverty, inequality and the weak state

Action to remedy underlying problems like poverty, inequality and weak states has frequently been very limited in the post-war period.

A classic example is the implementation of DDR programmes alongside macro-economic policies that reinvent the causes of wars. Like emergency aid, DDR has often been handled as a discrete programme, more or less isolated from a wider understanding of political and economic processes. In post-war Mozambique, aid workers and academics accused the World Bank and the IMF of imposing structural adjustment programmes that undermined economic opportunities just at the point when demobilized soldiers needed to be absorbed.[85] Feeding into this kind of schizophrenic approach has been a tendency to keep civilians ('good') and soldiers ('bad') in separate categories: insofar as civilians are seen as 'good' and soldiers as 'bad', this is unhelpful in understanding the circumstances that turn civilians *into* soldiers or that prevent soldiers from resuming life as civilians. Imagine for a moment that civilians are like water and that when grievances are sufficiently 'hot', the water turns into steam (combatants). We might want to turn the steam back into water (for example, through DDR); but the process would be severely undermined if we kept the heat turned on (for example, through international financial institutions' policies that deepened grievances).

In Sierra Leone, moves to tackle the underlying causes of the war have been rather weak.[86] An often abusive chieftaincy system has been revived. Privatization (which failed to revive the economy in the 1980s) has once more been wheeled out as the way forward. Corruption remains inadequately addressed, as do the low salaries that feed it. Joseph Hanlon notes that in post-war Sierra Leone, 'IMF spending caps prevent the essential expansion of education, and require civil service salaries to be so low that civil servants need additional income.'[87]

Pastor and Boyce suggested that the World Bank and IMF should prioritize equity issues in post-conflict situations so as to tackle root causes.[88] They argued that donors generally have an unusual degree of bargaining power when countries are weakened by war. In practice, however, the opportunity has often been spurned. The peace process in Cambodia is one example: although donors were contributing almost half the government's budget in 1996, corruption and authoritarian government were left largely intact.[89]

In the aftermath of wars in Central America, tackling the underlying causes of violence would have meant major land reform and major tax reform, among other measures. Yet land reform was low on major donors' list of favoured changes. In both El Salvador and Nicaragua, there were only limited land transfers after the civil wars.[90] In both, the failure to fulfil even the expectations of demobilized combatants jeopardized security and contributed to the high levels of post-war crime.[91] In Guatemala, one measure of continuing grievances has been the booming private security sector: ex-soldiers and ex-civil patrollers have played a key role in the armed protection of landed estates at risk from Mayan peasants who felt they got little from the long years of revolutionary war.

The case of Colombia shows how international pressure for social change can actually decline over time, as Luis Eduardo Fajardo argues. Almost 70 per cent of expenditure under the controversial Plan Colombia (announced in 1999 and ostensibly designed to bring peace to the country) has been military spending. By contrast, military spending made up less than 10 per cent of the US's Alliance for Progress under President Kennedy in the 1960s. The radical (and threatening) social reforms envisaged in the Alliance for Progress – notably land reform and tax reform – have been largely avoided in the Plan Colombia: the social element concentrates on coca crop substitution and emergency employment in urban areas. Even though Plan Colombia started with a significant element of social expenditure, the project has evolved into what is essentially a military and anti-drugs strategy. An important factor in this major shift of priorities has been the 9/11 terrorist attacks: with the FARC and ELN rebels now defined by the US as 'terrorists', the military drive against them has found new legitimacy and increased resources. One important development has been the US decision to remove legal restraints prohibiting the use of US-funded military hardware for counterinsurgency (as opposed to drug control operations).[92]

In most contemporary conflicts, tackling underlying causes also means rebuilding the state. We have seen how weak states breed grievances as well as an inability even to suppress insurgency. Institutions like the World Bank and IMF have often tended to denigrate the state and to push for privatiza-tion.[93] In post-war contexts (as in pre-war and even wartime contexts), the IMF and World Bank have tended to push for cuts in bureaucracy and for severe limits to social spending; yet consolidating peace will in all probabil-ity depend on quickly reducing inequalities and accommodating political factions with government positions.[94] Liberalizing trade may be particu-larly hazardous where states rely heavily on import taxes.[95]

The 'bloated' African state is something of a myth.[96] The ratio of civil servants to population in Sub-Saharan Africa has been estimated at around 1 per cent, compared to 7 per cent in richer countries.[97] The civil servants who do exist have seen their real pay hit by structural adjustment, increas-ing the temptations of petty corruption and involvement in the informal economy.[98] Without a rebuilding of the state, even the very positive initia-tives to rein in 'resource wars' will have difficulty taking hold. For example, diamond-certification schemes will always be partially undermined if senior army officers are themselves involved (a factor in Angola) or if traders can bribe underpaid civil servants to turn a blind eye (Sierra Leone).[99] Stan Hagberg reported that sustaining the salaries of civil ser-vants in Burkina Faso helped to minimize corruption and promote impar-tiality in arbitrating disputes (notably between farmers and pastoralists).[100] Raising salaries can help to reverse the 'brain drain' from Africa, a process that has seen some of the continent's best talent moving to richer countries.[101]

Liberalization programmes have often held out the prospect of long-term benefits if short-term suffering can only be endured. Even in peace-time, the promise often rang hollow. Under structural adjustment programmes in Africa, Kankwenda M'Baya suggested, citizens 'were expected to shut up, accept the burden and wait for the better tomorrow promised them, in which nobody believes any more'.[102] This burden could be especially heavy in countries such as Tanzania and Zambia, where struc-tural adjustment programmes were running down health infrastructure precisely when HIV/AIDS was tightening its grip.[103] Moreover, liberaliza-tion may powerfully fuel the violent expression of grievances (at the extreme, in warfare), with the result that these purported long-term bene-fits may never even have the chance to arrive.[104]

Meanwhile, liberalization packages continue to push African countries back to their 'historical' comparative advantage in primary products (copper for Zambia, gold and cocoa for Ghana, etc.).[105] Yet East Asian eco-nomic success was profoundly linked to industrialization and to the pro-tectionism and state intervention that made this possible.[106] African states have been dismissed as irredeemably corrupt and inept, but even some of the worst examples have shown a remarkable capacity to recover.[107] Thandika Mkandawire has pointed out that international pessimism about the 'corrupt' African state can have a perniciously self-fulfilling quality:

> To avoid clientalism and rent seeking, the state is squeezed fiscally and even politically. This weakened state then exhibits incapacity to carry out its basic functions (partly because of demoralization, moonlighting by the civil servants, corruption, etc.). This is then used to argue that the state in Africa is not capable of being developmental and therefore needs to be stripped down further and be buffeted by legions of foreign experts.[108]

In effect if not necessarily in intention, this would seem to be another example of Arendt's action-as-propaganda: propaganda about the state was only a partial truth; yet action based on this half-truth made the propaganda appear more and more plausible.

'Reconstruction'

In the aftermath of a war, a great deal of discussion typically centres on 'reconstruction', 'rehabilitation', 'rebuilding', 'resettlement' and all the various 're's' of post-conflict work. These tasks are not easy, but let us suppose they could all be achieved. If it were possible successfully to re-create and reconstruct the exact social and economic conditions prevailing at the outset of a civil war, would war not simply break out all over again – for the same reasons as before? Of course, there might have been external factors that originally precipitated conflict (like the incursion into Sierra Leone from Liberia), but these factors never operate in a vacuum: re-creating the old political economy risks a renewed conflagration from some renewed spark, whether external or internal. Mats Utas noted in relation to Liberia:

> Marginalisation appears to be the norm for a large proportion of young urbanites. Thus re-marginalisation and not reintegration is the natural outcome awaiting most ex-combatants. . . . Enlistment in the armies, in the first place, was envisaged as a move away from the margin and into the centre of society – a means of integrating in society, even if by force.[109]

Rather than simply reconstructing an economy, it would be more useful to try to reverse the process by which diverse groups took up arms or persuaded others to do so.

Another problem with simply rebuilding an economy is that people have often moved on in their thinking – and expectations – as a *result* of a war.

As Sierra Leone's war drew to a close, some human rights workers and aid workers in Sierra Leone were surprised to hear people beginning to talk of their 'rights'.[110] Areas subjected to high levels of violence seem to exhibit higher levels of political mobilization, for example in voter registration and attendance of community meetings.[111] One perceptive local aid worker with experience of many of the camps for displaced people told me in 2001:

> War has helped in creating awareness. For example, in relation to marketing, people now know the cost of food in Bo [a major town in the south] and are no longer ready to sell in their villages for much less than in Bo.[112] They can also take it to Bo themselves. And they have more political awareness. . . . In the camps, NGOs projects are going on. Before, people were not exposed. They would take the family to farm and come back home around 10. Now they know the facilities they were supposed to get. Some have time to listen to the news, and do reading. Now in the cities and camps they meet agencies, discuss issues. . . . Many people didn't know agencies like UNICEF, WHO. People are getting used to organizing themselves. They feel they should be one, like a community, and they can make a big fuss against an individual who says, 'Vote for me'.

Another significant change is that internal displacement has often led to more women taking on the major or exclusive role in providing for a household; these women may be unwilling to return to former domestic subservience when reunited with husbands in rural areas.[113]

One of the most useful tools for peacemaking may be for international aid workers and diplomats to listen to what people are saying, rather than to what these outside actors think people *ought* to be saying. Part of this involves outsiders refraining from assuming that young Africans, for example, want nothing more than to return to the traditional farming or pastoral lives that are often seen as their natural habitat. This is brought out in work by Mark Chingono on Mozambique and Gaim Kibreab on Sudan and Eritrea.[114] Rehabilitation should be more than an attempt to 'turn the clock back' to a rural idyll that perhaps never actually existed. As Paul Richards notes of Sierra Leone: 'Young people, modernized by education and life in the diamond districts, are reluctant to revert to this semi-subsistence way of life; many treat it only as a last stand-by.'[115] At the same time, some observers have noted the dangers in training young people for jobs that do not exist and the importance of ensuring a healthy rural sector.[116] Tackling underlying political problems in rural areas is likely to be critical, as with the often abusive chieftaincy system in Sierra Leone. A key cause of the war in Sierra Leone was that setting up a decent living as a farmer was proving increasingly impossible for many youths, especially younger sons, in the context of land shortages and control of access to land by abusive local chiefs. Many Sierra Leoneans suffered from the iron rule of abusive and unrepresentative local chiefs.[117] In line with Mamdani's analysis of 'decentralized despotism',[118] the power of these chiefs had been boosted under colonialism as a means of governing on the cheap. The experience of wartime (including the flight of some chiefs) means that many people are less prepared to put up with abuses than they were before the war. In these circumstances, the restoration of chieftaincies in Sierra Leone – backed by Britain-as-aid-donor rather than Britain-as-colonizer – may prove incendiary, not least through restoring the lack of representation for youth and for women that helped breed chiefs' abuses and fuel the conflict; it is no substitute for genuine decentralization and democratization.[119]

Also in grave danger of being reinvented and revived in Sierra Leone are several other phenomena that fed into the conflict. These include not only neoliberalism (with its privatization and devaluation) and endemic corruption but also continuing debt repayments, a neglect of industry, a dysfunctional legal system, and a focus of civil society activity and international assistance on Freetown.[120]

Backlash

Even interventions in the name of peace (often, in practice, a package of peace-plus-democracy) may have profoundly counterproductive effects, whether these projects are well intentioned or not. Interventions are typically mediated through deeply unequal power relations, and we have seen how famine relief operations can be subverted by (and may even reinforce) these power inequalities. Power inequalities may be very marked at the point when war is ending or democracy pending, and these inequalities will usually include a large imbalance between those who are armed and those who are not. To be accepted, any peace will probably need to accommodate power inequalities to some extent. If a peace agreement challenges these inequalities too drastically, we may expect a *backlash* of some kind.

External sanctions will also be mediated through unequal power relations, and may end up reinforcing them. Imposing justice at war's end may also prompt a damaging backlash – not least because the imposition of an external 'justice' agenda can smack of paternalism and colonialism.[121] Even imposing shame may be hazardous: we have seen the role of shame in driving extreme violence (see pp. 198–202 below). Finally, the whole enterprise of designing incentives so that others may be encouraged into 'good behaviour' can smack strongly of imperialism, and this can be a further source of unanticipated and undesirable 'side-effects'. Indeed, such interventions may feed strongly into the radicalization of the so-far non-violent (as in the 'war on terror').

Donor governments and others involved in humanitarian interventions frequently assume that 'all good things go together'.[122] It is always tempting to divide things into the good and the bad, and discussion of complex emergencies frequently falls into this simplistic paradigm (especially in media discussions). The good and the pure include victims, humanitarian actors, civilians and peace. The bad and the dirty include perpetrators, politics and warlords. A corollary of dualistic thinking is that we tend to 'lump' everything good together, and to lump everything bad together, imagining that all the good things tend to promote each other, and all the bad things also tend to promote each other. Thus, in the world of good things, we have peace, democracy, justice, human rights, self-determination and economic prosperity, and these are routinely assumed to reinforce each other. In the world of bad things, we have war, authoritarianism, injustice and collapsing economies, which again are seen as feeding into one another. Amartya Sen is one esteemed analyst who has tended to bracket 'good' things together – for example, in the argument that human development is good for growth.[123] An important contemporary manifestation of dualistic thinking has been a tendency to picture peace, democracy and capitalism as three cowboys riding hand-in-hand into the sunset at the dawn of a New World Order. How you get a sunset at dawn is the least of the problems with this perspective.

In reality, there may be important trade-offs between peace and self-determination, as well as between peace and democracy or peace and justice. Particularly where political reform and economic development are poorly advanced, imposing rapid change from the outside may be disastrous. This applies to military interventions (which may be designed, in part, to promote democracy) as well as to less violent pressures for democratization and liberalization. Roland Paris, Edward Mansfield and Jack Snyder have warned strongly against rushing too quickly towards competitive elections.

Western governments seem to be better at encouraging people to demand their rights than at protecting them against the consequences of doing so. US encouragement to the Kurds and Shi'ites to rise up against Saddam Hussein in 1991 was not matched by a willingness to protect them (especially the Shi'ites) from a violent government backlash. That chain of events ought to have given pause for thought to international 'democratizers' (especially in Washington) who were still riding a wave of confidence after the fall of communism. So too might the role of the international community in encouraging and recognizing declarations of independence by Croatia and Slovenia in 1991, declarations that helped to precipitate the wars in former Yugoslavia.

Another example that ought to have been sobering was Angola in 1992, when elections were rushed through at a moment when demobilization was very incomplete; UNITA rebels rejected the result and returned to war.[124] Then came Rwanda – the clearest example of a rush to democracy that tragically backfired. Recalling President Habyarimana's stalling on peace and power-sharing in 1993, Human Rights Watch reported:

> By late July [1993], the donor nations – including France – had lost patience and used the ultimate threat. In combination with the World Bank, they informed Habyarimana that international funds for his government would be halted if he did not sign the treaty by August 9. With no other source of funds available, Habyarimana was obliged to sign along with the other parties, on August 4, 1993.[125]

That meant accepting power-sharing during a transitional period leading to elections. Roland Paris notes that foreign donors were subsidizing at least 70 per cent of government's public investment at the time, so the external pressure was enormous.[126] Yet we have seen how the rush to democracy and power-sharing was ultimately resisted by Hutu extremists who were ready to resort to genocide. An exacerbating factor may have been the threat of prosecution against those named by UN investigators as responsible for previous massacres.[127]

Self-determination proved very hazardous for East Timor. Back in 1975, Western governments had supported the Indonesian annexation of this Portuguese colony, with the US in particular stymieing any effective resistance from the UN. President Suharto (who became President back in 1967) stepped down in 1998 after trying to resist IMF presssures for austerity. National elections followed in June 1999 and the West pushed successfully for a referendum on independence for East Timor in August 1999, a referendum that was supervised by Western observers. The East Timorese voted overwhelmingly for independence. Now this may have looked like progress. But the vote was to lead immediately to massive retaliation by pro-Indonesian militias linked to an army desperate to prevent the break-up of Indonesia.[128] Once again, the international community was very slow to offer protection against this backlash.

Understanding the possibility of a backlash against progressive reforms is linked to an understanding of the relationship between political freedom and economic power. What kinds of freedom are possible in what kinds of circumstances? Good policies can be seen as *outcomes* (of particular social formations) as well as *causes* (of particular development patterns).[129] The most famous example of this type of analysis is probably Barrington Moore's *Social Origins of Dictatorship and Democracy*, in which Moore suggested that the English aristocracy were able to accept a degree of democracy (and relatively free trade) because (in contrast to the Junker landowners in Prussia) they had no great need to prop up a tottering economic position with political levers (in part because they had diversified their economic interests beyond landed estates).[130]

Sanctions

Another potentially counterproductive intervention is the imposition of generalized trade and aid sanctions – a much-favoured instrument against abusive regimes in the 1990s in particular.

A well-known problem with sanctions directed at particular countries is that they tend to create suffering among ordinary people there.[131] Less well understood is the way that general sanctions can interact damagingly with a political economy of violence, often reinforcing the power and profits of an abusive elite. When sanctions are imposed, rulers may benefit economically from the manipulation of shortages and politically by emphasizing the existence of an 'external enemy' (probably with 'internal collaborators').

The former Yugoslavia illustrates the hazards of generalized sanctions. Indeed, during the late 1990s many intellectuals and aid workers in the Federal Republic of Yugoslavia (formed from the former Socialist Republics of Serbia and Montenegro in April 1992) argued that President Milošević and his cronies were actively courting international sanctions. Trading in key commodities was subject to monopolistic control, and sanctions on oil and other strategic goods tended to increase the profit margins for those whose political connections allowed them to breach these sanctions.[132] Smuggling and illicit economic activity were sometimes even celebrated as patriotic.[133] One local journalist based in Belgrade told me in 1999:

> Sanctions effected the destruction of the structured economy. The ruling elite didn't mind so much. They joined this process in a very enthusiastic way. . . . Sanctions were supposed to be an instrument that would put pressure to stop the war – in Bosnia, Croatia, Kosovo. But they created a political environment, a fertile soil for the ruling elite and some other groups and an alibi for the structural and deep criminalization of the society. You could get rich from a redistribution of national wealth.

Sanctions were also said to have reinforced a sense of siege in Serbia: designed to a large extent as a deterrent to violence, they seem to have ended up providing legitimacy for successive wars. At least during the mid- and late 1990s, sanctions helped Milošević to redirect discontent against external enemies (the people imposing the sanctions), whilst also helping him to stigmatize his opponents as collaborating with those who were imposing this hardship. The theory was that sanctions either would make Milošević change his behaviour or would encourage Serbs to rise up against him. But many people in Serbia resented the attempt to manipulate their behaviour through sanctions. One young Serbian woman working for an NGO said that many felt they were being experimented on like rats in a cage: 'Many people were against Milošević, but then reacted to sanctions by saying, "Don't tell me what I should be thinking and doing!" ' In conditions of hardship, the government's ability to provide jobs and other benefits to its security services proved a particularly valuable source of support for Milošević. Moreover, the impoverishment (and flight) of middle-class people weakened one of the forces that tends to be most vocal in demanding democracy.

With sanctions being blamed for every hardship, Milošević's regime was able to pursue all kinds of corrupt money-making schemes, including dubious public loan projects, pyramid schemes and simply printing money. Some intellectuals in Belgrade saw sanctions as providing an alibi for a lack of real transition to more democratic forms of government and a more genuinely competitive economy.

The criminalizing effects of sanctions spread from FRY to Albania, Romania, Bulgaria and Madeconia; paradoxically, the *lifting* of sanctions may have increased ethnic tensions in Kosovo and Albania, as local mafias and pyramid schemes had come to depend on the profits of sanctions-busting.[134]

It is possible that sanctions eventually played some part in getting rid of Milošević, who was deposed in October 2000. Even in 1999, there were those in Belgrade – apparently, a minority – who saw sanctions as ratcheting up the pressure on Milošević, particularly since he was by this time running out of plausible wars with which to boost the general sense of siege. A Western diplomat told me: 'Sanctions were ineffective before because Milošević had a military option – Bosnia, Kosovo. Does he still have an option? Theoretically, he could have an option against Montenegro or against his own people. But Milošević has been defeated in a war. In my mind he hardly has a military option.'

Even so, the many counterproductive effects of sanctions have to be taken seriously – and the case of Serbia is by no means an isolated one. In the early

1990s sanctions on Haiti seem to have reinforced that country's autocratic regime, whose security forces took control of the smuggling, the black market and the allocation of scarce resources. Sanctions were also reported to be squeezing out the Haitian middle class.[135] (Even Israel's punitive sanctions on Gaza and the West Bank, whilst further inflaming Palestinian anger, yielded windfalls for 'big-shots' in the Palestinian authority – and for well-placed Israelis – as (expensive) supplies regularly found their way through the relevant checkpoints.[136])

Under trade sanctions on Iraq from 1990, widespread bribery allowed Saddam's cabal to engage in exporting and importing, and the profits from these activities were again boosted by the large price differences that sanctions helped to create.[137] Dependence on state patronage seems to have become ever more important under conditions of scarcity created by sanctions, and Saddam meanwhile used his control of the media to put across the message that the West was entirely to blame.

Shame

Human rights work is based to a large extent on naming and shaming.[138] Such discourses create the possibility of accountability. At the same time, redistributing shame from victims to perpetrators may be very threatening and constitutes another possible source of backlash.

The distribution of shame is a vital – and potentially incendiary – element in wartime and in a post-war context. Systems of violence are often sustained, in part, by redistributing shame from the perpetrators (where it should properly reside) to the victims. This compounds the suffering of the victims, most obviously in the case of sexual violence; at the same time, the process may well encourage further atrocities by allowing the perpetrators to operate in a kind of 'shame-free' zone. The lack of shame among elements of the military can be remarkable. As one Guatemalan human rights worker put it to me, 'There is not one army official who has talked with regret about what they have done.' Hannah Arendt spelled out how the redistribution of shame can work:

> The SS implicated concentration camp inmates – criminals, politicals, Jews – in their crimes by making them responsible for a large part of the administration. . . . The point is not only that hatred is diverted from those who are guilty (the *capos* [prisoners working in lowly positions within the concentration camps] were more hated than the SS), but that the distinguishing line between persecutor and persecuted, between the murderer and his victim, is constantly blurred.[139]

Part of peacebuilding may be trying to lessen the burden of shame that has been loaded onto victims when violence has manufactured its own (spurious) 'legitimacy'. One woman who had studied the civil patrols in Guatemala was also involved in organizing 'returns' for displaced people after the 1996 peace accords. She emphasized the value, for surviving victims, of ceremonies commemorating the dead:

> They asked themselves why am I alive (when my wife died, my children died, the man standing beside me died). We have to show the people that we are not bad, to show they were not animals. They felt as though they were animals. When they were being driven to the mountains, they had to live like animals . . . .

Yet this process also carried a cost: 'One of the chiefs of the PAC [civil patrols set up by the government and responsible for many atrocities] started drinking that day and he went to the cemetery and he drank for fifteen days and he died . . . victims and perpetrators both come to recognize the humanity of the victims – it's part of the same process.'

In her study of war widows and the Guatemalan civil war, Judith Zur noted how the chiefs of the abusive civil patrol units have had a strong fear of the words of women (and war widows in particular). Part of this has been fear of physical and legal retribution, which women's condemnation was seen as making more likely. Zur also noted a strong fear of spiritual retribution and fear of the women's ridicule and laughter, with all this feeding into violence against women in 'peacetime' Guatemala. Civil patrol leaders have been reluctant to give up their authority, and levels of rural violence in general have been high.[140]

We saw in chapter 3 how attempts to impose shame on violent groups may sometimes provoke intensified violence. Based on extensive fieldwork in Sudan, Congo, Sierra Leone and Rwanda, Zoë Marriage questions the usefulness of condemning warring parties for breaking laws and norms to which they never subscribed in the first place. Such condemnation brings 'moral returns' to those pointing the finger, she argues, but has often proven useless or, worse, provocative – with warring factions sometimes reacting violently to condemnation and perceived hypocrisy.[141]

Part of the problem may be the redefinition of 'right' and 'wrong' that frequently accompanies the advent of peace. Soldiers' willingness to fight has typically been stoked up by inculcating them with the belief that their cause is just. If the world then turns around and re-labels them as perpetrators (and perhaps, by extension, re-labels their cause as unjust), then these ex-combatants may be more inclined to reject the world than to accept such stigma and shame.[142]

Who, in any case, has the right to impose shame? Tupac Shakur, an icon for many rebels in Sierra Leone, once wrote that 'Only God can judge me'. Officials in Washington and London have a tendency to regard themselves as bastions of propriety: cajoling or encouraging the world's more hot-headed populations into good behaviour; shaming, punishing and rewarding as they see fit. How this system looks 'at the other end' is a complex and neglected question, but we could do worse than go back to Shylock's defence – in *The Merchant of Venice* – of his right to the pound of flesh which was his 'property':

> What judgement shall I dread, doing no wrong?
> You have among you many a purchased slave,
> Which, like your asses and your dogs and mules,
> You use in abject and in slavish parts,
> Because you bought them: shall I say to you,
> Let them be free, marry them to your heirs?[143]

As a contemporary reminder of possible hypocrisy, this might be interpreted in a specific as well as a general way: memories of slavery, for example, are not as short in Africa as they are among the Western white establishment that issues moral admonishments on a regular basis. What is the moral authority of the West? If it exists, what kinds of actions have reinforced or eroded it? Particularly in the Arab and Muslim world, Western powers lost a great deal of credibility when they bypassed the UN in launching the 2003 Iraq war. So too, as UN Special Envoy to Sudan Jan Pronk observed after his expulsion by Khartoum, did the UN itself.[144] When the Sudan government has been condemned by the US and UK over human rights abuses in Darfur, the human rights abuses at Abu Ghraib have provided Khartoum with a convenient (if spurious) rebuttal. ICC referrals have so far focused on Africa, leading to a suspicion of bias against African leaders. Meanwhile at the UN Commission on Human Rights, many African governments have urged the international community not to be too harsh in criticizing Sudan. Some UN officials privately suggest that world politics is shaping up as the developing world saying, 'Don't tell us what to do!' Edward Said pointed out that history cannot be wiped clean so that American leaders can 'impose our own forms of life for these lesser people to follow'.[145] In October 2001, the then US Secretary of State Colin Powell expressed a related worry that the US was moving warlords around 'on a chessboard': 'Do they have any ideas about what they want to do, as opposed to what we think they ought to do?'[146]

What is the effect of condemnation if the condemned party already feels like a victim?[147] As one Serbian woman observed, where international criminal trials are seen as unfair, this can easily be seen as a continuation of a historical conspiracy towards the Serbs, and may even turn the accused into heroes. National justice systems, too, must be seen to be fair if they are not to exacerbate grievances.[148] If the analysis in previous chapters has suggested the importance of understanding how violence is perceived (not least by the participants), it will be equally important to consider how the *interventions* are perceived (not least by those capable of mobilizing violence in response to them).

Many Sierra Leonean combatants and ex-combatants projected an air of self-righteousness, and threatening them with shame could be useless or even (as psychiatrist James Gilligan would predict[149]) dangerous. One man taken hostage by Sierra Leone's West Side Boys said of the young combatants:

> Some of them really believe, even until now, that what they have done is absolutely right – mostly because of the indoctrination. If you seem to be justifying the violence, you make it hard for them to admit that it was wrong. But if you condemn them, they will not listen and will withdraw from you.

One key worker with ActionAid discussed with me a peace campaign called 'Never Again' in which that agency was active:

> When you go to ex-combatants and say you must demonstrate remorse, they will kill you. You have to time it. As far as he is concerned, he has done the right thing. . . . When they have evidence of their colleagues being reintegrated and their colleagues have not been in jail and have schools, jobs, they can use that as a basis to trust. So they can talk more openly and feel remorse. You have to examine your own self as someone who is not in any way responsible. If they suspect you're one of the people that caused the war, they can suspect you.

A surprising number of ex-combatants in Sierra Leone have expressed very idealistic career aims.[150] Researchers John and Valerie Braithwaite distinguished between 'stigmatizing' shaming and reintegrative shaming. They argued that the former makes crime worse and the latter reduces crime, and they explained: 'Stigmatization means shaming by which the wrongdoer is treated disrespectfully as an outcast and as a bad person. Reintegrative shaming means treating the wrongdoer respectfully and empathically as a good person who has done a bad act and making special efforts to show the wrongdoer how valued they are after the wrongful act has been committed.'[151] Of course, naming and shaming has a role in reducing impunity, and it would be wrong to blame the atrocities of, say, the RUF on those who publicly highlighted them. Even so, we should question the assumption that those condemned by the international community share the same moral universe as those who condemn them; we should also consider the possibility that condemnation without practical care can exacerbate violence.

International Actors: A Case of Failure?

To judge from the statements of leaders in richer countries, they have a strong concern with promoting peace and human rights around the world, and the main stumbling block comes from within the war-affected countries, perhaps because of the intractability of tribalism, the pervasiveness of poverty or the selfishness of 'extremists' and 'illicit power structures'. However, leaders in developed countries are better judged by their actions than their words. It is important to understand that peace and human rights may be just one priority (and not even a high one) among many that are being pursued simultaneously. Whatever the intentions of policy-makers in richer countries, blaming 'implementation' (or problems 'over there') may serve as a convenient 'escape route' (in Clay and Schaffer's terms[152]), legitimizing unhelpful policy practices that are nevertheless adhered to because they serve some other (generally unstated) function; yet poor outcomes will tend to reflect poor policy (chapter 7). As with our examination of policy within crisis-affected countries, it is important to avoid assuming that governments in powerful countries have *failed* when outcomes (in terms of human suffering) are poor.

Impunity has an important international dimension, both during complex emergencies and in the preceding period. International complicity in complex emergencies may begin long before the crisis, whether through the impact of colonialism or through support for abusive regimes during the Cold War. Colonialism and subsequent support for autocrats frequently set the scene for an explosion of grievances in the 1980s and 1990s and for a variety of elite attempts to channel grievances, politics and violence along ethnic lines.

Alex de Waal notes in his book *Famine Crimes* that the list of the largest African recipients of US bilateral assistance in 1962–88 reads like a roll-call of recent political emergencies: Sudan, Zaïre (DRC), Somalia, Liberia, Ethiopia, with semi-stable Kenya offering only a partial exception to the rule. Considering also the support from France in particular for the authoritarian government in Rwanda before the genocide, it appears that long-term aid has a great deal to answer for. Patrick McAuslan gives a flavour of Western powers' historical tendency to 'dance with dictators', noting the habit of paying lip-service to conditionality in long-term aid and military assistance whilst murmuring ' "not such a bad chap really, went to Sandhurst/The Middle Temple, must be all right"; "I knew his Permanent Secretary at University . . ." ', and so on.[153]

During a crisis, perpetrators frequently know how far they can go because they have 'tested the waters' beforehand. It has often been said that the Second World War was fought to save the Jews from the Nazis; however, international attitudes to the persecution of the Jews were actually highly ambivalent and this contributed to a significant degree of impunity for Nazi atrocities. Hannah Arendt observed of the victims of genocide:

> Only in the last stage of a rather lengthy process is their right to live threatened; only if they remain perfectly 'superfluous', if nobody can be found to 'claim' them, may their lives be in danger. Even the Nazis started their extermination of Jews by first depriving them of all legal status (the status of second-class citizenship) and cutting them off from the world of the living by herding them into ghettos and concentration camps; and before they set the gas chambers into motion they had carefully tested the ground and found out to their satisfaction that no country would claim these people. The point is that a condition of complete rightlessness was created before the right to live was challenged.[154]

Today, no-one seems to wish to claim the people of Chechnya, for example, as a collective concern: from 1994 onwards, Russia has been given a virtually free hand for its abuses of the civilian population there and UN agencies are routinely bullied if they try to bring up the issue of continuing abuses or internally displaced groups.[155]

In the case of Sudan, governments in Khartoum over the years have developed a sophisticated sense of what kind of abuses they can get away with (it helps if it looks like 'tribal warfare') and what kinds of concerns on the part of major powers (access to oil, humanitarian access, cooperation in the Cold War or the 'war on terror', cooperation in the north–south peace negotiations) can be exploited to secure international acquiescence (in practice, if not necessarily at the level of rhetoric). From a material point of view, the Security Council's resolve has been undermined by Russia's arms sales, by China's appetite for Sudanese oil, and by interest in the oil from both France and the US.[156] It is important to understand that Khartoum's gift for divide and rule applies externally as well as internally.

A senior aid official involved in Darfur commented: 'The international community has totally mishandled the Darfur situation. Its divisions have allowed the Khartoum government to play governments off against each other.'[157] Weak international action not only encouraged the persistence of attacks on civilians in Darfur but also allowed Khartoum to prevent a UN peacekeeping force from being sent to the region, with peacekeeping responsibilities offloaded onto an underfunded and ineffective African Union force. In contrast to earlier reticence over Rwanda, the US government did declare 'genocide' in Darfur in the summer of 2004;[158] yet subsequent failure to take protection seriously reinforced the impression (already fostered by the US-led invasion of Iraq in 2003) that the George W. Bush regime did not regard international law as binding.

In Rwanda in the early 1990s, donors did not reduce aid with specific reference to human rights violations in the run-up to the genocide, although the Belgian government threatened to do so; the emphasis was on structural adjustment and on promoting fiscal reform as well as on improved accountability for aid given. The French government gave active support to the Habyarimana regime. Military aid to Hutu extremists appears to have continued through June 1994, two months after the start of the genocide.[159] In April 1994, an already existing climate of impunity in Rwanda was further bolstered when the United States refused to call the violence an out-and-out genocide, apparently seeking to avoid commitments (which would follow naturally from the Genocide Convention) that threatened to lead the international community into 'another Somalia'.

The UN Secretariat denied the proactive role to peacekeepers from UNAMIR (United Nations Assistance Mission for Rwanda) – notably in searching for arms – that had been requested by UNAMIR commander General Romeo Dallaire. This was despite a detailed report in a now infamous cable from Dallaire to the UN's DPKO (Department of Peace-Keeping Operations in the UN Secretariat) in New York on 11 January 1994, which noted that a 'very important government official' had revealed plans to scare away the UN peacekeepers and for *interahamwe* militias, who had been training in camps outside the capital Kigali, to kill all the Tutsis in the city.[160] The information had come from a top-level organizer inside the *interahamwe* militia itself, and included horrific details such as a planned killing rate of 1,000 every twenty minutes.[161] Melvern reports that the US had argued for a small force to save money. Further:

> Under the terms of the [Arusha] Accords the peacekeepers were to ensure security throughout the country but the [Security] Council

decided that the peacekeepers should assist in ensuring the security of only the city of Kigali. Under the Accords, the peacekeepers were to confiscate arms and neutralize the armed gangs throughout the country. The US refused this provision and, mindful of the military fiasco in Somalia, insisted that the mission for Rwanda must be traditional peacekeeping, providing no more than a neutral buffer between two former enemies.[162]

As the crisis escalated in early 1994, UN Secretary-General Boutros Boutros-Ghali and the UN Security Council threatened to withdraw the UN's limited peacekeeping force if the 1993 Arusha peace agreement (of 1993) was not implemented – a bizarre move that failed to recognize that the now dominant Hutu extremists would actually be happy at such a withdrawal.[163] Security Council discussions focused on the war not the genocide. On 21 April 1994, in the midst of the genocide, the UN withdrew the bulk of what was in any case an inappropriately small peacekeeping force (and one focussed on Kigali), sending precisely the wrong signal to those perpetrating the genocide.[164]

After the Rwandan genocide, the international community effectively turned a blind eye to the damaging Rwandan and Ugandan invasions of the Congo and to the incitement of ethnic violence (notably by Ugandan forces) within that country. The focus was on the economic and political 'success stories' – the golden boys of Africa. Donors needed to point to success stories, and once large amounts of funding had been dispersed, this created a vested interest in insisting that this money had not been wasted. Rwanda and Uganda were devastating the DRC, yet Britain – the biggest bilateral funder for both Rwanda and Uganda – would not make their withdrawal a condition for continuing bilateral aid (in contrast to tougher sanctions on Mugabe, whose victims – as George Monbiot has pointed out – have included *white* people[165]). In particular, there was a conspicuous lack of sanctions on Uganda and Rwanda for their role in extracting conflict diamonds from the DRC. Meanwhile, Rwanda's activities in the DRC contributed to what Reyntjens calls 'a criminalization' of the Rwandan state and economy, and the suppression of opposition within Rwanda was allowed to pass with little international criticism, allowing grievances to fester and perhaps sowing seeds for renewed violence.[166] The lack of sanctions on Uganda and Rwanda over the DRC contrasted with the sanctions on Liberia in relation to its destabilizing role in Sierra Leone.[167] The latter had been encouraged by press reports that al-Qaida operatives in the Liberian capital of Monrovia had bought diamonds from the RUF.[168] Significantly, even the Liberian sanctions were weakened by richer countries' interests: China and France blocked timber sanctions for two years (until May 2003), reflecting their own substantial imports of Liberian timber.[169] Slightly earlier, in Sierra Leone, the NPRC military government of 1992–6 was able to present a façade of moral and financial probity in Freetown whilst tolerating and participating in increasingly violent forms of extortion elsewhere.[170]

During the conflict in Algeria in the 1990s, there was only weak pressure from UN bodies and other multilateral organizations in relation to the Algerian army's undemocratic rule and widespread abuses.[171] In fact, in 1994 Algeria secured the support of the IMF, the World Bank, the European Community and the G7 states to reschedule its debt – a package worth around $6,000 million. Key factors in this accommodation were Western fears of the 'Islamic peril' and its possible export to France in particular, combined with fears of mass migration to Europe if the Algerian regime collapsed. Journalist Chawki Amari commented, 'The generals are thus allowed to manage the crisis as they see fit – as long as they guarantee to keep it within their borders.' [172] On top of this, France, Spain, Italy and Portugal have been heavily dependent on Algerian oil and gas supplies, and there has been significant involvement in Algeria from Texas-based oil interests. Coming from desert areas away from the main conflict zones, these oil and gas supplies were unaffected by conflict. In fact, as Amari commented, 'European countries congratulate themselves on doing business with a partner so "reliable" that it succeeded in doubling exports in the middle of a civil war.'[173]

In many ways, the 'war on terror' is now reinventing Cold War-style impunity. Accommodations to abusive governments and groups, once done in the cause of anti-communism, are now routinely pursued in the cause of anti-terror. Sudan is just one example. Afghanistan is another. In November 2002, Human Rights Watch published a report highlighting human rights abuses (including torture) in western Afghanistan under a notorious Western-backed warlord, Ismail Khan.[174] The US commander in charge of coalition forces, Lt-Gen. Dan McNeill, responded that the US military would continue to work closely with Afghan warlords, stressing that they were providing stability in the absence of strong central government. Such relationships were forged when the US sought allies against the Taliban and have been bolstered by the need for physical protection for US Special Forces' compounds.[175]

Trade is another concern that frequently trumps human rights. Whilst developed countries can threaten abusive governments with sanctions, much less widely recognized is the fact that governments have sometimes threatened to impose their own sanctions – notably by restrictions on particular foreign multinationals – as means of softening criticism or watering down anti-corruption moves.[176]

In the early 1980s, the Reagan administration collaborated in the Guatemalan government's destructive counterinsurgency, giving covert CIA assistance to the Guatemalan government. Reagan's administration battled with the US Congress to restore (overt) military aid that had been cut from 1977.[177] An essentially genocidal project was presented – both nationally and internationally – as legitimate suppression of an insurgency.[178] Whilst a peace agreement was secured in 1996, human rights have continued to be some way down the list of international priorities. As so often before, economic reforms have taken precedence. In 2002, one senior donor indicated to me the prevailing international priorities:

> They [the government] are doing absolutely all what the IMF is asking for. They have very good macro-economic indicators. Even if the population is suffering more and more, statistically it looks like a paradise and it seems Guatemala is an excellent student. The only conditionality for an agreement with the IMF is the adoption of financial law – changing control of the Central Bank, of credit, of private banks. . . . The World Bank is trying to show it is very interested in the reduction of poverty. But how can you say that if what you are asking for is related to drastic economic reform which will affect the poorest people negatively? The model chosen is an old model – income through agricultural export products. . . . The international community of donors is giving a maximum of 700 million. The International Financial Institutions at least 1.3 billion. You can see the difference. Yes, it's a loan, but it's for the next government to pay back, so who cares?

This IFI funding should be seen alongside the funding that government actors can secure from criminal networks with which they are sometimes intimately involved.[179] A careful study of EU policy and democratization in Latin America concluded:

> [T]he degree to which the E.U. prioritized a defensive commercial interest gave Latin American governments a riposte to European strictures on human rights and democracy that, in practical terms, weakened the E.U.'s negotiating purchase. . . . European policymakers worked only on a basic assumption that the extension of market structures was likely to be broadly favourable to the extension of democratic rights.[180]

It should be noted that when it comes to tackling war economies, judicial action has been extremely limited. The Security Council did not refer the situation in Darfur to the ICC until March 2005 and the subsequent investigation took fully twenty months. Well-known sanctions-busters like arms trafficker (and former Soviet military officer) Victor Bout – who has supplied arms to conflicts in Angola, DRC and Liberia, for example – have retained virtual impunity; Bout's impunity will not have been harmed by his role – in contravention of Bush's executive order – as a supplier for the US military and its contractors in Iraq and for NATO forces in Afghanistan. By the end of 2004, one Bout company, Ibris, had flown more than 140 flights into Iraq for the US military and its contractors.[181]

Part of the motivation for China's weapons export drive may be a desire to find alternative sources of profit for a People's Liberation Army that is increasingly being forced out of its money-making domestic enterprises as China pursues economic reforms at home.[182] One can condemn (and one *should* condemn) the flow of arms to crisis zones from the former Soviet Union and from China, or the involvement of South African mercenaries in many African conflicts.[183] It is also important to understand how such flows may be (adaptive, abusive) responses to political changes within militarized countries, providing an outlet for potential 'spoilers' of domestic reforms within Russia, China, South Africa and elsewhere. Thus, the project of understanding (and making provision for) potential spoilers should not be limited to crisis-affected countries but should also be extended to richer countries where powerful actors may be seeking solutions for some of their own problems – or at least tolerating processes that offer such (damaging) solutions.

Concluding Remarks

The dualities of the good and the pure versus the bad and the dirty are very questionable. In general, a 'transition from war to peace' is likely to represent a realignment of political interests and a readjustment of economic strategies, rather than a clean break from violence to consent, from theft to production, or from repression to democracy.[184] Historically, the evolution of both democracy and capitalism was inextricably linked with violence of various kinds. Charles Tilly famously argued that state-formation is inseparable from warfare – in particular, from the need to raise taxes for warfare and the need to grant representation to tax-payers.[185] Charles Taylor's 'progress' from state official to rebel to President shows some of the continuities between peace and war. Before leading a predatory rebellion in Liberia, Taylor had escaped from a US prison where he was serving sentence for fraud. He subsequently rose to the status of rapacious warlord and eventually became President of Liberia.[186]

If war is *functional*, then peace will have to offer alternative routes to goals (perhaps respect or money or some other goal) that can be achieved through war. Even if war only holds out the *promise* of benefits, peace will have to be equally or more alluring. This way of thinking about peace is rather different from conceptualizing peace either as victory or as a compromise between warring factions.

The diverse aims of those involved in warfare (and in crimes during war) should be taken into account by those who are seeking to intervene in some way, whether such intervention takes the form of emergency aid, of attempts to broker a peace, or of rehabilitation efforts. Rather than simply concentrating on negotiations between the 'two sides' in a war, it is helpful to try to map the benefits and costs of violence for a variety of parties and to seek to influence the calculations they make. This can include attempts to reduce the economic benefits of violence (for example, through sanctions such as freezing bank accounts), to increase the economic benefits of peaceable activities (for example, through the provision of employment and more geographically even forms of development), and to reduce the legal (and moral) impunity that may be enjoyed by a variety of groups (for example, by publicizing abuses, initiating international judicial proceedings, and making aid explicitly conditional on human rights observance). We need to investigate what international interventions (aid, diplomacy, publicity, investment, trade) are doing to accelerate or retard the processes by which people fall below the protection of (national and international) law.

Protection can be improved by lobbying powerful governments to give genuine priority to human rights – in other words, holding these governments to account for their fine statements. Gaining clarity on this issue means questioning whether the policies of these governments have actually *failed* just because widespread suffering has occurred. A coordinated approach, using the UN, remains important. If Iraq shows all too clearly the dangers of unilateral or bilateral action, a longer-term trend in Sudan brings out a less obvious reason why a coordinated international approach is essential. The early 1990s saw major Western governments adopting an increasingly hostile attitude to the Sudanese government after Sudan's opposition to the 1991 Gulf War with Iraq and concerns over international terrorism compounded concerns over man-made famine in the south. But in many ways this drove Khartoum further into a Middle Eastern sphere of influence and also opened the way for a much closer relationship with China and Malaysia, particularly over oil. Massive human rights abuses proved perfectly compatible with this new balance of power. Addressing continuing abuses demands major diplomatic pressure on, and from, China and Russia in particular.[187]

Within a simple 'greed' framework, peace may come to be seen as a largely technical exercise – a question of altering the incentives for rebellion (notably, controlling the international trade in certain lucrative commodities). Trade controls do have an important role to play, but in peacebuilding it is vital to take politics seriously. This includes tackling the grievances that have fuelled violence and the agendas of a range of actors (again, not only the 'rebels') who may be interested in the perpetuation of various kinds of violence.

Along with economic and political agendas, psychological factors (and the psychological functions of violence) also have to be taken seriously. This means taking a holistic view of motivations and, correspondingly, of incentives. Whether for a warlord or an ordinary fighter, respect may be a more fundamental goal even than money, and money may be important for the respect it implies or facilitates. Sometimes the greatest care may need to be extended to those who have themselves been most uncaring. One UN worker in Sierra Leone said to me:

> In a way, what young people want, including rebels, is to be loved. If you look at the kids who come back to the Interim Care Centres, when they arrive they are aggressive. The really good care-givers are very good at defusing that. They are very nice to them, providing a degree of emotional stability. You can see the change.

'Behind the hatred', as British singer-songwriter Morrissey noted of 'The boy with the thorn in his side', 'there lies a murderous desire for love.' However, it would be naïve – and logically inconsistent – to imagine that those who have changed for the better because of a better environment cannot, in different circumstances, revert to a more violent incarnation.

As with respect, the role of excitement in warfare has also often been neglected. Commenting on UNDP demobilization plans in Sierra Leone in 1995, one very experienced British aid worker stressed to me the importance of employment – in whatever field – that offered some excitement: 'There's no realism about demobilization. Expatriates have [swimming] pools, and say, "Give us your gun and we'll give you a hammer." What kind of bribe are you going to give them? It is more exciting to fight than to be a carpenter. You've got to give people something that gives them an adrenalin kick.'

Another kind of reward for peace is to offer some kind of *political* benefits in terms of access to political power and changes in the law. This is in many ways a traditional way of thinking about – and engineering – peace in a civil war context. In Sudan, political rewards for the rebel SPLM/A – especially the promise of a referendum on independence – helped to make a north–south peace possible. In the context of Sierra Leone's civil war, a number of analysts have highlighted the importance of dealing with political and structural economic grievances.[188] This is also part of taking seriously the 'R' – reintegration – in DDR.

In contrast to the view of war and peace as *total opposites*, previous chapters have made it clear that war will rarely if ever represent either total collapse or unlimited conflict. War may be a *system* as much as a contest, and, conversely, peace may itself be quite violent. Both these qualifications have important implications for ending civil wars and reconstructing economies and societies.

While those on the political right have tended to condemn the state as anti-market, those on the left have often condemned the state as the oppressive tool of elites. Yet complex emergencies have frequently arisen from a partial collapse of the state, and it is important to think about how to put states back together so that they can provide physical and social security to their citizens. Improving the conditions of civil servants, police and soldiers can help to rein in corruption and can help states to harness their own economies for taxation and development; crucially, it can also help to tackle the problem of counterinsurgencies that implode into soldiers' or militias' attacks on civilians.

Development is often seen as providing some kind of insulation against conflict, and it is true that developed countries are relatively unlikely to experience civil war. Even so, it is always important to ask what kind of development has occurred, how this pattern of development may have fed into conflict, and whether an old dysfunctional mode of development is being revived in the aftermath of a war. In other words, there are grave dangers in reinventing a wheel that has already fallen off. The role of structural violence and of peacetime violence in creating conditions for war implies a need, in the aftermath of a war, to re-form a state, to re-form an economy, and to reorient development. This means taking grievances seriously, including the grievances of rebels and other groups in society.

The fact that violent groups often have shared goals and shared needs (for money, status, belonging, security) underlines the need to think of conflict resolution not only as a compromise between two divergent positions (and a zero-sum game) but as the simultaneous provision of what both sides need. This is one implication of work by John Burton, who sees conflict as an attempt to meet basic human needs not being met in peacetime.[189] Patterns of development and reconstruction that meet the needs of ordinary people – whether these are needs for resources, for education or for security – will tend to weaken the position of warlords, extremist politicians and faction leaders who offer to meet these needs through more violent means. Such measures can narrow the space for the greedy manipulation of grievances.

If the need to tackle underlying causes has been stressed in this chapter, so too has the importance of not provoking a dangerous backlash. There is some tension between these two suggestions: the more fundamental the social and political reform, the more incentive there may be for a backlash. What has too often been missing in international interventions is any sustained analysis of the social and political forces within a given society and of what kinds of change are possible and realistic in any given context. Such a project might be seen as giving comfort to autocrats. But sometimes *very significant* change will be realistic. Whilst nurturing democratic strands can make a difference to the power balance within a country, imposing sudden change without considering the groups who will be threatened has proven extremely hazardous. Military conquest is one form of imposition likely to create a backlash.

It is one thing to say that certain things are desirable – democracy, self-determination, human rights, justice. But how do you secure consent for them? Mansfield and Snyder are surely right to stress the importance of considering 'golden parachutes' (which might take the form of jobs or pensions) which could help clear the dangerous road to democracy by discouraging elites from the often-favoured strategy of appealing to nationalism or ethnic violence.[190] If you cannot secure consent for democracy, self-determination, and justice, how vigorously or hastily should you promote them? It may be highly risky to push for quick elections without significantly defusing ethnic tensions or taking steps to disarm and discourage groups who may be threatened by this process. What is your moral authority, moreover, as a promoter of morality among others, and how will perceptions of you impact on outcomes?

Using immunity to prosecution as a way of making peace more attractive than war has to be balanced against the need for some kind of justice and some kind of erosion of impunity. Using economic or political rewards to make peace more attractive than war has to be balanced against the dangers of institutionalizing corruption, neglecting grievances in the wider society, and even exacerbating these grievances. The dangers of a backlash also need proper consideration.

Balancing the needs and desires of civil society against the needs and desires of combatants and warlords may look like a 'zero-sum' game.

Balancing the need for reform against the dangers of backlash also appears to have elements of the 'zero-sum' game – or at least of the impossible dilemma. But the intelligent injection of resources can make a difference, helping to break free from the 'zero-sum' game and helping to secure the political space for reform. Programmes of austerity tied to liberalization in many ways do the opposite, and have proven particularly dangerous in moments of political transition. The need to move beyond a 'zero-sum' framework is underlined by Galtung's insight that conflict resolution is not simply about compromise; it is also about creative solutions that change the parameters of conflict and change the way people think.[191]

The injection of funding into post-Second World War Germany under the Marshall Plan is a successful model that has not subsequently been followed. Indeed, there has often been a contrast – noted by Menkhaus in relation to Somalia, for example[192] – between the very large sums spent on emergency relief and then the very small sums spent on rehabilitation once the cameras (and perhaps the international peacekeepers) have gone away. Such neglect of reconstruction may sow the seeds of future conflict, as when Russia failed to revive the Chechen economy after the war of 1994–6.[193]

Some of Collier's later work (with colleagues at the World Bank) is relatively helpful here. Collier, Elliott et al. found that the effect of socially inclusive policies in promoting growth in post-war countries has been significantly greater than the effect of macro-economic policies. They went on to suggest that such policies send a signal that the government intends to abide by the spirit of a peace settlement, and that this may help reassure investors that their investments will not be sabotaged by renewed conflict. In turn, growth insulates against conflict, especially growth in post-war countries. Aid usually falls during a civil war, but donors usually increase aid substantially in the first couple of post-war years (when publicity and goodwill are high); however, aid then tends to fall to below normal levels towards the end of the first decade. Collier, Elliott et al. say substantial aid during that first decade is crucial, and that it is unhelpful for the UN typically to see post-war interventions as two-year operations.[194]

In their book *Africa Works*, Chabal and Daloz point to what they call 'the politics of the mirror'. This is basically the system – beginning under colonialism and often continuing after independence – where elites in poor countries may appear to go along with the priorities of powerful foreign governments whilst simultaneously giving priority to private accumulation and to preserving power for themselves. Today, this may mean flattering external donors with the apparent pursuit of privatization, democratization, financial orthodoxy, and so on; and foreign governments and international financial institutions have often been content to accept the image or illusion of progress towards these goals. However, the reality may be very different. Just as privatization may sometimes be a way of transferring national assets to elite private groups, so also an apparent process of democratization may mask the arming of private militias designed to derail democracy – as, notably, in Rwanda. So long as policy is discussed in the manner critiqued by Clay and Schaffer – with a rigid distinction between policy (good) and implementation (a problem) – it can be relatively easy for local elites to get away with such tactics. Clay and Schaffer's analysis of development policy has much broader implications: for a whole range of international interventions before, during and after complex emergencies, we need to take very seriously their plea that 'obstacles to implementation' be taken into account in the design of policy.[195]

Let us suppose that you are lost and thirsty in the Arizona desert and you see a watering hole in the distance. The obvious course of action would seem to be to walk directly towards it. But the obvious is not always the best. In this case, you might end up falling directly into a Grand Canyon lurking (hypothetically) between you and your goal. Anticipating and negotiating obstacles along the way is a fundamental part of everyday life – and 'designing peace' should be no different.

9

Conclusion

In the aftermath of a war, paying insufficient attention to grievances tends to encourage the kind of reconstruction that ends up reconstructing the grievances that originally fuelled the conflict. Mindful of this danger, the current study has stressed the need to pay attention to longer-term political, economic and social grievances, as well as the grievances that soldiers may acquire in the course of a war.

Rather than necessarily contradicting the 'rational actor' framework, the book's exploration of emotional factors in violence is intended to complement it. We have seen that 'evil' is not a very useful way of explaining atrocities. A key danger with this approach is that it feeds into the view – integral to the 'war on terror' and many misguided counterinsurgencies – that evil must be rooted out and physically destroyed. The counterproductive 'war on terror' is one example where locating the source of the problem as some kind of extrinsic evil is unhelpful; understanding the West's role in nurturing and then rekindling terrorism offers much more room for manoeuvre in devising solutions. Further, when violence is depicted – à la Kaplan – as a kind of mindless evil, this can feed into a sense of apathy and hopelessness, where whole areas of the world may be deemed hardly worth bothering with.[1]

However, there is something about the concept of evil that is not so easily banished. In the middle of a horrible human disaster, I think, you can almost feel it. Perhaps it is the sense that anything can be done, that there are no consequences for bad actions, that abusers are emboldened by each other, that a particular group of people has no rights, and that violence may even be fun.[2] Anyone who has ever seen or experienced bullying at school – or taken part in it – will have at least some sense of how this works.

This kind of environment reminds us of why it is so important to register protest at early human rights abuses, and indeed at the language that paves the way for physical abuses.[3] Fascist and racist groups seem to like to send out 'feelers' (for example, in their use of dehumanizing language about particular targets) which serve the purpose of testing how much these abusive groups can get away with, how much they can abolish people's humanity in words before they do it in deeds, how much they can take away their rights before they take away their lives. Glover's study of the process of brutalization underlines the importance of addressing early indignities in an abusive process.[4] For those who see violence as the work of 'the others', the 'evil ones' or 'the savage ones', Christopher Browning's warning in *Ordinary Men* is worth heeding:

> There are many societies afflicted by traditions of racism and caught in the siege mentality of war or threat of war. Everywhere society conditions people to respect and defer to authority, and indeed could scarcely function otherwise. Everywhere people seek career advancement. In every modern society, the complexity of life and the resulting bureaucratization and specialization attenuate the sense of personal responsibility of those implementing official policy. Within virtually every social collective, the peer group exerts tremendous pressure on behaviour and sets moral norms. If the men of [the Nazis'] Reserve Police Battalion 101 could become killers under such circumstances, what group of men cannot?[5]

Alarmingly, we cannot really know whether our relatively moral behaviour in some relatively peaceful setting (if I may give myself and the reader the benefit of the doubt) is due to our moral scruples, or whether it stems from the likelihood of punishment – we would not know until the possibility of punishment was taken away, perhaps being replaced by a reward.

Failure and Its Failings

This book has stressed the need to be suspicious of the idea of 'failure' (as well as the related ideas of chaos, breakdown and tribal anarchy). What objectives are being achieved amidst apparent failure, chaos and breakdown? There is a pressing need to look at the diverse strategies of all involved. In the aftermath of a famine or a war, it is natural to ask the question: what went wrong? But it is also important to ask: what went right? Or to put it more neutrally in a simple but useful formula, 'What happened and why?'[6] This may sound obvious, but is actually rather different from the habitual emphasis on all the 'obstacles to implementation', all the reasons, constraints, condemnations and excuses that are routinely deployed to explain why things did not turn out 'as planned', a habit that generates an answer as consistent as it is unhelpful: namely, that all the bad people somehow – and somehow unexpectedly – got in the way of all the good people.

What are the diverse agendas of a range of actors creating a particular pattern of events? Who benefits from genocide and from racism more generally? Aid organizations may survive and even prosper in circumstances where their assistance is not very helpful. The containment of a (severe) crisis may be a success for donors anxious to limit refugee flows. Then there are those who actively profit from war and famine: these may be international arms traders or local military leaders who may use a war to justify their control of central government or their control of resource-rich areas; they may also be ordinary people who may see war as a short-cut to the benefits (money, status, power, even marriage) that development has perhaps failed to produce.[7]

Even counterproductive military operations (such as raids on civilians which make them more radical) should not be quickly dismissed as 'failures', particularly if continued war means continued profits or if violence is somehow exciting or if the prolongation of war facilitates the suppression of opposition and free speech in some kind of prolonged 'state of emergency'. Even the victims of a war or a famine – often refugees and displaced people – may have some degree of success in pursuing their own economic strategies in the midst of crisis, and it is important to understand what these strategies are if proper assistance is going to be provided.

If many people are achieving their goals even in the midst of disasters, we need to look at the reasons why disasters may not have negative consequences for them. This raises the issue of impunity. Local actors may be able to carry out acts of violence with little fear of punishment. Part of the reason is the 'cover' that war provides for human rights abuses, the spurious but significant 'legitimacy' that it is sometimes seen as bestowing on the suppression of political opposition, on violence against particular ethnic groups and even on violence against women and children. Again, within a climate of abuse, good behaviour may be punished and bad behaviour rewarded.

At the other end of the scale from impunity is not only justice but accountability: both at the local and national level, the presence or absence of democratic structures is likely to have a powerful impact on the degree of impunity that operates. To what extent is the international system democratic and accountable? Having five permanent members of the Security Council who can veto Security Council resolutions is hardly democratic. What sanctions exist – or should exist – for a failure to remedy humanitarian crises?

Civil wars have been dismissed as manifestations of mindlessness and madness, but even madness has its logic and its functions. Mental illness and psychosomatic symptoms may serve all kinds of functions for an individual, even as they cause great distress. One approach to healing is to try to render these damaging strategies *unnecessary* – by removing the problem or problems to which they are in some sense a solution. Similarly, ameliorating war and famine will be assisted if we think not only of combating them or relieving them but of rendering them unnecessary: in other words, if we attempt to put it place structures of support, status and security which will mean that people do not feel compelled to resort to damaging others (or themselves) in order to meet their needs. This includes not only ordinary citizens but also elites who may try to meet economic, social and political threats through abusive 'coping strategies'.[8] Perhaps the most pressing challenge for those attempting to facilitate peace is to try to nurture a society where normal human desires can be met without resort to violence and where, as a result, those who would try to manipulate these desires for violent ends are denied the space in which to operate.

It has recently become quite fashionable to say that 'greed' is driving civil wars, and this motive is not to be underestimated (particularly among elites). However, the word is unhelpful if we are trying to understand the abuses of those who are themselves caught up in an abusive system or the varied violence of those who themselves feel powerless in relation to some wider system of oppression, neglect and exploitation. A big step forward is reconstructing – or more often constructing – a state that can provide economic and physical security to all its citizens. A more general intellectual challenge is to take the various prevailing explanations of conflict – ethnicity, greed, and so on – and to investigate how these phenomena can themselves be explained. Even a motive like 'revenge' is hardly a fixed quantity: one man, who had had his leg amputated and was living in very bad conditions in the shamefully neglected amputees' camp in Freetown, Sierra Leone, said to me, 'The end of the conflict depends on the victims getting long-term benefit so that their relatives do not feel bad. If they go on struggling, what they will do is to revenge.' Greed feeds into grievance in complicated ways – and vice versa. For example, when a soldier or a rebel or a young man walking the streets is stigmatized as criminal or animal, he may be tempted to behave in ways that conform with this description. The victim may turn into a bully and an exploiter.[9] Of course, he may not be purely a victim, but shame is an unreliable route to reform, and humiliating a humiliator is likely to be as counterproductive as it is tempting.[10]

At present, interventions (for example, humanitarian aid; disarmament, demobilization and reintegration schemes; drives for democracy and/or market liberalization) tend to give too little attention to the functions that are served by dysfunctional phenomena like civil wars, famine, corruption, and so on. As a result, even well-meaning interventions are highly susceptible to appropriation, hijacking, distortion, subversion, and so on. In particular, international actors have focused excessively on what Bayart calls the '*pays legal*' – the formal institutions that are most readily visible and that tend to conform most closely to donors' favoured agendas – often ignoring the '*pays réel*'.[11] Elites who are threatened by peace and / or democracy have many times manipulated criminal economies and ethnic antipathies behind the scenes – subverting what are often more visible (if frequently illusory) signs of progress.

Also important to understand are the ways that violence is used to generate its own legitimacy – whether this is through fostering 'extremism', through making international law seem an irrelevance, or through redistributing shame from perpetrator to victim. That process can also be reversed through interventions that *delegitimize* violence and abuse. Drawing particularly on their fieldwork in Sierra Leone in 2000–1 in the area north of the Freetown–Bo road and adjacent to RUF-controlled territory, Archibald and Richards suggest not only that there is a new receptiveness to the idea of human rights but also that this needs to be encouraged and consolidated by aid practices which make these rights plausible and real.[12]

Language

A second major theme in the book has been *language*. What are the systems of language that surround complex emergencies, the words that surround what you might call these non-breakdowns? This issue involves not just the media (local and international) but also aid agency discussions (including early warning, needs assessment and evaluation), UN statements, government statements, international laws and declarations, and academic contributions.

In what ways has language contributed to or prolonged complex emergencies?[13] What statements, views and complaints (for example, against multinationals, arms manufacturers or states) are getting lost in the fashionable focus on 'rebel greed'? Are processes of forcible asset-transfer legitimized, for example, when famine is defined as starvation or war as a battle to win? Are we just throwing language at the problem? What kinds of false understandings and counterproductive interventions are ushered in when we aim a term like 'war' at such a wide variety of phenomena as criminal collusion, violent economic exploitation, genocide or one-sided international attacks? Terms like 'safe areas', 'empowerment', 'targeting' the most needy, 'protection by presence', and even the word 'peace' itself have often given the impression that fundamental problems were being tackled when in fact they were not.

Genocides have frequently been pursued in the name of genocide prevention: that is, the prevention of the genocide allegedly being plotted by the victim group. For those in immediate fear of their lives – and often heavily dependent on state propaganda for the definition of rational self-interest – how much more susceptible are they to the message that they must kill or be killed, or that only violence will keep the peace?

A recurring theme in the book has been the phenomenon of different actors in a sense agreeing to agree on a particular version of reality.[14] We have seen the dangers of collusion in the aid system, obscuring the causes of disasters and exaggerating the efficacy of relief – distortions that may also be favoured by states abusing their own people. We have seen various parties agreeing to depict war as 'ethnic' or as a straight fight between government forces and rebels. We have noted Chabal and Daloz's discussion of the 'politics of the mirror', which takes us back to local elites giving the appearance of acceding to internationally endorsed goals like peace, democracy and free markets, but working behind the scenes in favour of ethnic conflict, authoritarian rule and the creation of private monopolies. Rwanda, Sudan and Indonesia are among the governments that have claimed to be pursuing laudable goals like peace and democracy, whilst simultaneously encouraging the growth of militias designed to undermine these goals.

Most of these collusions and covert operations – in whatever sphere – have tended to shut out the voices of disaster victims. A key task for the researcher and the policy-maker – as Foucault would argue – is to bring to light these hidden or excluded views and visions. But those who do so may be seen as a significant threat – both to material interests and to comforting belief systems (both of which may depend on the ready identification of a particular enemy). A further disincentive to non-conformity is that in a crisis the best way to insulate yourself from persecution – whether as a rebel, witch, Tutsi, rogue international government or terrorist sympathizer – may be to join in the persecution.

Abusive systems will always be linked at some level with closed systems of thought. These closed systems (which are not simply mistakes but beliefs it is dangerous or disadvantageous to question) have to be understood and publicly challenged by outside researchers in support of people inside countries who are themselves trying to make this challenge. The forgotten and marginalized visions can themselves be self-fulfilling if they come sufficiently to prominence, so that it is, for example, the vision of ethnic nationalists that comes to seem far-fetched or even comical. Such revelations serve as useful 'counterpropaganda' to the propaganda of those who are manipulating the information that surrounds and ultimately prolongs particular crises.

Labelling extreme violence as 'evil' and 'other' may allow us to escape our own responsibilities in unfolding processes of violence. In an online discussion of corruption in Sierra Leone, one participant observed, 'When you subscribe to finger-pointing, three of your fingers are pointing at yourself.'[15]

A useful comparison can be made between disasters and infectious disease, which clearly serves important functions for the germs that flourish (perhaps temporarily) even as the patient falls sick. When it was recognized that disease had beneficiaries, that disease was often a complicated process of struggle between competing organisms rather than simply a set of symptoms, this realization facilitated major medical advances in the treatment of disease.

Yet every solution carries the seeds of a new problem. The manipulation of humanitarian aid and of sanctions are two examples. The backlash against 'democratization' is another. Just when 'enlightened opinion' was waking up to the dangers of 'conflict diamonds' and 'conflict timber' (dubbed the 'logs of war'), some governments in resource-rich countries were waging violent campaigns against ordinary people involved in these controversial trades. Philippe Le Billon has highlighted the Angolan government's violent deportation of tens of thousands of Congolese diamond diggers after its military victory over UNITA, as well as the Cambodian government's campaign to drive illegal loggers out of this sector in 1999.[16] All this underlines the need – again, as in medicine – to monitor and anticipate side-effects and to build them into the design (or re-design) of the intervention.

The need to be wary of every solution – and to think carefully about the relationship between war, crime and peace – is rather beguilingly touched on in an entry in a US competition where children were asked to come up with deep thoughts. One child wrote: 'If we could just get everyone to close their eyes and visualize world peace for an hour, imagine how serene and quiet it would be when the looting started.'

Notes

Introduction

1 Macrae and Zwi, p. 21.
2 Duffield, de Waal and the current author have been labelled as 'complex emergency theorists' (Edkins; Devereux).
3 On the latter problem, see Albala-Bertrand.
4 I still use the phrase.
5 Melvern, 2001, 2004a.
6 That vagueness has also sometimes been politically useful for aid agencies seeking not to offend host governments; no term is without its hazards.
7 IASC Working paper on Definition of Complex Emergencies, Inter-Agency Standing Committee Secretariat, New York, 9 December 1994, in OCHA, 1999. This definition was repeated in OCHA's 2003 'Glossary of Humanitarian terms (in Relation to Protection of Civilians in Armed Conflict)'.
8 OCHA, 1999.
9 *Joint Evaluation*.
10 Macrae and Zwi also link complex emergencies to 'the breakdown of the state' (p. 21).
11 See, notably, Duffield, 1994b.
12 Stern.
13 Oliver Burkeman, 'US says it will hunt down terrorists', *Guardian*, 14 May 2003.
14 Woodward, 2003, p. 67.
15 Woodward, 2003.
16 Galtung, 2004; and talk at Graduate Institute for International Studies, Geneva, 1 December 2006.
17 Bangura; see also Mkandawire, 2002.
18 Lary.
19 Adorno et al.; see also Moravia.
20 On this, (and especially Melanie Klein's work on preserving the image of the 'good mother'), see, for example, Likierman.
21 Lary. Part of the process of brutalization is that humans have a need to justify things they have done, making it easier to repeat them or to escalate the abuse (Glover). In his book *Hitler's Army*, Omer Bartov (2000) pointed to the *demand* for racist propaganda at the Russian front – notably to provide justification for atrocities already committed. Browning notes that for the Nazi's Reserve Police Battalion 101 in Poland, the killing became progressively easier (Browning, 1993).
22 Mamdani, 2001. Das notes that in a panic 'aggressors can experience themselves as if they were victims' (p. 109). Conversely, victims may be seen as the aggressors. For example, even when Sikhs took shelter in their temples during attacks by militant Hindus in Delhi in 1984 after the assassination of Prime Minister Indira Gandhi, rumours held that the Sikhs had amassed a vast weaponry there and would launch an attack from these temples (Das).

23 See, particularly, Marriage.
24 Woodward, 1995.
25 Collier, 2000. See Kelsall.
26 Keen, 1991a and 1994. See also Keen, 1998.
27 Collier, 1995.
28 Relevant texts include Duffield, 1994b; de Waal, 1994; and Reno.
29 Clay and Schaffer.

Chapter 1 War

 1 Uvin.
 2 Compare Galtung, 1996.
 3 See, for example, Deak. Arendt notes also that the mass persecutions in the Soviet Union were economically crippling.
 4 Duffield, 1994b.
 5 For a more detailed discussion, see Keen, 2006.
 6 *On War*, chapter 2, J.J. Graham translation at *www.clausewitz.com/CWZHOME/ VomKriege2/BK1ch02.html*.
 7 Fallows.
 8 See, for example, Keen, 1998; Kaldor.
 9 Apparently important to the rebel Renamo in Mozambique, for example, was that its violence should be seen to lack rationale and should be beyond comprehension or the belief that it could be managed or controlled (Wilson, 1991).
10 For a notorious example, see Kaplan, 1994a.
11 Turton.
12 Ibid.
13 Variations on this approach can be found in the work of Mark Duffield, William Reno, Alex de Waal and Mary Kaldor, for example.
14 When Foucault said that the Gulag should be looked at 'positively', he did not, of course, mean to convey any sense of approval; he meant looking at the Gulag as something that served certain purposes. That is also the approach that is adopted in the explorations of war and famine undertaken in this book.
15 Foucault, 1980, pp. 135–6.
16 In line with Foucault's approach, writers like James Ferguson, Arturo Escobar, Robert Chambers (1983), and Edward Clay together with Bernard Schaffer have stressed that what looks like the failure of development in terms of improving welfare may actually represent a success for a range of groups with other agendas, including the maintenance of order, the exercise of control over target groups, the preservation and expansion of bureaucracies, and so on.
17 For an interesting discussion, see Allen, 1999.
18 Kalyvas.
19 This term is not easy to define but in West Africa is often used to refer to unmarried males (who may be teenagers or significantly older) who lack power at the village (or other local) level; this group has been widely recruited into military factions in many parts of the world.
20 Keen, 2005a; Dolan.
21 Putin won a 'green light' for abuses in Chechnya, in part, from cooperation in US-led anti-Taliban operations in Afghanistan (Anderson, 2007).
22 See, notably, Ken Silverstein, 'Official pariah Sudan valuable to America's war on terrorism', *Los Angeles Times*, 29 April 2005 (accessed at *www.globalpolicy.org/empire/ terrorwar/analysis/2005/0429sudan.htm*). Longstanding cooperation between US security services and Khartoum over intelligence for the 'war on terror' has been growing

closer (Moorehead; Lavergne and Weissman). According to US officials, Major-General Salah Abdullah Gosh, suspected of planning the vicious counterinsurgency in Darfur, was flown by the CIA in a private jet to Virginia for debriefing; and the US pressed the UN not to include Gosh on the list of people who should be subject to UN sanctions – on the expectation that Gosh will continue to supply information about al-Qaida suspects, a topic on which he gained inside information as Osama bin Laden's main escort during bin Laden's 1990–6 stay in Sudan (John Prendergast and Don Cheadle, 'Our friend, an architect of the genocide in Darfur. The U.S. sacrifices moral leadership when it cozies up to killers for snippets of counterterrorism information', 14 February 2006 [*www.crisisgroup.org/home/index.cfm?id=3949*]). In March 2006, Gosh secretly visited London to meet senior British officials (Peter Beaumont, 'Darfur terror chief slips into Britain', *Observer*, 12 March 2006).

23 Silverstein, 'Official pariah Sudan' (see n. 22).

24 See, for example, Keen, 2005a and 2006.

25 The boundaries between these benefits or functions are not rigid. Not only are the desire for money and political power intimately related to each other, but these motivations can be seen as two among many possible psychological motivations. In one sense, *all* motivations are psychological.

26 Keen, 1994.

27 The International Crisis Group noted in December 2003: 'The latest attacks occurred deep inside the Fur tribal domain, against unprotected villages with no apparent link to the rebels other than their ethnic profile' (ICG, 2003b, p. 19). As earlier during counterinsurgency operations in Bahr el Ghazal (and it is tempting to put counterinsurgency into inverted commas), this pattern of attacks has helped spread rebellion to new groups: 'The government's heavy-handed counter-insurgency campaign has facilitated a major recruiting drive for the rebels, as suggested by the scarcity of young men in the refugee and IDP camps' (ICG, 2004b, p. 9). There is a widespread belief that the Zaghawa (an ethnic group spanning the Chad–Sudan border) provided the bulk of SLA military strength; the risks of attacking well-armed and mobile Zaghawa encouraged a 'counterinsurgency' focus on attacking Fur and Massaleit civilians (ICG, 2005b).

28 Zur.

29 See, for example, Nick Paton Walsh, 'Russia's man in reign of terror in Chechnya', *Guardian*, 13 January 2004.

30 John Aglionby, 'Inside Burma: fear and repression', *Guardian*, 23 May 2006.

31 The balance can change over time. For example, the first reaction of the Peruvian army to Shining Path insurgency (which started in 1980) was a 'scorched earth' policy. This alienated the local peasantry. Both the state and the Shining Path tended to direct attacks at the peasantry rather than engaging in open combat. But the army was able to change tactics from the mid-1980s, in effect constructing a political alliance with the peasantry in the form of the peasant-based self-defence forces (an alliance that can be seen as a revival of the army–peasant alliance for land reform after 1968). Force was now used primarily against the Shining Path itself, with better intelligence and with the self-defence forces in the forefront of the military campaign (Gutierrez, 2005).

32 Berdal and Keen, 1997; Le Billon, 2001a; Somerville. Elements of cooperation did not prevent great ruthlessness in warmaking, with oil constituting a rather indivisible resource. Government forces were involved in renewed and ruthless war in 1998–2002, including depriving UNITA areas of relief and forcing people from these areas into government-controlled assembly areas and camps where conditions were appalling and death rates high (Messiant).

33 Ellis, 1995 and 1999.

34 Badcock; Amari.

35 Badcock; see also interview with Souaidia in Gordon Campbell, 'The French Connection', *New Zealand Listener*, 14–20 February 2004.

36 See, for example, Bring's discussion of Kosovo.

37 See, notably, Shearer.

38 Adebajo 2002a and 2002b.

39 During civil war in Colombia, guerrilla demands were initially directed mostly at large landowners; however, as these large landowners increasingly fled the area, guerrilla groups increasingly extorted resources from smaller farmers, something that tended to undermine the guerrillas' political support base (Richani, 1997 and 2002).

40 Compare Beneduce et al.

41 Archibald and Richards, 2002a, 2002b, 2002c; Peters; Fanthorpe.

42 Keen, 2005a.

43 Kriger; Mitra.

44 Dolan.

45 Miller, 1996.

46 See, particularly, Dolan, Zur, Allen 1997, Nordstrom.

47 Zur, p. 103.

48 Zur, p. 71.

49 Violence in Colombia has served a function in intimidating human rights organizations and deterring collective organization (see, for example, Lopez Levy).

50 Shawcross, 1996.

51 Isabel Hilton, 'The heavy price of feudal nostalgia', *Guardian*, 26 May 2005. Democratic parties have been only weakly supported from outside.

52 At the same time, many within the military have been benefiting from drugs trading links with the Taliban in Afghanistan, a nexus threatened by pressure from the US and apparently defended in the October 1999 military coup (Emdad-ul Haq).

53 ICG, 2005a, p. i. The 2005 north–south peace agreement effectively spells the end of the SSDF (seen by the SPLA as having collaborated with Khartoum). Some SSDF might qualify for integration into security structures or civil institutions (ICG, 2005a).

54 Insofar as a peace agreement implies democracy is coming, this may itself be an incentive for kicking out and intimidating populations that are likely to support the opposition. Darfur is a stronghold for the Umma party, rival for the National Islamic Front, which has dominated politics in different guises for a decade and a half. The danger that democracy can be a spur for ethnic cleansing was underlined by renewed attempts aggressively to populate the contested Abyei area (oil-rich and set for a referendum on inclusion in north or south) with northern Arab Misseriya, combined with a long policy of depopulating it of Ngok Dinka (ICG, 2003b).

55 Judah, p. 62; Dolan; Keen, 2005a.

56 Discussion in Keen, 2005a.

57 Nzongola-Ntalaja; ICG, 2006a.

58 See, for example, Rogier.

59 Gordadze, p. 190.

60 See, for example, Keen, 2006.

Chapter 2 'Greed': Economic Agendas

1 Douglas Farah, 'Al Qaeda cash tied to diamond trade', *Washington Post*, 2 November 2001; Global Witness, 2003; Keen, 2005a; Le Billon, 2006.

2 See, for example, Cohen, 2006, p. 5.

3 Duffield, 2001, p. 132.

4 For a recent investigation, see Menkhaus, 2003.

5 See, notably, Jean and Rufin.

6 Keen, 1998.
7 Kosovar Albanian resistance to Serbia was funded to a significant extent by an informal payroll tax on Kosovar Albanians working in Germany (Addison et al.). The Tamil diaspora has provided substantial funds for the Tamil Tiger rebels in Sri Lanka (ICG, 2006f). Diaspora politicians may be more extreme than the population remaining in a country and may even assert their identity through an extreme position (Collier, Elliott et al.). Betty Bigombe saw the Ugandan diaspora as seeking to undermine her mediation efforts in northern Uganda in 1994, arguing that it was the war that was helping most of them to stay overseas (talk at Centre for Humanitarian Dialogue, Geneva, 14 December 2006).
8 See, notably, Bradbury, 1995a.
9 Wilson (1991) noted this pattern in relation to Renamo in Mozambique.
10 Le Billon, 2001b, p. 571.
11 Le Billon, 2001b.
12 Collier, 2000.
13 See, for example, Collier and Hoeffler, 1999.
14 Highly unequal societies (e.g. Chile, Kenya) may not suffer a civil war (Collier, Elliott et al.). Grievances may meet with successful repression (Hutchful and Aning). Stability may be more likely when ethnicity cross-cuts with inequality (Stewart, 2000, 2004; Klugman).
15 Collier, Hoeffler and Roehner, p. 18.
16 Ibid.
17 Ibid.
18 See, for example, Gutierrez, 2003, on Colombia. This chapter highlights economic agendas in the Chechnyan conflict, but this conflict cannot be understood without understanding the mass deportation of Chechens under Stalin in 1944, for example (e.g. Lieven). Frances Stewart (2000, 2004) emphasizes 'horizontal inequality' as a key driver of civil wars; horizontal inequality refers to group perceptions of inequality – it may be based on inequality between regions, ethnicities, religious groups or classes. In many parts of Latin America, trade patterns have conspicuously fuelled grievances and grievance-led rebellions, and ethnic and class divisions have often significantly coincided. The lure of export production (including coffee) encouraged settlers to seize large areas of land across the continent – a process that laid the basis for long-term political struggles over land. In Nepal, rebellion seems to correlate geographically with inequality (Murshed and Gates). For a discussion of the relationships between grievances and the environment, see Homer-Dixon.
19 See, for example, Galtung, 1996.
20 Duffield, 2001.
21 For a recent example, see the film *Blood Diamond*.
22 Ross. Botswana seems to have benefited from its deep-mined diamonds, which appear to be easier for the state to harness for development. Fearon found that where valuable smuggled commodities like drugs or diamonds were prominent, wars were particularly long-lasting.
23 Keen, 1994, 1998, 2005a; Ballentine and Sherman.
24 On this, see Berdal, 2003.
25 Humphreys and Weinstein (p. 29) observe that 'the potential wealth that could be gained from lucrative natural resource industries in Sierra Leone was not a core concern for most fighters. Their concerns were typically more mundane, focused on ensuring personal security and meeting basic needs' (p. 29).
26 On this distribution, see Humphreys and Weinstein.
27 Dolan.
28 Those attracted to the rebellion also included chiefly families excluded from local office.

29 Some ECOMOG troops became involved in diamond-trading in Sierra Leone and were even accused of collaborating with rebels (Keen, 2005a).

30 See, for example, Fitzgerald.

31 Keen, 2005a; compare Wilson, 1991, on the Naprama civil defence movement in Mozambique.

32 MacGaffey et al.; Keen, 1994 and 2005a.

33 In the 1980s (before the Liberian civil war began in 1989), a senior procurement official in President Doe's military government was building up his private contacts with foreign companies. His name was Charles Taylor, and when he became a rebel, he used these contacts to establish lucrative exports of iron ore, timber and agricultural products from territory he controlled as a warlord. These exports, in turn, boosted his military power (Ellis, 1995 and 1999). When Charles Taylor became Liberian President in 1997 (resuming his career as a government official) he used the profits of his warlordism to bolster his system of political patronage.

34 Lary.

35 Kaldor; Van Creveld, 1991a, 1991b; Lary; Berdal, 2003; Jacquin-Berdal.

36 Berdal and Keen.

37 See Chris Dolan's excellent study; also Judah; Bigombe talk (see this chapter, note 7 above).

38 Dolan.

39 Rebellion in the West may also have provided some opportunities.

40 Tangri and Mwenda.

41 Judah; according to Bigombe, 'A battalion should have 500 men and women, but there were actually only 200. Commanders were not happy when the [1994] peace process started. They were making a lot of money' (see this chapter, note 7 above).

42 Le Billon, 2001a.

43 Somerville, pp. 34–6.

44 Global Witness, 1998, 1999; Le Billon, 2001a.

45 Gerschman.

46 Naomi Klein, 'Stark message of the mutiny', *Guardian*, 15 August 2003.

47 McCulloch.

48 Human Rights Watch, 2006.

49 Simpson.

50 Gutierrez, 2005.

51 Richani, 1997 and 2002. Again, compare Lary.

52 Richani, 2002.

53 Gutierrez, 2005. Somewhat similarly, US-led attempts to eradicate poppy crops in Afghanistan risk turning impoverished farmers towards the Taliban (e.g. James Astill, 'US plans war on al-Qaida's Afghan opium', *Guardian*, 24 November 2003).

54 ICG, 2006a.

55 There were also hidden transfers from other ministries.

56 Compare Scheper-Hughes on Brazil.

57 Somewhat similarly, the reliance of warring parties in Afghanistan on opium trading began during the Cold War era.

58 Gordadze, pp. 191–2.

59 Gordadze, p. 193.

60 Gordadze.

61 Nick Paton Walsh, 'Russia's man in reign of terror in Chechnya', *Guardian*, 13 January 2004.

62 Gordadze, p. 188.

63 Gordadze, p. 189.

64 Gordadze, p. 190.

65 Something similar occurred in Ukraine, for example.
66 Castells; Cottrell.
67 Castells; see also Stille on the relationship between the Italian state and the mafia.
68 Duffield, 1998a; Varese, 1994; compare also Shearer, 1998.
69 Shearer, 1998.
70 Mitra, p. 24.
71 Faludi, p. 322. In his book *Ordinary Men*, Christopher Browning analysed the motivations of Reserve Police Battalion 101 – just under 500 men who took part in the rounding up and shooting of Jews in Poland in 1942–3. Browning rejected the view that those who carried out atrocities were forced to comply; nor were they subject to any particular indoctrination. They were ordinary men, who did terrible things for a variety of quite ordinary motives. Careerism was important: most of the men wanted to continue to pursue a career in the police, and those who actually declined to shoot sometimes pointed, as an explanation, to their own well-established civilian careers outside the police force to which they could return. To some extent, we can see atrocity as the working through of bureaucratic organizations, rather than the collapse of discipline and organizations (compare also Bauman). The Great Famine in China was caused partly by state bureaucrats trying to give a good impression by exaggerating local food production and maximizing requisitions (Becker).
72 Faludi, pp. 331–2.
73 Coghlan et al.
74 Fabienne Hara, 'Hollow peace hopes in shattered Congo', comment in Observer Online, 7 July 2002 (*observer.guardian.co.uk/worldview/story/0,,751002,00.html*).
75 Ibid.
76 James Astill, 'Rwandans wage a war of plunder', *Observer*, 4 August 2002; see also Report of the Panel of Experts (DRC).
77 Astill, 'Rwandans wage a war of plunder' (as note 76); see also ICG, 2002.
78 Report of the Panel of Experts (DRC).
79 Tangri and Mwenda.
80 Ibid.
81 Ibid.
82 Report of the Panel of Experts (DRC).
83 Collier, Elliott et al. citing Graduate Institute of International Studies, 2001.
84 Report of the Panel of Experts (DRC).
85 The US was hoping to isolate Iran from the oil supply and at the same time to assist the commercial interests of the Saudi-US company Unocal, in which George Bush senior has had a significant interest. Largely as a result, the US was initially supportive of the Taliban, though this support was eroded as increasing weight was given to the Taliban's links to international terrorism, particularly after September 11, 2001 (Rubin).
86 Duffield, 1995, 1996, 2001.
87 Simon Tisdall, 'Beijing makes friends and riches in Africa', *Guardian*, 22 April 2005.
88 Personal communication, Adekeye Adebajo.
89 De Beers was also buying directly in Angola (Le Billon, 2001a).
90 Report of the Panel of Experts (Sierra Leone).
91 RAID.
92 Malone and Nitschke.
93 Robert Verkaik, 'Government inquiry into firms "fuelling Congo war" attacked', *Independent*, 13 November 2006.
94 Fairhead.
95 E.g. Bower.
96 Hawley.
97 Addison et al.

98 Andreas.
99 Malone and Nitschke.
100 Hawley.
101 Watkins.
102 Curtis, p. 202.
103 Human Rights Watch, 2002a.
104 Terry.
105 Human Rights Watch, 2002a.
106 Hutchinson.
107 Terry, pp. 161–2.
108 Human Rights Watch, 2002a
109 Ibid.
110 Keen, 2005a and 2005b.
111 Rampton and Stauber. I am grateful to Joanna Macrae for making the link between picking 'winners' and the 'war on terror'.
112. See Duffield, 2001.

Chapter 3 Combatants and Their Grievances

1 See, for example, Gilligan, and valuable work by the NGO Human Dignity and Humiliation Studies (*www.humiliationstudies.org*).
2 Speech available at *www.jewishvirtuallibrary.org/jsource/Holocaust/hitjew.html*.
3 Compare also Rhodes.
4 Kaplan, 1994a.
5 See Richards, 1996a.
6 Bangura.
7 See Keen, 2005a; Richards, 1996a. A survey of over a thousand ex-combatants from various factions found that the vast majority were uneducated and poor. Many had left school before the war because they were unable to pay fees or because schools had closed. Many had lost one or both parents before the start of the war. Promises of education were an important incentive to join the various factions, especially the RUF (Humphreys and Weinstein). On collapsing education, compare the study of DRC by Beneduce et al.
8 Keen, 2005a; see also Berman. Humphreys and Weinstein noted that the average education levels of fighters declined through the war. One of the 'attractions' of joining an armed group may be the prospect of getting access to women, including forcibly through rape (e.g. Maass; Wilson, 1991; Keen, 2005a; Humphrey and Weinstein). Schools and universities were frequently targeted for violence, though the desire for education was usually strong.
9 Mamdani, 1996; Skelt, p. 47; compare Lord on forced labour; CARE International.
10 Bradbury, 1995a, p. 41; Atkinson et al. The public humiliation and execution of chiefs and Muslim Imams is also noted by Muana (p. 79).
11 Compare Kiernan.
12 Atkinson et al.
13 'Profiles' in Lord, 2000.
14 Hobsbawm, p. 65
15 Hobsbawm, p. 58.
16 Lary, p. 89. The Nazis' SA stormtroopers harboured significant social grievances, and Hannah Arendt observed: 'Behind the blind bestiality of the SA [stormtroopers], there often lay a deep hatred and resentment against all those who were socially, intellectually, or physically better off than themselves, and who now, as if in fulfilment of their wildest dreams, were in their power' (Arendt, p. 453).

17 Zur, p. 107.

18 Betty Bigombe, talk at Centre for Humanitarian Dialogue, Geneva, 14 December 2006.

19 Girard, p. 2.

20 Discussion in Keen, 2005a.

21 Richards, 1996a. Variations on the use of atrocity to cement 'loyalty' have been noted elsewhere. See, for example, Wilson (1991) on Renamo rebels in Mozambique. In northern Uganda, a 12-year-old boy was captured by the rebel Lord's Resistance Army and made to kill another boy. He was told, 'If you try to escape, the spirit of that boy will follow you wherever you go and kill you.' The boy did not believe this, but said that others do, and that this was one reason the LRA could hold so many in its thrall (Judah, p. 62).

22 Lord, p. 15.

23 RUF, 1995, p. 12.

24 RUF's apology to the nation, delivered on SLBS (Sierra Leone Broadcasting Service), 18 June 1997 (*www.sierra-leone.org/rufapology.html*).

25 Act 3, Scene 1. The years of single-party rule under President Siaka Stevens and the All People's Congress party were something of a school for villainy.

26 Act 3, Scene 1. Compare also Ignatieff, 1993: 'How many times in the weeks ahead do I meet Croats at checkpoints who say: "They call us Ustashe [a Croatian organization that collaborated with the Nazis in the Second World War]. Well then, that is what we are"' (p. 24).

27 This hostility could be compounded by drugs. One teenage boy told of his participation in the January 1999 attack on Freetown: 'My legs were cut with blades and cocaine was rubbed in the wounds. Afterwards, I felt like a big person. I saw the other people like chickens and rats. I wanted to kill them.' Although the violence was often depicted as drug-fuelled anarchy, drugs were often manipulated in a calculating way, particularly in the use of cocaine to make fighters more aggressive; marijuana was sometimes used to calm fighters in the aftermath.

28 Compare also Adebajo, 2002a.

29 Women were commonly so accused in Somalia, especially of passing secrets from their husband's group to their father's (Farah).

30 Compare Bartov, 2000; Robben.

31 Dixon; see also Emizet on Zaïre/DRC.

32 Mamdani, 2001, p. 188; see also, for example, Rodgers.

33 Amari, 252.

34 Short.

35 Independent International Commission on Kosovo.

36 Robben.

37 Messiant.

38 Faludi, p. 330.

39 Ibid. Michael Bernhardt, witness to the My Lai massacre in Vietnam, commented: 'What people think of you back home don't matter . . . What matters is how the people around you are going to see you. Killing a bunch of civilians in this way - babies, women, old men, people who were unarmed, helpless – was wrong. Every American would know that. [But] this group of people [one's comrades] was all that mattered. It was the whole world. What they thought was right was right. And what they thought was wrong was wrong. The definitions for things were turned round' (Glover, pp. 59–60). In these circumstances, Bernhardt recalled, an objector could come to think that he was the crazy one. Sympathy for civilians was seen as unmanly, he said: 'In Charlie Company, cowardice and courage was all turned around. If you showed any sign of caring, it was seen as a sign of weakness. If you were the least bit concerned about the civilians, you were considered pathetic, definitely not a man' (Faludi, pp. 351–2). He added, 'If you can define your manhood in terms of caring, then maybe

we can come back from this' (Faludi, p. 352). Well before the My Lai massacre in Vietnam, Bernhardt challenged the bullies within his own military company; he found they backed off relatively quickly: 'They were typically bullies, who are actually cowards, terrible cowards. Just being there after a while was enough. It wasn't that they were afraid of me – I don't think I look that dangerous, now or then. It was almost like Mom looking over your shoulder, I guess. . .' (Faludi, p. 334). As Browning showed in his analysis of atrocities in Poland by the Nazi's Reserve Police Battalion 101, perpetrators have sometimes defined virtue in terms of doing one's job and supporting one's colleagues. Those few reserve police soldiers who refused to participate in massacres of Jews in Poland tended to emphasize later that they had been too weak to engage in killing, rather than that they had been too good. Not shooting was seen as leaving the 'dirty work' to one's comrades and implied criticism of one's own tight-knit unit stationed abroad, on whom one depended for contact and support (Browning, 1993). One witness to the incursion into Freetown in January 1991 by rebels and rogue government soldiers told me that within the fighting group: 'Someone carrying out atrocities may be hailed as a hero, as brave, so others may want to show they can do it.'

40 Faludi, p. 330.
41 Faludi, p. 337.
42 Faludi, p. 336.
43 Faludi, p. 337
44 Gordadze, p. 190.
45 Gordadze, p. 191.
46 See, for example, Messiant.
47 Lary.
48 Osiel, p. 196.
49 Osiel, p. 195.
50 Collier, Elliott et al.
51 Chaumba et al.
52 Brett.
53 ICG, 2004e.
54 Ibid.
55 Human Rights Watch, 2005a.
56 Jézéquel; Human Rights Watch, 2005a.
57 ICG, 2004e.
58 ICG, 2004e, p. 11.
59 Russell, p. 380
60 Russell, p. 378.
61 Russell, p. 379.
62 Russell, pp. 385–6.
63 Russell, p. 386.
64 Hunt, p. 253.
65 Hunt, p. 265.
66 Military disaster also fed into a search for internal enemies in Turkey during the First World War and in Cambodia under the Khmer Rouge.
67 Bartov, 2000, pp. 95–6.
68 Waite, quoted in Barbara Ehrenreich's foreword in Theweleit, p. ix.
69 Mamdani, 2001, p. 207.
70 Mamdani, 2001, p. 210.
71 Human Rights Watch/International Federation of Human Rights, pp. 60–1.
72 Mamdani, 2001, p. 203. Mamdani also notes that the leadership of clan militias during conflict in Somalia in the 1990s came from army commandos who had earlier been demoralized by defeat by Ethiopian forces in the Ogaden war of 1977–8.

73 Human Rights Watch/International Federation of Human Rights.
74 Human Rights Watch/International Federation of Human Rights, p. 60. Compare Chingono.
75 See, for example, Ahmed Rashid's book *Taliban*.
76 Kepel, pp. 136–7.
77 Kepel, p. 298. Other conflicts where jihadists came to play a key role included Chechnya and Kashmir.
78 Schirmer.
79 Ibid.
80 In Guatemala, the army's attempts to secure finance from various kinds of relationships with organized crime goes back even to the 1970s.
81 See, for example, Boyce.
82 Keen, 2003, p. 20.
83 For example, Gear, section 9.
84 Gear, section 2.
85 I am particularly grateful to Tim Allen for conversations in this area.

Chapter 4 Defining the Enemy

1 Gordadze, p. 194. Gordadze notes that while the older generation of Chechen leaders often have close personal and cultural ties to Russia, the Kremlin's attempt to eradicate this leadership has risked leaving in charge a generation that is more vehemently anti-Russian.
2 Keen, 2006.
3 ICG, 2004e, p. 7.
4 See, for example, Allen and Eade.
5 Barth.
6 One example of this came in Zaïre/Congo. Here, the Banyarwanda (a group of relatively recent Tutsi and Hutu immigrants from Rwanda) were often in conflict with local people, who resented their land acquisitions and access to political power. It was only the influx of Hutu militias and soldiers of the old Rwandan army after the 1994 Rwandan genocide (and the attacks by these groups on Tutsi Banyarwanda) that drove a wedge between Tutsis and Hutus within the Banyarwanda (Emizet).
7 A related argument has been made in relation to Chechnya (Tishkov).
8 For example, Tajfel.
9 Turton.
10 Arendt.
11 See, notably, Robinson and Gallagher.
12 For a good, short explanation, see Charles Tripp, 'Iraq: the imperial precedent', *Le Monde Diplomatique*, 13 January 2003.
13 Other imperial powers also used local power structures when it suited them (e.g. Nugent, p. 128).
14 Hobsbawm and Ranger.
15 Mamdani, 1996.
16 See also Johnson on hardship in central Sudan feeding into exploitation of the south (p. 5).
17 Prunier (1995) makes this point strongly.
18 Ibid.
19 Alison.
20 Prunier, 1995.
21 African Rights, 1994.
22 Prunier, 1995, p. 9.

23 See, for example, Nzongola-Ntalaja on Zaïre/DRC.
24 Bartov, 2000.
25 Nazism as a 'lesser evil' also had some attractions internationally.
26 This account draws principally on work by Rakiya Omaar of African Rights (Africa Rights, 1994), Gerard Prunier (1995), René Lemarchand, and a Joint Evaluation of Emergency Assistance to Rwanda. Other informative accounts include those by Gourevitch and Human Rights Watch/International Federation of Human Rights.
27 Alison.
28 Prunier, 1995.
29 Lemarchand.
30 Joint Evaluation of Emergency Assistance to Rwanda.
31 Prunier, 1995, p. 269; African Rights, 1994.
32 Paris.
33 Mansfield and Snyder, 2005.
34 Ibid. The partition of India shows how ethnic animosities maybe easier to stir up than to control.
35 Paris.
36 See, for example, Keen, 1994. In northern Somalia, a somewhat similar process of indiscriminate state-led violence from 1988 tended to radicalize – and to legitimize the exploitation of – the Isaaq ethnic group (Africa Watch, 1990).
37 The 'Arab/African' dichotomy in the media is an oversimplification obscuring that the victims are Muslim and dark-skinned (Mahmood Mamdani, 'Darfur Crisis', *Black Commentator*, 28 October 2004).
38 In Darfur, the government of Sudan has been successful in driving a wedge between the SLA/M-Abdel Wahid (Sudan Liberation Army/Movement-Abdel Wahid Mohamed Nour) (mostly Fur) and the SLA/M-Minni (Minawi) (mostly Zaghawa) – in part by playing on fears that the Fur are being used as cannon fodder for the project of a Greater Zaghawa State in Sudan and Chad (ICG, 2006b).
39 ICG, 2006b, p. 3
40 See discussion in Prunier, 2005.
41 ICG, 2006b, p. 4.
42 See, for example, Jonathan Steele, 'Darfur wasn't genocide and Sudan is not a terrorist state', *Guardian*, 7 October 2005.
43 Ryle.
44 ICG, 2004d, p. 1. The ICG report added that ever since 1989 the government of Sudan has 'encourage[d] the perception that if serious pressure is applied, it would be counter-productive, giving advantages to putative "hardliners" or even causing the regime to crack, leaving a failed state in its wake' (ibid.). This echoes patterns in Sierra Leone, for example, where some donors feared pressuring the government to rein in abuses could lead to a failed state (Keen, 2005a).
45 Fareed Zakaria, 'Rethinking Iraq: the way forward', *Newsweek*, 6 November 2006, pp. 22–9.
46 Adebajo, 2002b; Ellis, 1999.
47 Reyntjens.
48 Moynihan; see also Kaplan, 1994b.
49 Turton
50 See, notably, Woodward, 1995; Chossudovsky; Ignatieff, 1993.
51 Woodward, 1995; Ignatieff, 1993.
52 E.g. Woodward, 1995.
53 Woodward (1995) stresses that the common focus on ethnicity and identity in post-Cold War conflicts tends to distract from the continuing importance of class conflicts.

Unemployment has been a key factor in conflicts in the Balkans, and remains a desta-bilizing element (Woodward, 1995 and 2002).

54 See, for example, Campbell; Ignatieff, 1993; Ali and Lifschultz.
55 See, for example, Ali and Lifschultz. There were lots of (largely unheard) strands of Serb opinion (like the Serb Civic Council in Bosnia-Herzegovina) that denounced Serbian nationalists as fascists and that articulated a vision of a multiethnic Bosnia capable of upholding the rights of everyone. There were also sizeable secret networks of Serbs that assisted victims of ethnic cleansing (Campbell), just as in Rwanda there were many Hutus who tried to save Tutsis from the genocide (African Rights, 1994).
56 The ideology that portrays Serbs as eternal victims, and the role of the Orthodox church in promoting this ideology, is well discussed in Branimir Anzulovic's book, *Heavenly Serbia: From Myth to Genocide*. Perhaps the nearest thing to a total fabrication was the Nazi construction of the Jewish threat.
57 Malcolm.
58 Ibid.
59 Dekmejian.
60 Zur.
61 Horowitz, 2000, p. 195.
62 Berman.
63 For example, Glazer and Moynihan.
64 African Rights, 1994.
65 Ignatieff, 1993.
66 Belgrade, 25 August 1999.
67 Ignatieff, 1993.
68 As Bosnian Muslim leader Alija Izetbegovic put it, 'By their oppression the Communists created this longing among people to express their religious or national identity' (Malcolm, p. 219).
69 Uvin. Abuses against Hutus in neighbouring Burundi were also a factor.
70 Mamdani, 2001, p. 233.
71 Bartov, 2000; Arendt. Alongside the Khmer Rouge's adoption of the language of purity (associated with Khmer culture) was a corresponding language of dirt and pollution (corresponding to Western, Chinese and Vietnamese influences) (Robins and Post). Participating in ethnic violence may sometimes be a way of proving that you are not part of the group being victimized.
72 At the global level, Western isolationism and hostility to immigration has been fed by fears of the expanding population in the developing world.
73 Bardhan.
74 Ibid.
75 For example, Keen, 1994.
76 African Rights, 1994; Prunier, 1995; also Platteau and André.
77 Uvin.
78 Mamdani, 2001.
79 Verwimp, p. 29.
80 Uvin.
81 Other European countries had also experienced major social and economic crises.
82 Arendt, p. 268
83 The analysis had quite strong similarities to that developed later by Susan Faludi in rela-tion to the contemporary US. Arendt, p. 356.
84 Arendt, p. 315.
85 See, for example, Scheff.
86 Scheff; Bartov, 2000.
87 Arendt, p. 225.

88 Rivalries *between* traders can also fuel ethnic conflict – as, for example, in India, where smaller Muslim traders have often tried to break the dominance of Hindu rivals (Bardhan).

89 Amy Chua, 'Our most dangerous export', *Guardian*, 29 February 2004.

90 Bardhan; Fischer; Chua (as in previous note); see also Chua, 2003.

91 Deng, 1973.

92 Zur.

93 Ignatieff, 1993. This also emerged from my own research in Belgrade in 1999.

94. Ignatieff, 1993, pp. 14–19. I am grateful to Dominique Jacquin-Berdal for conversations in this area (and many others).

95 Loza, p. 11, quoted in Campbell, p. 95.

96 Arendt, p. 363

97 Arendt, p. 333

98 Arendt, p. 352.

99 Arendt, p. 269

100 Arendt, p. 269. Adolf Hitler himself noted in *Mein Kampf* (chapter 6): 'When the nations on this planet fight for existence . . . then all consideration of humanitarianism and aesthetics crumble into nothingness . . . they become totally irrelevant to the forms of the struggle as soon as a situation arises where they might paralyze a struggling nation's power of self-preservation' (accessed at *www.hitler.org/writings/ Mein_Kampf/mkv1ch06.html*).

101 See discussion in Cohen, 2001.

102 Cohen, 2001, p. 16; Lerner.

103 Arendt, p. 446. Omer Bartov (2000) writes of the search, in Germany after the First World War, for 'an enemy . . . whose very persecution would serve to manifest the power and legitimacy of the victimizer' (p. 99).

104 See, notably, Buzan.

105 Vikram Dodd and Richard Norton-Taylor, 'Video of 7/7 ringleader says policy was to blame', *Guardian*, 2 September 2005.

106 A more extended discussion is in Keen, 2006.

107 Arendt; Bartov, 2000; cf. Keen, 2006.

108 Woodward, 2003, p. 17.

109 Woodward, 2003, p. 168.

110 Hersh.

111 Ikenberry.

112 Elworthy. Compare also Marsden.

113 Woodward, 2003, p. 338

114 Adolf Hitler, speech to Wehrmacht commanders-in-chief, 22 August 1939 (*www.union. edu/PUBLIC/HSTDEPT/walker/OldNSChronology/3686Walker02.html*). I am grateful to Edward Balke for bringing this statement to my attention.

115 Woodward, 2003, p. 341.

116 Keen, 2006.

117 Perle.

118 Independent International Commission on Kosovo.

119 David Hare, 'Don't look for a reason', *Guardian*, 12 April 2003.

120 Ron Suskind, 'Without a doubt', *New York Times*, 17 October 2004.

121 Fanon.

122 Jason Burke, 'Theatre of terror', *Guardian*, 21 November 2004; Burke, 2003, pp. 33–4. Chechen leader Shamil Basayev commented in early 2005 that his fighters would carry out more attacks like that on the school at Beslan, Russia, 'if only to show the world again and again the true face of the Russian regime', perhaps in part through their brutal reaction (Channel 4 News Special Report, Jonathan Miller, 'Another Beslan?', 3 February 2005 [*www.channel4.com*]).

123 See, for example, Gerges; Richard Norton-Taylor, 'Use and abuse of intelligence', *Guardian*, 19 July 2005; Rogers.
124 Burnham et al.
125 Michael Hoffman, 'The civilians we killed', *Guardian*, 2 December 2004.
126 See also Linker.
127 Woodward, 2003, p. 145.
128 Woodward, 2003, pp. 38–9; compare Theweleit.
129 Danner, p. 97. Perhaps feeding into the failure to understand 'bottom up' processes among their enemies was what Goff calls a 'ruling class myopia' in the Bush administration: 'They are constitutionally incapable of understanding history as a process that involves the masses', Goff suggests (p. 112).
130 For example, Anderson, 2004.
131 Keen, 2006.
132 Bob Dylan, 'License to Kill'.
133 Compare Graybill, p. 1126.
134 Video of peace campaign at Goderich, ActionAid, Freetown, *c*.2001.
135 Richards, 1996b, p. 13.
136 Rushdie, p. 117. Compare Arendt.
137 Solzhenitsyn, p. 168.
138 Robins and Post, p. 246.
139 Compare Orwell.

Chapter 5 Famine

1 Foucault, 1981, pp. 5–6.
2 Malthus, p. iv.
3 Sen, p. 1.
4 Poverty may also force people to live on a floodplain – or in a home that is vulnerable to earthquakes or hurricanes (Wisner et al.).
5 Dreze and Sen, p. 262.
6 Dreze and Sen, p. 22.
7 Dreze and Sen.
8 Edkins also noted that some element of coercion has often been involved even in natural disasters. The devastation of New Orleans by Hurricane Katrina in August–September 2005 saw widespread looting as well as security officials using force to control looting.
9 Africa Watch, 1991.
10 Ibid.
11 On the latter point, see Wolf.
12 De Waal, 1997. See also critique of the relief operations in Ethiopia, in Vaux.
13 Dreze and Sen, p. 17.
14 This point emerges from my study of Sudan and has been developed more comparatively by Eric Neumayer (Pluemper and Neumayer).
15 Control of food stocks (for example, for electioneering) becomes particularly pivotal in circumstances where the total available food has been run down (in Zimbabwe, when eviction of white farmers was not followed by significant government support for those who replaced them) (e.g. Rory Carroll, 'Police raze war veterans' farms as fresh land evictions rock Zimbabwe', *Guardian*, 18 October 2004; see also Brett). On famine in Zimbabwe, see McClelland.
16 E.g. Keen, 1994.
17 De Schweinitz.
18 Rangasami.
19 See discussion and references in Keen, 1994.

20 See discussion and sources in ibid.

21 On this famine, see, for example, Chamberlin; Oleskiw.

22 Africa Watch, 1991.

23 See discussion in Keen, 1994, pp. 184–7.

24 De Waal and Omaar, 1992; African Rights, 1993a.

25 De Waal, 1989.

26 De Waal and Whiteside. For a good, short overview, see Samuels and Simon.

27 Harrell-Bond; Ken Wilson, 'Enhancing refugees' own food acquisition strategies', Oxford nutrition symposium, March 1991.

28 See discussion and references in Keen, 1994.

29 Keen, 1991b.

30 African Rights, 1995, p. 49.

31 See, for example, Keen, 1993; de Waal, 1994.

32 This was at odds with the scenario envisaged by Peter Cutler (1984), who, based on his work in Ethiopia, predicted famine would spread from its 'epicentre' as grain moved in and people moved out.

33 De Waal has stressed the critical role in famines of increased exposure to infection and of local people's coping strategies; his analysis is discussed in more detail later in this chapter.

34 Keen, 1994.

35 Ibid. On slavery, see notably Jok, 2001.

36 Keen, 1994.

37 Under Operation Lifeline Sudan in the 1990s, vulnerability assessments in the south tended to neglect the vulnerability arising from wealth (and dispossession) – reflecting the common view that poverty lies at the root of famine. In his Ph.D. thesis, Luka Biong Deng (2003), a Dinka himself, found that particularly among those Dinka living adjacent to the north and well-known to their Arab militia attackers, the more wealthy were just as vulnerable to famine. They were particularly targeted in attacks (because of their wealth), and may have suffered greater trauma and been less well adapted to survival techniques such as consuming wild foods.

38 Human Rights Watch, 2005b; ICG, 2004a, 2004b, 2006b.

39 See, for example, Pantuliano and O'Callaghan.

40 Human Rights Watch, 2005b.

41 CIJ.

42 On Eronat, see David Leigh and Adrian Gatton, 'Briton named as buyer of Darfur oil rights', *Guardian*, 10 June 2005.

Chapter 6 Aid

1 Cutler.

2 Woodward, 2003, p. 130.

3 Prunier, 2005, p. 136.

4 Bennett; Terry.

5 Terry.

6 Jézéquel, p. 178.

7 See, for example, Duffield, 1998b and 2001.

8 Keen, 2005a.

9 Maass, p. 30.

10 Berdal, 1993.

11 One indication among many of the lack of diplomatic engagement was the absence of a British embassy; senior British officials later complained that they were getting poor information (Melvern, 2001).

12 ICG, 2004b, p. 13.
13 See the excellent paper by Pantuliano and O'Callaghan.
14 Keen, 1993a.
15 Woodward, 1995, p. 369.
16 Woodward, 1995.
17 Woodward, 1995, p. 320.
18 This applied to wars in Nigeria, Uganda, Sudan and Ethiopia, for example.
19 Duffield, 1994a.
20 Duffield, 2001; Woodward, 1995; Stevens.
21 Barutciski.
22 See discussion in Cunliffe and Pugh.
23 Allen and Morsink.
24 See, for example, Macrae and Harmer.
25 'Strangers at our gates', editorial, *Guardian*, 20 April 2006.
26 That was the conclusion drawn by independent lawyers at the charity Immigration Advisory Services. In 2003, only 5 out of 550 Algerians claiming asylum in the UK were granted it; the Home Office played down threats to returnees, yet Amnesty said torture of suspected subversives remained prevalent (Melanie McFadyean, 'A pile-up of shameful contradictions', *Guardian*, 24 November 2004).
27 Moorehead.
28 Lee.
29 Keen 1991b, 1994, 2005a; see also Africa Watch, 1991.
30 Amanda Ripley, 'How did this happen?', *Time*, 19 September 2005. The commercial sector proved to have more political clout that the principal victims, and one factor delaying evacuation in New Orleans as Hurricane Katrina approached seems to have been the city authority's fear of being held accountable for unnecessarily closing hotels and other businesses. Fear of loss of tourist income is also a consideration when issuing tsunami warnings.
31 See chapter 5, n. 30.
32 Mollat, pp. 8–9.
33 Keen, 1991b.
34 For example, the setting up of Jewish ghettos in Poland, the restriction of supplies to the ghettos and population movements in and out, and the eventual policy of annihilation all reflected the interaction of a very complex set of locally and centrally generated agendas, including the desire to *expel* the Jews, a concern with 'public health' (which perversely encouraged both the setting up and sealing off of ghettos), a desire to extract wealth from Jewish people by restricting food supplies, and, not least, the racial and genocidal ideology of the Nazis (see, notably, Browning, 1992).
35 Intention has been highlighted in the legal definition of genocide; but the world does not neatly conform to legal templates.
36 See, for example, Woodward, 1995; Keen, 1993b; Harriss.
37 For example, Rangasami; Keen, 1994.
38 On natural disasters, see Keen, 1991b.
39 De Waal, 1997; Farah.
40 African Rights, 1993a.
41 E.g. Maren on Somalia. In Bosnia, factions accused aid workers of funding their rivals (see, for example, David Pallister, 'When food relief comes out of the barrel of a gun', *Guardian*, 7 May 1994).
42 Menkhaus and Prendergast, pp. 4–5. This concern was also expressed in Liberia (Armon and Carl).
43 Maren.
44 James.

45 Keen, 2005a.
46 On this mechanism in Mozambique, see Chris McGreal, 'The land of drought, corruption and war', *Independent on Sunday*, 31 May 1992.
47 Naomi Klein, 'The rise of disaster capitalism', *The Nation*, 2 May 2005.
48 Leckie.
49 The city's reputation for 'sin' may also have been a factor. On these events and motives, see Giles Fraser, 'Betrayal of the Big Easy', *Guardian*, 2 January 2007, and Gary Younge, 'Gone with the wind', *Guardian Weekend*, 29 July 2006.
50 Duffield, 1994a.
51 Prunier, 2005, pp. 131–2.
52 ICG, 2004b.
53 Ibid.
54 Lavergne and Weissman.
55 Ibid.
56 Stremlau; Stevens.
57 See, particularly, Zolberg et al.
58 Shawcross, 1984.
59 Prunier, 1995.
60 Emizet.
61 Zaïrean President Mobutu had strong links with the Hutu extremists and was benefiting economically and diplomatically from Zaïre's role as a staging-post for humanitarian relief. (Despite all the impediments, some 200,000 had nevertheless repatriated to Rwanda from Goma camps by mid-January 1995, and civilian control over food distributions had improved by mid-1995 [Pottier].)
62 Pottier; Slim.
63 Emizet.
64 Goffman.
65 Allen and Turton.
66 Callamard.
67 Lee.
68 Zolberg et al., p. 277.
69 Marsden.
70 Compare Arendt.
71 Malkki.
72 Harrell-Bond.
73 See, for example, Kent; Wilson, 1992; Keen and Wilson.
74 ODI, 2006; Raikes; Kent.
75 Creti and Jaspers.
76 Keen and Wilson.
77 See also Marriage; Duffield, 2001; Bradbury, 1998.
78 Karim et al., p. 217.
79 Ibid.; African Rights, 1995.
80 De Waal, 1997. See also Karim et al.; Human Rights Watch, 1998; Lavergne and Weissman.
81 Shawcross, 1984, p. 48.
82 Ibid.
83 Moorehead.
84 See, for example, Bower.
85 See, for example, 'Introducing OHCA', *www.un.org.np/pdf/ochaen.pdf*.
86 Sudan Humanitarian Overview, 1 Jan.–1 Feb 2006, OCHA, vol. 2, issue 1 (*www.unsudanig.org*).
87 OCHA, 2006.

88 Gordadze, p. 207.
89 Ibid.
90 Messiant, pp. 125–6.
91 Jézéquel.
92 Summerfield.
93 Almedom.
94 Gibbs.
95 Van der Veer.
96 Graybill.
97 Lanzer.
98 See. notably, Hulme and Goodhand. According to Betty Bigombe, NGOs may also start living off a war and may undermine initiatives aimed at ending it (talk at Centre for Humanitarian Dialogue, Geneva, 14 December 2006).
99 Duffield, 2001. For example, Red Cross staff in Afghanistan (Ignatieff, 1998).
100 OCHA, 2006, p. 7.
101 Keen, 1993a.
102 Smith, p. 41; Keen, 1993a.
103 It would be difficult to object to 'empowerment'; yet in practice interventions helping the poor to claim their rights may prompt powerful local objections (Chambers, 1983); so too may cash relief that helps people to move more freely. OPEC's empowerment of oil-producing countries was seen in the West as disastrous.
104 Pantuliano and O'Callaghan, p. 18
105 Kevin Maguire, 'How British charity was silenced on Iraq', *Guardian*, 28 November 2003.
106 Ibid.
107 Ian Brown, 'This fatal compromise', *Guardian*, 19 November 2004.
108 See discussion in Duffield, 1994b, pp. 57–64.
109 Hanlon, 1996.
110 Keen, 1993a, p. 29.
111 Interview with Jan Birket-Smith.
112 De Waal, 1997; Bauer.
113 E.g. Keen, 2005a.
114 Duffield, 2001.
115 Keen, 2005a.
116 ODI, 2000.
117 MSF, p. 21.
118 Duffield highlighted this in Angola (1994a), and Karim et al. in Sudan.
119 Duffield, 2001.
120 Leach.
121 See discussion in Keen, 2005a.
122 Marriage; Cohen, 2001.
123 De Waal, 2003; Duffield, 2001.
124 Duffield, 1999.
125 Macrae and Leader.
126 Weissman; Keen, 2005a.
127 Lefort and Littell, pp. 10–11.
128 OCHA, 1997; Cortright et al., p. 176; Porter.
129 Messiant, p. 119.
130 Macrae, p. 8.
131 Stevens.
132 Whitaker.
133 Cunliffe and Pugh.

134 E.g. Stevens.

135 Keen, 1993a.

136 See, e.g., Stevens.

137 Whitaker.

138 Barnett.

139 Stevens.

140 Turton and Marsden; see also Lautze et al.

141 Turton and Marsden.

142 E.g. Duffield (1998a and 1998b) on 'postmodern' conflict and conditionality; Stockton; Macrae and Leader.

143 Stockton.

144 Pottier. About half a million refugees were forced out of former Zaïre. The US had strong ties to Rwanda's President Kagame and indeed had helped to train him before he assumed leadership of the RPF forces moving into Rwanda in October 1990 (Pottier). Once the mass repatriation from Zaïre began (some 500,000–700,000 refugees in a matter of days [Emizet]), the US quickly cancelled the plan for international intervention that would protect civilians in the area (Pottier; Emizet). Both the US and Rwanda were keen to declare the refugee crisis over and an international presence unnecessary (Pottier; Stockton). The US government said there was just one cluster of people who were 'in good shape' and who, moreover, could be assumed to be Hutu militiamen and members of the old Rwandan army implicated in genocide. But Oxfam's Nick Stockton said US aerial photos showed there were still about 500,000 displaced people – refugees plus a number of internally displaced – in various clusters in eastern Zaïre. In effect, Stockton reported, some 400,000 refugees and an unknown number of internally displaced Zaïreans were effectively 'air-brushed from history' (Stockton). US officials later admitted to Congress that some 400,000–500,000 Rwandan refugees had been left in Congo in late 1996 (Emizet). Moreover, only about 6 per cent of the Rwanda refugees in Congo were members of Hutu militias or the old Rwandan army (Emizet).

145 Emizet.

146 Emizet, p. 183.

147 Slim, p. 251.

148 Slim, p. 252.

149 Interestingly, de Waal actually comes back to hints of a deontological position at the end of his analysis in *Famine Crimes*, namely that aid organizations should tell the truth. Of course, he sees this as a necessary path if welfare is to be maximized, but at some level perhaps the 'ifs' and 'buts' of consequentialism have proven too burdensome; the lure of a definite and unchanging maxim is hard to resist.

150 Stockton; Shearer, 2000.

151 See, notably, Shearer, 2000.

152 Crisp and Jacobsen, p. 27.

153 Richards, 1996a. See also Anderson, 1999.

154 De Waal, 1997; compare Maren.

155 Betts; Chambers, 1986; Harrell-Bond; Wilson, 1991.

156 The Sphere project – spearheaded by the Red Cross and Red Crescent movement, Oxfam and other NGOs.

157 Tong; see also Hofmann et al.

158 OCHA, 2006, p. 8.

159 Hofmann et al.

160 Atkinson and Leader.

161 ICG, 2004d, p. 3.

162 Slim.

163 Rangasami.
164 From the 1970s Saddam Hussein attempted to divide and weaken the Kurds, and to make them dependent on him, by undermining their economy. His economic boycott on the north was a continuation of this policy, whose effects were exacerbated by international sanctions on Iraq as a whole.
165 See, for example, Bradbury, 1995b.
166 Keen, 1994.
167 De Waal, 1997.
168 Women's Commission for Refugee Women and Children.
169 Lee; see also Agier and Boucher-Saulnier.

Chapter 7 Information

 1 Deng, 1980, p. 296.
 2 Dreze and Sen.
 3 E.g. Opondo; Prunier, 1995.
 4 Benthall; Kaplan,1994a; Huntington, 1993, 1998, 2004.
 5 It is uncomfortable to hold two contradictory thoughts at once, and one way of preventing this is to 'censor' new information so that it fits with what you think already.
 6 Allison.
 7 Chomsky, 1992.
 8 With mounting US casualties in Iraq, the first slogan was subverted in the banner:* 'Support our troops: Bring them home!'.
 9 Incidentally, Chomsky says you can have a genuine debate on abortion because it does not threaten the power elite.
10 IRC survey, published 2003.
11 Meera Selva, 'Rwanda's army accused of killing civilians after mass grave of hundreds is uncovered in Congo', *Independent*, 5 October 2005.
12 Baudrillard.
13 Allen, 1999.
14 See, for example, Chomsky, 1991.
15 Aburish.
16 E.g. Keen, 1993b.
17 Herman and Chomsky.
18 The total has been much disputed, but it is now widely accepted that the total was in excess of 3 million. The problem of under-reporting was compounded when the North Vietnamese authorities minimized casualties, in part to boost morale.
19 Chomsky, 2002, p. 35.
20 This process has found echoes in the treatment of criminal suspects. Looking at copies of Britain's *Sun* newspaper in the 1980s reveals that the paper repeatedly used dehumanizing language about people committing violent crimes, then polled its readers on whether they should be hanged, then cited the poll findings as showing overwhelming support for the death penalty.
21 See, for example, Rampton and Stauber; Massing.
22 The clearest expositions, perhaps, are in *Discipline and Punish* and *Power/Knowledge*. Compare also Allison on organizational norms helping to shape policy through the production of certain kinds of information.
23 Foucault, 1977.
24 Foucault, 1981.
25 Mustafa Kemal Ataturk, Turkey's first President, strongly opposed Turkish dress.
26 Saint-Exupéry, p. 16.
27 Dreyfus and Rabinow. For a general discussion, see also Smart.

28 Wood.
29 Schaffer.
30 Schaffer, pp. 188–9.
31 Foucault 1977, 1978, 1981.
32 Schaffer, p. 152.
33 Clay and Schaffer; Schaffer.
34 Schaffer 1984, p. 177.
35 Keen, 1994 and 2005a.
36 Robinson. On threats to NGO independence, see also de Torrente; Stockton; Tong; and Duffield, 2001.
37 Keen, 1993a.
38 Correspondence between EEC and SCF officials accessed at SCF archives, Khartoum, 1987.
39 Comments cited in Keen, 1992; see also Hofmann et al.
40 Keen, 1993a.
41 Jok, 1996; see also Jok, 2001. Disillusionment with NGOs can arise from an assumption that questions imply an undertaking to do something (Tsunami Evaluation Coalition, Joint Evaluation of the International Response to the Indian Ocean Tsunami, Synthesis Report, July, p. 71).
42 A promising initiative is donors' Good Humanitarian Donorship project (see, for example, Graves and Wheeler).
43 Duffield, 2001; compare also Tong.
44 See discussion in Keen, 1994, chap. 5.
45 Ibid.
46 Foucault, 1980, p. 85. Foucault was questioning Marxism and psychoanalysis in particular.
47 An example is figures for regional distribution of aid in Sudan, showing the severe neglect of the south (Keen, 1994).
48 'Grown-ups love figures. When you tell them that you have made a new friend, they never ask you any questions about essential matters. They never say to you, "What does his voice sound like? What games does he love best? Does he collect butterflies?" Instead, they demand: "How old is he? How many brothers has he?" ' (Saint-Exupéry, p. 16).
49 See, notably, Duffield, 1994b.
50 NGOs may also take refuge in the 'policy/implementation' divide, arguing that they were 'only the implementers' (Chris Dolan, personal communication; see also Dolan).
51 Cutler, 1989; Keen, 1994; Prunier, 2005.
52 Media coverage can provide an impetus to withdrawal or isolationism. For example, coverage of the killing of US soldiers in Somalia in October 1993 seems to have fed powerfully into a period of isolationism that included shameful inaction on the 1994 Rwandan genocide.
53 Sontag,
54 Ignatieff, 1988; Keen and Ryle.
55 Nicholas Kristof, 'All ears for Tom Cruise, all eyes on Brad Pitt', *New York Times*, 26 July 2005.
56 George Monbiot, 'Threat of unreality TV', *Guardian*, 22 October 2002.
57 Benthall.
58 Oxfam and Save the Children Fund have stressed the value of positive images of developing countries.
59 Madeleine Bunting, 'A hall of mirrors', *Guardian*, 17 January 2005.
60 African Rights, 1994.
61 Atkinson, 1996
62 Bell.

63 McNulty; African Rights, 1994; Article 19.
64 Thompson; Sofos.
65 Thompson.
66 Research, Belgrade, 1999.
67 Ugrešić.
68 Kemal.
69 See also Knightley; Opondo.
70 See, for example, 'The Dirty Thirty', a list of allegedly dangerous UCLA academics (*www.uclaprofs.com/articles/dirtythirty.html*).
71 Baudrillard.
72 To its credit, CNN chose to cover some of the civilian suffering arising from allied bombing.
73 E.g. Save the Children Fund.
74 Sontag.
75 On Evans' views, see Evans, 1978 and 2003.
76 E.g. Joint Evaluation of Emergency Assistance to Rwanda.
77 David Teather, 'Katrina uncovers the forgotten queues at America's soup kitchens', *Guardian*, 17 October 2005.
78 Uvin, p. 2.
79 Sen. Who can buy what kinds of information and what kinds of silence?
80 See, notably, Prunier, 1995.
81 Linda Melvern, 'The west did intervene in Rwanda, on the wrong side', *Guardian*, 5 April 2004. Melvern's book is *Conspiracy to Murder*.
82 Melvern, 2001.
83 Melvern, 2001, p. 103.
84 Ndiaya
85 Owen, p. 16.

Chapter 8 Peace

1 Schivelbusch. One can see elements of this dynamic in the response to major terrorist attacks. A major attack may lead to a search for those who can be targeted in retaliation – and 9/11 would appear to be a case in point. On the other hand, an attack may lead – as in Madrid – to hostility towards a domestic regime that is seen as having ultimate responsibility for the disaster.
2 Keen, 2005a.
3 Fithen and Richards; see also Utas on Liberia.
4 Galtung, 1996.
5 Scheper-Hughes. She links this to a climate of fear that was heightened when democratization made the poor seem less easily controlled.
6 Nordstrom.
7 Some forms of rape – for example, a husband raping his wife – may not be taken very seriously even in peacetime (Human Rights Watch, 2003).
8 Mazurana; for an interesting discussion, see Allen, 1997.
9 Le Billon, 2001b, p. 562; Rodgers.
10 Betty Bigombe, talk at Centre for Humanitarian Dialogue, Geneva, 14 December 2006.
11 One case where capturing the leader severely weakened a terror/rebel organization was the capture of Shining Path leader Abimael Guzman in 1992. The Peruvian rebel leader had cultivated an extreme personality cult and a centralized organization (Gutierrez, 2005).
12 Kevin Toolis contrasts Israel's policy of assassinating Hamas leaders with Britain's refraining from assassinating IRA leaders in Northern Ireland even as the IRA tried to

decapitate the British cabinet (as in the Brighton hotel bombing of 1984). In fact, MI6 was secretly negotiating with the IRA's Martin McGuiness (sowing seeds for the 1998 Good Friday agreement) (Kevin Toolis, 'You can't make a deal with the dead', *Guardian*, 10 September 2003).

13 See, for example, Gordadze on Chechnya.
14 This idea is explored in Keen, 2001.
15 Shawcross, 1996; Berdal and Keen.
16 Keen, 2005a.
17 The Antwerp trade's governing body, the Diamond High Council, announced in 1999 that independent experts would verify that diamonds were not from war zones, but in 2000 Antwerp buyers were still prepared to purchase diamonds billed as 'from Sierra Leone with no papers' (Jason Burke, Chris McGreal, Ed Vulliamy and Nick Paton Walsh, 'Diamonds: Africa's deadly wealth', *Observer*, 14 May 2000). Tel Aviv was even less regulated (*Africa Confidential*, 23 June 2002, p. 2). See also Report of the Panel of Experts (Sierra Leone), p. 1.
18 Keen, 2005a.
19 On the rather limited impact of UN sanctions on UNITA (which included sanctions on arms, fuel, travel, financial assets as well as diamonds), see Le Billon, 2001a.
20 Porteous.
21 King.
22 Hawley.
23 E.g. ICG, 2004b. The US imposed some in May 2007.
24 See, for example, Ken Silverstein, 'Official pariah Sudan valuable to America's war on terrorism', *Los Angeles Times*, 29 April 2005 (accessed at *www.globalpolicy.org/empire/terrorwar/analysis/2005/0429sudan.htm*).
25 See, for example, Flint and de Waal. The assets of suspected terrorists were frozen after the foiling in August 2006 of a major bomb plot directed at some ten planes and hatched in the UK and Pakistan.
26 See, for example, the work of Saferworld, Oxfam, International Action Network on Small Arms (IANSA) and the Small Arms Survey research project at the Graduate Institute of International Studies, Geneva; see also Human Rights Watch, 2002a.
27 Dennis Bright, Commission for Consolidation of Peace in Sierra Leone, 'Sierra Leone: The Conflict and the World', CODEP conference, 18–20 June 2001, SOAS.
28 See, for example, Le Billon, 2003.
29 Shawcross, 1996; Le Billon, 2000; Berdal and Keen.
30 Shawcross, 1996.
31 Berdal and Keen.
32 Le Billon, 2000.
33 Keen, 2005a.
34 King.
35 See Berdal, 1996, on demobilization.
36 'Lip service' to the need to support agriculture has been common (e.g. Hanlon, 2005).
37 ICG, 2006a.
38 Simon Robinson and Vivienne Watt, 'The deadliest war in the world', *Time*, 5 June 2006, p. 35.
39 ICG, 2006a, pp. 25–6.
40 ICG, 2006a.
41 Ibid.
42 Ibid.
43 Ibid.
44 Human Rights Watch, 2005b.
45 Allen, 2006.

46 Rory Carroll, 'Court orders Uganda to pay Congo damages', *Guardian*, 20 December 2005.
47 Hilton.
48 ICG, 2006d.
49 See, for example, Human Rights Watch, 2003; and discussion in Keen, 2005a.
50 King.
51 Bigombe is more ambivalent (Bigombe, see n. 10). Mawson.
52 Bigombe, see n. 10.
53 Shawcross, 1996.
54 Priscilla Hayner also discusses the degree and type of accountability it may be realistic to expect in different post-conflict situations, and the possible role of truth commissions in these processes.
55 ICG, 2006d.
56 Lunn, p. 13; see also Boyce.
57 See, for example, work by the NGO Tiri at *www.tiri.org*.
58 On one example of this process, see Andreas.
59 See, for example, Armon and Carl. In Liberia, many members of the transitional government (2003–5) were known warlords determined to extract what they could from holding state power (ICG, 2004e).
60 Le Billon, 2000; see also Malone and Nitschke.
61 ICG, 2004e.
62 Giustozzi.
63 Hoffman; see also Sarah Chayes, 'Dangerous liaisons', *Guardian*, 7 July 2003.
64 Chayes (as previous note).
65 Hilton.
66 Ibid. (see also ICG, 2006d). Loyalist paramilitary groups in Northern Ireland remain involved in drugs supply, counterfeiting, smuggling and armed robbery, often using pubs, clubs and taxi firms as cover and employing tactics of intimidation developed early in the conflict. The Provisional IRA leadership has made an effort to rein in criminal activities by its members, but some such activities remain. Meanwhile, dissident republican groups are reportedly heavily involved in crime (Organised Crime Task Force). In parts of Belfast, some people continue to look to paramilitaries for resolving petty disputes in a context where going to the state can be seen as less effective and even as 'snitching' (visit, August 2006). The IRA's encouragement (and taxing) of criminal activity has helped to leave a legacy of organized (and often drug-related) crime in Belfast and Dublin. On Russian oligarchs moving into politics, see Cottrell.
67 This argument has been taken to an extreme by Alan Dershowitz, who argues that addressing the root causes of terrorism is precisely the *wrong* approach, since it signals that 'terrorism works'.
68 Amnesty International.
69 Keen, 2005a.
70 Compare also Hanlon, 2005; Marriage.
71 ICG, 2003b.
72 I am grateful to Valpy FitzGerald for this formulation. See also Voutira and Brown.
73 See Voutira and Brown.
74 See, for example, *www.tiri.org*.
75 Keen, 2001; Andreas.
76 Menkhaus and Prendergast.
77 African Rights, 1993b.
78 Some people in Guatemala interpreted the 1996 peace agreement as a kind of collusion between rebel elites (mostly Ladino) and government-plus-business.

79 Rogier; ICG, 2005a.

80 Steve Mbogo, 'Oil disputes raise tension among Southern Sudan factions', *World Politics Watch*, 26 September 2006 (*www.globalpolicy.org*).

81 ICG, 2006a.

82 Johnson.

83 Ibid.; Keen, 1994. A 2006 Coalition for International Justice report noted Sudan's long history of damaging mechanized farming and observed, 'In agriculture, as in other aspects of its policies, the NIF [National Islamic Front, predecessor of the ruling NCP] has implemented policies that are, broadly speaking, similar to those of its predecessors, but more aggressive, more virulent and more hurtful to rural communities' (CIJ, p. 47). Key areas here have been Upper Nile, Blue Nile and Southern Blue Nile. The long-standing pattern of rewarding political supporters with mechanized farming concessions has been continued.

84 ICG, 2006f.

85 See, notably, Hanlon, 1996; compare also Hanlon, 2005.

86 Hanlon, 2005; ICG, 2004e; Fanthorpe; Keen, 2005a.

87 Hanlon, 2005, p. 461.

88 Pastor and Boyce.

89 Shawcross, 1996.

90 Pastor and Boyce; Boyce.

91 Pastor and Boyce; Rodgers.

92 This analysis comes from an excellent paper by Fajardo.

93 Keen, 2005b; Woodward, 2002; see also Hanlon, 2005, on Sierra Leone. While the World Bank now recognizes an important role for the state in development, it is not clear that a fundamental rethink has occurred, and in practice the World Bank has often deferred to IMF targets on budget deficits (Woodward, 2002).

94 See, notably, Woodward, 2002.

95 Hesselbein et al.

96 Sender.

97 Hawley.

98 Ibid.; Keen, 2005b.

99 Keen, 2005a.

100 Hagberg.

101 Mkandawire, 2001.

102 M'Baya, p. 74.

103 Baylies and Bujra.

104 See, for example, Keen, 2005a and 2005b.

105 Mkandawire, 2001.

106 Arrighi; Wade. Another factor was privileged access to the US domestic market.

107 To a degree, Uganda and Ghana are examples (e.g. Hutchful and Aning).

108 Mkandawire, 2001, p. 306.

109 Utas, pp. 150–1; war could offer a better chance of marrying. Compare also the discussion of the Rwandan genocide in Alison.

110 Talk by Zainab Bangura, second UCL conference, 1996.

111 Bellows and Miguel.

112 Compare also Fithen and Richards, p. 131.

113 Similar dynamics were discovered during the civil war in Mozambique by Mark Chingono.

114 Chingono; Kibreab.

115 Richards, 1996a, p. 51. Compare also the reluctance of Liberian fighters to take up agricultural work (ICG, 2004e); see also Sommers.

116 Utas.

117 Mamdani, 1996.

118 Ibid.

119 See, for example, ICG, 2003a.

120 Hanlon, 2005. Raising awareness of human rights without providing them may be an important source of violence (Lindner; Keen, 1993a).

121 Lunn.

122 See, for example, Duffield, 2001. Another example is that development is increasingly claimed to be necessary for 'security' (Duffield, 2001; Berdal, 2005).

123 By contrast, analysts who have stressed conflicts between competing goods (rather in contrast to Sen) have included Karl Marx, who stressed that limitations on human development were often good for growth (or 'capitalism'). One right may conflict with another. For example, the right to security may conflict with the right to liberty (see, for example, Ignatieff, 2001).

124 Berdal, 1996; Paris.

125 Human Rights Watch/International Federation of Human Rights, p. 125.

126 Paris.

127 On this, see Alex de Waal, Transcript of Seminar Eight, Bard College, 11 March 2000.

128 Ignatieff, 2001.

129 See particularly Acemoglu et al.

130 Moore. This kind of analysis can sometimes help to explain why civil war is averted: arguably, the largely non-violent transition to majority rule in South Africa was only possible because the diversification of the economy meant that the income of large numbers of white people was no longer dependent on apartheid (Ignatieff, 2001; Teddy Brett, personal communication). Analysis on these lines may also help to explain how war can be brought to an end. In the discussion of trade in chapter 3, it was noted that trade could encourage or discourage war. Jack Snyder and Robert Jervis (1999) argue that coffee growers in El Salvador saw that war was hitting their coffee production, but also 'they came to see that, in the era of economic globalization, profits from other kinds of commercial and manufacturing enterprises would be even better than the benefits of repression-based agriculture' (p. 32). In Guatemala by the early 1990s a combination of physical disruption, increased taxes and a US and regional threat of increasingly restricted access to international markets meant that important elements of the business sector in Guatemala were beginning to see that peace might suit their economic interests better than war. Those who were not depending on the hyper-exploitation of indigenous Mayan migrant workers in coffee and sugar plantations had less reason to use extreme violence in order to maintain their economic position (Keen, 2003). If analysis of the economic 'substructure' can help to explain how peace becomes possible, it can also help to explain why peace is frequently more violent than we would imagine. In South Africa, the economic interests of many white farmers and businessmen went unchallenged with the end of apartheid; continuing inequalities have fuelled crime and may yet erupt into widespread political violence. In Guatemala, high levels of intimidation against human rights workers and trade unionists have continued. The plantation sector remains important and still depends to a large extent on the intimidation of labour. The European Union has been involved in promoting non-traditional exports and part of peacebuilding may lie in trying to change the economic substructure in ways that reduce the dominance of sectors that depend on hyper-exploitation of labour and hence, ultimately, on violence and intimidation.

131 See, for example, Cortright and Lopez.

132 See, notably, Andreas, 2005; compare also Woodward, 1995.

133 Andreas, 2005.

134 Ibid.

135 Cortright and Lopez, p. 20.

136 Elon, citing Richard Ben Cramer 'How Israel lost'.
137 E.g. Le Billon, 2005.
138 See, for example, de Waal, 2003.
139 Arendt, p. 353.
140 Zur.
141 Marriage.
142 Again, compare Gilligan.
143 Act 4, Scene 1.
144 Jan Pronk, interviewed on BBC World, 21 December 2006.
145 Edward Said, 'A Window on the World', *Guardian* (G2), 2 August 2003.
146 Woodward, 2003, p. 275.
147 See, for example, de Waal, 2005.
148 In Rwanda, a danger of 'victor's justice' has arisen, with local *gacaca* courts specifically excluding from trial those Tutsis involved in massacring civilians as the RPF gained control of Rwanda (Corey and Joireman).
149 Gilligan.
150 For example, a 16-year-old girl captured by the RUF said she had helped to chop off people's hands; now she wanted to become a nurse (interviewed by Ambrose James, in Lord, p. 48).
151 Braithwaite and Braithwaite, 2001, p. 5.
152 Clay and Schaffer; Schaffer.
153 McAuslan.
154 Arendt, p. 296.
155 On the international 'green light', see, for example, Anderson, 2007.
156 ICG, 2004b; *Wall Street Journal*, 'Cynical in Sudan', editorial, 28 July 2004. See also Lavergne and Weissman.
157 ICG, 2004b, p. 4.
158 Events in Darfur were labelled a genocide by the US Congress, Secretary of State Colin Powell and President George W. Bush.
159 Joint Evaluation of Emergency Assistance to Rwanda.
160 Ibid.
161 Adelman.
162 Melvern, 2001, p. 104.
163 See, notably, Joint Evaluation of Emergency Assistance to Rwanda.
164 Melvern, 2001 and 2004a.
165 George Monbiot, 'A truckload of nonsense', *Guardian*, 14 June 2005.
166 Reyntjens.
167 Chapter 'Controlling War Economies' in Pugh and Cooper. Belatedly, Britain cut its budget support to the Ugandan government in December 2005, citing concern over the arrest and trial of opposition leader Kizza Besigye and delays in the government's road-map for political transition (though not the war in the north). Other European donors have also cut budget support.
168 Farah; Global Witness, 2003; Le Billon, 2006.
169 Pugh and Cooper; Malone and Nitschke.
170 Keen, 2005a.
171 Amari.
172 Amari, p. 260.
173 Amari, p. 261.
174 Human Rights Watch, 2002b.
175 Chayes, 'Dangerous liaisons' (see n. 63 above); British Agencies Afghanistan Group, 'Afghanistan: Monthly Review', November, 2002.
176 See Messiant on Angola, and Massey and May on Chad.

177 Jonas, pp. 120–1.
178 Zur, p. 89.
179 Keen, 2003; see also Boyce.
180 Youngs, p. 127.
181 Farah and Austin.
182 'China's Hand in Africa's Wars', Global Intelligence Update, *www.Stratfor.com*, 22 August 2000.
183 Given almost total international neglect, Executive Outcomes provided a degree of security, but it should not come to this.
184 Keen, 2001.
185 Tilly.
186 Whilst Taylor's rebellion in Liberia had a predatory aspect, Philippa Atkinson has argued that he was concerned to construct a viable economic system in areas he controlled, limiting outright abuses (e.g. 1999). In Mancur Olson's terms, he was arguably a 'stationary bandit' (with some interest in longer term exploitation) as much as a 'roving bandit', and this might explain how he was able to win a Presidential election in Liberia (Olson). Compare also Lary on early twentieth-century China; and MacKinlay.
187 Western pressure on the Burmese junta is one thing; but pressure from Burma's main trading partners, China and India, would be more effective. See, for example, John Aglionby, 'Inside Burma: fear and repression', *Guardian*, 23 May 2006.
188 See, notably, Richards, 1996; Peters; also Keen, 2005a.
189 Burton.
190 Mansfield and Snyder. In the disastrous transition from Communism in former Yugoslavia, a missed opportunity to secure to the pensions of JNA (Yugoslav People's Army) officers fed into the willingness of many to support Milosevic's greater Serbia as their best bet of financial security (Glenny). Nzongola-Ntalaja comments on Zaïre/DRC, 'Since Mobutu's power relied heavily on the security forces, it was amazing how little thought went into the matter of how to manage the transition with military chiefs who were against it' (p. 200). Many feared prosecution as well as loss of privileges.
191 Galtung, 1996.
192 Menkhaus.
193 Lieven.
194 Collier, Elliott et al.
195 Clay and Schaffer.

Chapter 9 Conclusion

1 Kaplan, 1994a; compare also Enzensberger.
2 For example, Peter Maass argues that war in the former Yugoslavia removed the constraints that normally deter men from sexual violence.
3 On dehumanizing the enemy, see, for example, Staub.
4 In his book *Humanity: A Moral History of the Twentieth Century*, Jonathan Glover explored the mechanisms by which people's sense of morality and humanity was overridden so that it became possible for them to commit atrocities: 'People slide by degrees into doing things they would not do if given a clear choice at the beginning' (Glover, p. 35). The process may include dehumanizing victims through propaganda; downplaying the abuse through the use of euphemisms and jargon; dividing the abuse into different 'tasks' (and so removing a sense of individual responsibility); blindfolding the victim (to provide a kind of distancing from his or her humanity and gaze). Inflicting a relatively minor humiliation may prepare the perpetrator to do something worse. Compare also Cohen, 2001.

5 Browning, 1993, pp. 188–9.
6 I am grateful to Gavin Williams for this formulation.
7 Utas; Keen, 2005a. This may also apply to crime (see, for example, Castells, pp. 204–5; Beneduce et al. on the DRC; and Rodgers on Nicaragua).
8 See, particularly, Duffield, 2001.
9 See, for example, Reyntjens.
10 See particularly Human Dignity and Humiliation Studies (*www.humiliationstudies.org*).
11 Bayart.
12 Archibald and Richards, 2002a, 2002b, 2002c; see also Fithen and Richards.
13 Marriage.
14 Young.
15 Leonenet (*www.leonenet.net*), archive, 1995–6. If Sierra Leone has been haunted by the RUF, in a way it has been haunted by its own shadow. In 2000, one experienced human rights activist working in Sierra Leone went so far as to observe: 'The solution lies in the non-RUF areas. In a sense, the RUF is almost irrelevant. As in Uganda, the key issue is the government. In Uganda, you have a very powerful government and a rather pathetic rebel movement and you have to ask why does the conflict continue.'
16 Le Billon, 2006 and 2000.

Bibliography

Aburish, Said. 1997. *A Brutal Friendship: The West and the Arab Elite*. London: Victor Gollancz.

Acemoglu, Daron, Simon Johnson and James Robinson. n.d. 'An African Success Story: Botswana'. Unpublished manuscript (*econ-www.mit.edu/faculty/acemoglu/files/papers/Botswanafinal.pdf*).

Addison, Tony, Philippe Le Billon and S. Mansoob Murshed. 2001. 'Finance in Conflict and Reconstruction', United Nations University, WIDER Discussion Paper 2001/44, August.

Adebajo, Adekeye. 2002a. *Building Peace in West Africa: Liberia, Sierra Leone, and Guinea-Bissau*. International Peace Academy Occasional Paper Series. Boulder, CO: Lynne Rienner.

Adebajo, Adekeye. 2002b. *Liberia's Civil War: Nigeria, ECOMOG and Regional Security in West Africa*. Boulder, CO: Lynne Rienner.

Adelman, Howard. 1999. 'Early Warning and Prevention: The United Nations and Rwanda', in Frances Nicholson and Patrick Twomey (eds), *Refugee Rights and Realities: Evolving International Concepts and Regimes*. Cambridge: Cambridge University Press.

Adorno, Theodor, Else Frenkel-Brunswik, Daniel Levinson and R. Nevitt Sanford. 1950. *The Authoritarian Personality*. New York: Harper and Brothers.

Africa Watch. 1990. *Somalia: A Government at War With Its Own People. Testimonies About the Killings and the Conflict in the North*. New York: Africa Watch.

Africa Watch. 1991. *Evil Days: Twenty Years of War and Famine in Ethiopia*. New York, Washington, Los Angeles and London: Africa Watch.

African Rights. 1993a. *Somalia – Operation Restore Hope: A Preliminary Assessment*. London: African Rights.

African Rights. 1993b. *Land Tenure, the Creation of Famine, and Prospects for Peace in Somalia*. Discussion Paper no. 1, October. London: African Rights.

African Rights. 1994. *Death, Despair and Defiance*. London: African Rights.

African Rights. 1995. *Facing Genocide: The Nuba of Sudan*. London: African Rights.

Agier, Michel and Françoise Boucher-Saulnier. 2004. 'Humanitarian Spaces: Spaces of Exception', in Fabrice Weissman (ed.), *In the Shadow of 'Just Wars': Violence, Politics and Humanitarian Action*. London: C. Hurst and Co.

Albala-Bertrand, José Miguel. 2000. *What is a 'Complex Humanitarian Emergency'? An Analytical Essay.* Working Paper no. 420, Dept. of Economics, Queen Mary, University of London.

Ali, Rabia and Lawrence Lifschultz. 1994. 'Why Bosnia?', *Third World Quarterly*, 15, 3, pp. 367–401.

Alison, Miranda. 2007. 'Wartime Sexual Violence: Women's Human Rights and Questions of Masculinity', *Review of International Studies*, 33, pp. 75–90.

Allen, Tim. 1997. 'The Violence of Healing', *Sociologus*, 47, 2, pp. 101–28.

Allen, Tim. 1999. 'Perceiving Contemporary Wars', in Tim Allen and Jean Seaton (eds), *The Media of Conflict: War Reporting and Representations of Ethnic Violence:* New York: St Martin's Press.

Allen, Tim. 2006. *Trial Justice: The International Criminal Court and the Lord's Resistance Army.* London: Zed; Claremont, SA: David Phillip Books.

Allen, Tim and John Eade. 2000. 'The New Politics of Identity', in Tim Allen and Alan Thomas (eds), *Poverty and Development into the 21st Century*. Oxford: Oxford University Press.

Allen, Tim and Hubert Morsink. 1994. *When Refugees Go Home.* Geneva: UNRISD; London: James Currey.

Allen, Tim and David Turton. 1996. 'Introduction: In Search of Cool Ground', in Tim Allen (ed.), *In Search of Cool Ground: War, Flight and Homecoming in Northeast Africa.* Geneva: UNRISD; London: James Currey; Trenton, NJ: Africa World Press.

Allison, Graham. 1971. *Essence of Decision: Explaining the Cuban Missile Crisis.* Boston: Little, Brown and Co.

Almedom, Astier. 2004. 'Factors That Mitigate War-Induced Anxiety and Mental Distress', *Journal of Biosocial Science*, 36, pp. 445–61.

Amari, Chawki. 2004. 'Algeria: The Utility of Terrorism', in Fabrice Weissman (ed.), *In the Shadow of 'Just Wars': Violence, Politics and Humanitarian Action.* London: C. Hurst and Co.

Amnesty International. 1998. *1998 UN Commission on Human Rights – Building on Past Achievements.* London, 1 January.

Anderson, Mary B. 1999. *Do No Harm: How Aid Can Support Peace – Or War.* Boulder, CO: Lynne Rienner.

Anderson, John Lee. 2004. 'Out on the Street', *New Yorker*, 15 November.

Anderson, Perry. 2007. 'Russia's Managed Democracy', *London Review of Books*, 25 January, pp. 3–12.

Andreas, Peter. 2005. 'Criminalizing Consequences of Sanctions: Embargo Busting and Its Legacy', *International Studies Quarterly*, 49, 2, pp. 335–60.

Anzulović, Branimir. 1999. *Heavenly Serbia: From Myth to Genocide.* New York: New York University Press.

Archibald, Steve and Paul Richards. 2002a. 'Seeds and Rights: New Approaches to Post-war Agricultural Rehabilitation in Sierra Leone', *Disasters*, 26, 4, pp. 356–67.

Archibald, Steve and Paul Richards. 2002b. 'A Window for Human Rights? War, Humanitarianism and Justice in Rural Central Sierra Leone'. Mimeo.

Archibald, Steve and Paul Richards. 2002c. 'Conversion to Human Rights? Popular Debate about War and Justice in Central Sierra Leone', *Africa*, 72, 3, pp. 339–67.

Arendt, Hannah. 1951. *The Origins of Totalitarianism*. New York: Harcourt.

Armon, Jeremy and Andy Carl. 1996. *Accord: The Liberian Peace Process, 1990–1996*. Conciliation Resources, London, issue 1.

Arrighi, Giovanni. 2000. 'The African Crisis: World Systemic and Regional Aspects', *New Left Review*, 15, May–June, pp. 5–35.

Article 19. 1996. *Broadcasting Genocide: Censorship, Propaganda and State-Sponsored Violence in Rwanda, 1990–1994*. London: Article 19.

Atkinson, Philippa. 1996. 'The Liberian Civil War – Images and Reality', in Tim Allen, Kate Hudson and Jean Seaton (eds), *War, Ethnicity and the Media*. London: School of Education, Politics and Social Science, South Bank University.

Atkinson, Philippa. 1999. 'Deconstructing Media Mythologies of Ethnic War in Liberia', in Tim Allen and Jean Seaton (eds), *The Media of Conflict: War Reporting and Representations of Ethnic Violence:* New York: St Martin's Press.

Atkinson, Philippa and Nicholas Leader. 2000. 'The "Joint Policy of Operation" and the "Principles and Protocols of Humanitarian Operation" in Liberia', HPG report 3, London: ODI, March.

Atkinson, Philippa, Anabel Hoult and David Mills. 1991. *Sierra Leone – A Security Crisis: '99% of your life is ours'*. Oxford: Refugee Studies Programme.

Badcock, James. 2002. 'Out of the Dark, Into the Courts', *Index on Censorship*, 27 July (*www.indexonline.org/en/news/articles/2002/3/out-of-the-dark-into-the-courts.shtml*).

Ballentine, Karen and Jake Sherman (eds). 2003. *The Political Economy of Armed Conflict: Beyond Greed and Grievance*. Boulder, CO: Lynne Rienner.

Bangura, Yusuf. 1997. 'Understanding the Political and Cultural Dynamics of the Sierra Leone War: A Critique of Paul Richards' *Fighting for the Rain Forest*', *African Development*, 22, 2– 3, Special Issue on Sierra Leone, pp. 117–47.

Bardhan, Pranab. 1997. 'Method in the Madness? A Political-Economy Analysis of Ethnic Conflicts in Less Developed Countries', *World Development*, 25, 9, pp. 1381–98.

Barnett, Michael. 2001. 'Humanitarianism with a Sovereign Face: UNHCR in the Global Undertow', *International Migration Review*, 35, 1, pp. 244–77.

Barth, Fredrik (ed.). 1969. *Ethnic Groups and Boundaries: The Social Organization of Cultural Difference*. Boston: Little, Brown and Co.

Bartov, Omer. 1991. *Hitler's Army: Soldiers, Nazis, and War in the Third Reich*. New York and Oxford: Oxford University Press.

Bartov, Omer. 2000. *Mirrors of Destruction: War, Genocide and Modern Identity*. Oxford: Oxford University Press.

Barutciski, Michael. 1998. 'Tensions between the Refugee Concept and the IDP Debate', *Forced Migration Review*, 3, December, pp. 11–14.

Baudrillard, Jean. 1995. *The Gulf War Did Not Take Place* (trans. Paul Patton). Bloomington: Indiana University Press.

Bauer, Peter. 1971. *Dissent on Development: Studies and Debates in Development Economics*. Cambridge, MA: Harvard University Press.

Bauman, Zygmunt. 1989. *Modernity and the Holocaust*. Cambridge: Polity Press.

Bayart, Jean-François. 1993. *The State in Africa: The Politics of the Belly*. London: Longman.

Baylies, Carolyn and Janet Bujra. 2000. *AIDS, Sexuality and Gender in Africa: Collective Strategies and Struggles in Tanzania and Zambia*. London: Routledge.

Becker, Jasper. 1996. *Hungry Ghosts: Mao's Secret Famine*. New York: Henry Holt and Co.

Bell, Martin. 1996. *In Harm's Way*. New York: Penguin.

Bellows, John and Edward Miguel. 2006. 'War and Institutions: New Evidence from Sierra Leone', *African Economic Development*, 96, 2, pp. 394–9.

Beneduce, Roberto, Luca Jourdan, Timothy Raeymaekers and Koen Vlassenroot. 2006. 'Violence with a Purpose: Exploring the Functions and Meaning of Violence in the Democratic Republic of Congo', *Intervention*, 4, 1, pp. 32–46.

Bennett, Jon. 1999. *North Korea: The Politics of Food Aid*. Network Paper no. 28, Humanitarian Practice Network. London: Overseas Development Institute, March.

Benthall, Jonathan. 1993. *Disasters, Relief and the Media*. London: I.B. Tauris Books.

Berdal, Mats. 1993. *Whither UN Peacekeeping? An Analysis of the Changing Military Requirements of UN Peacekeeping with Proposals for Its Enhancement*. Adelphi Paper no. 281. London: International Institute for Strategic Studies / Brassey's.

Berdal, Mats. 1996. *Disarmament and Demobilisation after Civil Wars*. Adelphi Paper no. 303. London: Oxford University Press for the International Institute for Strategic Studies.

Berdal, Mats. 2003. 'How "New" Are "New Wars"? Global Economic Change and the Study of Civil War', *Global Governance*, 9, pp. 477–502.

Berdal, Mats. 2005. 'The UN's unnecessary crisis', *Survival*, 47, 3, Autumn, pp. 7–32.

Berdal, Mats and David Keen. 1997. 'Violence and Economic Agendas in Civil Wars: Some Policy Implications', *Millennium: Journal of International Studies*, 26, 3, pp. 795–818.

Berman, Bruce. 1998. 'Ethnicity, Patronage and the African State: The Politics of Uncivil Nationalism', *African Affairs*, 97, 388, pp. 305–41.

Betts, T.F. 1984. 'Evolution and Promotion of the Integrated Rural Development Approach to Refugee Policy in Africa', *Africa Today*, 31, 1, pp. 7–24.

Bower, Tom. 1997. *Nazi Gold: The Full Story of the Fifty-Year Swiss–Nazi Conspiracy to Steal Billions from Europe's Jews and Holocaust Survivors*. New York: HarperCollins.

Boyce, James K. 2002. *Investing in Peace: Aid and Conditionality after Civil Wars*. Adelphi Paper no. 351. London: Oxford University Press for the International Institute for Strategic Studies.

Bradbury, Mark. 1995a. *Rebels without a Cause? An Exploratory Report on the Conflict in Sierra Leone*. Report for CARE International, April.

Bradbury, Mark. 1995b. *Aid under Fire: Redefining Relief and Development Assistance in Unstable Situations*. Wilton Park paper no. 104, London

Bradbury, Mark. 1998. 'Normalizing the Crisis in Africa', *Disasters*, 22, 4, pp. 328–38.

Braithwaite, John and Valerie Braithwaite. 2002. 'Shame, Shame Management and Regulation', in Eliza Ahmed, Nathan Harris, John Braithwaite and Valerie Braithwaite (eds), *Shame Management through Reintegration*. Cambridge: Cambridge University Press.

Brett, E.A. 2005. 'Authoritarian Patrimonialism and Economic Disorder: The Politics of Crisis and Breakdown in Uganda and Zimbabwe'. Crisis States Programme workshop, London, 30 August–1 September.

Bring, Ove. 2002. 'International Humanitarian Law after Kosovo: Is *Lex Lata* Sufficient?', *Nordic Journal of International Law*, 71, pp. 39–54.

Browning, Christopher R. 1992. *The Path to Genocide: Essays on Launching the Final Solution*. Cambridge: Cambridge University Press.

Browning, Christopher R. 1993. *Ordinary Men: Reserve Police Battalion 101 and the Final Solution in Poland*. New York: HarperPerennial.

Burke, Jason. 2003. *Al Qaeda: Casting a Shadow of Terror*. London and New York: I.B. Tauris.

Burnham, Gilbert, Riyadh Lafta, Shannon Doocy and Les Roberts. 2006. 'Mortality after the 2003 Invasion of Iraq: A Cross-sectional Cluster Sample Survey', *The Lancet*, 368, pp. 1421–8.

Burton, John. 1990. *Conflict: Resolution and Provention*, New York: St Martin's Press.

Buzan, Barry. 2002. 'Who May We Bomb?', in Ken Booth and Tim Dunne (eds), *Worlds in Collision: Terror and the Future of Global Order*. Houndmills: Palgrave Macmillan.

Callamard, Agnes. 1999. 'Refugee Women: A Gendered and Political Analysis of the Refugee Experience', in Alastair Ager (ed.), *Refugees: Perspectives on the Experience of Forced Migration*. London: Continuum.

Campbell, David. 1998. *National Deconstruction*. Minneapolis and London: University of Minnesota Press.

CARE International. 2002. *Food Security: Rights Based Approach Project, Peace and Rights Days Analysis Report*. Freetown/London. April-May.

Castells, Manuel. 1998. *End of Millennium*. Malden, MA, and Oxford: Blackwell Publishers.

Chabal, Patrick and Jean-Pascal Daloz. 1999. *Africa Works: Disorder as Political Instrument*. Oxford: James Currey.

Chamberlin, W.H. 1935. *Russia's Iron Age*. London: Duckworth.

Chambers, Robert. 1983. *Rural Development: Putting the Last First*. Harlow: Longman.

Chambers, Robert. 1986. 'Hidden Losers? The Impact of Rural Refugees and Refugee Programs on Poorer Hosts', *International Migration Review*, 20, 2, Special Issue: Refugees: Issues and Directions, pp. 245–63.

Chaumba, Joseph, Ian Scoones and William Wolmer. 2003. 'New Politics, New Livelihoods: Agrarian Change in Zimbabwe', *Review of African Political Economy*, 30, 98, December, pp. 585–608.

Chingono, Mark. 1996. *The State, Violence and Development: The Political Economy of War in Mozambique, 1975–92*. Ashgate: Avebury.

Chomsky, Noam. 1991. *Deterring Democracy*. London: Verso.

Chomsky, Noam. 2002. *Media Control: The Spectacular Achievements of Propaganda*. New York: Seven Stories Press.

Chossudovsky, Michel. 1997. *The Globalization of Poverty: Impacts of IMF and World Bank Reforms*. Penang: Third World Network; London: Zed Press.

Chua, Amy. 2003. *World on Fire: How Exporting Free-Market Democracy Breeds Ethnic Hatred and Global Instability*. London: Heinemann.

CIJ (Coalition for International Justice). 2006. *Soil and Oil: Dirty Business in Sudan*. Washington, DC: Coalition for International Justice, February.

Clay, Edward and Bernard Schaffer. 1984. 'Introduction: Room for Manoeuvre: The Premise of Public Policy', in Edward Clay and Bernard Schaffer (eds), *Room for Manoeuvre: An Exploration of Public Policy in Agriculture and Rural Development*. London: Heinemann Educational Books.

Coghlan, Benjamin, Rick Brennan, Pascal Ngoy, David Dofara, Brad Otto, Mark Clements and Tony Stewart. 2006. 'Mortality in the Democratic Republic of Congo: A Nationwide Survey', *Lancet*, 367, pp. 44–51.

Cohen, Craig. 2006. *Measuring Progress in Stabilization and Reconstruction*. Washington, DC: United States Institute of Peace.

Cohen, Stanley. 2001. *States of Denial: Knowing about Atrocities and Suffering*. Cambridge: Polity.

Collier, Paul. 1995. *Civil War and the Economics of the Peace Dividend*. Centre for the Study of African Economies, Working Paper Series no. 26.

Collier, Paul. 2000. 'Doing Well out of War: An Economic Perspective', in Mats Berdal and David Malone (eds), *Greed and Grievance: Economic Agendas in Civil Wars*. London: Lynne Rienner.

Collier, Paul and Anke Hoeffler. 1999. 'Justice-Seeking and Loot-Seeking in Civil War'. Mimeo. Washington, DC: The World Bank.

Collier, Paul, V.L. Elliott, Havard Hegre, Anke Hoeffler, Marta Reynal-Querol and Nicholas Sambanis. 2003. *Breaking the Conflict Trap: Civil War and Development Policy*. World Bank Policy Research report, vol. 1.

Collier, Paul, Anke Hoeffler and Dominic Rohner. 2006. 'Beyond Greed and Grievance: Feasibility and Civil War', Centre for the Study of African Economies, Oxford, WPS/2006-10, 7 August.

Corey, Allison and Sandra Joireman. 2004. 'Redistributive Justice: The Gacaca Courts in Rwanda', *African Affairs*, 103, 410, pp. 73–89.

Cortright, David and George A. Lopez. 2000. *The Sanctions Decade: Assessing UN Strategies – the 1990s*, Boulder, CO: Lynne Rienner.

Cottrell, Robert. 2003. 'Putin's trap', *New York Review of Books*, 4 December.

Creti, Pantaleo and Susanne Jaspers. 2006. *Cash-Transfer Programming in Emergencies*. Oxford: Oxfam.

Crisp, Jeff and Karen Jacobsen. 1998. 'Refugee Camps Reconsidered', *Forced Migration Review*, 3, December, pp. 27–30.

Cunliffe, S. Alex and Michael Pugh. 1996. 'The UNHCR as Lead Agency in the Former Yugoslavia'. University of Plymouth (*www.jha.ac/articles/a008.htm*).

Curtis, Mark. 1998. *The Great Deception: Anglo-American Power and World Order.* London: Pluto.

Cutler, Peter. 1984. 'Famine Forecasting: Prices and Peasant Behaviour in Northern Ethiopia', *Disasters*, 8, 1, pp. 48–56.

Cutler, Peter. 1989. 'The Development of the 1983-85 Famine in Northern Ethiopia', Ph.D, University of London.

Danner, Mark. 2003. 'Delusions in Baghdad', *New York Review of Books*, 18 December.

Das, Veena. 1998. 'Official Narratives, Rumour, and the Social Production of Hate', *Social Identities*, 4, 1, pp. 109–30.

de Schweinitz, Karl. 1961. *England's Road to Social Security: From the Statute of Laborers in 1349 to the Beveridge Report of 1942*. New York: Perpetua (first published 1943).

de Torrente, Nicolas. 2004. 'Humanitarian Action Under Attack: Reflections on the Iraq War', *Harvard Human Rights Journal*, 17, pp. 1–29.

de Waal, Alex. 1989. *Famine that Kills: Darfur, Sudan, 1984–1985*. Oxford: Clarendon Press.

de Waal, Alex. 1994. 'Some Comments on Militias in Contemporary Sudan', in M. Daly and A.A. Sikainga (eds), *Civil War in the Sudan*. London: I.B. Tauris.

de Waal, Alex. 1997. *Famine Crimes: Politics and the Disaster Relief Industry in Africa*. Oxford: James Currey.

de Waal, Alex. 2003. 'Human Rights Organizations and the Political Imagination: How the West and Africa Have Diverged', *Journal of Human Rights*, 2, 4, December, pp. 475–94.

de Waal, Alex. 2005. 'Who are the Darfurians? Arab and African Identities, Violence and External Engagement', *African Affairs*, 104, 415, pp. 181–205.

de Waal, Alex and Rakiya Omaar. 1992. 'The Lessons of Famine', *Africa Report*, November/December, pp. 62–5.

de Waal, Alex and Alan Whiteside. 2003. ' "New Variant Famine": AIDS and Food Crisis in Southern Africa', *The Lancet*, 362, pp. 1234–7.

Deak, Istvan. 2004. 'Improvising the Holocaust', *New York Review of Books*, 23 September.

Dekmejian, R.H. 1986. 'Determinants of Genocide: Armenians and Jews as Case Studies,' in Richard Hovannisian (ed.), *The Armenian Genocide in Perspective*. New Brunswick, NJ: Transaction Press.

Deng, Francis. 1973. *Dynamics of Identification: A Basis for National Integration in the Sudan*. Khartoum: Khartoum University Press.

Deng, Francis. 1980. *Dinka Cosmology*. London: Ithaca Press.

Deng, Luka Biong. 2003. *Confronting Civil War: A Comparative Study of Household Livelihood Strategies in Southern Sudan During 1990s*. Ph.D. dissertation, Brighton: University of Sussex, Institute of Development Studies (IDS).

Dershowitz, Alan. 2002. *Why Terrorism Works*. New Haven and London: Yale University Press.

Devereux, Stephen. 2000. *Famine in the Twentieth Century*. IDS Working Paper no. 105. Brighton: Institute of Development Studies.

Dixon, William Nah [Bishop] 1992. *Great Lessons of the Liberian Civil War, and What Did We Learn? A Personal View*. Monrovia: Feed My People.

Dolan, Chris. 2006. *Understanding War and its Continuation: The Case of Northern Uganda*. Ph.D., LSE (Berghahn Books, forthcoming).

Dreyfus, H. and P. Rabinow. 1982. *Michel Foucault: Beyond Structuralism and Hermeneutics*. Brighton: Harvester Press.

Dreze, Jean and Amartya Sen. 1989. *Hunger and Public Action*. Oxford: Clarendon Press and Oxford University Press.

Duffield, Mark. 1994a. *Complex Political Emergencies, with Reference to Angola and Bosnia: An Exploratory Report for UNICEF*. University of Birmingham, March.

Duffield, Mark. 1994b. 'The Political Economy of Internal War', in Joanna Macrae and Anthony Zwi (eds), *War and Hunger: Rethinking International Responses to Complex Emergencies*. London: Zed Books and Save the Children, UK.

Duffield, Mark. 1995. 'The Fate of Information in the Disaster Zone'. Paper presented at Workshop on the Fate of Information in the Disaster Zone. Oxford University: North East African Seminar, 27 September.

Duffield, Mark. 1996. 'The Symphony of the Damned: Racial Discourse, Complex Political Emergencies and Humanitarian Aid', *Disasters*, 20, 3, pp. 173–93.

Duffield, Mark. 1998a. 'Post-modern Conflict: Warlords, Post-adjustment States and Private Protection', *Civil Wars*, 1, 1, spring, pp. 65–102.

Duffield, Mark. 1998b. *Aid Policy and Post-Modern Conflict: A Critical Review*. Occasional Paper 19. Birmingham: University of Birmingham, School of Public Policy.

Duffield, Mark. 1999. 'Lunching with Killers: Aid, Security and the Balkan Crisis', in Carl-Ulrich Shierup (ed.), *Scramble for the Balkans: Nationalism, Globalism and the Political Economy of Reconstruction*. London: Macmillan.

Duffield, Mark. 2001. *Global Governance and the New Wars: The Merging of Development and Security*. London: Zed Books.

Edkins, Jenny 1996. 'Legality with a Vengeance: Humanitarian Relief in Complex Emergencies', *Millennium: Journal of International Studies*, 25, 3, pp. 547–75.

Ellis, Stephen. 1995. 'Liberia 1989–1994: A Study in Ethnic and Spiritual Violence', *African Affairs*, 94, 375, pp. 165–97.

Ellis, Stephen. 1999. *The Mask of Anarchy: The Roots of Liberia's War*. New York: New York University Press.

Elon, Amos. 2004. 'War without End', *New York Review of Books*, 15 July.

Elworthy, Scilla. 2005. 'Tackling Terror by Winning Hearts and Minds', 20 July (*opendemocracy.net*).

Emdad-ul Haq, M. 2000. *Drugs in South Asia: From the Opium Trade to the Present Day*. Basingstoke: Macmillan.

Emizet, Kisangani. 2000. 'The Massacre of Refugees in Congo: A Case of UN Peacekeeping Failure and International Law', *Journal of Modern African Studies*, 38, 2, pp. 163–202.

Enzensberger, Hans Magnus. 1994. *Civil War*. London: Granta.

Escobar, Arturo. 1994. *Encountering Development: The Making and Unmaking of the Third World*. Princeton: Princeton University Press.

Evans, Harold. 1978. *Pictures on a Page: Photojournalism and Picture Editing*. New York: Holt, Rinehart and Winston.

Evans, Harold. 2003. *War Stories: Reporting in the Time of Conflict from the Crimea to Iraq*. Boston and London: Bunker Hill.

Fairhead, James. 2000. 'The Conflict over Natural and Environmental Resources', in E. Wayne Nafziger, Frances Stewart and Raimo Vayrynen (eds), *War, Hunger, and Displacement: The Origins of Humanitarian Emergencies: Vol. 1. War and Displacement in Developing Countries*. Oxford: Oxford University Press.

Fajardo, Luis Eduardo. 2003. 'From the Alliance for Progress to the Plan Colombia: A Retrospective Look at US Aid to Colombia'. Crisis States Programme, DESTIN, LSE, paper presented at annual workshop, University of Witwatersrand, Johannesburg, 14–18 July.

Fallows, James. 1996. *Breaking the News: How the Media Undermine American Democracy*. New York: Pantheon.

Faludi, Susan. 1999. *Stiffed: The Betrayal of the Modern Man*. London: Chatto and Windus.

Fanon, Frantz. 2001. *The Wretched of the Earth* (trans. Constance Farrington). London: Penguin Classics.

Fanthorpe, Richard. 2006. 'On the Limits of Liberal Peace: Chiefs and Democratic Decentralization in Post-War Sierra Leone', *African Affairs*, 105, 418, pp. 27–49.

Farah, Ahmed Yusuf (with I.M. Lewis). 1993. *Somalia: The Roots of Reconciliation*. London: Action Aid.

Farah, Douglas and Kathi Austin. 2006. 'Air America', *New Republic*, 23 January.

Fearon, James. 2002. 'Why Do Some Civil Wars Last So Much Longer Than Others?', *Journal of Peace Research*, 41, 3, pp. 275–301.

Ferguson, James. 1990. *The Anti-Politics Machine: 'Development', Depoliticization and Bureaucratic Power in Lesotho*. Cambridge: Cambridge University Press.

Fischer, Andrew. 2005. *State Growth and Social Exclusion in Tibet: Challenges of Recent Economic Growth*. Copenhagen: Nordic Institute of Asian Studies Press.

Fithen, Caspar and Paul Richards. 2005. 'Making War, Crafting Peace: Militia Solidarities and Demobilization in Sierra Leone', in Paul Richards (ed.), *No Peace, No War: An Anthropology of Contemporary Armed Conflicts*. Oxford: James Currey; Athens: Ohio University Press.

Fitzgerald, Valpy. 2000. 'Paying for the War: Economic Policy in Poor Countries', in Frances Stewart and Valpy Fitzgerald (eds), *War and Underdevelopment, vol. 1: The Economic and Social Consequences of Conflict*. Oxford: Oxford University Press.

Flint, Julie and Alex de Waal. 2005. *Darfur: A Short History of a Long War*. London: Zed.

Foucault, Michel. 1977. *Discipline and Punish: The Birth of the Prison* (trans. Alan Sheridan). London: Penguin Books.

Foucault, Michel. 1978. 'Politics and the Study of Discourse', *Ideology and Consciousness*, 3, pp. 7–26.

Foucault, Michel. 1980. *Power/Knowledge: Selected Interviews and Other Writings, 1972–1977* (ed. Colin Gordon). Brighton: Harvester.

Foucault, Michel. 1981. 'Questions of Method: An Interview with Michel Foucault', *Ideology and Consciousness*, 8, pp. 3–14.

Frank, Thomas. 2004. *What's the Matter with America? The Resistible Rise of the American Right*. London: Secker and Warburg.

Galtung, Johan. 1996. *Peace by Peaceful Means: Peace and Conflict, Development and Civilization*. London: Sage; Oslo: International Peace Research Institute.

Galtung, Johan. 2004. *The Security Approach and the Peace Approach* (*www.gipri.ch/spip/IMG/pdf_GALTUNG_Johan.pdf*).

Gear, Sasha. 2002. *Wishing Us Away: Challenges Facing Ex-combatants in the 'New' South Africa*. Johannesburg: Centre for the Study of Violence and Reconciliation, Violence and Transition Series, vol. 8 (*www.csvr.org.za/papers/papvtp8a.htm*).

Gerges, Fawaz. 2005. *The Far Enemy: Why Jihad went Global*. Cambridge: Cambridge University Press.

Gerschman, John. 2002. 'Is Southeast Asia the Second Front?', *Foreign Affairs*, July/August, 81, 4, pp. 60–74.

Gibbs, Sara. 1997. 'Postwar Social Reconstruction in Mozambique: Reframing Children's Experiences of Trauma and healing', in Krishna Kumar (ed.), *Rebuilding Societies after Civil War*. Boulder, CO: Lynne Rienner.

Gilligan, James. 2000. *Violence: Reflections on Our Deadliest Epidemic*. Forensic Focus No. 18. London: Jessica Kingsley Publishers.

Girard, René. 1977. *Violence and the Sacred* (trans. Patrick Gregory). Baltimore: Johns Hopkins University Press.

Giustozzi, Antonio. 2004. *Respectable Warlords? The Politics of State-Building in Post-Taliban Afghanistan*. Working paper 33, Crisis States Programme, DESTIN, LSE.

Glazer, Nathan and Patrick Moynihan. 1970. *Beyond the Melting Pot*. Cambridge, MA: MIT Press.

Glenny, Misha. 1992. *The Fall of Yugoslavia: The Third Balkan War*. Harmondsworth: Penguin.

Global Witness. 1998. *A Rough Trade: The Role of Companies and Governments in the Angolan Conflict*. London: Global Witness.

Global Witness. 1999. *The Role of the Oil and Banking Industries in Angola's Civil War and the Plunder of State Assets*. London: Global Witness.

Global Witness. 2003. *For a Few Dollars More: How Al Qaeda Moved into the Diamond Trade*. London: Global Witness.

Glover, Jonathan. 1999. *Humanity: A Moral History of the Twentieth Century*. London: Jonathan Cape.

Goff, Stan. 2004. *Full Spectrum Disorder: The Military in the New American Century*. New York: Soft Skull Press.

Goffman, Erving. 1961. *Asylums: Essays on the Social Situation of Mental Patients and Other Inmates*. New York: Doubleday Anchor.

Gordadze, Thorniké. 2004. 'Chechnya: Eradication of the Enemy Within', in Fabrice Weissman (ed.), *In the Shadow of 'Just Wars': Violence, Politics and Humanitarian Action*. London: C. Hurst and Co.

Gourevitch, Philip. 1999. *We Wish to Inform You That Tomorrow We Will Be Killed With Our Families: Stories from Rwanda*. New York: Picador.

Graduate Institute of International Studies. 2001. *Small Arms Survey 2001: Profiling the Problem*. Oxford: Oxford University Press.

Graves, Sue and Victoria Wheeler. 2006. 'Good Humanitarian Donorship: Overcoming Obstacles to Improved Collective Donor Performance', discussion paper, December.

Graybill, Lyn. 2004. 'Pardon, Punishment, and Amnesia: Three African Post-conflict Methods', *Third World Quarterly*, 25, 6, pp. 1117–30.

Gutierrez Sanin, Francisco. 2003. *Criminal Rebels: A Discussion of War and Criminality from the Colombian Experience*. Crisis States Programme, Working Paper no. 27, DESTIN, LSE, April.

Gutierrez Sanin, Francisco. 2005. 'Diverging Paths: Comparing Responses to Insurgent Challenges in Colombia and Peru'. Paper presented at annual workshop, Crisis States Research Centre, LSE, 30 August–1 September.

Hagberg, Stan. 2005. 'Dealing with Dilemmas: Violent Farmer–Pastoralist Conflicts in Burkina Faso', in Paul Richards (ed.), *No Peace, No War: An*

Anthropology of Contemporary Armed Conflicts. Oxford: James Currey; Athens: Ohio University Press.

Hanlon, Joseph. 1996. *Peace without Profit: How the IMF Blocks Rebuilding in Mozambique*. Oxford: James Currey.

Hanlon, Joseph. 2005. 'Is the International Community Helping to Recreate the Preconditions for War in Sierra Leone?', *The Round Table*, 94, 381, September, pp. 459–72.

Harrell-Bond, Barbara. 1986. *Imposing Aid: Emergency Assistance to Refugees*. Oxford: Oxford University Press.

Harriss, John (ed.). 1995. *The Politics of Humanitarian Intervention*. London: Pinter Press.

Hawley, Susan. 2000. *Exporting Corruption: Privatisation, Multinationals and Bribery*. The Corner House, Sturminster Newton, June.

Hayner, Priscilla. 2001. *Unspeakable Truths: Confronting State Terror and Anarchy*. London and New York: Routledge.

Herman, Edward and Noam Chomsky. 1998. *Manufacturing Consent: The Political Economy of the Mass Media*. New York: Pantheon Books.

Hersh, Seymour. 2003. 'Selective Intelligence', *New Yorker*, 12 May (*www.newyorker.com/archive/2003/05/12/030512fa_fact*).

Hesselbein, Gabi, Frederick Golooba-Mutebi and James Putzel. 2006. *Economic and Political Foundations of State-Making in Africa: Understanding State Reconstruction*. Working Paper no. 3. Crisis States Research Centre, LSE.

Hilton, Isabel. 2005. 'Alvaro Uribe's gift: Colombia's Mafia Goes Legit' (*www.OpenDemocracy.net*), 25 October.

Hobsbawm, Eric. 1972. *Bandits*. Harmondsworth: Penguin.

Hobsbawm, Eric and Terence Ranger (eds). 1982. *The Invention of Tradition*. Cambridge: Cambridge University Press.

Hoffman, Bruce. 2004. 'The Pragmatist', *Atlantic Monthly*, July / August.

Hofmann, Charles-Antoine, Les Roberts, Jeremy Shoham and Paul Harvey. 2004. *Measuring the Impact of Humanitarian Aid: A Review of Current Practice*. HPG Report 17, ODI, London, June.

Homer-Dixon, Thomas. 1994. 'Environmental Scarcities and Violent Conflict: Evidence from Cases', *International Security*, 19, 1, summer, pp. 5–40.

Horowitz, Donald. 2000. *Ethnic Groups in Conflict*. Berkeley: University of California Press (first published 1985).

Hulme, David and Jonathan Goodhand. 2000. *NGOs and Peace Building in Complex Political Emergencies: Final Report to the Department for International Development*. Manchester: Institute for Development Policy and Management (IDPM).

Human Rights Watch. 1998. *Famine in Sudan, 1998: The Human Rights Causes*. New York: Human Rights Watch (written by Jemera Rone).

Human Rights Watch. 2002a. *The NATO Summit and Arms Trade Controls in Central and Eastern Europe*. November 15.

Human Rights Watch. 2002b. *All Our Hopes are Crushed: Violence and Repression in Western Afghanistan.* New York, November.

Human Rights Watch. 2003. *'We'll Kill You If You Cry': Sexual Violence in the Sierra Leone Conflict.* New York.

Human Rights Watch. 2005a. *Youth, Poverty and Blood: The Lethal Legacy of West Africa's Regional Warriors.* New York, March.

Human Rights Watch. 2005b. *Entrenching Impunity: Government Responsibility for International Crimes in Darfur.* New York, December.

Human Rights Watch. 2006. *Too High a Price: The Human Rights Cost of the Indonesian Military's Economic Activities.* New York.

Human Rights Watch/International Federation of Human Rights. 1999. *Leave None to Tell the Story: Genocide in Rwanda.* New York: Human Rights Watch; Paris: International Federation of Human Rights.

Humphreys, Macartan and Jeremy Weinstein. 2004. *What the Fighters Say: A Survey of Ex-combatants in Sierra Leone, June–August 2003.* Colombia University/Stanford University/PRIDE, Freetown, July.

Hunt, Tristram. 2003. *The English Civil War: At First Hand.* London: Orion.

Huntington, Samuel. 1993. 'The Clash of Civilizations', *Foreign Affairs*, 72, 3, summer, pp. 22–49.

Huntington, Samuel. 1998. *The Clash of Civilizations and the Remaking of World Order.* London: Touchstone.

Huntington, Samuel. 2004. *Who Are We? The Challenges to America's National Identity.* New York: Simon and Schuster.

Hutchful, Eboe and Kwesi Aning. 2004. 'The Political Economy of Conflict', in Adekeye Adebajo and Ismail Rashid (eds), *West Africa's Security Challenges: Building Peace in a Troubled Region.* Boulder, CO: Lynne Rienner.

Hutchinson, Sharon. 1996. *Nuer Dilemmas: Coping with Money, War and the State.* Berkeley: University of California Press.

ICG (International Crisis Group). 2002. *Storm Clouds over Sun City: The Urgent Need to Recast the Congolese Peace Process.* Nairobi/Brussels, 14 May.

ICG (International Crisis Group). 2003a. *Sierra Leone: The State of Security and Governance.* Freetown/Brussels, 2 September.

ICG (International Crisis Group). 2003b. *Sudan: Towards an Incomplete Peace.* ICG Africa Report no. 73. Nairobi/Brussels, 11 December.

ICG (International Crisis Group). 2004a. *Darfur Rising: Sudan's New Crisis.* ICG Africa Report no. 76. Nairobi/Brussels, 25 March.

ICG (International Crisis Group). 2004b. *Sudan: Now or Never in Darfur.* ICG Africa Report no. 80. Nairobi/Brussels, 23 May.

ICG (International Crisis Group). 2004c. *Darfur Deadline – A New International Action Plan.* ICG Africa Report no. 83. Nairobi/Brussels, 23 August.

ICG (International Crisis Group). 2004d. *Sudan's Dual Crises: Refocusing on IGAD.* Africa Briefing no. 19, 5 October.

ICG (International Crisis Group). 2004e. *Liberia and Sierra Leone: Rebuilding Failed States*. Africa Report no. 87, 8 December.

ICG (International Crisis Group). 2005a. *The Khartoum–SPLM Agreement: Sudan's Uncertain Peace*. Africa Report no. 96, 25 July.

ICG (International Crisis Group). 2005b. *Unifying Darfur's Rebels: A Prerequisite for Peace*. Africa Briefing no. 32, 6 October.

ICG (International Crisis Group). 2006a. *Security Sector Reform in the Congo*. Nairobi/Brussels, 13 February.

ICG (International Crisis Group). 2006b. *To Save Darfur*. Nairobi/Brussels, 17 March.

ICG (International Crisis Group). 2006c. *Sudan's Comprehensive Peace Agreement: The Long Road Ahead*. Africa Report no. 106, 31 March.

ICG (International Crisis Group). 2006d. *Uribe's Re-election: Can the EU Help Colombia Develop a More Balanced Peace Strategy?* 8 June.

ICG (International Crisis Group). 2006e. *Darfur's Fragile Peace Agreement*. Africa Briefing no. 39, 20 June.

ICG (International Crisis Group). 2006f. *Sri Lanka: The Failure of the Peace Process*. Colombo/Brussels, 28 November.

Ignatieff, Michael. 1993. *Blood and Belonging: Journeys into the New Nationalism*. London: BBC Books and Chatto and Windus.

Ignatieff, Michael. 1998. *The Warrior's Honor: Ethnic War and the Modern Conscience*. New York: Metropolitan Books.

Ignatieff, Michael. 2001. *Human Rights as Politics and Idolatry*. Princeton: Princeton University Press.

Ikenberry, G. John. 2002. 'America's Imperial Ambition', *Foreign Affairs*, September–October, 81, 5, pp. 44–60.

Independent International Commission on Kosovo. 2003. *The Kosovo Report* (accessed at *www.reliefweb.int/library/documents/thekosovoreport.htm*).

Jacobs, Dan. 1987. *The Brutality of Nations*. New York: Knopf.

Jacquin-Berdal, Dominique. 2004. 'How New are Africa's New Wars? An Historical Sketch'. LSE, mimeo.

James, Wendy. 1996. 'Uduk Resettlement: Dreams and Realities', in Tim Allen (ed.), *In Search of Cool Ground: War, Flight and Homecoming in Northeast Africa*. London: James Currey.

Jean, François and Jean-Chrisophe Rufin (eds) 1996. *Economie des guerres civiles*. Paris: Hachette.

Jézéquel, Jean-Hervé. 2004. 'Liberia: Orchestrated Chaos', in Fabrice Weissman (ed.), *In the Shadow of 'Just Wars': Violence, Politics and Humanitarian Action*. London: C. Hurst and Co.

Johnson, Douglas H. 2003. *The Root Causes of Sudan's Civil Wars*. Oxford: James Currey.

Joint Evaluation of Emergency Assistance to Rwanda. 1996. Copenhagen: Danida.

Jok, Madut Jok. 1996. 'Information Exchange in the Disaster Zone: Interaction between Aid Workers and Recipients in South Sudan', *Disasters*, 20, 3, September, pp. 206–15.

Jok, Madut Jok. 2001. *War and Slavery in Sudan*. Philadelphia: University of Pennsylvania Press.

Jonas, Susanne. 2000. *Of Centaurs and Doves: Guatemala's Peace Process*. Boulder, CO: Westview Press.

Judah, Tim. 2004. 'Uganda: the secret war', *New York Review of Books*, 23 September.

Kaldor, Mary. 1998. *New and Old Wars*. Cambridge: Polity Press.

Kalyvas, Stathis. 2004. 'The Urban Bias in Research in Civil Wars', *Security Studies*, 13, 3, spring, pp. 1–31.

Kaplan, Robert. 1994a. 'The Coming Anarchy', *The Atlantic Monthly*, February, pp. 44–74.

Kaplan, Robert. 1994b. *Balkan Ghosts: A Journey through History*. New York: Vintage.

Karim, Ataul, Mark Duffield, Susanne Jaspars, Aldo Benini, Joanna Macrae, Mark Bradbury, Douglas Johnson and George Larbi. 1996. *OLS: Operation Lifeline – a Review*. Geneva: Department for Humanitarian Affairs, July.

Keen, David. 1991a. 'A Disaster for Whom? Local Interests and International Donors during Famine among the Dinka of Sudan', *Disasters*, 15, 2, pp. 58–73.

Keen, David. 1991b. 'Targeting Emergency Food Aid: The Case of Darfur in 1985', in Simon Maxwell (ed.), *To Cure All Hunger: Food Policy and Food Security in Sudan*. London: Intermediate Technology Publications.

Keen, David. 1992. *Refugees: Rationing the Right to Life: The Crisis in Emergency Relief*. London: Zed Books.

Keen, David. 1993a. *A Comparative Study of Some Donor Countries' Experiences with NGOs*. Sub-report of the Evaluation Study: NGOs as a Channel of Norwegian Development Aid. Centre for Development Studies, University of Bergen.

Keen, David. 1993b. *How Safe is their Haven Now? The Kurds in Iraq*. London: Save the Children Fund.

Keen, David. 1994. *The Benefits of Famine: A Political Economy of Famine and Relief in Southwestern Sudan, 1983–89*. Princeton: Princeton University Press.

Keen, David. 1998. *The Economic Functions of Violence in Civil Wars*. Adelphi Paper no. 320. London: Oxford University Press for the International Institute for Strategic Studies.

Keen, David. 2000. 'Incentives and Disincentives for Violence', in Mats Berdal and David M. Malone (eds), *Greed and Grievance: Economic Agendas in Civil Wars*. London: Lynne Rienner.

Keen, David. 2001. 'War and Peace: What's the Difference?', in Adekeye Adebajo and Chandra Lekha Sriram (eds), *Managing Armed Conflicts in the 21st Century*. Special Issue of *International Peacekeeping*, 7, 4, pp. 1–22.

Keen, David. 2003. *Demobilising Guatemala*. Crisis States Programme Working Paper no. 37, LSE, November (*www.crisisstates.com*).

Keen, David. 2005a. *Conflict and Collusion in Sierra Leone*. Oxford: James Currey; New York: Palgrave, with International Peace Academy.

Keen, David. 2005b. 'Liberalization and Conflict', *International Political Science Review*, 26, 1, pp. 73–89.

Keen, David. 2006. *Endless War? Hidden Functions of the 'War on Terror'*. London: Pluto / Michigan University Press.

Keen, David and John Ryle. 1996. 'Editorial: The Fate of Information in the Disaster Zone', *Disasters*, 20, 3, pp. 169–72.

Keen, David and Ken Wilson. 1994. 'Engaging with Violence', in Joanna Macrae and Anthony Zwi (eds), *War and Hunger: Rethinking International Responses to Complex Emergencies*. London: Zed Books and Save the Children, UK.

Kelsall, Tim. 2006. Review of David Keen, *Conflict and Collusion in Sierra Leone*. *International Affairs*, 82, 4, pp. 820–1.

Kemal, Yasar. 1997. 'The Dark Cloud over Turkey', in W.L. Webb and Rose Bell (eds), *An Embarrassment of Tyrannies: 25 Years of Index on Censorship*. London: Victor Gollancz.

Kent, Randolph C. 1987. *Anatomy of Disaster Relief: The International Network in Action*. London: Pinter Publishers.

Kepel, Gilles. 2002. *Jihad: The Trail of Political Islam*. London / New York: I.B. Tauris.

Kibreab, Gaim. 1996. *People on the Edge in the Horn: Displacement, Land Use and the Environment in the Gedaref region of Sudan*. Oxford: James Currey.

Kiernan, Ben. 1996. *The Pol Pot Regime: Race, Power and Genocide in Cambodia under the Khmer Rouge, 1975–1979*. New Haven: Yale University Press.

King, Charles. 1997. *Ending Civil Wars*. Adelphi Paper no. 308. London: Oxford University Press for the International Institute for Strategic Studies.

Klugman, Jeni. 2000. 'Kenya: Economic Decline and Ethnic Politics', in E. Wayne Nafziger, Frances Stewart and Raimo Vayrynen (eds), *War, Hunger and Displacement: The Origins of Humanitarian Emergencies*. Oxford: Oxford University Press.

Knightley, Phillip. 1989. *The First Casualty: From the Crimea to the Falklands: The War Correspondent as Hero, Propagandist and Myth Maker*. London: Pan Books (first published 1975).

Kriger, Norma. 1992. *Zimbabwe's Guerrilla War: Peasant Voices*. Cambridge: Cambridge University Press.

Lanzer, Toby. 2005. 'Has the Tsunami Affected Funding for Other Crises?', *Forced Migration Review*, special issue, July, p. 17.

Lary, Diana. 1985. *'Warlord Soldiers': Chinese Common Soldiers 1911–1937*. Cambridge: Cambridge University Press

Lautze, Sue, Neamat Nojumi and Karem Najim. 2002. *Qaht-e-Pool, 'A Cash Famine': Food Security, Malnutrition and the Political Economy of Survival: A*

Report from Kabul, Haert and Qandahar, Afghanistan. Medford: Tufts University, February.

Lavergne, Marc and Fabrice Weissman. 2004. 'Sudan: Who Benefits from Humanitarian Aid?', in Fabrice Weissman (ed.), *In the Shadow of 'Just Wars': Violence, Politics and Humanitarian Action*. London: C. Hurst and Co.

Le Billon, Philippe. 2000. 'The Political Ecology of Transition in Cambodia, 1989–1999: War, Peace and Forest Exploitation', *Development and Change*, 31, pp. 785–805.

Le Billon, Philippe. 2001a. 'Angola's Political Economy of War: The Role of Oil and Diamonds, 1975–2000', *African Affairs*, 100, pp. 55–80.

Le Billon, Philippe. 2001b. 'The Political Ecology of War: Natural Resources and Armed Conflicts', *Political Geography*, 20, 5, pp. 561–84.

Le Billon, Philippe. 2003. 'Buying Peace or Fuelling War: The Role of Corruption in Armed Conflicts', *Journal of International Development*, 15, 4, pp. 413–26.

Le Billon, Philippe. 2005. 'Corruption, Reconstruction and Oil Governance in Iraq', *Third World Quarterly*, 26, 4–5, pp. 685–703.

Le Billon, Philippe. 2006. 'Fatal Transactions: Conflict Diamonds and the (Anti)Terrorist Consumer', *Antipode*, 38, 4, pp. 778–801.

Leach, Melissa. 1992. *Dealing with Displacement: Refugee–Host relations, Food and Forest Resources in Sierra Leonean Mende communities during the Liberian Influx, 1990–91*. Research Report no. 22. Brighton: Institute of Development Studies, April.

Leckie, Scott. 2005. 'The Great Land Theft', *Forced Migration Review*, July, pp. 15–16.

Lee, Vivian. 2002. 'Chronicle of a Scandal Foretold: Humanitarian Food Aid Policies and Practices for Refugees in West Africa'. M.Sc. dissertation, LSE.

Lefort, Pascal and Jonathan Littell. 1998. 'Food and Terror in Sierra Leone', Action Internationale Contre La Faim, mimeo.

Lemarchard, René. 1995. 'Rwanda: The Rationality of Genocide', in Obi Igwara (ed.), *Ethnic Hatred: Genocide in Rwanda*. London: ASEN Publishing.

Lerner, Mervin. 1980. *The Belief in a Just World: A Fundamental Delusion*. New York: Plenum Press.

Lieven, Anatol. 1999. *Chechnya: Tombstone of Russian Power*. New Haven: Yale University Press.

Likierman, Meira. 2001. *Melanie Klein: Her Work in Context*. London and New York: Continuum.

Lindner, Evelin. 2006. *Making Enemies: Humiliation and International Conflict*. Westport: Praeger.

Linker, Damon. 2006. *The Theocons: Secular America under Siege*. New York: Doubleday.

Lopez Levy, Marcela. 1999. 'Introduction', in Constanza Ardila, *The Heart of the War in Colombia* (trans. Alice Jay). London: Latin America Bureau.

Lord, David. 2000. *Paying the Price: The Sierra Leone Peace Process*. London: Conciliation Resources.

Loza, Tihomir. 1993. 'A People with Tolerance, a City without Laws', *War Report*, 21 (August/September).

Lunn, Jon. 2005. *The Power of Justice, Justice as Power: Observations on the Trajectory of the International Human Rights Movement*. Crisis States Development Research Centre, DESTIN, LSE, Discussion Paper no. 12, September.

Maass, Peter. 1996. *Love Thy Neighbor: A Story of War*. London and Basingstoke: Papermac

McAuslan, Patrick. 2001. 'Take this aid and shove it: it ain't working here no more'. Mimeo.

McClelland, Cary. 2006. 'Political Capital Deficits in Zimbabwean Famine: National and International Responsibility for Prevention Failure', *Journal of International Affairs*, 59, 2, pp. 315–32.

McCulloch, Lesley. 2003. 'Greed: The Silent Force of the Conflict in Aceh'. Melbourne: University of Deakin, mimeo.

MacGaffey, Janet, Vwakyanakazi Mukohya, Rukarangira Wa Nkera, Brooke Grundfest Schoepf, Makwala Ma Mavambu Ye Beda, Walu Engundu. 1991. *The Real Economy of Zaïre: The Contribution of Smuggling and Other Unofficial Activities to National Wealth*. London: James Currey.

MacKinlay, John. 2002. *Globalization and Insurgency*. Adelphi Paper no. 352. London: Oxford University Press for the International Institute for Strategic Studies.

McNulty, Mel. 1999. 'Media Ethnicization and the International Response to War and Genocide in Rwanda', in Tim Allen and Jean Seaton (eds), *The Media of Conflict: War Reporting and Representations of Ethnic Violence*. London: Zed Books.

Macrae, Joanna. n.d. 'The Politics of Coherence: The Formation of a New Orthodoxy on Linking Aid and Political Responses to Chronic Political Emergencies'. Mimeo *(fletcher.tufts.edu/humansecurity/con2/ws4/macrae.pdf)*.

Macrae, Joanna and Adele Harmer. 2003. *Humanitarian Action and the 'Global War on Terror': A Review of Trends and Issues*. Humanitarian Policy Group, HPG Report no. 14. London: ODI, July.

Macrae, Joanna and Nicholas Leader. 2000. *The Politics of Coherence: Humanitarianism and Foreign Policy in the Post-Cold War Era*. Humanitarian Policy Group, HPG Briefing no. 1. London: ODI, July.

Macrae, Joanna and Anthony Zwi. 1994. 'Famine, Complex Emergencies and International Policy in Africa: An Overview', in Joanna Macrae and Anthony Ziwi (eds), *War and Hunger: Rethinking International Responses to Complex Emergencies*. London: Zed Books and Save the Children, UK.

Malcolm, Noel. 1996. *Bosnia: A Short History*. Second edition. London: Papermac. (First edition published 1994.)

Malkki, Liisa. 1995. *Purity and Exile: Violence, Memory and National Cosmology among Hutu Refugees in Tanzania*. Chicago: University of Chicago Press.

Malone, David M. and Heiko Nitzschke. 2005. *Economic Agendas in Civil Wars: What We Know, What We Need to Know*. Discussion Paper no. 2005/07, WIDER, United Nations University.

Malthus, Thomas. 1798. *An Essay on the Principle of Population*. London: J. Johnson/St Paul's Church-Yard.

Mamdani, Mahmood. 1996. *Citizen and Subject: Contemporary Africa and the Legacy of Late Colonialism*. Princeton: Princeton University Press.

Mamdani, Mahmood. 2001. *When Victims Become Killers: Colonialism, Nativism, and the Genocide in Rwanda*. Oxford: James Currey.

Mansfield, Edward and Jack Snyder. 1995. 'Democratization and the Danger of War', *International Security*, 20, 1, summer, pp. 5–38.

Mansfield, Edward and Jack Snyder. 2005. *Electing to Fight: Why Emerging Democracies Go to War*. Boston: MIT Press.

Maren, Michael. 1997. *The Road to Hell: The Ravaging Effects of Foreign Aid and International Charity*. New York: Free Press.

Marriage, Zoë. 2006. *Not Breaking the Rules, Not Playing the Game: International Assistance to Countries at War*. London: C. Hurst and Co./Palgrave Macmillan.

Marsden, Peter. 1998. *The Taliban: War, Religion and the New Order in Afghanistan*. Lahore: Oxford University Press; London: Zed.

Massey, Simon and Roy May. 2006. 'The Crisis in Chad', *African Affairs*, 105, 420, pp. 443–49.

Massing, Michael. 2004. 'Now They Tell Us', *New York Review of Books*, 26 February.

Mawson, Andrew. 2004. 'Children, Impunity and Justice: Some Dilemmas from Northern Uganda', in Lisa Carlson, Megan Mackeson-Sandback and Tim Allen (eds), *Children in Extreme Situations: Proceedings from the Alistair Berkley Memorial Lecture*, DESTIN Working Paper no. 00-05 (*www.lse.ac.uk/collections/DESTIN*).

Mazurana, Dyan, 2006. *Women in Armed Opposition Groups in Africa and the Promotion of International Humanitarian Law and Human Rights*. Report of a workshop in Addis Ababa, Geneva Call/Program for the Study of International Organization(s), 23–6 November 2005.

M'Baya, Kankwenda. 1995. 'The Economic Crisis of Adjustment and Democracy in Africa', in Eshetu Chole and Jibrin Ibrahim (eds), *Democratization Processes in Africa*. Dakar: CODESRIA.

Melvern, Linda. 2001. 'The Security Council: Behind the Scenes', *International Affairs*, 77, 1, pp. 101–11.

Melvern, Linda. 2004a. 'A Conspiracy to Murder: The Rwandan Genocide', notes from a parliamentary lecture, 18 May (*www.lindamelvern.com/articles.htm*).

Melvern, Linda. 2004b. *Conspiracy to Murder: The Rwandan Genocide*. London: Verso.

Menkhaus, Ken. 2003. 'State Collapse in Somalia: Second Thoughts', *Review of African Political Economy*, 30, 97, pp. 405–22.

Menkhaus, Ken and John Prendergast. 1995. *Political Economy of Post-Intervention Somalia*. Somalia Task Force Issue Paper no. 3, April (*www.netnomad.com/menkhaus.html*).

Mermin, Jonathan. 1999. *Debating War and Peace: Media Coverage of U.S. Intervention in the Post-Vietnam Era*. Princeton: Princeton University Press.

Messiant, Christine. 2004. 'Angola: Woe to the Vanquished', in Fabrice Weissman (ed.), *In the Shadow of 'Just Wars': Violence, Politics and Humanitarian Action*, London: C. Hurst and Co.

Miller, Arthur. 1996. *The Crucible: Text and Criticism*, ed. Gerald Weales. Harmondsworth: Penguin (first published 1952).

Mitra, Gopal. 2006. 'Kashmir: Perspectives of Conflict and Violence'. M.Sc. dissertation, LSE.

Mkandawire, Thandika. 2001. 'Thinking about Developmental States in Africa', *Cambridge Journal of Economics*, 25, pp. 289–314.

Mkandawire, Thandika. 2002. 'The Terrible Toll of Post-colonial "Rebel Movements" in Africa: Towards an Explanation of the Violence against the Peasantry', *Journal of Modern African Studies*, 40, 2, pp. 181–215.

Moeller, Susan. 1999. *Compassion Fatigue: How the Media Sell Disease, Famine, War and Death*. New York: Routledge.

Mollat, Michel. 1986. *The Poor in the Middle Ages: An Essay in Social History*. New Haven and London: Yale University Press (first published 1978).

Moore, Barrington, Jr. 1974. *Social Origins of Dictatorship and Democracy: Lord and Peasant in the Making of the Modern World*. Harmondsworth: Penguin University Books (first published 1966).

Moorehead, Caroline. 1998. *Dunant's Dream: War, Switzerland and the History of the Red Cross*. London: HarperCollins.

Moravia, Alberto. 2000. *The Conformist*. Hanover, NH: Steerforth (first published 1951).

Moynihan, Patrick. 1993. *Pandaemonium: Ethnicity in International Politics*. New York: Oxford University Press.

MSF (Médecins Sans Frontières). 1995. 'Review of the Programme of Food Assistance to Liberian and Sierra Leonean Refugees in Guinea', December, draft.

Muana, Patrick. 1997. 'The Kamajoi Militia: Violence, Internal Displacement and the Politics of Counter-Insurgency', *Africa Development*, 22, 3–4, pp. 77–100.

Murshed, S. Mansoob and Scott Gates. 2005. 'Spatial-Horizontal Inequality and the Maoist Insurgency in Nepal', *Review of Development Economics*, 9, 1, pp. 121–34.

Ndiaya, B.W. 1993. *Extrajudicial, Summary or Arbitrary Executions*. Report on mission of 8-17 April 1993, Commission on Human Rights, UN, 11 August.

Nordstrom, Carolyn. 1999. 'Girls and War Zones: Troubling Questions', in Doreen Indra (ed.), *Engendering Forced Migration: Theory and Practice*. New York: Berghahn Books.

Nugent, Paul. 2004. *Africa since Independence: A Comparative History*. Basingstoke: Palgrave Macmillan.

Nzongola-Ntalaja, Georges. 2002. *The Congo from Leopold to Kabila*. London: Zed Books.

OCHA (Office for the Coordination of Humanitarian Affairs, UN). 1997. *Inter-agency Assessment Mission to Sierra Leone: Interim Report*. Final draft, Claude Bruderlein, 10 February.

OCHA (Office for the Coordination of Humanitarian Affairs, UN). 1999. *OCHA Orientation Handbook on Complex Emergencies*. August (*www.reliefweb. int/library/documents/ocha__orientation__handbook_on__.htm*).

OCHA (Office for the Coordination of Humanitarian Affairs, UN). 2006. *Inter-agency Real-Time Evaluation of the Humanitarian Response to the Darfur Crisis*. January.

ODI (Overseas Development Institute). 2000. *Reforming Food Aid*. ODI Briefing Paper, January.

ODI (Overseas Development Institute). 2006. *Saving Lives through Livelihoods: Critical Gaps in the Response to the Drought in the Greater Horn of Africa*. HPG Briefing Note, May.

Oleskiw, Stephen. 1983. *The Agony of a Nation: The Great Man-Made Famine in Ukraine, 1932–33*. London: The National Committee to Commemorate the 50th Anniversary of the Artificial Famine in Ukraine 1932–3.

Olson, Mancur. 2002. *Power and Prosperity: Outgrowing Communist and Capitalist Dictatorships*. New York: Basic Books.

Opondo, Enoch. 1996. 'Representation of Ethnic Conflict in the Kenyan Media', in Tim Allen, Kate Hudson and Jean Seaton (eds), *War, Ethnicity and the Media*. London: South Bank University.

Organised Crime Task Force. 2006. *Annual Report and Threat Assessment 2006: Organised Crime in Northern Ireland*. UK government (*http://www.octf. gov.uk/uploads/publications/OCTF%20Annual%20Report%20and%20Threat% 20Assessment%202006.pdf*).

Orwell, George. 1992. *Nineteen Eighty-Four*. New York: Everyman's Library (first published 1949).

Osiel, Mark J. 1999. *Obeying Orders: Atrocity, Military Discipline and the Law of War*. London: Transaction Publishers.

Owen, Ursula, 1997. 'Preface', in W.L. Webb and Rose Bell (eds), *An Embarrassment of Tyrannies: 25 Years of Index on Censorship*. London: Victor Gollancz.

Pantuliano, Sara and Sorcha O'Callaghan. 2006. *The 'Protection Crisis': A Review of Field-Based Strategies for Humanitarian Protection in Darfur.* HPG Discussion paper, London: ODI, December.

Paris, Roland. 2004. *At War's End: Building Peace after Civil Conflict.* Cambridge: Cambridge University Press.

Pastor, Manuel and James Boyce. 2000. 'El Salvador: Economic Disparities, External Intervention, and Civil Conflict', in E. Wayne Nafziger, Frances Stewart and Raimo Vayrynen (eds), *War, Hunger, and Displacement: The Origins of Humanitarian Emergencies, vol. 2.* New York: Oxford University Press.

Perle, Richard. 2003. 'United They Fall', *The Spectator*, 22 March (*www.benadorassociates.com/article/287*).

Peters, Krijn. 2006. *Footpaths to Reintegration: Armed Conflict, Youth and the Rural Crisis in Sierra Leone.* Proefschrift, Ph.D., Wageningen University.

Platteau, J.-P. and C. André. 1998. 'Land Relations under Unbearable Stress: Rwanda Caught in the Malthusian Trap', *Journal of Economic Behavior and Organization*, 34, 1, pp. 1–47.

Pluemper, Thomas and Eric Neumayer. 2007. *Famine Mortality, Rational Political Inactivity, and International Food Aid.* Social Sciences Research Network, Working Paper series, February (*papers.ssrn.com/sol3/papers.cfm?abstract_id=920852*).

Porteous, Samuel. 2000. 'Targeted Financial Sanctions', in Mats Berdal and David Malone (eds), *Greed and Grievance: Economic Agendas in Civil Wars.* London: Lynne Rienner.

Porter, Toby. 2003. *The Interaction between Political and Humanitarian Action in Sierra Leone, 1995 to 2002.* Geneva: Centre for Humanitarian Dialogue, March.

Pottier, Johan. 1998. 'The "Self" in Self-Repatriation: Closing Down Mugunga Camp, Eastern Zaïre', in Richard Black and Khalid Khoser (eds), *The End of the Refugee Cycle? Refugee Repatriation and Reconstruction.* Oxford: Berghahn Books.

Prunier, Gerard. 1995. *The Rwanda Crisis: 1959–1994. History of a Genocide.* London: Hurst and Co.

Prunier, Gerard. 2005. *Darfur: The Ambiguous Genocide.* London: Hurst and Co.

Pugh, Michael and Neil Cooper (with Jonathan Goodhand). 2004. *War Economies in a Regional Context: Challenges of Transformation.* Boulder, CO: Lynne Rienner.

RAID (Rights and Accountability in Development). 2004. *Unanswered Questions: Companies, Conflict and the Democratic Republic of Congo.* Oxford, April.

Raikes, Philip. 1991. *Modernising Hunger: Famine, Food Surplus and Farm Policy in the EEC and Africa.* London: Catholic Institute for International Relations with James Currey (London) and Heinemann (Portsmouth, NH).

Rampton, Sheldon and John Stauber. 2003. *Weapons of Mass Deception: The Uses of Propaganda in Bush's War on Iraq.* London: Robinson.

Rangasami, Amrita. 1985. '"Failure of Exchange Entitlements" Theory of Famine: A Response', *Economic and Political Weekly,* XX, 41, 12 October and 42, 19 October, pp. 1747–51 and 1797–800.

Rashid, Ahmed. 2000. *Taliban: Islam, Oil and the New Great Game in Central Asia.* London: I.B. Tauris.

Reno, William. 1995. *Corruption and State Politics in Sierra Leone.* Cambridge: Cambridge University Press.

Report of the Panel of Experts (DRC). 2002. *Final Report of the Panel of Experts on the Illegal Exploitation of Natural Resources and Other Forms of Wealth of the Democratic Republic of the Congo.* Report to UN Security Council, 16 October.

Report of the Panel of Experts Appointed Pursuant to UN Security Council Resolution 1306. 2000. Paragraph 19 in Relation to Sierra Leone, December.

Reyntjens, Filip. 2004. 'Rwanda, Ten Years On: From Genocide to Dictatorship', *African Affairs,* 103, pp. 177–210.

Rhodes, Richard. 2000. *Why They Kill: The Discoveries of a Maverick Criminologist.* New York: Vintage Books.

Richani, Nazih. 1997. 'The Political Economy of Violence: The War-System in Colombia.' *Journal of Interamerican Studies and World Affairs,* 39, 2, pp. 37–81.

Richani, Nazih. 2002. *Systems of Violence: The Political Economy of Violence in Colombia.* Albany: State University of New York Press.

Richards, Paul. 1996a. *Fighting for the Rain Forest: War, Youth and Resources in Sierra Leone.* Oxford: James Currey.

Richards, Paul. 1996b. 'Violence as Cultural Creativity: Social Exclusion and Environmental Damage in Sierra Leone'. Mimeo.

Robben, Antonius. 1999. 'The Fear of Indifference', in Kees Koonings and Dirk Kruijt (eds), *Societies of Fear: The Legacy of Civil War, Violence and Terror in Latin America.* London: Zed Books.

Robins, Robert S. and Jerrold M. Post. 1997. *Political Paranoia: The Pyschopolitics of Hatred.* New Haven: Yale University Press.

Robinson, Mark. 1991. 'An Uncertain Partnership: The Overseas Development Administration and the Voluntary Sector in the 1980s', in Anuradha Bose and Peter Burnell (eds), *Britain's Overseas Aid since 1979: Between Idealism and Self-Interest.* Manchester: Manchester University Press.

Robinson, Ronald and John Gallagher (with Alice Denny). 1978. *Africa and the Victorians: The Official Mind of Imperialism.* Basingstoke: Palgrave Macmillan (first published 1961).

Rodgers, Dennis. 2006. 'Living in the Shadow of Death: Gangs, Violence and Social Order in Urban Nicaragua, 1996–2002', *Journal of Latin American Studies,* 38, pp. 267–92.

Rogers, Paul. 2005. 'A Jewel for al-Qaida's Crown', 11 August (*opendemocracy.net*).

Rogier, Emeric. 2005. *Designing an Integrated Strategy for Peace, Security and Development in Post-Agreement Sudan.* The Hague: Netherlands Institute for International Relations, 'Clingendael', April.

Ross, Michael. 2002. *Oil, Drugs, and Diamonds: How Do Natural Resources Vary in Their Impact on Civil War?* For International Peace Academy, New York (*www.polisci.ucla.edu/faculty/ross/OilDrugs.pdf*)

Rubin, Barnett. 2000. 'The Political Economy of War and Peace in Afghanistan', *World Development*, 28, 10, pp. 1789–803.

RUF (Revolutionary United Front). 1995. *Footpaths to Democracy* (see *sierra-leone.org/footpaths.html*).

Rushdie, Salman. 1997. 'Last Chance?' in W.L. Webb and Rose Bell (eds), *An Embarrassment of Tyrannies: 25 Years of Index on Censorship*. London: Victor Gollancz.

Russell, Conrad. 1971. *The Crisis of Parliaments: English History 1509–1660*. Oxford: Oxford University Press.

Ryle, John. 2004. 'Disaster in Darfur', *New York Review of Books*, 12 August (*middleeastinfo.org/article4650.html*).

Saint-Exupéry, Antoine de. 1971. *The Little Prince* (trans. Katherine Woods). New York: Harcourt, Brace and World, Inc. (first published 1943).

Samuels, Fiona and Sara Simon. 2006. *Food, Nutrition and HIV: What Next?* Briefing Paper no. 7. London: ODI, August.

Save the Children Fund 1998, *Dispatches from Disaster Zones: The Reporting of Humanitarian Emergencies*. A record of the public conference at Church House, London, on 27 May.

Schaffer, Bernard. 1984. 'Towards Responsibility', in Edward Clay and Bernard Schaffer (eds), *Room for Manoeuvre: An Exploration of Public Policy in Agriculture and Rural Development*. London: Heinemann Educational Books.

Scheff, Thomas J. 1994. *Bloody Revenge: Emotions, Nationalism, and War*. Boulder, CO: Westview Press.

Scheper-Hughes, Nancy. 1992. *Death without Weeping: The Violence of Everyday Life in Brazil*. Berkeley: University of California Press.

Schirmer, Jennifer. 1999. 'The Guatemalan Politico-Military Project: Legacies for a Violent Peace?', *Latin American Perspectives*, 26, 2, pp. 92–107.

Schivelbusch, Wolfgang. 2003. *The Culture of Defeat: On National Trauma, Mourning and Recovery* (trans. Jefferson Chase). New York: Metropolitan Books.

Sen, Amartya. 1984. *Poverty and Famines: An Essay on Entitlement and Deprivation*. Oxford: Oxford University Press and Clarendon Press.

Sender, John. 1999. 'Africa's Economic Performance: Limitations of the Current Consensus', *Journal of Economic Perspectives*, 13, 1, pp. 89–114.

Shawcross, William. 1984. *The Quality of Mercy*. London: André Deutsch Limited.

Shawcross, William. 1996. 'Tragedy in Cambodia', *New York Review of Books*, 14 November, pp. 41–6, and 19 December, pp. 73–4.

Shearer, David. 1998. *Private Armies and Military Intervention*. Adelphi Paper no. 316. London: Oxford University Press for the International Institute for Strategic Studies.

Shearer, David. 2000. 'Aiding or Abetting? Humanitarian Aid and Its Economic Role in Civil War', in Mats Berdal and David Malone (eds), *Greed and Grievance: Economic Agendas in Civil Wars*. London: Lynn Rienner.

Short, Philip. 2004. *Pol Pot: The History of a Nightmare*, London: John Murray.

Simpson, John. 1994. *In the Forests of the Night: Encounters in Peru with Terrorism, Drug-Running and Military Oppression*. London: Arrow.

Skelt, Joanna. 1997. *Rethinking Peace Education in War-Torn Societies: A Theoretical and Empirical Investigation with Special Reference to Sierra Leone*. Master's thesis, International Extension College, Cambridge.

Slim, Hugo. 1997. 'Doing the Right Thing: Relief Agencies, Moral Dilemmas and Moral Responsibility in Political Emergencies and War', *Disasters*, 21, 3, pp. 244–57.

Smart, Barry. 1988. *Michel Foucault*. London and New York: Routledge.

Smith, Brian. 1983. *US and Canadian Non-profit Organizations (PVO's) as Transnational Development Institutions*. Institute for Social and Policy Studies, Yale University, August.

Snyder, Jack and Robert Jervis. 1999. 'Civil War and the Security Dilemma', in Barbara F. Walter and Jack Snyder (eds), *Civil Wars, Insecurity, and Intervention*. New York: Columbia University Press.

Sofos, Spyros. 1999. 'Culture, Media and the Politics of Disintegration and Ethnic Division in Former Yugoslavia', in Tim Allen, Kate Hudson and Jean Seaton (eds), *The Media of Conflict: War Reporting and Representations of Ethnic Violence*. London: Zed Books.

Solzhenitsyn, Alexander. 1974. *The Gulag Archipelago: 1918–1956* (trans. Thomas P. Whitney). New York: Harper and Row.

Somerville, Keith. 1997. 'Angola – Groping Towards Peace or Slipping Back towards War?', in William Gutteridge and Jack Spence (eds), *Violence in Southern Africa*. London: Frank Cass.

Sommers, Marc. 2006. *Fearing Africa's Young Men: The Case of Rwanda*. Social Development Papers, Conflict Prevention and Reconstruction, Paper no. 23. World Bank, January.

Sontag, Susan. 1977. *On Photography*. New York: Farrar, Straus and Giroux.

Stanford, Peter. 1996. *The Devil: A Biography*. New York: Henry Holt and Co.

Staub, Ervin. 1992. *The Roots of Evil: The Origins of Genocide and Other Group Violence*. Cambridge: Cambridge University Press.

Stern, Nicholas. 2007. *Stern Review: The Economics of Climate Change*. London: HM Treasury/Cabinet Office.

Stevens, Jacob. 2006. 'Prisons of the Stateless: The Derelictions of UNHCR', *New Left Review*, 42, November–December, pp. 53–67.

Stewart, Frances. 2000. 'The Root Causes of Humanitarian Emergencies', in E. Wayne Nafziger, Frances Stewart and Raimo Vayrynen (eds), *War, Hunger and Displacement: The Origins of Humanitarian Emergencies*. Oxford: Oxford University Press.

Stewart, Frances. 2004. *Development and Security*. DESTIN Crisis States Programme, Research Seminar Series (*www.crisisstates.com/News/seminars4.htm*).

Stille, Alexander. 1996. *Excellent Cadavers: The Mafia and the Death of the First Italian Republic*. New York: Vintage.

Stockton, Nick. 1998. 'In Defence of Humanitarianism', *Disasters*, 22, 4, pp. 352–60.

Stremlau, John. 1977. *The International Politics of the Nigerian Civil War, 1967–1970*. Princeton: Princeton University Press.

Summerfield, Derek. 1996. *The Impact of War and Atrocity on Civilian Populations*. Network Paper no. 14, London: ODI (*www.torturecare.org.uk/UserFiles/File/publications/Summ_4.rtf*).

Tajfel, Henri. 1982. 'Social Psychology of Intergroup Relations', *Annual Review of Psychology*, 33, pp. 1–39.

Tangri, Roger and Andrew Mwenda. 2003. 'Military Corruption and Ugandan Politics since the late 1990s', *Review of African Political Economy*, 98, pp. 539–52.

Terry, Fiona. 2004. 'North Korea: Feeding Totalitarianism', in Fabrice Weissman (ed.), *In the Shadow of 'Just Wars': Violence, Politics and Humanitarian Action*. London: C. Hurst and Co.

Theweleit, Klaus. 1987. *Male Fantasies* (trans. Stephen Conway). Cambridge: Polity.

Thomas, Keith. 1978. *Religion and the Decline of Magic*. London: Penguin Books.

Thompson, Mark. 1999. *Forging War: The Media in Serbia, Croatia, Bosnia and Hercegovina*. Luton: University of Luton.

Tilly, Charles. 1985. 'War Making and State Making as Organized Crime', in Peter Evans, Dietrich Rueschemeyer and Theda Skocpol (eds), *Bringing the State Back In*. New York: Cambridge University Press.

Tishkov, Valery. 2001. *Understanding Violence for Post-Conflict Reconstruction in Chechnya*. Geneva: Centre for Applied Studies in International Negotiations. January.

Tong, Jacqui. 2004. 'Questionable Accountability: MSF and Sphere in 2003', *Disasters*, 28, 2, pp. 176–89.

Turton, David. 1997. 'Introduction: War and Ethnicity', in David Turton (ed.), *War and Ethnicity: Global Connections and Local Violence*. New York: University of Rochester Press.

Turton, David and Peter Marsden. 2002. *Taking Refugees for a Ride? The Politics of Refugee Return to Afghanistan*. Afghanistan Research and Evaluation Unit, December.

Ugrešić, Dubravka. 1998. *The Culture of Lies: Antipolitical Essays* (trans. Celia Hawkesworth). London: Phoenix House.

Utas, Mats. 2005. 'Building a Future? The Reintegration and Re-marginalization of Youth in Liberia', in Paul Richards (ed.), *No Peace, No War: An Anthropology of Contemporary Armed Conflicts*. Oxford: James Currey; Athens: Ohio University Press.

Uvin, Peter. 1998. *Aiding Violence: The Development Enterprise in Rwanda*. West Hartford, CT: Kumarian Press.

Van Creveld, Martin. 1991a. *On Future War*. London: Brassey's.

Van Creveld, Martin. 1991b. *The Transformation of War*. New York: Free Press.

van der Veer, Guus. 1998. *Counselling and Therapy with Refugees and Victims of Trauma: Psychological Problems of War, Torture and Repression*. Chichester: John Wiley and Sons.

Varese, Federico. 1994. 'Is Sicily the Future of Russia? Private Protection and the Emergence of the Russian Mafia', *Archives Européennes de Sociologie*, XXXV/2, summer, pp. 224–58.

Vaughan, Megan. 1987. *The Story of an African Famine: Gender and Famine in 20th-Century Malawi*. Cambridge: Cambridge University Press.

Vaux, Tony. 2001. *The Selfish Altruist: Relief Work in Famine and War*. London: Earthscan.

Verwimp, Philip. 2003. 'An Economic Profile of Peasant Perpetrators of Genocide: Micro-level Evidence from Rwanda'. Catholic University of Leuven/Yale University, November.

Voutira, Efthia and Shaun Brown. 1995. *Conflict Resolution, A Cautionary Tale: A Review of Some Non-governmental Practices*. Oxford: Refugee Studies Programme.

Wade, Robert. 2003. *Governing the Market: Economic Theory and the Role of Government in East Asian Industrialization*. Princeton: Princeton University Press (first published 1990).

Waite, Robert. 1952. *Vanguard of Nazism: The Free Corps Movement in Postwar Germany 1918–1923*. Cambridge, MA: Harvard University Press.

Watkins, Kevin. 1995. *Oxfam Poverty Report*. Oxford: Oxfam.

Weissman, Fabrice. 2004. 'Sierra Leone: Peace at Any Price', in Fabrice Weissman (ed.), *In the Shadow of 'Just Wars': Violence, Politics and Humanitarian Action*. London: C. Hurst and Co.

Whitaker, Beth. 2002. *Changing Priorities in Refugee Protection: The Rwandan Repatriation from Tanzania*. New Issues in Refugee Research. Working Paper no. 53. Geneva: Evaluation and Policy Analysis Group, UNHCR.

Wilson, Ken. 1991. 'Cults of Violence and Counter-Violence in Mozambique', *Journal of Southern African Studies*, 18, 3, special issue, pp. 527–82.

Wilson, Ken. 1992. *A State of the Art Review of Research on Internally Displaced, Refugees and Returnees from and in Mozambique*. Stockholm: Swedish International Development Cooperation Agency.

Wisner, Ben, Piers Blaikie, Terry Cannon and Ian Davis. 1994. *At Risk: Natural Hazards, People's Vulnerability and Disasters*. London: Routledge.

Wolf, Daniel. 2004. 'What Happened to the Fucking Money?', *The Spectator*, 23 October.

Women's Commission for Refugee Women and Children. 2006. *Beyond Firewood: Fuel Alternatives and Protection Strategies for Displaced Women and Girls*. New York, March.

Wood, Geoff (ed.). 1989. *Labelling in Development Policy: Essays in Honour of Bernard Schaffer*. London: Sage Publications.

Woodward, Bob. 2003. *Bush at War*. New York: Simon and Schuster.

Woodward, Susan L. 1995. *Balkan Tragedy: Chaos and Dissolution after the Cold War*. Washington, DC: Brookings Institution.

Woodward, Susan L. 2002. 'Economic Priorities for Successful Peace Implementation', in Stephen J. Stedman, Donald Rothchild and Elizabeth M. Cousens (eds), *Ending Civil Wars: The Implementation of Peace Agreements*. Boulder, CO: Lynne Rienner.

Young, Allan. 1995. *The Harmony of Illusions: Inventing Post-traumatic Stress Disorder*. Princeton: Princeton University Press.

Youngs, Richard. 2002. 'The European Union and Democracy in Latin America', *Latin American Politics and Society*, 44, 3, pp. 111–39.

Zolberg, Aristide R., Astri Suhrke and Sergio Aguayo (eds). 1989. *Escape from Violence: Conflict and the Refugee Crisis in the Developing World*. Oxford: Oxford University Press.

Zur, Judith N. 1998. *Violent Memories: Mayan War Widows in Guatemala*. Boulder, CO: Westview Press.

Index